MW01053798

World's Greatest Direct Mail Sales Letters

Herschell Gordon Lewis
Carol Nelson

World's Greatest Direct Mail Sales Letters

Printed on recyclable paper

NTC Business Books
a division of *NTC Publishing Group* • Lincolnwood, Illinois USA

Library of Congress Cataloging-in-Publication-Data

Lewis, Herschell Gordon, 1926–
The world's greatest direct mail sales letters / Herschell Gordon Lewis, Carol Nelson.
p. cm.
Includes index.
ISBN 0–8442–3570–9
1. Sales letters. 2. Direct marketing. I. Nelson, Carol.
II. Title
HF5730.L483 1995
808'.066658—dc20 95–11303
CIP

Published by NTC Business Books, a division of NTC Publishing Group
4255 West Touhy Avenue
Lincolnwood (Chicago), Illinois 60646-1975, U.S.A.

Manufactured in the United States of America.

6 7 8 9 ML 0 9 8 7 6 5 4 3 2 1

Contents

Preface

Don't expect to see a lot of fancy rhetoric in this book.

The letters we've chosen represent every facet of direct mail communication. You'll see letters selling land, vacuum cleaners, siding, steaks, and other prosaic commodities, as well as the highest level of fund raising and business-to-business offers.

Rather than apologize for including communications for a Las Vegas casino and an erotic stimulator, we rejoice in the opportunity to make this a representative collection of the most effective and successful direct mail letters ever written, regardless of their subjects.

We should also add: regardless of their age. Some of the great letters of the twentieth century were composed 20 to 40 years ago, and we have been lucky enough to capture a few of them.

Our personal philosophy is that paragraphs in letters should be indented . . . that no paragraph should be longer than seven lines . . . that some reference to the actual offer should appear early on. We have ignored our personal preferences in cases in which we knew a letter had performed well. After all, the purpose of this book is not to project our individual criticism, but rather to supply templates for every kind of persuasive letter-writing.

Whenever we could possibly do so, we have named the writer of the letter. Not every letter has this information, and this is for two reasons: First, in some cases we simply were unable to get the name, despite repeated requests. Second, the originators of some letters did not want their identities disclosed because of competitive conflicts or changes in their professional circumstances.

An invitation to the reader who may recognize his or her handiwork, unsung: Let us know who you are and in subsequent editions of this book, you will receive the recognition you certainly deserve.

A challenge to those not represented in these pages, who feel they have authored a letter which deserves inclusion: Send us that letter and it may appear in a future edition of this book.

An apology to the hundreds or perhaps thousands of talented writers of whose letters we simply have been unaware: To create this book we mailed an invitation to every listed direct response writer and advertising agency. If our invitation did not reach you, blame the post office and the various directories, not us.

Herschell Gordon Lewis
Carol Nelson

Acknowledgments

Much as we would like to, we can't publicly acknowledge all the participants whose works appear in this book because we have promised anonymity to some. But you know who you are and we offer our sincere gratitude.

Our thanks to the editorial staff at NTC Business Books, and especially to Ms. Anne Knudsen and Mr. Richard Hagle who authorized this project and helped nurse it to completion.

We owe a debt of gratitude to Margo Lewis for her tireless help in collecting and classifying exhibits.

To those who responded to our request for samples, we owe more than thanks; we owe them this book itself.

We're looking forward to leaning on all of you good people for the next edition!

Chapter 1

What Makes a Great Letter "Great"?

Too many observers, critics, and even teachers gauge the effectiveness of direct mail letters by the wrong criteria.

Unless you actually earn your living by trying to convince someone you've never met—someone who may never have heard of you before . . . someone who ten seconds ago had no idea what you're "pitching"—you may judge a letter by its grammar or its use of flashy adjectives or its rhetorical symmetry.

In the world of direct response all three—careful grammar, Roget-driven adjectives, and attention to form instead of substance—can *suppress* response, not enhance it.

Or you may, logically enough, award accolades to a letter which uses techniques you've never seen before.

Hold it! Save that award until you've been able to gauge how the techniques *worked,* because unless innovation is tied to successful response it's the result of dilettante-dabbling, not marketing expertise.

To us, editing this compendium of sales letters, greatness stems from the first rule of direct marketing:

> The purpose of a direct response message is to convince the reader, viewer, or listener to perform a positive act, as the direct result of having absorbed the message.

How Does a Letter Convince the Reader?

A good letter-writer has to be a good instinctive psychologist. Not a *professional* psychologist, who may depend on pre-announced personal stature and a knowledge of technical terminology to convince a patient or an onlooker (who may be the same person) to adopt a state of mind, but a *practicing* psychologist, able to drive the message-recipient in the proper direction.

We've often compared the world of "force-communication"—the technique of generating the response you want—to controlling rats in a maze. Put a rat into a maze, and it will flounder, eventually collapsing in exhaustion.

But place a piece of cheese in one corner: The rat scampers toward the cheese. Touch the rat with an electric prod: The rat runs directly away from the prod. Open a gate: The rat goes through the gate and out of the maze. Our job, as "Ratmasters," is to supply the cheese, the prod, the gate.

An absolute rule for those who think descriptive ability parallels sales ability:

> *Description and salesmanship are NOT parallel.*

A description is a clerk. One walks into a department store, selects a shirt or blouse, and takes it to the clerk. I want this one. Has the clerk *sold* that shirt or blouse? Without the department store ambience, the clerk would have no shirt or blouse to ring up.

But a salesperson! In some business organizations, a salesperson will make more money than the head of the company. Why not? Cash flow comes from sales. And sales stem from *description PLUS buying rationale,* not description alone.

Too Much Description, Not Enough Salesmanship

One of the approximately two thousand letters we read, sorting and selecting for this book, begins:

> Dear Fellow Investor:
>
> You can guarantee a more secure and comfortable financial future for you and your family by investing in high-quality investments. As a non-profit educational association serving more than 65,000 individual investors, we are in a unique position to help you improve your investing. You are invited to join us.

You can see immediately why this letter isn't included as an example of superlative letter-writing. Some letters can be condescending and still succeed, because the reader accepts the authoritative position of the writer. Some letters can be self-applauding and still succeed, because the reader acknowledges the superior position of the writer. Some letters can generalize and still succeed, because the subject matter has a delicacy-factor which makes specifics too brutal.

Can a letter be condescending, self-applauding, and generalized and still succeed? In our opinion, any success will be fractional compared with the potential success of a dynamic, targeted, rapport-building letter loaded with specifics.

Suppose we *phone* you instead of writing to you. We use the same wording this letter uses, to open the conversation. We say, "You can guarantee a more secure and comfortable financial future for you and your family by investing in high-quality investments." You reply (or certainly think), "So what else is new? Of course I can guarantee a more secure and comfortable financial future that way. You're telling me something I already know, as though I were some sort of idiot. And what else would I invest in other than investments?"

We continue: "We are in a unique position to help you improve your investing." You reply, "How? What will you do? What do you know about my investment history?"

Are we about to convince you? Or are we exasperating and alienating you?

Deep in the letter is solid grist for our word-mill. The organization has computer software for the individual investor, and it's so masterful Wall Street professionals use this same software. (Can you sense a potent opening from this buried point?) Buried even deeper are:

- the capability of buying stocks direct from corporations, avoiding brokers' fees;
- discounts on financial publications well in excess of membership dues;
- advanced online trading software;

. . . and half a dozen other benefits. But the reader is long gone.

The point, as we explain in more detail in Chapter 2: Open with dynamite or the reader disappears.

Greatness Isn't in Vocabulary Mastery

Don't be surprised to see letter after letter that doesn't have a single brilliant adjective in it. Nouns and verbs make greatness far more than adjectives do.

Oh, we're not discarding adjectives. What we're discarding is the notion that the writer has to show off a mastery of vocabulary. Word use, yes, absolutely. Vocabulary, a "maybe" at best.

We've all received letters which used words (or, our pet peeve, unexplained acronyms) we didn't understand. (Just in case, so we won't be guilty of that same sin: An acronym is a group of letters representing what words beginning with each of these letters represents: NRA = National Rifle Association; MADD = Mothers Against Drunk Driving.) If we respond to these letters, is it because we're in awe of the big words or despite them?

The writer who can create a word-picture, clear and focused in the reader's brain, is writing a great sales letter. The writer who smashes home a point so directly and so vigorously the reader shakes with the impact is writing a great sales letter. The writer who forces open the reader's interest, grabs it like a pit-bull, and doesn't let go until the last word of the p.s. is writing a great sales letter.

Don't Look for a Pattern

Many "authorities" will teach, "Write like I do." What results from the keyboards of their disciples is a sameness unrelated to persuasion.

We're disciples of short sentences and short paragraphs. Some of the entries in these pages have long sentences and long paragraphs.

We think a single P.S. on a letter represents an optimum "kick" at the end. Some of the entries in these pages have a P.P.S.; one has a P.P.P.S.

We believe a multi-page letter should specify the offer on page one, leaving ample time and room for justification. Some of the entries on these pages never specify a price, leaving that chore to other components of the mailing.

Disagreement with our own principles is certainly no reason for exclusion. If all writers employed identical force-communication philosophies, all letters would look the same. (And, quickly, breakaway approaches would command reader attention.)

So the common thread justifying all the letters in this book isn't subscription to a single set of parameters, a group of edicts laid down by the editors, an arbitrary judgment based on personal prejudices. The basis for inclusion is more prudent—and more obvious—than these flawed criteria.

In one word: The key to letter-writing greatness is *persuasion.*

Chapter 2

How to Write an Effective Direct Mail Letter

The examples in this book run a wide gamut. Some are high-pressure, some are low-pressure; some are folksy; some are deliberately austere (we eliminated inadvertent or amateurish austerity); some are eight pages long, some are shorter than a single page.

What do these letters have in common . . . if anything?

Do You Know Your Prospect?

Direct mail is the only mass advertising discipline using a personalized approach—*we* or *I* to *you.*

When a professional letter-writer sits down to write a direct mail letter, he or she says to the fingertips: Write it as though I'm communicating with someone I know . . . someone who either wants or needs the information I'm writing about. The target group becomes one person.

One perilous qualifier: The writer doesn't know the prospect. And our best prospects are so accustomed to receiving boilerplate direct mail letters that unless the writer grabs the prospect's attention immediately, the letter is likely to end up in the round file before the writer has fired the first shot.

So the first rule of letter-writing has to be:

1. Aim your message squarely at the reader's interests and then massage that interest until the reader pants with desire.

Simple? Of course not. Anyone can write a letter. Not everyone can write an effective letter.

Other standards of professional letter-writing:

2. Hit the reader early on with the strongest benefit of what you're selling—what's in it for him or her.

Once you have the reader's attention, you have no surer way of holding it than answering the foremost question in any reader's mind: "What's in it for me?"

3. Speak in the reader's language.

You should know the people you're trying to reach, and you should know the language they're accustomed to using. Establish rapport with them by speaking colloquially in words they would use themselves. That means if you're writing a business-to-business letter, know the lingo. If you're writing strictly to women, write to them on their terms, over a woman's signature if the offer has to do with gender. The language you'd choose to write to a 7-year-old is absolutely different from the language you'd choose to write to that 7-year-old's parents.

(**Warning:** If the reader thinks you're being condescending or not the person you claim to be, you're a loser.)

4. Avoid "in" jargon.

Avoiding the wrong words is as important as choosing the right ones. If you're writing for a technical product or membership group, be sure to explain any technical terms or "in" talk.

5. Make the reader feel singled out, unique, a special person.

It's a letter. Letters should appear to be personal. Whether computer-personalized or not, give it a personal, me-to-you feel. You're writing only to this one individual. As marketers, we want thousands of responses. As professional letter writers, we need to say "Only you." An appeal based on exclusivity not only is easy to construct; it does work.

6. Avoid arm's-length copy except when you can claim an Olympian position.

The god Zeus can throw thunderbolts. If the reader recognizes you as Zeus, go ahead and heave them. If the reader might resent your posturing and strutting, you're safer putting your arm around the prospect's shoulder as you're writing.

7. Sprinkle your text liberally with that magic word, *you.*

Here we can use rhetorical tricks. We can start by referring to what we're selling with the article *the.* As the text progresses, we gradually replace *the* with *your,* invisibly increasing the concept of reader possession.

Can you over use *you?* Sure, you can; but unsuccessful letters more often under use it than overuse it.

8. Assume the reader is enthusiastic.

Don't write like a loser. Enthusiasm is contagious. So is apathy.

What happens when a professional writer breaks some of these rules? The same result a professional poker player gets when changing cards. The result can be a royal flush, an "inside straight," or a pair of deuces—in other words, either complete, unqualified success or near-total disaster. And, note, please: These are professionals. If you're not yet stained with the blood of a competitor or yourself from the direct mail wars, play it safe. Open your sales argument with as many of your strongest sales points as possible. The reader, your partner, will know how to respond.

An Effective Letter Should Have . . .

Any "blanket" type of categorization is dangerous. Still, inspecting the letters in this collection, we can categorize effective letters into a dozen different groups:

1. How lucky you are to be among the first to know about this . . . *or* You're invited.
2. I want you to have this, but if I don't hear from you I'll have to offer it to somebody else.
3. I have something you want . . . or certainly should want.
4. At last you have an edge over (somebody) (everybody) else.
5. You're in a unique position (to make a difference) (to be supreme) (to save a child or a nation) (to know what nobody else knows) (to have what nobody else has).
6. (Especially for fund raising) The situation is desperate. You and I have very little time.
7. This is important to you, and here's why.
8. Remember when . . . ? Good times are here again.
9. You can still (get rich) (get in on this).
10. Quit worrying. Here's the solution to your problem.
11. Are you making these mistakes?
12. Let others suffer. You don't have to.

Variations of these exist, of course, and some successful letters are difficult to categorize. But those are the huge bins into which most fall. They seize the reader and play an emotional rat-a-tat-tat through one of the great motivators of our time—*fear, exclusivity, greed, guilt,* and *need for approval,* plus occasional astute use of the two "soft" motivators, *pleasure* and *convenience.* (Don't forget: fund raisers writing to single-issue groups have another motivator in their arsenal: *anger.*)

And the Difference Is . . .

Many—no, make that <u>most</u> direct mail letters of any professionalism use one of those 12 approaches. What drops the less-effective letters into a lower echelon? What makes them less effective in the first place?

The answer, invariably:

Letters that hit and run are losers.

What's a hit and run? A letter that says,

- "How lucky you are to be among the first to know about this"—but doesn't give us any proof . . .
- A letter that says, "I want you to have this, but if I don't hear from you I'll have to offer it to somebody else,"—and doesn't convince us we should have it . . .

- A letter that says, "I have something you want"—and doesn't persuade us that yes, we do want it . . .
- A letter that crows, "At last you have an edge over somebody else"—and leaves us apathetic about this questionable or useless edge.

This is the difference between amateurish puffery—make a claim and hope the reader believes it—and professional puffery—make a claim and apparently prove it.

How Do We Do That?

The technique is a lot simpler than the casual letter-writer, untrained in the tempering discipline resulting from immersion in the fires of competition, might imagine.

Transforming amateurish puffery into professional puffery is as simple as forcing evidence out of your keyboard.

Add one of these to a claim, and you can't leave the reader dangling on the unraveling thread of an unproved claim:

- *Here's why.*
- *That's because . . .*
- *I can prove it to you this way:*
- *I'll tell you what John A. Sample says about this.*
- *This is what will happen.*
- *When you do that, the result will be . . .*
- *You'll never again be [WHATEVER] because . . .*
- *This is why I've chosen you for this offer:*
- *I'll explain the difference:*

Analyze what these statements have in common, and you'll probably be able to add another batch. There's no mystery here. The difference between the amateur and the professional is the difference between a strident claim of superiority or effectiveness or necessity and the convincing proof of superiority or effectiveness or necessity.

Mini-tricks for Effectiveness

Only after a couple of hundred years of seat-of-the-pants experimentation are we learning the value of punctuation.

- Open with a question . . . you've involved the reader.
- End a comment with a colon . . . the reader knows an explanation will follow.
- Use exclamation marks judiciously . . . the reader will exclaim with you.

- Use a semicolon after a statement . . . the reader knows what follows relates to what preceded.
- Put a sentence or phrase or single word or number within a pair of parentheses . . . the reader subordinates the parenthetical thought.
- Tie an adjective which also can be a noun to the next word with a hyphen (example: *force-communication*) . . . the reader's speed and comprehension both are improved.

These procedures have little to do with grammar. They're all components of the force-communications mix, and the more a writer recognizes which punctuation if any to use, the more in command that writer becomes.

Chapter 3

Subscriptions Are the "Bellwether"

Any compendium of "great" direct mail letters has to be skewed heavily in favor of subscriptions and books.

One reason is that some of the titans of direct mail letter-writing, such as Bill Jayme, Gary Bencivenga, Ed McLean, and the late Mel Martin, have written exclusively or most frequently for publications.

Convincing someone who opens an envelope without having any prior desire to subscribe to a publication or to buy a book is the height of direct response psychology. Why? Because subscriptions and books aren't parallel to "product" whose romance is more easily described.

The letters in this section are the best work by some of the best writers. We're saying "some" because even we couldn't know or reach every writer, and some we did reach were too modest or diffident to share their rhetorical treasures. (Others were terrified that we'd print letters their bosses or clients didn't want replicated.)

The Two "Faces" of Circulation Promotions

Circulation promotions have two faces: "hard offers" and "soft offers." Hard offers say, in effect, "Pay us and we'll send you the magazine." Soft offers, much more in vogue, say, "We'll send you one issue free. If you like what you see, pay the bill and we'll send you more. If not, just write 'Cancel' on the bill and that will be the end of the matter." Always, in soft offers, gross response—total requests for a free issue—will be considerably higher than net response.

Mailer: **The Wall Street Journal**

Key Words: **"On a beautiful late spring afternoon"**

(© The Wall Street Journal)

Writer: **Martin Conroy**

The Challenge

A newspaper has an image. In this case the image is that of an elitist publication, aimed at and circulating to captains of industry.

To broaden the circulation base, the newspaper has to target and convince the next lower echelon of potential reader. How to do this, without compromising the image of the publication? What is the reason to subscribe in the first place?

The Implementation

The Wall Street Journal shows a fictional, but logical episode justifying subscription. By writing the letter in first-person singular, the approach became avuncular, acceptable advice from someone who has been there and experienced the success the letter suggests.

Comment

This letter has endured for more than 20 years! That alone makes it worthy of inclusion in *any* compendium of great letters. Some estimate it has resulted in more than $1 billion in subscription orders.

The writer points out what the analyst assumes: The letter is aimed at middle management—those aged 25 to 45, on their way up the corporate ladder.

Figure 3–1. ***The Wall Street Journal***

THE WALL STREET JOURNAL.

World Financial Center, 200 Liberty Street, New York, NY 10281

Dear Reader:

On a beautiful late spring afternoon, twenty-five years ago, two young men graduated from the same college. They were very much alike, these two young men. Both had been better than average students, both were personable and both—as young college graduates are—were filled with ambitious dreams for the future.

Recently, these men returned to their college for their 25th reunion.

They were still very much alike. Both were happily married. Both had three children. And both, it turned out, had gone to work for the same Midwestern manufacturing company after graduation, and were still there.

But there was a difference. One of the men was manager of a small department of that company. The other was its president.

What Made The Difference

Have you ever wondered, as I have, what makes this kind of difference in people's lives? It isn't a native intelligence or talent or dedication. It isn't that one person wants success and the other doesn't.

The difference lies in what each person knows and how he or she makes use of that knowledge.

And that is why I am writing to you and to people like you about The Wall Street Journal. For that is the whole purpose of The Journal: to give its readers knowledge—knowledge that they can use in business.

A Publication Unlike Any Other

You see, The Wall Street Journal is a unique publication. It's the country's only national business daily. Each business day, it is put together by the world's largest staff of business-news experts.

Each business day, The Journal's pages include a broad range of information of interest and significance to business-minded people, no matter where it comes from. Not just stocks and finance, but anything and everything in the whole, fast-moving world of business. . .The Wall Street Journal gives you all the business news you need—when you need it.

Knowledge Is Power

Right now, I am looking at page one of The Journal, the best-read front page in America. It combines all the important news of the day with in-depth feature reporting. Every phase of business news is covered. I see articles on new taxes, inflation, business forecasts, gas prices, politics. I see major stories from Washington, Berlin, Tokyo, the Middle East. I see item after item that can affect you, your job, your future.

(over, please)

A classic "control" letter, aimed at second-echelon ladder-climbers. *(Continued)*

And there is page after page inside The Journal, filled with fascinating and significant information that's useful to you. The Marketplace section gives you insights into how consumers are thinking and spending. How companies compete for market share. There is daily coverage of law, technology, media and marketing. Plus daily features on the challenges of managing smaller companies.

The Journal is also the single best source for news and statistics about your money. In the Money & Investing section there are helpful charts, easy-to-scan market quotations, plus "Abreast of the Market," "Heard on the Street" and "Your Money Matters," three of America's most influential and carefully read investment columns.

If you have never read The Wall Street Journal, you cannot imagine how useful it can be to you.

A Money-Saving Subscription

Put our statements to the proof by subscribing for the next 13 weeks for just $44. This is among the shortest subscription terms we offer—and a perfect way to get acquainted with The Journal.

Or you may prefer to take advantage of our better buy—one year for $149. You save over $40 off the cover price of The Journal.

Simply fill out the enclosed order card and mail it in the postage-paid envelope provided. And here's The Journal's guarantee: should The Journal not measure up to your expectations, you may cancel this arrangement at any point and receive a refund for the undelivered portion of your subscription.

If you feel as we do that this is a fair and reasonable proposition, then you will want to find out without delay if The Wall Street Journal can do for you what it is doing for millions of readers. So please mail the enclosed order card now, and we will start serving you immediately.

About those two college classmates I mention at the beginning of this letter: they were graduated from college together and together got started in the business world. So what made their lives in business different?

Knowledge. Useful knowledge. And its application.

An Investment In Success

I cannot promise you that success will be instantly yours if you start reading The Wall Street Journal. But I can guarantee that you will find The Journal always interesting, always reliable, and always useful.

Sincerely,

Peter R. Kann
Publisher

PRK: id
Encs.

P.S. It's important to note that The Journal's subscription price may be tax deductible. Ask your tax advisor.

subscribing...then keep that big issue as our gift to you. You will pay nothing, and there will be no further obligation of any kind.

Now let me answer more fully the question you undoubtedly have...

With literally hundreds of American magazines to choose from, why should you subscribe to The Illustrated LONDON NEWS?

What can it bring to your life, to your understanding of the world around you that Time, Newsweek...The New Yorker, Harper's...or other such reputable domestic publications cannot?

Global perspective.

You see, The Illustrated LONDON NEWS is not primarily about London. It is about the world. It gives you unbiased, international viewpoints on the vital issues of the day. The Mid-East, Iran, OPEC, SALT. Inflation, taxation, pollution.

You will be surprised at the quantity of U.S. coverage, with typical articles on: President Carter - his rating abroad...Herbert Hoover's nightmare - could Wall Street crash again?...Ft. Ross - the remains of Russia's little-known outpost in California.

In-depth illustrated feature articles take you to worlds you might not otherwise explore: the primitive lives of the Cayapa Indians of Ecuador...the dramatic peak-scaling attempt up savage Latok 2 in the Himalayas...Arabia's Pirate Coast...or the lonely world of the successful cartoonist.

Here, for example, are the varied topics you would have discovered in a single recent issue:

- President Carter: How's He Doing?
- Hang Gliding in Southern Utah
- The pros and cons of reprocessing nuclear fuel
- Return to Latok 2 in the Himalayas
- Parasites and Hyperparasites
- The Cartoonists - their successful and lonely lives
- Renovation of Covent Garden
- Welsh Rugby loses its prince - the great Gareth Edwards
- The Gold of Eldorado - the legend and search it inspired
- The Laser Supersleuth - the police use of lasers to detect indiscernible fingerprints
- The Hard Grind of London's Acting Schools

(Continued)

- Research into Egyptian Tomb Sculpture
- The Earth as Seen from Space
- For Collectors - Creations in Glass
- The spread of Victorian Jewelry
- A Lively Market in Precious Stones
- Travel - Siberia in Winter

PLUS - pages and pages of columns and articles on:

art...opera...recent books, fiction and other...theatre ...cinema...ballet...wine...food...bridge...chess... gardening...money...property...and even a complete Motor Show Guide!

All this - in a single information-packed issue of The Illustrated LONDON NEWS.

You will appreciate this unique monthly newsmagazine for its incisive reporting. For its impartial commentary - unpressured by American lobbies, big business, and political influences.

Your life will be enriched by the generous cultural nourishment it provides month after month.

And - above all - you will appreciate its scope.

Interested in the inventions of Leonardo...the latest findings on the Loch Ness Monster...West Germany's futuristic dashboard display that may soon drive your car automatically?

Like to know more about Hong Kong's Water People...the new "invisible" gamma ray astronomy that is uncovering mysteries of outer space...Paul Mellon's views on art collecting?

You will find it all - and a good deal more - in The Illustrated LONDON NEWS.

ACCEPT THIS SPECIAL NO-RISK SATISFACTION-GUARANTEED
OFFER FROM THE PUBLISHER...

You are invited to join a select group of discerning Americans and examine The Illustrated LONDON NEWS...entirely without risk.

Let us send you the first big 9" x 12" full-color issue to enjoy at your leisure. Spend a few moments with it in the comfort of your living room. Or tuck it under your arm and take it along to work for lunch-hour

(please turn)

(Continued)

reading diversion.

If you are not as delighted with your introductory issue as I believe you will be, then simply cancel the bill...pay nothing...and keep the first issue as our no-obligation gift to you.

Otherwise, we will enter your year's subscription for 12 monthly issues at the rate of just $20, with this further guarantee:

> At any time, for any reason, you may cancel and receive a refund on the unused portion of your subscription.

IN ADDITION - for subscribing now - we will include the special year-end Christmas issue - making it not 12, but 13 giant-sized issues in all for the same reasonable annual cost.

After 150 years, The Illustrated LONDON NEWS remains for many the international newsmagazine of our time.

You be the judge. Try it. Simply mail the enclosed no-risk subscription card in the postpaid envelope provided.

Sincerely,

Rodney Winston

Rodney Winston
U.S. Subscription Manager

RW:cm

Mailer: **Worth Magazine**
Key Words: **"It was Scott Fitzgerald"**
Writer: **Bill Jayme**
Art Director: **Heikki Ratalahti**

The Challenge

How many publications are aimed at the moneyed investor?

This group of targets is a rich lode because of buying power and diversity of interests. The result is a seemingly endless parade of periodicals, most of which make the same claims.

How can a new publication not only make a different claim, but appear to be more readable, more sprightly, and more relevant than its host of competitors?

The Implementation

The giant word "FREE" dominates the beginning of this communication. The basic sales argument is quickly condensed into a comparison chart which, despite being split through pagination, makes a potent point without irritating the reader.

Added to the mixture is a quiet challenge—a series of questions, the answers to which are difficult enough that no recipient can say, "Oh, I know the answer to that already."

The letter concludes with a triple punch—"Send no money"; "Owe nothing"; and "Low Charter Rate." This combination of sales tools has seldom been used in concert so smoothly.

Comment

The synergy between copy and art is seldom apparent in a letter because most writers simply write text. The celebrated partnership between Bill Jayme and Heikki Ratalahti produces letters which are a *gestalt*—the eye reacts to the appearance as much as it does to the actual text. One quick look at the "disadvantages of being rich" and the "advantages of being rich" on the first page of this 4-page letter has to give many writers that "Why didn't I think of this?" reaction. And note the handwritten circle around the single "advantages" entry on page 2.

A positioning statement: Tested against "traditional" serious letters, this one was the runaway winner.

Figure 3–3. *Worth Magazine*

It's the sophisticated new magazine about you and money—making it, investing it, enjoying it.

You're invited to reserve Charter Perks & Freebies and to preview our next issue without cost or obligation.

Dear Reader:

It was Scott Fitzgerald who observed, "The rich are different from us."

It was Ernest Hemingway who then shot back, "Yes. They have more money."

But money isn't all that the rich have more of. They also have more worries...

...so before you accept this invitation to move up higher financially, you may want to consider some of the pros and cons:

DISADVANTAGES of being rich	ADVANTAGES of being rich
You'll start hearing from long-lost cousins looking for loans.	
You won't be able to get away with sending the Red Cross just $10.	
Total strangers will corner you to ask which stocks to buy.	
You'll be expected to use the Full Service pumps, to buy Super, and to tip.	

(over, please)

A master imparts creative synergy to maximize impact. *(Continued)*

DISADVANTAGES	ADVANTAGES
You'll have to dress for the opera.	
Whenever you throw a dinner party, you'll be expected to provide valet parking.	
No guest will ever again show up bearing a bottle of wine.	
Political candidates will want to be introduced to you.	
None will want voters to see you together.	
You'll feel obliged to buy the Forbes 400 issue each year to see if you've made the list of America's richest.	You'll have tons more money.

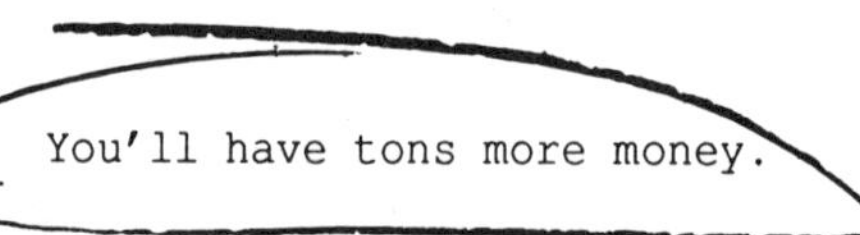

So, now then. Do you really still want to be rich? You do? Great! And I think you're going to feel right at home immediately with WORTH, the sophisticated new personal finance magazine that encourages you to think rich, live rich, and be rich.

FREE EXAMINATION ISSUE

The next issue of WORTH will be out momentarily, with our exclusive guide to the best brokerage firms. Who has the best research, the best service, fewest investor complaints, the most innovative products? WORTH will tell you.

> Additional goodies. If you like the first issue, you can then enjoy other Charter freebies and perks including a special survival guide to help you protect and enhance your lifestyle, plus a timely round-up of expert opinion on how best to structure your investments for the 21st century. Read on!

WORTH is backed by the publishing subsidiary of Fidelity Investments, one of the nation's most prestigious financial institutions. The magazine operates totally independently. It's totally unfettered. Totally unbiased. And I think you'll find that it's also totally unique.

Unlike other personal finance publications, WORTH is written and edited

(Continued)

for a very special kind of individual. The assumptions we've made about you are these:

> If you're not already living on Easy Street, you're by now only a block or two away.
>
> Your day-to-day investing decisions are being handled quite capably by various professionals in your employ – a money manager, stock broker, banker, et al.
>
> You enjoy being a part of the investing decisions made on your behalf – reading about them, discussing them, often making recommendations of your own.
>
> And ... being human, you can't help wondering at times if you couldn't be doing even better.

Helping you to do better is precisely where WORTH comes in. The magazine is written for lay persons in easy-to-grasp, conversational English – not industry jargon. But it brings you information, ideas and advice that are normally reserved for professionals. And it takes the long-term view, not the short.

For example:

o when the nation finally rebounds from recession, which market sectors will be first to reward investment?

o what opportunities lie waiting in international markets as European markets integrate, and as Hong Kong reverts to China?

o which products and services stand to make the most money from the greying of America – the elderly and retired?

o where might you invest to help meet the needs of America's newest immigrants – housing, education, day care centers?

o which U.S. companies stand to profit most from the rebuilding of Russia and Eastern Europe?

o what's ahead for technology issues – genetics, communications, transportation, space?

o how might you turn a penny or two when the government finally decides to overhaul the nation's health care system?

o as the environmental movement gathers force, what investments should you maybe think about dumping?

We live in exciting times! And from the standpoint of making money,

(over, please)

(Continued)

nowhere will you get better answers to questions like these than from the stories and columns in WORTH.

> Features like The Advisor — financial management tips, investment opportunities, money myths. Intrigue — the inside scoop on the movers and shakers, the deals they're putting together.
>
> ROI (Return on Investment) about getting the most value for your money — vacation hideaways, high-tech toys, lifestyle gear, food and wine. And our private sage and seer, Contrarious, written under a nom-de-plume with the knowing outlook of a 30-year investing veteran ...

...but come experience WORTH for yourself on us — compliments of the house.

The magazine is published six times a year, not weekly or monthly, so as to give you plenty of time for absorbing one issue fully before going on to the next ... for gaining in-depth perspective on strategies ... for mulling over new opportunities, ideas, avenues and options. I think you'll find it enormously stimulating ... and quite a bit of fun.

> SEND NO MONEY. When you mail the enclosed card promptly, you'll receive a copy of our very next issue for your examination. No cost. No obligation.
>
> OWE NOTHING. If for any reason you feel that the magazine is not for you, just return the subscription bill marked "cancel," and that's that. You've spent nothing. You owe nothing.
>
> LOW CHARTER RATE. But if, on the other hand, you find WORTH to be pertinent - interesting, informative, relative to your interests and goals - your price as a Charter Subscriber is just $9.97 for a full year.

PLUS OTHER FREEBIES & PERKS. By reserving now, you save from the very start. You save in perpetuity. You have a full refund guarantee at all times on all copies still to go. And in the special flyer I'm enclosing, you'll read about other valuable Charter benefits that include a free survival guide, and a special investing handbook.

EARLY POSTMARK. Only so many copies of the next issue are being printed - no more. In fairness, first come, first served. Avoid disappointment. Mail the card at your earliest convenience. Why not be rich just as soon as you can? Or at least a bit richer?

Yours cordially,

John M Boyd

John Boyd
Publication Director

worth

The net result of intelligent investing

Mailer: **The Bonanza Report**
Key Words: **"Are you prepared to be very, very rich?"**
Writer: **Ruth Sheldon**

The Challenge

The typical investor is immediately wary of publications purporting to transmit money-making information on the stock market.

That's because the typical investor has already suffered through subscriptions to such publications, most of which sank into speculative opinions unbacked by solid research.

Cracking this wall of skepticism—skepticism based on negative experiences and negative newspaper articles about the entire field of fiduciary advice—is indeed a major challenge.

To compound the problem, this publication embraces penny stocks, which, for investors, are the most suspect of all investments.

The Implementation

The pre-letter statement of position makes an extraordinary claim:

> Several years ago, I bought 100,000 shares in a venture capital company that looked as if it was going places. It went. I paid 3 cents a share. Three months later the stock was trading at $3 a share. That's a profit of $297,000 before taxes.

The subheads progress in proper sequence, concluding with a no-risk offer and a guarantee. The P.S. reinforces the free gifts included with the offer.

Comment

Some critics might wonder whether having so much text before the greeting impedes quick readership. We would wonder, too, if the writer had not pointed out the letter achieved a 17% response rate. Had the letter not been written (ostensibly) by an individual who reinforces the claim in the opening text with his own picture, the results might not have been so strong.

Figure 3–4. The Bonanza Report

THE BONANZA REPORT

ABSOLUTELY NOT FOR THE TIMID, THE TENTATIVE OR THE ME-TOOer!

I've always been fascinated by penny stocks. It started when I was a stock broker and blossomed into a love affair during the 16 years I was president of my own Wall Street brokerage firm. My buddies thought I was crazy, until they realized, I was crazy like a fox.

Several years ago, I bought 100,000 shares in a venture capital company that looked as if it was going places. It went. I paid 3 cents a share. Three months later the stock was trading at $3 a share. That's a profit of $297,000 before taxes. Not bad for an initial investment of $3,000. As my friends will now tell you, because of my many successes with penny stocks, I now live the good life with more money than I will ever need.

If I've made you even a little curious about one of the most exciting and lucrative investment markets in the world, I'd like to send you two issues of **THE BONANZA REPORT** -- the only independent monthly newsletter of penny stock recommendations -- ABSOLUTELY FREE. No strings. No obligations. It's on me.

Dear Friend,

Are you prepared to be very, very rich? It **can** happen. Without your having lots of money to invest. Without your ever having been an investor before. I'm talking about the penny stock market where the risks are high but the potential for making lots of money with a small initial investment is as real as the bank accounts of those who continue to reap windfalls.

But penny stocks are not for everyone. They're not for the faint-hearted or "me-tooers" who wait for everyone else to jump on the bandwagon before they make their move. But I don't think you're that kind of person.

If my research and intuition are correct, you're exhilarated by challenge and have the foresight to take a calculated risk when the rewards warrant it.

That's why I want you to see first-hand how **THE BONANZA REPORT** gives you the potential of converting a small investment into profits that can exceed 1,000% in 90 days! Right now two issues of my newsletter are reserved in your name FREE. To receive them, all you do is return the enclosed Reservation Card. But more of that in a minute.

(over, please)

Breaking through the Wall of Cynicism to get a "Bonanza." *(Continued)*

-2-

How the Leverage Factor Can Make You Rich

You studied it in science. The leverage principle works the same way with penny stocks. A small investment effort results in proportionally much greater returns.

Think about it. If you were to invest $500 in AT&T, you would own less than 20 shares. The same $500 buys you 50,000 shares of a stock costing a penny. If both stocks went up ten cents (not at all uncommon with penny stocks), you would have made a $2.00 profit with your AT&T stock and a $4,500 profit on your penny stock investment! That's even better than moving a boulder with a crowbar.

The Leverage Factor and Power

Now consider the leverage of power and influence. Owning 20 shares of AT&T doesn't make you a very important stockholder. Try calling AT&T's president and you'd be lucky to get past a secretary in the investor relations department.

It's a whole new ball game when you own 50,000 shares or maybe 500,000 shares of a Belaire Energy, for example. Its president would probably keep you on the phone for an hour discussing OPEC, the future of the oil industry, and the possibility of your paying a visit to the company.

Your opinion counts! You're an important person in the life of Belaire's President because you are a major stockholder. He wants to keep you informed... and happy. What you do with your controlling shares can have a significant impact on the direction of his company. And no CEO lets this go by unnoticed.

What Do You, T. Boone Pickens and Carl Icahn Have in Common?

How do the fat cats make their money? It's basically simple. Their big bucks buy mega numbers of shares in a company they think has potential. They could be acting on news of a merger, a new discovery or just intuition. Because of their financial clout, they stand to make a bundle even when there's only a modest rise in a stock's price.

The same principle of buy-a-lot-and-make-a-killing holds true with penny stocks. Because they're usually priced at under two dollars, penny stocks let you do precisely what Icahn and Pickens do -- only on a smaller scale.

Just imagine the fun of telling your friends you bought 20,000 shares of stock in an oil company because you think the price of oil will firm. Then watch their expressions when you tell them your stock went up from 25 cents a share to $5.25 as Altex Oil did...or from 25 cents to $4.75 as Silver King Mines did...or from 85 cents to $34.50 as Toys 'R' Us did.

What The Bonanza Report Gives You That No Other Monthly Publication Can

Unlike other publications, **THE BONANZA REPORT** is not a lazy rehashing of

(Continued)

-3-

broker's tips, or press releases from company "hopefuls" who pay for the coverage they receive. We don't forecast the market because our recommendations are based on a company's growth potential which is equally valid in any financial climate.

Each and every month **THE BONANZA REPORT** gives you independent, concrete recommendations on specific penny stocks we think can easily double, triple and even go up ten times in value within six months to a year. In plain and simple English, I tell you which stocks to buy, which to sell, which to hold.

And even if you decide never to invest a cent, you'll get an insider's view of the future. You'll learn which companies hold promise and why. How to deal with brokers. Why some companies go belly up while others blossom. How to avoid the slumps and surges of the marketplace. And so much more.

The Numbers Don't Lie: THE BONANZA REPORT's Track Record

Subscribers often ask why so many of my recommendations are right on target. The answer is hard work -- and plenty of it. After many years of experience -- plus extensive contacts in the investment community -- I'm able to spot companies where merger or acquisition activities are happening. Where management has positioned a company for explosive growth in sales, profits and returns on shareholders'investments.

Before you read about it in **THE BONANZA REPORT**, my staff and I thoroughly research a company, analyze its financials, talk with its executives and in some cases with suppliers, banks and customers.

And as you can see below, our investigative footwork pays off royally. For example, recent **BONANZA** recommendations like Checkrobot went from $2 per share to $3.63 (a gain of 82% in 12 months)...Environmental Diagnostics Inc. went from 59 cents per share to $3.06 (a gain of 419% in 21 months)...Great Western Systems Inc., went from 50 cents per share to $1.44 (a gain of 251% in 9 months)...and the list goes on.

Of course, not all of our recommendations are this successful. I once recommended a stock in a company promoting a surgical pin that was developed in Russia. This product was considered a great success by top European physicians and promised to be a winner in this country. The day after we made our recommendations, the Russian-Korean airliner tragedy occurred. No one wanted to have anything to do with a Russian product. Our stock hit rock bottom.

There's always the chance that an unforeseen event like this can upset a very promising applecart. But that's part of what makes owning penny stocks so exciting.

But in order to limit your downside risks as much as possible, our recommendations are designed to help you build a diversified, well-balanced portfolio. And we naturally follow up all our selections so you're alerted whenever we think the time has come to cash in your chips on a particular stock.

(over, please)

(Continued)

And Now For My No-Risk Offer

Please accept as my gift to you, two issues of **THE BONANZA REPORT**, normally a $12 value, absolutely free. Instead of paying the regular one-year subscription price of $72, you'll receive the next 12 issues for just $60. But if you act right now, I'll do even better than that. I'll reduce your subscription price even further to only **$49**! That's a savings of 32% off the regular price.

Or, you can subscribe for two years, and save even more. Pay only $79 for 24 issues. **That's a savings of 45% off the regular price.**

You'll receive exclusive recommendations on our **Aggressive Investor's Stock** (with the potential of doubling or better within 6-12 months)...**Speculator's Pick of the Month** (riskier but with a chance of appreciating even more)...**Follow Up Advice** (the latest news and developments on stocks we've recommended)...and **New Issues to Watch** (advice about issues being sold for the first time.)

But that's not all...

Because I believe information is an investor's best friend, I'll also send you Alan Horowitz's informative introductory booklet, The Low-Price Stocks Guide ...plus...an invaluable directory of brokers who handle penny stocks in your area. And as I said before, there are no strings. This material is yours to keep FREE by just returning the Reservation Card. You can read more about your free gifts in the enclosed flyer.

Our Guarantee to You

If for any reason, **THE BONANZA REPORT** fails to live up to your expectations, just cancel for a full refund on all unmailed issues. No questions asked.

For fastest service, VISA or MASTERCARD card holders may order by calling 1-800-628-7954 toll free, weekdays, 8AM-4PM, Pacific Standard Time.

I look forward to your reply in the return mail.

Sincerely,

James Bartel

James Bartel

P.S. Remember, even if you decide NOT to subscribe, two issues of **THE BONANZA REPORT**, the National Stock Broker Directory, and The Low-Price Stocks Guide are yours to keep as my gift to you!

Mailer: Men's Health

Key Words: "He has a certain male magic"

The Challenge

This magazine shares a challenge with all personal health magazines: Using a combination of fear and curiosity about one's own health, fitness, and sexual prowess without lapsing into insult or foolishness.

The problems the publication promises to solve have to be ones the target recognizes as potentially damaging to him.

The Implementation

In a single letter the writer encapsulates within two words—"male magic"—just about every problem that might face today's half-macho, half-frightened man.

So references are made to igniting a woman's sex drive, super-charging the man's sex drive, increasing chest size, lowering risk of disease, looking better-groomed, having a more successful career, and to cap off the promises of improvement, combating thinning hair.

The book, *101 Men's Health Secrets,* is described as a special "FOR MEN ONLY" report, suggesting secret inside information. The second report, "New Sex Secrets for the Modern Man," is carefully sandwiched between that first report and "How to drop 10 pounds fast." Had the writer given any more emphasis to this second report, it might have caused some unease and discomfort. By cleverly positioning it as one of three, the writer avoids any negative reaction.

Comment

What's *your* opinion of using typeset instead of a typewriter face for a letter? Ours is usually negative, but what this writer has done has been to give the reader a visually exciting, easy-to-read message. Note the power words such as, "ignite," "supercharge," and—as noted in "The Implementation"—"sex secrets."

Figure 3–5. *Men's Health*

Men's Health

Emmaus, PA 18098

"He has a certain . . . male magic!"

Dear Sir,

Do you know about "male magic"?

Do you know how to tap the secret powers locked within your own body and mind?

The mysterious power to IGNITE a woman's sex drive when her libido is almost nonexistent?

The nutritional power to SUPERCHARGE your potency, sex drive, immunity and wound healing with a single magic substance . . .

The secret power to build a BIGGER, STRONGER chest and arms in just minutes a day?

You don't know about these powers?

Then you haven't been reading MEN'S HEALTH® magazine.

At MEN'S HEALTH, we're dedicated to giving you comprehensive, reliable information on how to unleash the astonishing male powers locked inside you.

And I'm here to tell you how EASY it is to take a FREE look at what you've been missing. Just say the magic word, and I'll send you the current issue of MEN'S HEALTH -- with my compliments.

It won't cost you a penny.

You could be enjoying your newfound male powers in a matter of days -- at no cost or risk to you . . .

SEXUAL POWER to not only satisfy your lover every time, but bring both of you to new heights of orgasmic pleasure . . .

(over, please)

A visually exciting, easy-to-read message creates "mail magic." *(Continued)*

How to get AWESOME ABS in

FITNESS POWER to not only avoid injury in your workouts, but get maximum strength and endurance from the simplest exercises . . .

NUTRITIONAL POWER to not only lower your risk of disease, but live a supercharged life . . .

HEALTH POWER to not only resist aging, but gain new strength and vigor at any age . . .

RELATIONSHIP POWER to not only get along with the opposite sex, but develop winning relationships with women . . .

GROOMING POWER to not only look your best, but be the best-looking man in any crowd . . .

CAREER POWER to not only survive in your career, but unleash creative forces that will lift you to the pinnacle of success!

More than a million men turn to each issue of MEN'S HEALTH for immediately useful information about these important male issues. Want some specific examples? Just look:

* Five vitamins that ERASE AGE like magic.
* Explicit instructions on how to have TWO OR MORE orgasms without losing your erection.
* The mysterious secret of the best time to ask for a RAISE.
* How to get AWESOME ABS in just 20 minutes a week.
* How to choose from among the new medical advances for THINNING HAIR.
* The easy diet trick that ELIMINATES MILD DEPRESSION.
* The POTENCY PILL that stimulates the brain's sexual pleasure center.
* The magic way to banish a POTBELLY and BACK PAIN in just minutes a day.
* The magic way to make your child feel SECURE.
* Doctor's secret way to tell whether you should EXERCISE with that cold.
* The pill to take before a workout to head off SORE MUSCLES.
* How to spot VENEREAL DISEASE on a partner.

(Continued)

just five minutes every other day.

* Secret one-minute trick to REVERSE the effects of STRESS.

* And more!

MEN'S HEALTH readers tell us that we make fitness fun. We make health a pleasure. And we make medical news relevant and fascinating -- as well as practical and easy to apply to busy modern lives.

Thanks to what they see and read in MEN'S HEALTH, our readers tell us that they look and feel better, stronger, healthier, sexier.

They've unlocked male powers within their own bodies and minds.

Now you can too!

Powers that make your life better in every way. Healthier. Happier. Sexier. More successful.

TRY THE FIRST ISSUE FREE!

Sound good? We think it does. That's why we made it so EASY for you to try MEN'S HEALTH. Absolutely FREE.

On the newsstand, MEN'S HEALTH costs $2.95 per issue. But when you mail back the enclosed reply card, I'll send you the latest issue absolutely free.

But if the magazine is not for you, you won't need magic to end the matter. All you have to do is mark "cancel" on the subscription invoice and return it. Keep the first issue free with my thanks.

But I really believe you'll be as excited about MEN'S HEALTH as I am. If you are, just pay the SPECIAL INTRODUCTORY RATE for a full year's subscription.

PLUS — RECEIVE A FREE BOOK
101 Men's Health Secrets
(Absolutely no purchase necessary!)

Here's a FREE BONUS to sweeten the deal and help you come into your own male magic even faster:

Mail the enclosed card right away, and I'll send you a copy of 101 Men's Health Secrets ABSOLUTELY FREE!

This is a special "FOR MEN ONLY" report filled with secret tips and instructions for unleashing your male powers in all matters of life and love.

(over, please)

- →

(Continued)

It's yours FREE, with my compliments, just for taking a **free look** at the latest issue of MEN'S HEALTH magazine. NO COST! NO RISK! NO OBLIGATION!

DOUBLE BONUS! You'll also receive a FREE second special report: New Sex Secrets for the Modern Man . . . PLUS: an additional FREE special report: How to Drop 10 Pounds FAST.

ALL THREE SPECIAL REPORTS ARE YOURS TO KEEP WITHOUT OBLIGATION . . . EVEN IF YOU DO NOT SUBSCRIBE!

Don't miss this special opportunity to UNLEASH the MALE MAGIC that lies inside of you.

Mail the enclosed card now!

To your good health,

Michael Lafavore

Michael Lafavore
Executive Editor

P.S. Your satisfaction is guaranteed . . . 100 percent! If MEN'S HEALTH ever lets you down, for any reason, just let us know . . . and we'll issue you a full refund with no questions asked!

You're under NO OBLIGATION at all. Why? Because we're sure that once you've had a taste of your own male magic, you'll want to unlock more and more of it. See for yourself -- mail back the enclosed postage-paid reply card today!

-- M. L.

Printed in USA

MH17488B

- -

Mailer: **Movieline**
Key Words: **"It's Shocking"**
Writer: **Lauren Brenner-Katz**

The Challenge

A generation ago, movie magazines glorified, glamorized, and often fictionalized the lives of movie stars. That was before the days of investigative reporting.

Today, enough exposé-type information appears in supermarket tabloids and television "tell it all" programs to make glamorization passé. This evolution also makes movie magazines as a genre semi-passé. To seize and exploit interest in the Hollywood colony today, a publication has to provide shock and secrets beyond those the public is now accustomed to expect.

The Implementation

The words the writer uses to describe this magazine:

> Probing. Cynical. Thought-provoking. Penetrating. Clever. Surprising. Snide.

The text builds on these points, especially "snide"—note the boxed comment by actress Daryl Hannah. Phraseology such as "Hollywood with its pants down" and "Who has Hollywood cooties?" generate a tone of irreverence that mirrors 1990s reader-cynicism.

Because the writer of this letter obviously is targeting those within and younger than "Generation X" (under age 30), the terminology is in sync. Example: "You'll giggle. You'll groan. You'll gasp."; "When your mother asks why . . . you'll be smart and sassy."

Comment

We have included this letter with and without the "sticky note." These pasted-on notes have, in the last few years, been terrific response-boosters, and this one is no exception. The purpose of these notes is to literally drag the reader into the letter itself. Jan Edwards-Pullen, circulation consultant for the publication, points out that repeated attempts to unseat this letter have failed.

Figure 3–6. The *Movieline* Post-It Note

Movieline

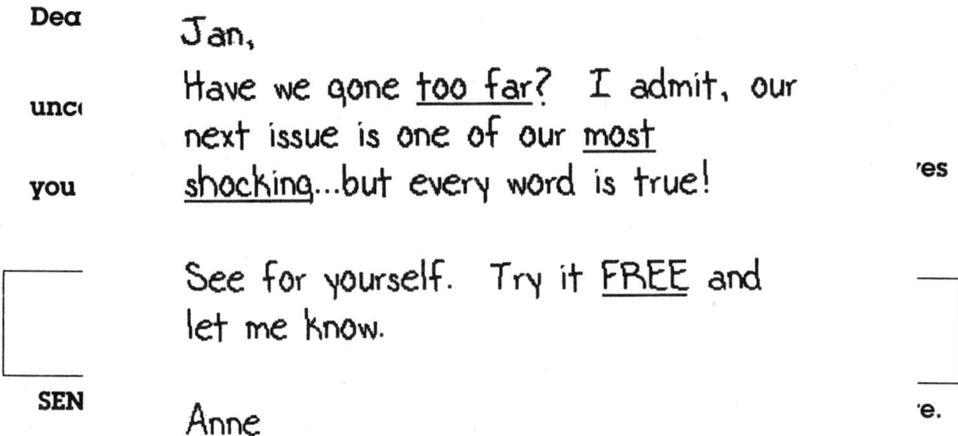

Surp

It's not for the casual moviegoer. It's for people who want to enjoy the glamour and glitz of Hollywood with eyes and minds wide open. We show you the film world like no other publication has ever dared.

WE'RE NOT AFRAID OF GETTING OUR HANDS DIRTY...

Of telling it like it is. Of printing it the way it's said. We're not afraid to dig. To laugh. To offend. To tell you the sometimes wacky and often tacky truth about what's happening on--and behind--the scenes.

> "As soon as I get hired, they start talking about "Oh and in the nude scene..." "What nude scene? It's just a drag. There are some definite sleazebags around."
> Daryl Hannah, Actress. In the November issue.

WAAAAY BEHIND THE SCENES!

We deliver Hollywood with its pants down and its tongue wagging. In-depth interviews ask stars the questions you really want to know. Photos show you the Hollywood parties you really want to see. Features and columns tell you what you really want to hear about today's big names. Special reports tell you what really happened to the golden stars of yesteryear.

* You'll meet actors, actresses, directors and producers where they live, eat and rock and roll.
* See the fashions, trends and events that shape the movie biz.
* Read honest, piercing, enlightening reviews on the latest movies, videos and books.
* Know who's in, and who's on the way out.

Plus, you'll discover:

A simple but effective response booster.

(Continued)

* Who has Hollywood cooties;
* The latest addiction of young Hollywood;
* What the famous do when their stars begin to fade;
* How things really get done in the town without pity;
* Where the hip and trendy wine, dine, sleep and party in LaLaLand;
* Who's making movies...who's making money...and who's making who in movieland.

With *Movieline*, you'll be the first to hear about the top celebs' personal lifestyles. Their crises, challenges and triumphs. Their career moves. Deals in the works.

You'll giggle. You'll groan. You'll gasp.

Above all, you'll be smart and sassy about the ins-and-outs, the ups-and-downs of everyone's favorite industry.

* When your friends talk about this week's leading man, you'll know exactly how he got where he is.
* When others rave about the box office smash, you'll be able to tell them where, when and for how much it was made.
* When know-it-all co-workers critique the latest release, you'll have more than two cents to put in about the script, casting, production and more.
* When your mother asks why you aren't making ten mil' a year, you'll be able to tell her precisely why she'd rather not have you in Hollywood.

WHO SAYS THERE'S NO FREE LUNCH IN HOLLYWOOD?

Return the enclosed card with the yellow sticker attached and we'll send you a FREE ISSUE of *Movieline*. NO RISK. NO STRINGS. NO OBLIGATION. NO KIDDING. If you like it (and you will), pay just $7.50 for 11 more issues (12 in all).

You save 50% off the regular subscription price. And 69% off the newsstand price!

And remember, there's no risk. You send no money now. If you decide not to subscribe, just write "cancel" on your bill and we'll go away.

We guarantee it's the best movie deal you'll get all year.

Sincerely,

Anne Volokh

Anne Volokh
Publisher

P.S. Hurry, place the yellow sticker on your order card today to get your free issue!

Figure 3–7. *Movieline*

Movieline

Dear Friend:

It's shocking. Witty. Sexy. Hilarious. Intelligent. And totally uncensored.

It's *Movieline*, the off-beat, high-style hot new magazine that gives you the inside line on the fascinating world of movies.

The people. The places. The dreams. And the real dirt.

> **"One sits in front of the TV all day watching sports and the other is obsessed with sex. I'll let you decide which is which."**
> Michelle Phillips on Jack Nicholson and Warren Beatty in the November issue.

SEND FOR YOUR FREE ISSUE NOW. NO RISK OR OBLIGATION. But beware. *Movieline* isn't for everyone.

It's probing. Cynical. Thought-provoking. Penetrating. Clever. Surprising. And snide.

It's not for the casual moviegoer. It's for people who want to enjoy the glamour and glitz of Hollywood with eyes and minds wide open. We show you the film world like no other publication has ever dared.

WE'RE NOT AFRAID OF GETTING OUR HANDS DIRTY...

Of telling it like it is. Of printing it the way it's said. We're not afraid to dig. To laugh. To offend. To tell you the sometimes wacky and often tacky truth about what's happening on--and behind--the scenes.

> **"As soon as I get hired, they start talking about "Oh and in the nude scene..." "What nude scene? It's just a drag. There are some definite sleazebags around."**
> Daryl Hannah, Actress. In the November issue.

WAAAAY BEHIND THE SCENES!

We deliver Hollywood with its pants down and its tongue wagging. In-depth interviews ask stars the questions you really want to know. Photos show you the Hollywood parties you really want to see. Features and columns tell you what you really want to hear about today's big names. Special reports tell you what really happened to the golden stars of yesteryear.

* You'll meet actors, actresses, directors and producers where they live, eat and rock and roll.
* See the fashions, trends and events that shape the movie biz.
* Read honest, piercing, enlightening reviews on the latest movies, videos and books.
* Know who's in, and who's on the way out.

Plus, you'll discover:

Appealing to reader-cynicism to overcome subscriber cynicism. *(Continued)*

- Who has Hollywood cooties;
- The latest addiction of young Hollywood;
- What the famous do when their stars begin to fade;
- How things really get done in the town without pity;
- Where the hip and trendy wine, dine, sleep and party in LaLaLand;
- Who's making movies...who's making money...and who's making who in movieland.

With *Movieline*, you'll be the first to hear about the top celebs' personal lifestyles. Their crises, challenges and triumphs. Their career moves. Deals in the works.

You'll giggle. You'll groan. You'll gasp.

Above all, you'll be smart and sassy about the ins-and-outs, the ups-and-downs of everyone's favorite industry.

- When your friends talk about this week's leading man, you'll know exactly how he got where he is.
- When others rave about the box office smash, you'll be able to tell them where, when and for how much it was made.
- When know-it-all co-workers critique the latest release, you'll have more than two cents to put in about the script, casting, production and more.
- When your mother asks why you aren't making ten mil' a year, you'll be able to tell her precisely why she'd rather not have you in Hollywood.

WHO SAYS THERE'S NO FREE LUNCH IN HOLLYWOOD?

Return the enclosed card with the yellow sticker attached and we'll send you a FREE ISSUE of *Movieline*. NO RISK. NO STRINGS. NO OBLIGATION. NO KIDDING. If you like it (and you will), pay just $7.50 for 11 more issues (12 in all).

You save 50% off the regular subscription price. And 69% off the newsstand price!

And remember, there's no risk. You send no money now. If you decide not to subscribe, just write "cancel" on your bill and we'll go away.

We guarantee it's the best movie deal you'll get all year.

Sincerely,

Anne Volokh

Anne Volokh
Publisher

P.S. Hurry, place the yellow sticker on your order card today to get your free issue!

Mailer: **Catnip**
Key Words: **"Because your cat is counting on you"**
Writer: **Barbara Harrison**

The Challenge

Cat owners take their role as surrogate parents for their cat very seriously. A lighthearted approach is not likely to sell a magazine.

On the other hand, a deadly serious approach is at war with the whole concept of pet ownership. So a publication has to balance its appeal between being serious enough to warrant consideration and lighthearted enough to avoid a stodgy, pedantic image.

The Implementation

The first sentence—four words—disarms the reader. In fact, this sentence could apply to many first-person "mock confession" letters. Paw prints and (deliberately?) non-professional-looking photographs say to the reader, "This is for you."

The publication says it takes the mystery out of cat behavior, explains the cat's body language, and offers information on a psychological level as well as a physical level. This positioning is crucial for generating subscriptions in the crowded field of pet publications.

Comment

Guilt is a potent motivator. To a cat owner, the combination of "because your cat is counting on you" and "a Newsletter for Caring Pet Owners" had to be highly motivational. Proof? The letter successfully launched, of all things, a newsletter about cat care.

Figure 3–8. *Catnip*

Because your cat is counting on you...

Please accept from Tufts University School of Veterinary Medicine,
CATNIP:
a Newsletter for Caring Cat Owners.

The next issue is yours absolutely FREE!

Dear Cat Lover,

Okay, I'll admit it.

I leave the radio on when I go out because my three cats find classical music soothing.

And every night, Nicholas the Ridiculous lulls me to sleep by purring in my left ear. The bed gets crowded when Nicholas and Perdita join me and my husband, so Aunty Nina usually heads downstairs to sleep.

(She has so many extra claws that it sounds like someone's clumping down the steps in heavy boots!)

We all have different ways of demonstrating our love for our cats, but we all share the desire to keep them healthy and happy. That's why the experts at the Tufts University School of Veterinary Medicine invite you to ...

> Sample CATNIP, the new monthly newsletter of <u>total cat care</u>. This unique guide helps you understand and respond to your cat's changing medical, behavioral and nutritional needs. Your cat's health and happiness could depend on it.

Best of all, CATNIP is upbeat and entertaining. Fun to

(over, please ...)

A disarming and effective appeal to guilt. *(Continued)*

read. And a charter issue is yours absolutely FREE.

Fascinating reading. No fluff.

CATNIP goes beyond the scope of glossy magazines. Each timely, topical article tackles an important aspect of communicating with, and caring for, the creature you love. And because it carries no advertising, CATNIP is free to give you the honest, independent view of what's really best for your cat. Unbiased reviews of new cat foods and products. Straightforward health advice from one of the nation's leading schools of veterinary medicine.

Starting with your first free issue, you'll love the way CATNIP:

> helps you respond to your cat's changing nutritional needs. Find out how to ensure that even a finicky cat eats a balanced diet.
>
> takes the mystery out of cat behavior, showing you what it means, and how you can modify it.
>
> clues you in to your cat's body language and vocal expressions. What does an upright tail with a curl at the end mean? What's the message in a cat's blink?
>
> improves communications with your veterinarian, a time- and money-saver that could even save your cat's life.
>
> reveals the best ways to prevent, detect and treat common cat ailments and injuries. Learn what to do yourself, and when it's time to call the vet.
>
> helps you maintain a satisfying relationship with your cat.

From whiskers to tail, and from kittenhood to old age, CATNIP helps you do what is best for your cat.

If it's part of loving care, you'll find it in CATNIP.

Everything that concerns your cat is a topic for CATNIP. In-depth articles, short features, regular departments, a reader's forum and lively snippets of cat lore make the eight-page newsletter "must reading" for everyone who cares for a cat.

You'll love the easy-reading, breezy style, free of jargon or technical talk.

Meet mythical cats. Cats out of history. Cat stars of stage and screen. Celebrities and the felines who share their

(Continued)

-3-

fame. Explore cat metaphors (why "cat on a hot tin roof?"). Uncommon cat names (tell us yours!) and much more.

Safeguard your cat's good health.

Watch for an update on rabies. Effects of neutering on cat health and disposition. A guide to preventing and treating internal parasites. Promising new research on feline leukemia.

Discover how to control dander so even an allergic person can cohabit with cats. Master feline first aid for cat scratches and bites. Clean your cat's teeth without losing a few fingers.

Know how to react in an emergency. And what not to do.

CATNIP takes you on a guided tour of your cat's anatomy. See through your cat's eyes to understand its vision. Explore the wonders of whiskers. Sharpen your knowledge of claw care.

(You'll finally find out how the design of a cat's ear lets it hear the opening of a can of food from incredible distances!)

Understand your cat's behavior.

Clearly, your cat understands you. But how well do you understand your cat?

What does it mean when cats roll around in catnip? Why do they eat your socks? CATNIP reveals the surprising explanations behind baffling behavior.

Learn how to prevent your couch from becoming a scratching post. Choose a cat litter that's to your cat's liking. Introduce a new cat without making the resident cat pack its bags.

Be alert to hidden health hazards in everything from mothballs to antifreeze (its sweet taste is attractive to cats).

Live compatibly with cats.

Should your cat come along on your vacation? Who's happier and healthier, the indoor or outdoor cat? How can natural enemies like cats and dogs, birds or hamsters learn to be friends?

A FREE issue of CATNIP is reserved in your name.

The next issue will mail soon and I don't want you to miss

(over, please ...)

(Continued)

it. To receive your free copy, please return the enclosed card today in the postpaid envelope.

That's all. No cost. No risk. No obligation.

If you're delighted with CATNIP, and your cat loves all the extra attention, pay the invoice and keep it coming all year long. Just $16 for 12 more issues (13 in all). Otherwise, write "cancel" on the bill and return it. The free issue is yours with our compliments.

You enjoy the delightful newsletter. Your cat reaps the health benefits for the rest of its life.

To your cat's health and happiness!

Gloria Parkinson

Gloria Parkinson
Editor

P.S. Our Board of Advisors really should include the "cat consultants" who share my office. From left to right, meet Aunty Nina, Perdita and Nicholas. I couldn't get all three in one photo because Aunty Nina refuses to be seen with the riffraff.

(Maybe CATNIP needs a feature on how to persuade cats to sit still for the camera...)

Mailer: **Marlin Magazine**

Key Words: **"You feel a jolt on the line"**

Writer: **Ed McLean**

The Challenge

The big game fisherman regards himself as the elite among anglers—to the extent that an ordinary fly fisherman who is unlucky enough to be aboard with a group of big game veterans becomes the butt of what might be the equivalent of "tenderfoot" jokes. So a publication aimed at this elitist group faces the difficult task of having the reader nod his head "Yes!" as he leafs through the text.

The Implementation

The first paragraph is pure poetry, the way Ernest Hemingway might have written it. It sets a tone the big-game fisherman accepts: "Yes, that's who I am."

As the letter progresses it moves into areas of information and instruction. No matter how experienced a fisherman might be, some of the bullets have to be enticing.

Would the letter appeal to the beginner? Unquestionably, if that beginner intends to masquerade as an experienced big-game fisherman. By showing parts of the covers in the margin of the center spread, the writer not only makes the letter more readable, but whets the appetite of the prospective subscriber.

Comment

Ed McLean is the master of bringing the reader into the letter and no better example exists than his "Dear Sportfisherman" letter for *Marlin.* The response to the reader-involving "You feel a jolt on the line" opening was phenomenal for letters of this type—better than 9% from cold lists.

Figure 3–9. *Marlin*

Wade Leftwich
Publisher

Dear Sportfisherman:

You feel a jolt on the line and it whips up and out of the water as your reel screams. A hundred feet back, an immense blue monster explodes from the sea, thrashing from side to side, walking on its tail toward you before plunging from sight.

"Marlin!" shouts the mate from the fly bridge. The rod bends and you suck in your breath, bracing yourself. You set the drag and the line straightens. You crank the reel in, then abruptly let out slack. Someone yells advice and encouragement but you can't understand a word of it.

Your mind, your body, your entire being are concentrated on just one thing now. And that is to win the battle that has begun.

It could go on for hours or end suddenly, in minutes, with a snapped line or slipped hook. But, for as long as this struggle lasts, you'll give it everything you've got.

When the battle is over and you've vanquished your marlin, you ask the mate to tag and release it -- to help make sure future generations of sportfishermen are not denied the sheer enjoyment of doing battle, as you have, with a mighty creature of the sea.

Sheer enjoyment: that's what Marlin, the magazine of big game fishing, is all about. And if that's what you're looking for in the favorite sport of Ernest Hemingway, Zane Grey and other seekers of adventure, I hope you'll accept our special money-saving offer.

Send no money now. Try one issue of Marlin before you

(turn page, please...)

Exploiting the exclusivity angle . . . for anglers. *(Continued)*

-2-

decide whether or not you wish to continue receiving Marlin. If you decide Marlin's not for you, just write "cancel" on the invoice and mail it back to us. Keep the first issue, with our compliments. You'll owe nothing. But if you like what you see, pay the invoice for $22 for one year (total: six issues) and you'll get Marlin in the year ahead.

If you enjoy pitting your skills against the superb fighting qualities of marlin, swordfish, bluefin tuna, sailfish, shark, dorado, wahoo and other scrappy blue water fish, I'm confident you'll like what you see in your first issue of Marlin.

"I enjoy reading in Marlin about areas of big game fishing all over the world," writes Steve Schumacher of Alaska.

Steve's not alone in this. Our readers want to be taken where the big fish are. So Marlin takes you to the 'hot spots' of big game fishing in each issue. Recently, we've reported on --

Cozumel	Trinidad	Madeira	Cabo San Lucas
Montauk	Hawaii	Block Island	Cayman Islands
Tahiti	Venezuela	Tobago	Daytona Beach
Azores	St. Thomas	Ocean City	New Zealand
Grenada	Bimini	Mauritius	Florida Keys
Chile	Australia	Walker's Cay	Ecuador

In these in-depth reports, you get details on dockage and charter boat availability as well as restaurants, accommodations, and best fishing spots.

"I recently caught my first blue marlin," writes Tim LaPella of Pennsylvania. "Without the valuable information in Marlin, I never would have won the battle of one hour and 52 minutes."

The valuable information to which Tim refers is found in every issue of Marlin. It's one reason so many of our subscribers save their copies, referring back often to useful "how-to" articles in well-thumbed issues to settle questions that can come up even in a cockpit of seasoned fishermen. Such as how to choose, test and tie the best light tackle knots and the secret of making live bait attractive to sailfish. Plus --

* Tactics that can bring in bigeye tuna
* Avoiding broken lines: helpful tips from the experts
* How not to lose fish on the strike
* Drag setting reduced to a science

Illustration by John Carroll Doyle. Courtesy of Sherrill Poulnot, Jr.

"A quality publication in every way..."

Guy Harvey

"Try one issue...before you decide..."

"The fishing tips are great..."

(Continued)

"Tactics that bring in sailfish..."

-3-

* How to replace lure skirts in a jiffy
* A veteran angler's tips for raising the billfish you sight
* How New Zealanders prepare tail-rigged skip baits -- fast
* Fly-fishing for billfish: some techniques worth knowing
* Secrets of successful lures
* A Hawaiian charter boat mate reveals how he gets sailfish and swords to go for live bait
* Packing big game fishing gear for airline travel
* Lure-rigging and crimping tips from a master

The pros and cons of subjects discussed by your fellow sportfishermen the world over are covered in Marlin so you can hold your own (with facts) when the conversation turns to such matters as --

-- a 200 lb. minimum for landing billfish?
-- artificial lures versus live bait?
-- tag and release, or dockside weigh-ins?
-- those trolling birds: help or hoax?

Marlin informs you on what's being done worldwide to conserve the endangered stock of big game fish. In each issue, our Conservation Comments feature alerts readers to the threat posed by foreign fishing vessels ("longliners"), seabed strip mining off Hawaii, the dumping of toxic wastes near some of the best fishing grounds, and depletion of food fish habitat areas.

In our News Line feature, we keep you up to date on all the good news, too. Major billfish sightings ...helpful new research...boat shows worth attending... new breakthroughs in tackle design...and more.

"Marlin is the very best big game fishing magazine in the world," writes Lawrence DeBono of Australia. "I enjoy reading it from front to back and often I read it twice clear through. The stories are excellent, the fishing tips are great, and the color photos are fine!"

Accept our "get-acquainted" offer now and you'll see what Lawrence is talking about. We're proud of the fact that color pages from Marlin are tacked up on fishing boat bulkheads from Pensacola to Papeete.

Ours is a quality publication in every way: great photography and painting reproductions on top quality paper stock that are suitable for framing. Plus useful, interesting articles you won't find elsewhere.

"I want to thank Marlin and its helpful Charter

(Continued)

Boat Listing feature for assisting me in locating a great boat and crew in Venezuela," writes Bill O'Keefe of Lake Worth. "The fishing was great and we had a wonderful time!"

Thanks, Bill. As active sportfishermen ourselves here at Marlin, we try to offer our readers the same kind of useful, practical tips and features we value. We've been told by our readers that our love of big game fishing shows up on every page of Marlin. And maybe that's why we get so many letters like this one from reader Edward Olana of New Jersey:

"Your magazine is the best fishing magazine there is. I know, I read them all. I was a charter boat captain for years. My specialty was live bait blue marlin or sail. I know all about boats and big game fishing. And Marlin is by far the best!"

See for yourself if Ed Olana is right. There's no risk, no cost to you if you decide, after looking over your first issue, that you don't agree with him.

Here's the deal: Send no money now. Just send in the Acceptance Card bearing your name and address. When your first issue arrives, kick off your shoes, sit back and relax with Marlin. Browse through its colorful yet informative pages. Read the issue clear through, if you like.

If, after this, you decide Marlin's not for you (and you're the sole judge of that), just write "cancel" on the invoice you get with your first issue. Return the invoice but keep the first issue. And that will be that. You'll owe nothing.

But if your first issue pleases you and you wish to continue as a subscriber, pay the invoice within 10 days.

Please act on this special money-saving offer now, while you're thinking of it. Thank you.

Yours for great fishing,

Wade Leftwich

Wade Leftwich

P.S. Do something for yourself today. Mail back your Acceptance Card. Marlin will bring you many hours of interest and pleasure...
Or for faster service, call our toll-free number 1-800-MARLINS.

P.O. BOX 12902 PENSACOLA FLORIDA 32576-9985

Mailer: **Arizona Highways**
Key Words: **"A National Treasure Is Yours to Enjoy"**
Writer: **John Lyle Shimek**

The Challenge

Magazines which have no commercial or self-help overtone have to find another way to justify their existence.

Most people give lip-service to the beauty of nature, but these same people are not an easy target for a subscription offer tied to such an exalted appeal.

So a subscription letter for a publication which founds itself on the concept of natural beauty has to generate a highly emotional reaction if it is to compete.

The Implementation

With a series of nine bullets and a listing of six unusual areas of subject matter, the writer of this letter justifies the claim of the Johnson Box: "A National Treasure is yours to enjoy." (See page 152 for a description of "Johnson Box".)

The magic of this letter is its appeal, not only to Arizona residents, but to those outside the state as well. This magic is accomplished by provocative references and carefully chosen colorful adjectives.

By aiming the text at "you," the writer accomplishes reader-involvement beyond the range of what one might expect from a publication whose appeal is picturesque, rather than event-oriented.

Comment

Every teacher and every text tells the student writer to mention, early on, what's being sold. For the master writer, rules become flexible. They become tools for creating stronger presentations and higher response rates. Not until the second paragraph of the second page does this writer give the reader a clue. But his technique works.

Figure 3–10. *Arizona Highways*

```
* * * * * * * * * * * * * * * * * * * * * * * *
*                                             *
*  A NATIONAL TREASURE IS YOURS TO ENJOY      *
*                                             *
*  and you can enjoy it every month when      *
*  you accept this invitation to subscribe    *
*  to the world's most beautiful magazine     *
*  -- the incomparable ARIZONA HIGHWAYS       *
*                                             *
* * * * * * * * * * * * * * * * * * * * * * * *
```

Yes, dear reader --

-- you are richer -- infinitely richer -- than you think, if you love the beautiful, the unusual, the mysterious and the enchanting. And I am inviting you today to discover a wonderful way to enjoy the boundless wealth that is already yours without ever leaving home unless you choose to do so.

Forty-five per cent of Arizona is <u>your</u> land, reserved for your pleasure -- forever -- and if you are not taking advantage of this unusual heritage, more's the pity, for here are just some of the odd, the beautiful, the humorous and the awesome things you may be missing --

- a land of cliffs and canyons where, if you want to (and if you have the courage to) you can spit a mile straight down.
- a land with a town named Bumble Bee, a mine named Total Wreck, a creek called Quien Sabe?, a valley named Horse Thief Basin, a fort named Misery (and rightly so), a town named Show Low (high though it may be in Arizona's White Mountains).
- the world's oldest living trees (the bristlecone pines) and its oldest dead ones, too (the 180-million-year-old denizens of the famous Petrified Forest.
- canyons that take you to the rim of history while they take your breath away and one, the Grand Canyon, which for sheer awe and beauty yields to none. Others like Oak Creek and Sycamore and Canyon de Chelly prove again and again the outstanding fact about Arizona -- that here is one place where Mother Nature didn't stint herself.
- a land of sophisticated cities and untouched natural beauty.
- a land where you can find turquoise exquisitely crafted onto great scallops of silver by Indian artists who are today more sought after than some of the artists of New York and Paris.
- a land where natural history is spread out everywhere with casual extravagance and you have your choice of colors.
- a land of dreamy distances -- and Indians who think nothing of saddling up to ride 20 miles to the trading post for a pound of coffee.
- a land of dozens of natural bridges -- PLUS one imported from London, of all places. (How's <u>that</u> for carrying coals to Newcastle?)

I could go on about this land where big is beautiful and beautiful is

Involving the reader with masterful use of *you*. *(Continued)*

far too big to enjoy with one quick glance through the windows of an air-conditioned car. But if you've read this far, you may already suspect that here is just another Western apostle of the Big Brag trying out his tall tales on the city dudes.

I can't say that I blame you. Arizona and the Southwest have always had to be seen to be believed, anyway. So if my tall-sounding tales fall on skeptical ears, I invite you, then, to <u>look</u> -- to look again -- to look to your heart's content and see and feel for yourself the wonderful experience that awaits you each month in the pages of ARIZONA HIGHWAYS and its unsurpassed color photography.

But ARIZONA HIGHWAYS is more than sensational scenery sensitively photographed. I think you'll enjoy <u>reading</u> it, too -- will be both informed and entertained by its well written articles on such subjects as --

-- solar energy and how Arizona is taking the lead in its development.

-- the gemstones of Arizona and how and where to find them

-- Indian basketry in Arizona and why this art is dying

-- the night people who probe the stars in Arizona's observatories

-- the sound of Arabian hoofbeats in Arizona and what it means to horselovers the world over.

-- the strange and fascinating new discoveries about the pre-historic Southwest.

I believe you will enjoy seeing and reading ARIZONA HIGHWAYS every month. And if you've not yet gotten around to visiting Arizona and the rest of the great Southwest there's no need to wait another moment to start your appreciation of this scenic wonderland.

You'll find a turquoise token on the enclosed card. All you need to do to begin your 12 vacations to Arizona in the coming year is punch out the token, put it in the "YES" slot on the Sunshine Certificate and send the certificate to me. You can send your remittance now or we can bill you later. Either way, all you pay is

((ONLY $8.00 FOR A FULL YEAR OF ARIZONA HIGHWAYS))

If, however, you are unable to accept my offer at this time, I'd appreciate your placing the turquoise token in the "NO" slot and returning the card to me so that we may extend this invitation to someone else.

Your copies of ARIZONA HIGHWAYS contain no advertising. They sell at no special rates. Every page of every issue is devoted to giving you a memorable monthly visit to a land no one should miss. So you don't miss another lovely issue, why not use your turquoise token to tell me to start ARIZONA HIGHWAYS coming your way -- TODAY?

Sincerely,

[signature]

For ARIZONA HIGHWAYS

ARIZONA HIGHWAYS

2039 West Lewis Avenue • Phoenix, Arizona 85009

Mailer: **Ohio Magazine**

Key Words: **"Whose mother makes the best cheesecake . . ."**

Writer: **Paul Stiga**

The Challenge

Ohio does not have the picturesque image Arizona has, so a magazine dedicated to this state has to find intramural areas of interest.

With every daily newspaper incorporating a "state" section and most Sunday supplements including some local travel topics, a magazine has to combine the exploitation of citizen love for the state with oddities people cannot find described or covered elsewhere.

Along with this, the publication has to represent itself as offering information of genuine worth.

The Implementation

The very first question, "Whose mother makes the best cheesecake in Ohio (and what's her recipe)?" not only isolates Ohio, but also, by including the recipe, offers information many who would never subscribe to a cooking publication might find useful. In fact, each of the six questions that precede the "Dear Ohioan" greeting attracts a different area of interest.

The letter makes much of what appears to be a large editorial and pictorial staff so the reader will not think this is a dilettante publication. Included are areas of history as well as current events, including those most readers regard favorably—scandals.

The occasional touch of humor keeps the letter from becoming preachy, as do words and phrases such as, "Nope." and "So here's the deal."

Comment

Capitalizing on a common interest is a winning psychological ploy, and this writer's use of such psychology resulted in a subscription letter that has worked for more than ten years. He positions the magazine as an information service rather than as something to read.

Figure 3–11. *Ohio Magazine*

Whose mother makes the best cheesecake in Ohio
(and what's her recipe)?

Where can you buy a 100-acre island for $125,000
-- or scrumptious beef burgundy for $2.60?

What room in Ohio did the Beatles stay in -- and
how much will it cost you to stay in it?

Which of your neighbors is within six countries
of beating his own Guinness world record?

Where's the best place to catch walleye (up to
18 pounds in weight and 30 inches long)?

When's the next big hot-air balloon festival...
threshers' reunion...Sweet Corn Festival
(the sweet corn, with butter, is free)?

Dear Ohioan,

The fact that you live in the most wonderful place in the world doesn't make one iota of difference to you

...unless you know what's really out there

...exactly how to find it

...just how much it should cost you

...and what you can do to squeeze every last drop of joy, beauty, value, pleasure and profit out of it to give yourself the happiest life possible.

So there's a service that supplies you with all the things -- and exactly the things -- you need to know.

And all it costs is 83¢ a month.

It's called

because

Using common interest to garner uncommon results. *(Continued)* that's <u>all</u> it's about. It won't make you an authority on the cleanup problems in Chernobyl...vacation hideaways in the Aleutian Islands...or the best black truffles in Lyons.

But it <u>will</u> make you something of an expert on

...the cleanup problems in Ohio's rivers ("even the notorious Black River--where the river itself is carcinogenic, at least to the catfish--is no longer monitored continuously")

...vacation hideaways within a day's drive (like the wonderful guide we published to elegant old-time hotels, from Toledo to Marietta, Cincinnati to Cleveland Heights)

...and hamburgers in Akron so juicy "extra napkins are supplied" with them..."real hamburgers made by real people with real ground chuck" in Columbus..."quality beef that is ground fresh--hourly, not daily" in Dayton ...hamburgers in Findlay so good "the lines start forming before noon and can be a block long."

Every day, our own OHIO staff, reporters, photographers, and critics are all over the state searching out the best, most, happiest, cheapest, hottest, least-known and most-likely-to-succeed of <u>everything</u>. And once a month we pack the pick of their crop into the pages of OHIO Magazine and ship it directly to your door.

What's in it for you?

<u>OHIO points out the terrific things sitting right at your doorstep</u>.

How much do you honestly know about the next town or city down the road from you, let alone the treasures and pleasures an hour or two's drive away?

- OHIO did a special listing of 30 places around the state you could go for fresh, for-real organically grown produce.

- We regularly visit terrific towns like Findlay, where you can see the original "Old Mill Stream" beloved by barbershop quartets.

- Our special <u>Ohioguide</u> at the back of every issue lists times, places and prices of everything from once-in-a-lifetime events around the state to annual fairs and festivals.

<u>OHIO gives you a sense of what Ohio was like "back when"</u> -- fascinating glimpses into such bits of Ohio history as the crash of the dirigible <u>Shenandoah</u> in Ava...the ruckus caused when Norman Vincent Peale's <u>Power of Positive Thinking</u> was first published...and the story of Cincinnati's own arsenic-and-old-men murderer, Anna Marie Hahn.

<u>OHIO regales you with little things you didn't know about Ohio</u> like how many strawberries you can get from a one-acre crop (5,400 pounds) and which spots scored highest (Cincinnati

(Continued)

and Toledo at 122) and lowest (Cleveland at 65) on Ohio's Ragweed Pollen Index.

More importantly, OHIO keeps you informed on issues that can affect your finances...the quality of your life... the entire future of your family...

- how efficiently -- and honestly -- the state legislature functions, for example;

- how the Toledo brokerage firm of Bell and Beckwith managed to hide the largest stock brokerage fraud in SEC history for so long;

- why Sir James Goldsmith backed down from his attempted Goodyear takeover (and whether it could happen again);

- what our own smartest Ohio farmers think could be done about the farm crisis.

The exact economics of the Cleveland/Columbus/Cincinnati High Speed Rail Plan...the sorry conditions of Ohio's highways...the still-devastating problems of toxic wastes and poisoned waters. We cover them all. And when we think you're getting a raw deal, we say so, in no uncertain terms.

OHIO introduces you to your neighbors -- all kinds of people you'd like to get to know better: Star coaches and high school quarterbacks...self-made millionaires and maverick politicians...world-class celebrities like Centerville's best-selling author, syndicated columnist, and Good Morning, America regular Erma Bombeck...

"'Of course, I still do housework,' she told us, 'and not just to keep my hand in, for heaven's sakes -- to keep the board of health from the door.'"

and the nice guy who sells you worms in Dayton...

"People will come in and ask, 'Do you have worms?' And I say, 'Well, I sell worms.' And they get indignant about it. But I have a reason for answering that way. Once a man came in and said, 'Do you have worms?' and I said 'Yes,' and he said, 'Well, you'd better see a doctor.' From that time on, I've never been trapped again."

Do you want to taste some of the best food in the world? OHIO tells you where you can find it:

A fresh shrimp cocktail in Cleveland that has 16 fresh shrimp in it...produce picked fresh from a Boardman restaurant's own 2-acre garden... a spot in Columbus where people line up to sit in a dining room half the size of the restaurant's kitchen...pies so good at an airport that the pilots often fly off with the whole pie.

over, please

(Continued)

Those are a few of literally thousands of tips we've passed on to readers in our monthly Statewide Dining Out Guide. And if your taste is more toward Dining In, that's a monthly feature, too: Not fancy stuff, but old-fashioned down-home favorites like Caramel Popcorn Balls, Potato Pancakes, and the most sadly neglected of them all, Chipped Beef.

And included in your subscription will be our Annual OHIO Restaurant Guide -- 124 pages last September.

Have I told you what OHIO Magazine is all about?

Nope, I've barely scratched the surface.

I haven't talked about the photography, which is beautiful, a lot of it in full color...the look and feel of the magazine, which is very fine...or the emotions you feel when you go through a copy of OHIO. (Can you read about the city workers in Dayton who are voluntarily donating their own sick days to benefit a terminally ill police officer and not feel a little thrill of pride that you're an Ohioan? That's one example.)

The point is, you can't truly know how much OHIO can add to your day-to-day life without reading OHIO.

So here's the deal.

Mail in the card enclosed, and I'll send OHIO Magazine to you for 45% less than what everyone pays who buys it in a store or on a newsstand:

83¢ per issue.

That's also ONE-THIRD off the regular subscription price.

Send $10 for the next full year. Or we'll bill you. Either way, if you're ever dissatisfied, let me know, and you'll get a full pro-rated refund on all unmailed copies.

I can tell you, it's a guarantee just about no one has ever taken us up on.

OHIO is that good.

Proof? Tuck the token in the card, the card in the envelope, and mail it off today.

Sincerely,

Robert B. Smith
Editor-in-Chief

P.S. Just to clear up one critical matter: It's Bob Trebilcock's mother who makes the best cheesecake in Ohio.

OHIO 40 SOUTH THIRD STREET, COLUMBUS, OHIO 43215

Mailer: **Vermont Magazine**

Key Words: **"You have an issue reserved in your name"**

Writer: **Josh Manheimer**

The Challenge

The Green Mountain State has a reputation, whether earned or not, of being conservative in its social views and occasionally liberal in its political views. A magazine aimed at residents of the state avoids controversy and deals in natural splendors and cultural events.

Are these enough of an incentive to justify a subscription?

The Implementation

Is colorful coverage of natural splendors and cultural events enough of an incentive to justify a subscription? The ability to do this is why this letter is included.

Making these elements seem to be strong enough incentive and peppering the offer with references to "the involved citizen in you" and "the naturalist in you" broaden the appeal.

The P.S. is unusually strong because it brings up areas of interest even most lifelong Vermonters might not have known about before.

Comment

Paralleling the *Ohio* letter is this one for *Vermont Magazine.* With the references about the Ice Age returning, tire ruts in mud season, and black flies in August, Vermonters have to be nodding their heads and saying yes, not only to the anecdotes, but to the subscription offer.

The writer points out that this letter, in a mini-booklet format, has far outpulled other approaches and formats tested against it.

Figure 3–12. ***Vermont Magazine***

VERMONT

You have an issue reserved in your name.
May we send it to you?

* Did you know one of Vermont's best restaurants is in the back of an old school bus? Do you know where the bus is parked?

* Do you know what's really happening in the Vermont economy and the State House? What kind of health care, education, and environment we can expect in the Green Mountain State?

* Did you know our state has 50 museums, 45 concert series, 12 theaters, 35 art galleries, and one wild game reserve? Do you know where to find them?

* Do you know how to garden beautifully in our tough climate? What ideas the state's best architects have for affordable, practical homes? Which resort lets beginners ski for free?

Dear Fellow Vermonter,

When you're staring at your thermometer in February, wondering if the Ice Age has finally returned for good...

When you're measuring your tire ruts in mud season, wondering whether whole deer will disappear down them forever...

When you're swatting black flies in August, wondering whether they will leave any blood for the Red Cross this year...

...smile.

For two reasons.

Conviviality and colorful verbalisms broaden the appeal. *(Continued)*

One, of course, is these minor inconveniences keep tourists from moving here permanently. The other reason?

> You have an issue of an exciting new magazine reserved in your name.
>
> It's called VERMONT MAGAZINE. May we send you a sample copy to thumb through at our expense?

Written by Vermonters for Vermonters, the second you peek inside its delightful covers, you'll realize you are holding far more than just a fancy, state-sponsored, travel brochure.

> Rather, you'll find handy, down-to-earth information that tips you off and turns you on to everything that is exciting in our state, and thoughtful in-depth journalism that goes far beyond the picture-postcards of Vermont.

FOR THE GOURMET IN YOU: You'll discover where to savor broiled swordfish with avocado lime butter in Bristol. Where to sample the famous bean supper in Brownsville. How to create exciting meals with fresh Vermont-grown ingredients.

FOR THE INVOLVED CITIZEN IN YOU: You'll learn why Vermont's small rural hospitals are in trouble. How well Act 250 is working. The current status of Lake Champlain's endangered environment. And which towns are making real progress on waste disposal, land use, the preservation of agriculture, town plans, and education reform.

FOR THE ADVENTURER IN YOU: You'll schuss down the best little-known ski trails. Canoe from inn to inn along the Battenkill River. Rub noses with a Pot-Bellied Pig at the World's Fair in Tunbridge.

FOR THE INVESTOR IN YOU: You'll know all about the state's economy and politics, the environmental regulations and laws that keep the Green Mountains green -- and affect property values.

FOR THE NATURALIST IN YOU: You'll rediscover moose in Vermont, and exotic species from loons to rare wildflowers. And see natural Vermont in spectacular photographs.

(Continued)

FOR THE ARTIST IN YOU: You'll go behind the scenes at the Marlboro Music Festival. Meet great artists like Tasha Tudor and Ed Koren. Find out who's teaching the hottest jazz dance classes in downtown Montpelier and how to attend a spinning and weaving retreat in Marshfield.

Whether we are tipping you off to an inept government program in Rutland or a buttery chicken tetrazzini in Middlebury, our journalists will keep you posted on what's happening. To whom. When. Where. And, most important, why.

> You see, before VERMONT MAGAZINE, to find out what was really going on in our state, you either had to know a lot of folks or get on the mailing list of every organization.
>
> Now, however, our reporters fan out across the state and report back to you from the front lines.

Together you and I will discover which diners serve the best breakfasts and which town hosts the annual sheepdog herding contest.

You'll learn which Vermonter will make you a custom guitar in Bennington. A custom jigsaw puzzle in Norwich. A custom sweater in Chester. A custom car bumper in Winooski.

You'll travel the back roads and find out who's milking sheep these days in Jeffersonville. Who's writing plays for Broadway in Calais. Who's saving tropical rain forests from Strafford.

You'll find out where to visit a Morgan horse worth half-a-million dollars in Manchester Center. How to find the orchardist in Monkton who still sells old-time apple varieties.

> Well, so far I've given you some idea of all you can expect inside this exciting, new magazine.

But you'll never really know until you send for your issue of VERMONT MAGAZINE.

(Continued)

To get your free issue ... SEND NO MONEY!

To have your FREE trial issue of VERMONT MAGAZINE rushed into your hands, simply mail back your Special Invitation in the enclosed postage-free envelope.

If you like what you see, pay our invoice for just $14.95 and receive 5 more issues (6 large bimonthly issues in all). You'll save a full 15% off the newsstand price.

As a special bonus, we'll send you a beautifully silk-screened canvas tote bag by Vermont artist Woody Jackson -- free with your paid subscription.

> OUR IRON-CLAD GUARANTEE. If, however, you decide -- for any reason whatsoever -- that our magazine is not for you, just write "Cancel" across our bill, return it, and that's that. You will always be entitled to a full cash refund on all unmailed issues.

You can keep your free sample issue regardless. It's our way of saying, "Thanks for at least giving VERMONT MAGAZINE the once-over."

With so much to gain -- and not a thing to lose -- isn't it worth taking a free look?

Cordially,

Sarah E Roman

Sarah E. Roman
Circulation Director

P.S. Did you know that before adopting the Constitution of the United States, the Republic of Vermont coined its own money, carried on foreign trade, regulated weights and measures, naturalized citizens, and fought off claims from New York, New Hampshire, and Massachusetts with its own militia?

What are proud, independent-minded Vermonters inventing, crafting, cooking, fighting for next?

Your free issue of VERMONT MAGAZINE will tell you. Why not send for it today?

LT-100

Mailer: **Air & Space/Smithsonian**
Key Words: **"You're cleared for takeoff"**
Writer: **Tom McCormick**

The Challenge

Smithsonian supporters regard the museum as a historical repository.

While this is a definite benefit for most Smithsonian activities, it can be an obstacle to the introduction of a new area of editorial coverage.

AIR & SPACE/Smithsonian is a departure into a more contemporary editorial sphere. The challenge of this introduction was to create a new area of interest, within the existing ranks of Smithsonian supporters.

The Implementation

The letter is loaded with action words, from the very first sentence. It educates invisibly by answering the question it asks so the reader does not feel left behind. Using short paragraphs and many double-indented paragraphs, it holds interest, even among those who have had no prior interest in aerospace.

By emphasizing adventure as much as information, the writer holds the reader solidly throughout four pages of glamorized fact. The Smithsonian never damages its image and yet achieves, in this publication, a more contemporary status.

Comment

This classic "you are there" letter positions the magazine as parallel to a test flight. We didn't count the number of times the writer used the word *you* in this very readable letter, but the word or an imperative with *you* implied does appear in practically every paragraph.

Figure 3–13. *Air & Space/Smithsonian*

YOU'RE CLEARED FOR TAKEOFF

on an action-packed ride to the high frontiers of flight!

(Go ahead. You needn't pay a cent.)

Dear Smithsonian Associate:

You've been chosen to take one of our sleek new creations for a trial spin...to open it up, ride it aloft, and experience all the powerful excitement we've built into it.

So when it arrives, just pull back the cover, settle in, and GO!

Check its dramatic scope of action -- from sprints back through time to watch legendary civil and military craft blaze their way into history, to steep ascents into orbit for deep-probing missions into the eery void beyond.

Note its revealing breadth of view -- sweeping vistas of our world in miniature far below...close-ups of tomorrow's fantastic aircraft being tested today...sightings of strange new worlds out beyond our own solar system.

Enjoy its hours of wide-reaching range -- unhurried hours filled with detailed studies of developments like the Soviet space shuttle, UFO reports, the "stealth" fighter, VSTOL craft, and lots more...all in the same issue.

If that sounds like impressive performance, wait until you actually get into your test issue of AIR & SPACE/Smithsonian. For this is one magazine that's guaranteed to keep you riveted to your seat with endlessly fresh, vividly authentic flights of discovery.

Take the "scramjet," for instance -- a new kind of engine now being developed to power the X-30.

What's the X-30? A "space plane." An airliner that will skim the edge of space at 4,000 miles per hour!

Is that the sort of thing you'd like a close look at? Then you would surely be intrigued by all the non-stop adventures aloft that await you in AIR & SPACE/Smithsonian.

Imagine a fighter that turns so fast it needs a computer to sense pilot black-out, and take over the flying.

Imagine a space ship that takes off like a plane instead of

Putting the reader at the controls.

(Continued)

launching like a missile. (It's being developed now!)

Imagine satellites with telescopic cameras so powerful that there's concern about them violating your privacy.

Better yet, don't imagine such things. See them in all their reality.

You'll find advances like these graphically detailed in every edition of AIR & SPACE/Smithsonian -- including the "test flight" issue we're about to send you. It's yours without obligation or commitment!

I can't tell you exactly where your complimentary copy will carry you. But I can promise that you'll have a hard time putting it down.

Because once you open the cover, you'll find yourself caught up in the working world of the "professionals." Pilots. Astronauts. Aviation historians. Aerospace scientists. Engineers. Flight technicians.

You might, for example, suddenly find yourself looking down at the entire Middle East from 13 miles up as your pilot in a top-secret SR-71 'spy plane' slows to 1,000 m.p.h. to turn for Europe.

After that, you could be deposited amid a tangle of power cables beneath the floodlit bulk of the space shuttle Atlantis as technicians ready her for mounting on a massive Mobile Launch Platform.

Then you might be aloft again -- strapped under the wing and tiny motor of a 150-pound "ultralight" airplane -- lazily exploring the fields and meadows that pass a few dozen feet beneath your bucket seat.

Next, you could be on hand for tests of a new hybrid craft...half helicopter, half airplane...as its rotors lift it off the ground, then stop to form an X-shaped wing while a jet engine drives it forward in flight.

Following that, you might sit in on the launch of a space telescope able to detect celestial objects 14 billion light years away -- a telescope that could well reveal the very beginnings of creation.

Whatever adventures await you in your trial issue of AIR & SPACE/Smithsonian, you can be sure of one thing. They'll all be vividly alive!

For this graphic magazine doesn't just "cover" the world of aviation and space flight. It captures the reality of it all. The craft, the feats, the technology.

Here, for example, is a publication that gets you so close to a B-52 during in-flight refueling that you can see the rescue-hatch releases, the screws holding down an access panel, even the wrinkles in the aging bomber's aluminum skin. (Yes, old airplanes also get wrinkles.)

Here too is a view of what the pilot of the future will see through the visor of his electronic helmet...a computerized display of approaching

(Continued)

terrain, plus his altitude, airspeed, heading, and navigation checkpoints.

And here is a cutaway rendering of Grumman's X-29, the radical flying experiment now blazing a path to hypersonic aircraft capable of maneuvers unheard of today -- plastic aircraft with built-in intelligence.

Then, of course, there are the endless surprises.

For example, are you aware that Germany had a perfectly workable space plane under development in 1940?

> Early versions of its advanced rocket engines were actually being tested when Hitler's costly invasion of Russia put a fortunate end to the "America Bomber" project.

Do you know how close NASA came to losing the crew of the Apollo 13 moon mission?

> A sudden loss of power forced the astronauts to shut down all but the most essential systems and take refuge in the freezing lunar module while frantic controllers turned the ship back towards earth.

Have you any idea what Navy fliers experience every time they take off from an aircraft carrier?

> The steam catapult that hurls them off the deck whips them from a standstill to over 150 m.p.h. in under two seconds! Anything less and they won't gain the speed essential for flight.

Are you interested in knowing what it's like to fly an airliner that's been in regular service for over 50 years?

> The plane is "Old 36," a DC-3 built in 1937. After ten different owners, it recently passed its 100,000th hour of flight time carrying passengers for Provincetown-Boston Airline. And it's a sweet-handling ship, thank you.

As you can see, the adventures awaiting you in AIR & SPACE/Smithsonian will be every bit as diverse and arresting as you have a right to expect from a magazine with its pedigree.

For it comes to you from the Smithsonian Institution's National Air and Space Museum -- the single most popular museum in the entire world.

> No other organization can match this unique living monument to flight in bringing you graphically detailed, often never-before-revealed insights into aeronautical developments and exploits to date . . . or the craft and missions being readied now to open new modes of flight, to take us to unknown new worlds.

But see for yourself! Take AIR & SPACE/Smithsonian for a test hop.

(Continued)

If you enjoy it, you're invited to continue on a non-stop ride to ever new heights of discovery in each crisp new edition. You'll even join us in membership.

But first I definitely want you to try the next hefty issue of our magazine without the least obligation. That way you'll have a chance to size it up personally before you make any decisions.

To accept, just attach the enclosed "TEST FLIGHT" token to the reply card provided, and return them in the postage-free envelope.

When your sample issue arrives, page through it at your leisure. See for yourself if AIR & SPACE/Smithsonian isn't every bit the stirring, captivating experience I've promised you.

> In the unlikely event you decide that this unique magazine isn't for you -- no matter the reason -- just write "cancel" on the invoice we'll send you, return it, and owe nothing. The sample issue is then yours to keep as a gift.

But if it casts the spell over you that I'm sure it will...if you want to continue riding with it to the frontiers of flight, the beckoning reaches of space...just settle back and turn the flying over to us.

We'll send you five more issues, a total of six, for the special Smithsonian Associates' fee of just $16 -- 10% less than the regular non-Associate rate. What's more, we'll make you a full member of the National Air and Space Museum, entitled to all benefits and privileges, at no additional cost to you whatever!

> First, though, accept our invitation to try a test flight along the loftiest frontiers of human experience without obligation or commitment.

All you need to get underway is that "TEST FLIGHT" token enclosed. Just return it with the accompanying reply card, and your trial issue of AIR & SPACE/Smithsonian will arrive before you know it.

Sincerely,

Joseph J. Bonsignore

Joseph J. Bonsignore
Publisher

JJB/tdl

P.S. Please note that there's a deadline date on your order card. To be absolutely certain of receiving the non-obligating issue promised you, be sure to return the token together with the reply card well in advance of that date.

Mailer: **HeadsUp**

Key Words: **"Today, information is a strategic weapon"**

Writer: **Don Hauptman**

The Challenge

Many publications claim to keep their readers up to date with changes in the business community. To stand apart, a new entry in this field has to do more than imply that it includes information—or access to information—others don't cover.

In the late 1990s the medium is as exploitable as the message, provided the reader understands what the publication has to offer. The challenge is one, then, of convincing the reader, first, that the service is worthwhile and, second, that the service is unique.

The Implementation

The writer builds a case for what he calls "information overload"—12,310 articles about technology in business generated each day. The comparison is a strong one: The President of the United States, who has many staffers among whom this information is split; and you, the typical business executive, who has no such filters.

The publication is sent by fax rather than by post or delivery system. This in itself adds an element of timeliness beyond that which any conventional publication might be able to claim.

Paralleling the editorial approach one expects of the publication itself, wording is terse, crisp, pointed, and aimed at the business professional.

Comment

Although the nameplate is "Individual," the subscription being sold is to a newsletter—actually to a "news service" titled *HeadsUp.* This may cause some confusion, and confusion is the enemy of response. The writer, of course, has no control over what appears at the top of page 1; and the proper way to keep score is not by theory, but by actual response. This letter beat the previous control by 62.8%.

Figure 3–14. *HeadsUp*

84 Sherman St., Cambridge, MA 02140

Mr. Richard M. Osborne
U.S.A. Direct, Inc.
2901 Blackbridge Road
York, PA 17402-9708

Dear Mr. Richard M. Osborne,

Today, information is a strategic weapon.

A market niche, a sales opportunity, a competitive tactic. A technology breakthrough or product development. Or a major purchase decision.

Advance knowledge of important events can give you a jump on everyone else -- and enhance the fortunes of your company and your career.

In technology today, change is the only constant. More than ever before, the winners will be those with the right information -- and who possess it early enough to act. Missing an important fact or trend, however, or learning about it too late, might prove fatal!

But how can you keep up with the flood of information? That's the big problem.

Did you know that 12,310 articles about technology and business are generated each day? It's the familiar "information explosion" dilemma. As the amount of data escalates, it seems impossible to absorb it all.

Fortunately, a solution is at hand.

Think for a moment about the President of the United States, and what he needs to know. Now there's the ultimate information overload situation!

The President, however, has help. A department staffed by people who do nothing but read all the news sources, then compile a daily summary that's tailored exclusively for him.

Now imagine that, like the President, you had an employee whose job is to gather, review, and synthesize all the news in your field. A kind of "personal reader" who knows your interests as well as you do. Who is perceptive enough to select only those items that are relevant to you, and then presents them to you each morning in a neat one-page summary.

Wouldn't that be an enormous benefit?

(over, please)

Loading up with action words. *(Continued)*

A Dramatic Cure for Information Overload.

Such a scenario is no longer a fantasy. A remarkable new service does exactly what I've just described. It's called HeadsUp.

> Simply stated, HeadsUp is the first and only truly personalized and interactive daily news service devoted to business and technology.

HeadsUp is not a magazine or newspaper or newsletter. It's a whole new kind of information medium. A customized news report.

Just tell HeadsUp what you want, and it goes into action. It sifts literally millions of words each day, searching for and capturing just those items that fit your specifications -- and screening out the rest.

Each morning via fax, you receive a compact one-page report. It contains between 18 and 20 capsule summaries of industry articles and news releases that are pertinent to your interests. Each is condensed into a single paragraph that conveys its most important points. You can read the entire report in five minutes, over your morning cup of coffee!

In most cases, everything you need to know about the development is in the summary. But if you want more detail on any item, a toll-free call brings you the original full text, on demand.

HeadsUp is a uniquely personal news service. Timely. Quick-reading. Action-oriented.

It's the perfect, logical, elegant solution to the information overload problem. Finally, a way to gain control over information -- instead of letting the information control you.

> What you don't see is as important as what you do. HeadsUp eliminates the irrelevant, the immaterial, the trivial. It delivers only what's germane to your interests, exactly as you specify them.

The result: You read less -- but more efficiently!

What's more, HeadsUp is a kind of "insurance policy." It virtually guarantees that you won't miss news that's potentially important to your work, to your company, to your career.

Access to Knowledge With a Bottom-Line Payoff.

One HeadsUp subscriber, an Information Systems manager with a major retail chain, requested that we track the following topics: Groupware, Client/Server Computing, PenBased Computing, Database Software...and six other categories.

Each morning when he arrives for work, his HeadsUp report, summarizing developments in precisely these areas, is waiting for him.

(continued)

(Continued)

- 3 -

The benefits he enjoys can be yours, too. For instance:

> Many stories will reach you earlier -- anywhere between one day and one week before they appear in the industry and general business press.

That's because we receive trade news and company releases directly from the original sources, in electronic form, well before they are set in type, printed, and distributed. Couldn't that window give you a tremendous edge?

Our coverage is comprehensive. HeadsUp methodically scans more than 300 news sources: major newspapers, wire services, and computer and telecommunications industry trade publications, both U.S. and worldwide.

Today, following events in global markets is no longer optional. It's essential. With HeadsUp, you'll be able to monitor international high-tech developments more closely than ever before. Our worldwide coverage is superior to that of any other service.

Your daily HeadsUp reports are a terrific source of competitive intelligence -- keeping you abreast of company product launches, pricing plans, distribution techniques, selling strategies...and more.

You'll follow the moves of key players: your customers, prospects, suppliers, and rivals. You'll spot new sales opportunities and new markets. You'll be prepared to make better buying decisions. You'll forge valuable industry contacts.

And you'll be able to identify important trends, often in their embryonic stages. A broader perspective enables you to see wider, farther, and clearer.

> Subscribers tell us that HeadsUp makes them smarter. Their thinking is better focused. They avoid mistakes.

The reason is simple. When you know all the facts early enough, you reduce the level of uncertainty and risk, and gain the confidence to make the right decisions.

Charter Invitation: FREE 30-Day Trial.

Your first HeadsUp report can be on your desk tomorrow morning. Ready to make you more knowledgeable, more surefooted, more competitive -- while relieving you of the burden of those unread stacks of publications.

HeadsUp is unique. There is nothing else like it. It's a one-stop, single-source solution to the information deluge.

You can be among the first to harness the potential of the information revolution -- while avoiding its downside. Join us on the cutting edge of a brand-new information medium.

(over,please)

(Continued)

- 4 -

Consider: How else could you ensure that you're covering 61,550 business and technology news items each week -- 12,310 every working day? If you tried, you wouldn't have time to do anything else!

At last, there's a more efficient way to process the flow of information you need to know. The time HeadsUp saves can be put to better use. Try this innovative service, and watch your performance and your productivity soar.

Perhaps the biggest benefit of all is the reassuring sense that you'll never again miss something important. You won't feel anxious about not keeping up, or guilty that you lack the time to read what others are reading. Can you put a price on that?

Here's my offer:

> Try HeadsUp FREE for 30 days. Prove for yourself that it delivers all the advantages I've promised. You incur no costs, no risks, and no obligations.

What's more, during your trial period, you will have unlimited full-text retrieval privileges. You may request as many original articles as you wish, without charge.

After the 30-day trial ends, you may elect to continue as a subscriber, or you may cancel -- for any reason or for no reason -- without owing a dime. It's entirely your decision.

I can't think of an offer that's more fair, can you?

To begin your FREE Charter trial, all you have to do is tell us your interests. Simply complete the enclosed form, indicating up to ten subjects, as listed in the Topic Selection Guide. Then fax or mail it back. Even the reply is free of charge.

Welcome to HeadsUp. Once you've tried it, I think you'll agree: You've never seen the world in quite this way before.

Sincerely,

John Zahner

John Zahner,
Vice President

P.S. Any questions? If so, please call a HeadsUp representative toll-free at 1-800-414-1000. We'll help with your topic selections, or answer any other questions. Of course, there is no obligation.

Remember: Respond today by fax and your FREE HeadsUp trial will begin tomorrow. You'll have an entire month to judge its value, without charge.

Mailer: **Utne Reader—The Alternative Press**
Key Words: **"Reading and Dining Salon"**
Writer: **Bill Jayme**

The Challenge

To someone who does not know the name, "Utne," a communication from someone of that name is regarded as a curiosity rather than a serious sales letter. So the writer has to overcome an attitude: "What kind of name is that? And what does it have to do with me?"

The Implementation

The writer recognizes the unusual name and, in marvelous fashion, exploits it by including a "lift note" which makes much of that very point. In fact, within three paragraphs, the reader feels he knows Eric Utne very well. The apparent artlessness of the approach is infectious, and within a matter of one to two minutes the unknown not only has become familiar; it has become desirable.

Notice that the letter has a handwritten signature, without the name having been typed below and, to preserve the one-to-one image, the letter has no postscript.

Comment

As is true of many of Bill Jayme's letters, this letter has been the control (as of this writing) for a decade or more. The first paragraph hurls down a targeted gauntlet for the ideal *Utne Reader* subscriber—the young idealist with dual goals: to help cure the ills of the world and to lead the good life. (The lift note points out that in Norwegian, *Utne* means "far out"; "Alternative Press Reading & Dining Salon" is explained in the lift note as an "in-group" roundtable from which each edition of the Utne Reader springs full-blown.)

Figure 3–15. Alternative Press

T H E   A L T E R N A T I V E   P R E S S

READING & DINING SALON

invites you to sample the bill of fare of

U T N E   R E A D E R

by sending for the next issue without cost or obligation

F R E E

Dear Reader:

If you believe that exercise will help you live longer...that small companies are better to work for than big ones...and that you can't possibly make money while maintaining your principles...

...there's something you should know. It won't. They aren't. You can. And if revelations like these contradict axioms you learned at your mother's knee, there are more surprises to come. Just open UTNE READER to any page. Overturned truisms. Shattered shibboleths. Debunked bromides. Truth!

UTNE READER? Yes, UTNE READER. It's the new magazine that rekindles the kind of intellectual excitement we all enjoyed here in America before complacency set in. The magazine that's got people making up their own minds again instead of swallowing ideas whole. The magazine that gives you perspective. Opens your eyes. Saves you time and money.

> Free issue. When you mail the enclosed card promptly, you'll get the next issue of UTNE READER with our compliments. No cost. No commitment. Free. If you like it? Subscribe and save yourself some silver. Read on!

UTNE READER was created a little over five years ago to bring you the best of the alternative press. Economic forecasts like you find in Dollars and Sense. Lifestyle how-to like you get from Mother Earth News. Politics -- American Spectator, Mother Jones, The Nation. Activism -- Ms., Earth First!, Dissent. Commentary -- The New Statesman, Foreign Policy, The Guardian.

> The Cutting Edge -- The Village Voice, Washington Monthly, Rolling Stone. Fitness and Health -- Medical SelfCare, American Health, Whole Life Times. Science, Technology and the Environment --Audubon, Resurgence, Orion. Any and everything you ought to know about that you won't find in mainstream media.

UTNE READER isn't slick -- no glossy paper, no centerfolds, no scratch-and-sniff perfume packets -- but it is designed to please the eye as well as the mind. It's where more and more of the brightest movers and shakers are congregating. And what our magazine is doing for them, it can also do for you.

(over please)

Exploiting both medium and message. *(Continued)*

UTNE READER adds to your perspective. Here's Barbara Ehrenreich on today's crazed pursuit of "excellence." Ken Kesey on coming to terms with the death of his 20-year-old son. Alice Walker on saying goodbye to a dying friend. Gary Snyder on life in general. The meaning of marathoning according to Hunter Thompson. The jogger's prayer according to Tom Wolfe.

Here's Chris Mullin on Vietnam today. Allen Ginsberg on Nicaragua. Deena Metzger on careers in prostitution. Jonathan Rowe on Ralph Nader. Noam Chomsky on disarmament. Garrison Keillor on porches. "A good porch," Keillor observes, "lets you smoke, talk loud, eat with your fingers...without running away from home."

UTNE READER opens your eyes. Child abuse -- how parents can scar their kids worse than any molester. Dieting -- why are health authorities now telling you to forget it? Central America -- how is the administration censoring the news? Nazis -- if you think that they're ancient history, why should you think again? AIDS -- what's more dangerous than the disease?

Family farms -- how does saving them start at your supermarket? World peace -- what might you be doing? Stress -- how can you lessen it by taking on more responsibility? All these have been the focus of UTNE READER stories that reveal the facts without bias, pull no punches, help you get at the truth.

UTNE READER saves you time and money. The New York Times notes that the Lord's Prayer contains 56 words, the 23rd Psalm 118 words, the Gettysburg Address 226 words, and the Ten Commandments 297 words, while the U.S. Department of Agriculture directive on pricing cabbage weighs in at 15,629 words.

If you go for gospel over gobbledegook, brevity over bombast, pith over prolixity, our magazine can save you hours in reading time. It can also save you big bucks. Instead of paying $18, $24, $30 a year apiece for all the publications that interest you, you get the best of all of them with a single subscription to UTNE READER.

Send no money. To get a taste of UTNE READER, just mail the enclosed card. If the magazine goes down easy, your introductory price for a full year's subscription (6 bimonthly issues in all) is only $18. Single copy costs come to $24. You save a full $6.00.

Owe nothing. If UTNE READER doesn't sit well, though, just return the subscription bill marked "cancel," and that's the end of the matter. You've spent nothing. You owe nothing. You're under no further obligation. The issue is yours to keep with our thanks.

Early postmark. Only so many copies of each issue are published, and no more. In fairness, first come, first served. Avoid disappointment. Mail card quickly. Our gratitude. And bon appetit.

Cordially yours,

Carolyn Adams

Carolyn Adams
For the Alternative Press
READING & DINING SALON

Utne Reader • P.O. Box 1974 • Marion, Ohio 43306

Figure 3–16. Utne Reader Lift Note

ERIC UTNE

Dear Reader:

Utne rhymes with chutney. In Norwegian, it means far out. And "far out!" is what you'll probably say when I tell you how we publish UTNE READER.

The magazine comes to you six times a year from a converted warehouse here in Minneapolis. We have an editorial staff of four. Myself. Our executive editor, Jay Walljasper. Our task-master, Lynette Lamb. Our resident generalist, Helen Cordes. And in the best tradition of feisty little journals, our friends and relatives volunteer time to help plan the magazine.

> There's Nina, my bemused wife. There's a Buddhist anti-nuclear activist. There's a socially responsible philanthropist. A Jungian dream analyst. An Amish quilt merchandiser. An anarcho-punk theorist. A hog farmer. Plus a dozen or so other stalwart media junkies who are nice enough to lend a hand.

For two months, we all read and clip whatever we find of interest in more than 1,000 alternative publications. Political exposés. How-to lifestyle pieces. Money advisories. Interviews with unusual people. Stories about the environment, survival, shenanigans in high places. Any and everything that you're not likely to find in mainstream newspapers and magazines.

Then, round about deadline time, we all get together in an all-night gathering that's come to be known as The Alternative Press Reading & Dining Salon. We discuss what we've read. We talk. We argue. We nibble on pizza and popcorn. And by dawn's early light, we've got it -- what we feel is one of the most exciting, yet useful, magazines you can read today.

> UTNE READER is independent, unbiased, revealing, irreverent, comprehensive, authoritative, spirited, visionary, forthright, honest, and a blueprint for social betterment. It's also fun to read in the tub...

...but come see for yourself on us. When you mail the enclosed card promptly, you get the next issue free. If you like it, you'll save $6.00. If you don't, just say so and that's that. You've spent nothing. You owe nothing. No nerd will knock at your door to try to change your mind. No computer will bug you. You have the oath of a Viking Son. Jeg lover -- I promise!

May we look for your reply by return mail? There's not much storage space here in the office, and we have only so many copies to hand out free. Avoid disappointment by mailing the card before sundown. Thank you,

Cordially yours,

Eric Utne

"Utne? What's that?" This writer makes the most of it. *(Continued)*

Why the "Alternative Press Reading & Dining Salon"?

Why the **"Utne Reader"**? *Why "Utne"?*

Mailer: **Story Magazine**

Key Words: **"You may know the story"**

Writer: **Josh Manheimer**

The Challenge

Many social critics believe that we are moving into a post-literate society in which good writing, especially fiction, is becoming obsolete.

A publication which attempts to combat this attitude has to reach a select readership segment, a segment which is (because it is select) the target of many similar appeals within this shrinking marketplace.

The Implementation

Quite properly, the letter underscores the exclusivity of the group to which the recipient belongs—those who cherish good stories by top writers.

Using the touchstone technique, the letter capitalizes on names such as Carson McCullers and Norman Mailer. In fact, the first words one sees, above any sales copy, are names of writers first published in *Story Magazine*—J.D. Salinger, Tennessee Williams, William Saroyan, Truman Capote, et al.

The letter positions the premiere revival issue as a collector's item and combines standard successful subscription techniques—the word "Charter" and "Send no money"—with reader status.

Comment

The reintroduction of a literary magazine is an "iffy" gamble at best. This publisher, who also publishes the *Writer's Digest* group of books and magazines, was the perfect candidate to take such a gamble. The writer reports a 14% gross response to a letter whose appeal is highly literate—which suggests exquisite list selection as a major factor (as it always should be, but too often isn't, in targeting message-recipients) in making a letter successful.

Figure 3–17. ***Story Magazine***

The magazine that *first* published J.D. Salinger, Tennessee Williams, William Saroyan, Kay Boyle, Elizabeth Janeway, Nelson Algren, Erskine Caldwell, Truman Capote, Norman Mailer. . .

. . . has just made a resounding return!

Introducing. . . the new. . .

STORY

You have the Premier Issue reserved in your name.

May we send it to you free?

Dear Friend,

You may know the story.

Fifty-eight years ago in Vienna, the first issues of a magazine were cranked out on an old mimeograph machine.

However, buried within those ink-smudged pages were gems of fiction no other publication at the time could touch.

The magazine was called STORY.

Now, in the most talked about revival in

Combining traditional appeals with reader status. *(Continued)*

-2-

the history of publishing, STORY magazine will return to bring you today's most compelling voices in literature.

Riveting. Captivating. Talk-to-me-later-I'm-busy stories.

Whether you enjoy the quiet thrill of discovering an unknown 24-year-old who promises to be the next Carson McCullers...

> ...or relish a sliver from Norman Mailer's soon to be published new novel, you'll cherish this Premier collector's copy.

No essays. No reviews. No poetry. Just stories. Brilliant short fiction that will make you shout across the room, "You've really got to read this!"

Frankly, before the return of STORY, to enjoy today's top fiction, you had to hunt through countless, hard-to-find, literary journals -- an undertaking of considerable effort and expense.

Now, however, you'll soon have at your fingertips an assemblage of gripping, spellbinding, humorous, tantalizing tales that you can devour in minutes.

> No other mainstream publication today can offer you this unique experience.

Short fiction has always been the seed bed for promising new authors.

As a Charter Subscriber to STORY, you will be able to count yourself among the small discerning audience who appreciates the deep

(Continued)

-3-

satisfaction one gains by keeping abreast of the current climate in literature.

> Printed on heavy premium paper and sturdily bound, STORY is meant to be read, dog-eared, borrowed, but above all -- cherished and collected for years to come.

Great stories endure.

Soon you can treat yourself to fiction of extraordinary stature in just minutes.

I know of no other feeling like it.

<u>Correction.</u>

I do know of <u>one</u> other feeling...

Becoming a part of literary history.

<u>To get your free Premier Charter Issue...</u>

...SEND NO MONEY. Simply mail back the enclosed R.S.V.P. and we'll rush you the Premier issue at absolutely no charge.

If you like what you see and want more, we'll sign you up for the full year at the low introductory Charter rate of just $15 and forward 4 additional quarterly issues (making 5 you'll receive in all)!

<u>Your Risk-Free Guarantee</u>:

> If you decide not to continue as a Charter subscriber, simply jot "No Thanks" across our bill, return it, and that will be that.

(Continued)

-4-

Keep the free Premier issue regardless, as our way of saying, "Thanks for at least giving STORY a look."

Cordially,

Richard Rosenthal
Publisher

P.S. Your Free Premier Charter issue of STORY is bound to be a collector's item. Because only so many will be printed, we can hold onto your personal copy for a short period before we must offer it to someone else.

To assure your free Premier copy reaches you without delay, please return your R.S.V.P. by the earliest possible postmark. Thanks. R.R.

Mailer: **Shutterbug**

Key Words: **"I was reading an article"**

Writer: **Herschell Gordon Lewis**

The Challenge

With dozens of publications aimed at amateur photographers, positioning has become increasingly difficult. For a magazine to create and justify a new niche, a publication must find an area of interest not being oversold by its competitors and justify that area of interest as a reason for the individuals to subscribe.

This suggests comparisons. And for a comparison to succeed, it must be, to the reader, not only clear, but apparently advantageous.

The Implementation

Marginal notes, which have come to full flower as a direct response device in the 1990s, lead the reader through this letter. Beyond that advantage, they lend additional power to the paragraphs opposite which they appear.

If the reader pays attention only to the marginal notes, he or she still will have the basic sales story for this magazine.

Note the second marginal note on the first page:

> Did you know this? I didn't.

Touches such as this build rapport between the signatory—the magazine's publisher—and the potential subscriber.

Comment

We included this letter by one of the book's co-authors because it represents a successful experiment in design. The handwritten marginal note is a well-established technique, but using these notes as subheads had not been tried previously. This letter, without a brochure, had a response ratio comparable to a longer letter with a brochure. Response ranged from 6% to better than 10%, depending on the list used.

Figure 3–18. ***Shutterbug***

shutterbug®

I'll keep this open for you for 30 days. Please read

Dear Fellow Photographer,

I was reading an article about digital imaging systems in a recent issue of SHUTTERBUG.

I've been publisher of this magazine (and of course a photographer) for years, but I admit — even though I had heard about digital imaging systems, I thought they were still "a gleam in somebody's eye."

Digital IS here now!

I hadn't realized digital imaging is here now. And you can buy this spectacular 21st century development now. Oh, sure, it still costs more than the typical photographer wants to pay. But give it a year or two and we'll all be swarming to upgrade. My point: I wouldn't know what the new developments are if I didn't read SHUTTERBUG.

Did you know this? I didn't

Another article was about Panatomic X. Kodak doesn't make this film any more. What's a logical replacement, and what chemicals do you use to develop that replacement? (Kodak recommends T-Max-100 film, but our columnist preferred another stock, explained why, and covered the developer for both.)

Like all the articles in SHUTTERBUG, the information was so clear a beginner could follow it easily. And the subjects were so useful a professional could benefit from them. (We have letters to prove it.)

Will You Look at a Free Issue?

I invite you to become a subscriber to SHUTTERBUG, at a very special price ... far, far below the cover price.

Please, before you make a quick decision to toss this mailing into the wastebasket, understand what I'm offering you. Yes, I want you to become a subscriber. No, I don't want you to decide — yes or no — until you've seen a sample issue.

I'll tell you why: I can sit here all day,

A successful experiment in building rapport. *(Continued)*

writing about SHUTTERBUG, and not be able to transmit a fraction of what you can expect to find in the pages of this magazine.

For example, if you think photo magazines are "burned out" ... if you think they aren't giving you any new information (except camera and equipment manufacturers' press releases) you're right about some of them ... but you aren't right about SHUTTERBUG. This magazine just keeps getting brighter and brighter, more and more informative. And our writers are incorruptible. They give you straight information, not rehashed news releases.

I think you'll especially like our most popular regular column: "HELP."

Try getting these answers anywhere else

This column is a combination of Action Line, Find-the-Source, and technique know-how. One recent column tackled reader questions ranging from "Where can I find Kaiser adjustable shoulder stocks for the Nikon F4s?" (tough question, but we found the answer: HP Marketing Corp., Pine Brook, NJ) to "Is there a U.S. source for 6x7 projection equipment?" (sure there is, and Mamiya America Corp. has lots of them) ... to — well, that's enough. You get the idea, and I haven't described half the column.

Shutterbug is the big photo magazine

Every issue of SHUTTERBUG is loaded with useful facts, not obscure theory that might interest one of 100 readers.

And we're a big magazine — more than 250 jumbo pages, not the "standard" size, in every issue.

You really get your money's worth in SHUTTERBUG. One issue easily can save you ten times your low subscription cost. I'll prove that to you in a minute.

But first, here's my deal for you:

12 Huge Issues for Just...

Compare Shutterbug with these

At $3.50 an issue SHUTTERBUG just may be the best bargain in the world of photography.

Another magazine, also $3.50, has about 72 standard (8"x10-1/2") pages. Yet another has 105 standard pages. A third has 90 standard pages. Compare these with the mighty SHUTTERBUG, 250+ jumbo pages (10"x13").

(Continued)

In size and in content, SHUTTERBUG is a terrific bargain at $3.50.

But you won't pay that.

Newsstand price: $42.00
Your price: $15.95

IF you decide to subscribe ... and I've capitalized the word IF so you'll understand we're talking about a 100% free look ... you can get SHUTTERBUG for a whole year — 12 mammoth issues — for just $15.95. You save $26.05 off the newsstand price!

This means each issue is yours for just a little more than 1/3 the cover price.

Take a Good Look, at OUR Risk

I want to send you a sample issue. You know by now how enthusiastic I am about SHUTTERBUG. What matters is whether you'll be enthusiastic. I'll certainly take that risk.

You'll get the current issue brimming with useful articles ... articles filled with tips you can start using that same day, and crammed with ads that make SHUTTERBUG the biggest photographic bazaar of all time. (I'm coming to that.)

You take absolutely no risk

If you decide to continue, you'll get a full year — twelve giant issues — for just $15.95. If not, just write one word — "cancel" — and that will be the end of the matter.

A Marketplace-Wonderland

Save ten times your subscription cost

I've saved the best for last. I told you a single issue could easily save you ten times the cost of your annual subscription.

Ready for some proof?

Two quick questions:

Here's your proof

1. What would you expect to pay for a mint condition Bronica GSI?

2. What would you expect to pay for a Minolta 7000i demo in perfect condition?

If the answer to question 1 is more than $699, or if the answer to question 2 is more than $250, you have less than 1/1000 of the proof I'm talking about.

(Continued)

SHUTTERBUG's pages carry ads for thousands and thousands of cameras, lights, meters, filters, strobes, lights, tripods, film, cases, video gear, and every photographic item you can think of. We're loaded with ads reflecting the hot new interest in Leicas.

You'll find experts who repair cameras nobody else would touch because "parts aren't available." You'll find books on exotic subjects. You'll find notices of clubs — so many that some have to be in your neighborhood.

Are you a collector?

If you're a collector, riffling through the pages of SHUTTERBUG is like being in Wonderland. I'm not just talking about old Zeiss and Leica and Graphic cameras. I'm talking about cameras you may have thought have disappeared forever — Alta, Chiyoka, Hirsch, Reid.

If they ever existed at all, you'll find them in SHUTTERBUG. SHUTTERBUG is more than the world's biggest photographic discount supermarket. We're the ultimate source, with more information, more ads, more offers than anybody.

Limited Offer: Take Advantage of It NOW!

Take me up on this. Getting your no-risk issue of SHUTTERBUG means at worst you'll have a free copy of the most dynamic magazine in the photographic universe. At best you'll get the best, every month.

Don't "file" this. Mail Card now so you won't miss out.

Getting 12 giant issues for just $15.95 is the bargain of bargains.

But I can't guarantee this offer beyond the next few weeks. Mail your Free Issue Card now. You don't even need a stamp. So please do mail that Card.

For the Number One Photographic Showplace and Marketplace,

Christi Ashby

Christi Ashby, Publisher

P.S. Even if you have no intention of subscribing, I want you to have your free issue so you'll be familiar with SHUTTERBUG. I'll look for your Free Issue Card. Thanks.

Mailer: **The Menninger Clinic Newsletter**

Key Words: **"Why have I chosen you?"**

Writers: (two approaches) **Jack Walsh (A), Herschell Gordon Lewis (B)**

The Challenge

A newsletter dealing in mental health has to strike a delicate balance between appearing to be pedantic—beyond the informational plane available to the typical layperson—and simplistic in which people say, "I can get that information in one of the newspaper columns."

The Menninger Clinic has an exalted reputation, and the temptation would be to overuse that reputation to the detriment of any popular appeal a mental health newsletter might achieve.

By assigning two writers to this project, the Menninger Clinic was able to test two approaches, both of which showed an awareness of the challenge, and two different themes. This type of testing is completely logical when a mailer intends to mount a major marketing campaign that has no prior indication of which approach might pull best.

The Implementation

Walsh version (A):

By referring to the newsletter as "Your National Resource for Mental Health" and by, in the bullet copy, avoiding technical terminology, the writer succeeds in appealing to many levels of information and interest.

On page 3 of the letter we have a lengthy sampling of articles, chosen with exquisite care to cover the many facets of experience and interest which the newsletter promises to discuss.

All these areas of experience and interest are engrossing on multiple levels, ranging from the mental health professional to the casually-interested layperson.

Lewis version (B):

This approach to marketing the newsletter is peppered with "Did you know?" boxes. The intention is to tantalize the reader with episodes lifted from copies of the newsletter. The last box, shortly before the letter closes, adds a startling fact about cholesterol, a subject very much in the minds of those who would be prime prospects for any health or medical newsletter. Notice how the technique of boxing a paragraph seizes the eye.

The rubber stamp on the first page is a technique which, as other entries in this collection illustrate, adds timeliness and excitement without betraying the mailer's position of dignity.

Comment

The Menninger Clinic, in Topeka, Kansas, has a well-deserved reputation among mental health professionals; but it is not widely known to the general public. A newsletter aimed at the general public has to justify itself through examples the typical person understands, which may be why the first sentence of the letter—"Why have I chosen you to be among the first to receive the Menninger Letter?"—worked so well in this instance.

Conferring status to the reader is an almost infallible sales tool.

Figure 3–19a. The Menninger Clinic

The Menninger Clinic

BOX 829 • TOPEKA, KS 66601-0829

Yours free. . . the premiere issue of The Menninger Letter: Your National Resource for Mental Health -- from the doctors who have been helping people attain and maintain stability since 1925.

And, if you deem it to be as effective as we plan it to be, you'll enjoy the next year of monthly issues at half the regular annual subscription rate.

Either way, Volume I, Number 1 is yours absolutely free.

Dear Charter Subscriber-Elect:

Why have I chosen you to be among the first to receive The Menninger Letter?

To begin with, let me tell you that for every person I'm writing today, I have quite literally eliminated thousands. I did so by looking for those I thought would have an interest in. . .

- learning practical ways to promote individual growth;
- recognizing and managing mental health issues in their own lives and in the lives of those close to them;
- understanding psychological principles;
- keeping abreast of research and treatment dealing with various emotional disorders;
- examining media coverage of mental health issues and knowing what other publications are saying;
- becoming more inquisitive.

These being our criteria, I had no choice but to write you.

Even if you never took Psych. 101, I believe you, especially, will profit from the Letter because it deals with what I'm convinced is the most fascinating thing on the planet, bar none -- the human mind.

Yours, mine, and everyone else's.

And there is no one better equipped to do it. To say that

Appealing to multiple interest levels. *(Continued)*

The Menninger Clinic is preeminent in the field of mental health is as accurate as it is immodest. It's been said that our facility is "a national resource" and that "no other institution in the land offers the breadth of services available here in treatment, education, research and prevention."

Of these four endeavors, I think you'll find the Letter stresses prevention the most. For, if nothing else, ours is a practical publication, filled with information that you will use every day to maintain psychological equilibrium -- and to apply what you've learned in dealing with others.

And it will be presented in non-technical, readable, even conversational English. For while we assume that anyone who has an interest in our subject is of more than average education and intelligence (they don't always go hand-in-hand, which we'll write about). . . we will not assume you know what, say, Fregoli's or Munchausen's syndrome is. And in a future issue we'll explain both these fascinating dysfunctions.

> The bulk of our articles, however, will need no explanation at all:
>
> Grieving Anger deals with the inability to complete the grieving process, often because of unresolved ambivalence toward the deceased. The situation is usually characterized by denial, hostility, depression or over-activity, or all four.
>
> Biofeedback can be used with remarkable success to control migraine and tension headaches, relieve daily stress, enhance performance and alleviate urinary incontinence.
>
> Hypnosis for the highly motivated only. If you qualify, it can help you break nervous habits like nail-biting and smoking, relieve pain and nausea, and overcome trauma.
>
> Parenting is, of course, a matter of making the right choices. How do you handle the child who cheats? Whose pet dies? Who has no friends? Doesn't sleep through the night? Or explain sex, AIDS, death, divorce, remarriage? (It was Dr. Karl Menninger who said, "What's done to children, they will do to society.")

Phobias, which almost all of us have at one time or another, will be a recurring topic in our Letter. Common ones are fears of public speaking, high places, open places and closed spaces. There's even erythrophobia -- a fear of blushing. Interestingly, one can be acrophobic (fearing high places) yet have no fear of flying. We'll discuss how -- and if -- they should be treated. Incidentally, women are twice as likely to suffer from less complex phobias.

(Continued)

But it's balanced by men being far more likely to experience sleep terrors. Which are different from nightmares. The former are repeated episodes of abrupt awakening in the first third of sleep that are characterized by a scream. Whereas nightmares are repeated awakenings from the second half of sleep with detailed recall of frightening dreams, causing significant distress.

Your childhood sibling position is undoubtedly affecting your behavior even today, no matter what your age. Let us explain this effect in your one-on-one relationships (friendships, romance, marriage), in work situations, in social groups.

> One of the recurring buzzwords these days is "self-esteem." How important is it, really? How can you improve it? Can you have too much of it? When should you worry about it?

"How to Avoid Being Manipulated"
"The Difference between 'Aloneness' and 'Loneliness'"
"Is Unwed Motherhood Contagious?"
"Stress: Make It Work for You"
"How Parental Perceptions of Siblings Influence Offspring"
"The Effects of Late-Life Divorce"
"How Much Sleep Do You Really Need as You Age?"
"Is There Any Hope for a National Health Insurance Plan?"
"Tips on Choosing a Therapist"
"Turning Old into Gold"
"Saving a Failing Marriage"
"Facing Death -- Your Own or a Loved One's"
"Interpreting Your Dreams"
"Aging Couples in Dual-Career Families"
"Why Do Young People Use Drugs?"
"In Therapy, How Long Is Too Long?"
"Life Cycles of Mothers and Daughters"
"Does Alcohol Have Any Redeeming Value?"
"Rules for Rearing Children"
"A Bright Light in Depression"
"The Uses of Pornography"
"Obtaining Mental Health Care Inexpensively"
"Religious Beliefs and Psychiatric Treatment"
"Marital Happiness of Care-givers to the Elderly"
"12-Step Programs -- Don't Trip"
"The Role of Fantasy"
"What We Know -- and Do Not Know -- about Eating Disorders"
"Creativity Defined -- Maybe"
"Homosexuality -- Its Causes and Effects"
"The Stepfamily Imbroglios. . . in the Plural"
"Fear of Failure -- Fear of Success!"
"Dealing with Sexual Harassment without a Lawyer"

These are just a sampling of the articles you may discover in your

(Continued)

money-saving Charter Subscription. And the monetary advantages go beyond your reduced Charter rates:

If, through The Menninger Letter, you perform in the workplace better -- and get fellow workers to do the same -- you'll certainly be money ahead.

And because it is indisputable that mental health is intimately related to physical health. . . you'll be hedging against the punishing cost of you or a loved one being ill.

But these reasons for subscribing are very poor seconds to what I believe you'll find the most compelling reason for having done so:

> An expanded self-confidence and renewed peace of mind. The knowledge that you have the counsel of an institution whose authority is unexcelled in its field. . . easily retrieved through an exhaustive, cross-referenced annual index.

Best of all, you can test my words and your satisfaction free.

Just return the enclosed Charter Subscription Reservation Form (with the "I Accept" seal affixed, please) at our expense and we'll send you the premiere issue of The Menninger Letter to examine, judge, use.

If it is not everything I have suggested and you surmised, you can write "Cancel" on the bill when it arrives, return it and that is that.

You not only can cancel, you should.

Far more likely, however, you'll find it so useful, down-to-earth and reassuring that you'll happily pay just $12.00 for 11 more issues (a total of 12) -- saving some 50% on the regular price of $24.00.

Do mail the Form today, please. Being experts on memory, we know that delaying even one day dramatically increases the chances of it never being mailed at all.

Thank you for reading my letter and I do hope to hear from you in just a day or two.

Sincerely,

Glen O. Gabbard, M.D.

Glen O. Gabbard, M.D.

P.S. Please remember that it's just about as easy to write "Cancel" on the bill as it is to put the "I Accept" seal on the Reservation Form. So your risk in doing the latter is all but non-existent. A reminder to you that is psychologically -- and practically -- very prudent.

Figure 3–19b. The Menninger Clinic

The Menninger Clinic
P.O. Box 829
Topeka, KS 66601-0829

Good Morning!

I'm delighted to issue you this private invitation:

We invite you to enjoy a personal subscription to a publication I guarantee is unlike any you've seen and read before: The Menninger Letter. I'm ready to send you a free sample issue. And if I hear from you within the next 15 days, I'll include our privately printed "Candid Answers to Candid Questions" -- a booklet you'd never be able to get elsewhere.

> DID YOU KNOW? Recent studies of persons with schizophrenia indicate they find it difficult to visually follow a spot of light across a screen. This also is true of their relatives and children. What does this mean? You'd know all about it if you read The Menninger Letter.

You've heard the line "This isn't for everyone" hundreds of times, I know -- usually as an advertising ploy. Believe me, The Menninger Letter isn't for everyone. It's for alert, educated, informed individuals who want information about psychological developments ... mental health issues ... and an expanding universe of knowledge that can open new vistas of well-being and communication you'll certainly want to explore.

Why Others Can't Share This Information

Others won't know what you know because I'm sending this private Invitation to just a fraction of potential subscribers. Among your benefits is getting the Letter for half-price. Instead of the $24 others will pay for a full year's subscription (and it's a bargain at that price!), The Menninger Letter is yours for only $12.

Only one possible source could produce The Menninger Letter. That's The Menninger Clinic, which for decades has been listed among the very best psychiatric centers in the world.

Now, don't let that term "psychiatric center" get in the way of your perception of what you'll get in each month's issue of The Menninger Letter. What you'll get is inside insight, on a totally readable level in plain English. And reports in The Menninger Letter are copyrighted and protected. You'll have this exclusive "inside insight" months before the general public.

Involving the public through tantalizing questions. *(Continued)*

DID YOU KNOW? Exercise seems to aid the memory function in the elderly and seems to slow the rate of age-linked mental deterioration. You'd know all about it if you read The Menninger Letter.

What's New in Hypnosis? In Parenting? In Biofeedback?

Is The Menninger Letter a newsletter? Oh, yes. Every month its eight pages are crammed with news ... but not the kind of political or financial news the standard newsletter brings you. The Menninger Letter is the authoritative voice of news you just couldn't ferret out if you weren't a subscriber.

I suppose you'd benefit from a newsletter telling you which mutual funds have performed well over the past year. But wouldn't you benefit more from a newsletter telling you how much better YOU might perform over the NEXT year?

DID YOU KNOW? The "Old Wives' Tale" that women talk more than men may have some basis in fact. The splenium, part of the brain linked to verbal fluency, is larger in women than in men. You'd know all about it if you read The Menninger Letter.

I don't have to tell you that hypnosis, once regarded as the province of charlatans and stage magicians, has proved its clinical worth. What does that have to do with you? The Menninger Clinic is in the vanguard of research associated with the human mind. Much of the massive storehouse of knowledge to which our incomparable medical staff contributes daily is yours to see in the pages of The Menninger Letter.

And The Menninger Letter deals with subjects you want to know about. This isn't some obscure, arcane, incomprehensible scientific treatise. It's a monthly treasure-house of news and reports I guarantee you'll find not just fascinating, but also useful.

How Can I GUARANTEE You'll Like What You See?

It's easy enough for me to guarantee you'll be looking forward to the unique compendium of information you get each month in the fact-packed pages of The Menninger Letter.

That's because I'm going to send your first issue free. Look it over. See for yourself. If you don't like what you see, just write "cancel" on the bill and that will be the end of it. If you do like what you see and recognize how useful and informative The Menninger Letter will be for you, we'll send eleven more issues -- a whole year -- for half the published issue price. Others will pay $24. Your subscription is just $12.

(Continued)

DID YOU KNOW? When a child hates to go to school, the reason may be "separation anxiety" -- anxiety over being separated from the primary caretaker. This differs from "school phobia." What to do? Counseling? Medication? Maybe both. You'd know all about it if you read The Menninger Letter.

Answers to Your Questions

Perhaps the most popular feature in The Menninger Letter is the column "On Call." In this column, our experts answer questions you, our subscribers, ask.

Some of the questions -- such as biofeedback to strengthen muscles in muscular dystrophy or other weaknesses ... weight control ... sex education ... depression ... rape and sexual abuse -- these are personal problems in which expert advice is literally invaluable. Other questions, such as whether it's safe to drink alcohol while taking Prozac (it is, in moderation) and how to discuss sex with a 14-year-old, are both interesting and educational.

DID YOU KNOW? Since it was the subject of a number of "L.A. Law" programs, Tourette's syndrome -- involuntary vocal and body "tics" -- has become a popular subject. Haldol has shown promise in treating Tourette's syndrome, but precautions are in order. You'd know all about it if you read The Menninger Letter.

And our experts are top experts -- heads of departments and clinical directors at The Menninger Clinic itself, as well as distinguished mental health professionals from around the country. Advice and counsel comes from authorities to whom you'd pay hundreds of dollars for individual sessions. No wonder so many readers turn first to see what's in this month's "On Call."

An Extra Gift For You ...

I've been authorized to add yet another sweetener to this special invitation to you:

If you mail your Direct Invitation Form within the next 15 days, we'll include with your first issue a most unusual booklet -- "Candid Answers to Candid Questions." In its pages is invaluable information from our "On Call" experts, culled from many issues of The Menninger Letter ... answers to questions you won't find elsewhere -- such as, "Should I confront my 15-year-old son about the girlie magazines I found in his closet?" and "What can I do to help my sister get over her bitterness about her divorce?" and "What are the current guidelines for nudity in the home among family members?"

(Continued)

"Candid Answers to Candid Questions" is yours to keep with the compliments of The Menninger Letter.

So you see, you aren't getting this communication by accident. I think you're the kind of person who will see the benefit -- no, the usefulness and the power -- of The Menninger Letter. You must be pleased.

A Service Whose Time Has Come

For years a whole group of newsletters has discussed physical well-being. That's good, because our bodies need all the help they can get.

Now, at last, here's a newsletter that covers an even more crucial subject -- mental well-being. When I say "At last," I'm pointing out how much more your mind can contribute to your well-being (or lack of well-being) than your body. And beyond that, as an informed and educated individual, you're very much aware that the mind can not just affect the body's well-being but can also actually control it.

> DID YOU KNOW? Everybody seems to want to lower his or her cholesterol; but a low cholesterol level can lead to depression and even thoughts of suicide. You'd know all about it if you read The Menninger Letter.

What I'm offering you is a monthly gourmet feast for your mind. I'm offering it to you at the very best rate anyone could have -- the special limited-time half-price Subscription rate.

Best of all, I'm offering you a no-risk look at the publication that can be as significant to your future happiness, future relationships, and future peace of mind as you'll ever be able to enjoy.

Won't you at least take a look at a sample issue, with my compliments? I think after examining your free issue you'll agree you've made a wise choice.

For The Menninger Letter,

Glen O. Gabbard, M.D.

Glen O. Gabbard, M.D.

P.S. Just place the "I Accept" sticker in its box and mail your Direct Invitation Form in its postage-free envelope within the next 15 days to guarantee that you'll get your copy of "Candid Answers to Candid Questions." The booklet is yours to keep whether or not you decide to subscribe. Thank you.

Mailer: The Chronicle of Philanthropy
Key Words: "New demands from donors"

The Challenge

Fund raisers, a highly sophisticated group of professionals, often feel they should be writing advice to their contemporaries rather than paying for a subscription to a publication which gives them advice.

Convincing a fund raiser that a publication has information which will add substantially to his or her professional stature and capabilities is not only a challenge; it is a *major* challenge.

The Implementation

The postscript encapsulates the sales argument for this publication: "If The Chronicle of Philanthropy helps you get one grant, provides the fund-raising idea that brings in one additional gift, or leads you to the job you've always wanted, it will more than pay for itself."

Within the letter, the writer attacks many of the problems non-profit organizations face, especially those which have no single "pat" solution.

The Chronicle of Philanthropy balances its appeal on three bases: hard news; legislation; and trends in fund-raising techniques.

Comment

Although we aren't enchanted with the overline—the line above "Dear Colleague"—we include this letter because, except for that sentence, the letter is both targeted and dynamic.

Why do we make a negative comment about the overline? Because it is a generic statement common to all business and fund raising.

Note the first paragraph, which begins with—and gains strength from—partial sentences.

Figure 3–20. *The Chronicle of Philanthropy*

THE CHRONICLE OF PHILANTHROPY
The newspaper of the non-profit world

To succeed in today's non-profit world, you need to know what's going on.

Dear Colleague:

New demands from donors. Changing foundation priorities. Reduced government funds. Threats of more regulation. Never before have you and your organization faced such challenges -- and opportunities.

The key to being effective in times like these is information like:

* Why the new tax law will encourage charitable giving -- and how you can take advantage of it.

* How the technological revolution will change everything you do -- from delivering services to raising money.

* How controversies over charity and foundation salaries will affect all non-profits including yours.

Now you can have that kind of information without paying hundreds of dollars. Everything you need is in one reasonably priced publication, The Chronicle of Philanthropy. It's not like any other publication in the non-profit world.

* It is timely. Published every other week on a fast-closing schedule, it gives you the news while you still have time to do something about it.

* It is easy to scan -- and a pleasure to read. Written by a staff of first-rate professional journalists, it's a paper you'll look forward to seeing.

* Above all, it is useful. The Chronicle is full of information: lists of grants, fund-raising ideas, job opportunities, deadlines, texts, regulations, IRS rulings, statistics, and much, much more.

A no-risk offer for you.

And because I'm so confident that you'll find The Chronicle of Philanthropy absolutely essential, I'll send you the next four issues to try before you decide to buy. But more about that later. Once you

Talking to professionals in their own language. *(Continued)*

subscribe, you'll know why the Grantsmanship Center declares The Chronicle "essential." In the last few weeks our readers have learned:

- Why corporations are cutting back on philanthropy -- and how you can get gifts anyway.

- Why a flurry of bad press is making things tough for charities nationwide.

- How health-care reform will affect non-profits -- and donations to health causes.

- How charities are <u>making connections with celebrities</u> in sports and popular music.

Chronicle readers also know about the latest regulatory actions: How the federal government plans to crack down on fraudulent mailings by charities and what new accounting standards will mean for fund raising. We'll even tell you <u>how to cope with an IRS audit</u> -- and how to avoid one in the first place.

We write about the people and organizations who do the Good Works that are the heart of philanthropy: The low-key entrepreneur who helps people in third-world countries start their own businesses, the San Diego shelter for battered women considered one of the nation's most effective non-profits, the Detroit woman whose organization helps people like herself who have lost children to street violence.

The latest trends in fund raising.

You'll also be up to date on the latest trends and ideas in fund raising. You'll know:

- Why banks and other financial institutions are moving in on planned giving -- and what it means for charities.

- Whether it's better to write long fund-raising letters or short ones.

- Why charitable trusts are <u>the hottest things in fund raising</u> today.

- Why some experts believe charities are wasting time collecting useless information about potential donors.

And we'll give you lots of other hints on how to make your

(Continued)

organization more effective: How to cut costs when budgets get tight. How to get advice without hiring expensive consultants. Why charities' health-insurance costs have soared -- and what you can do about it.

What companies and foundations are thinking.

As a Chronicle reader, you'll know all about the latest thinking at the nation's foundations and corporations. We've taken our readers inside foundations like Ford, MacArthur, Weinberg, and Wallace. And when major foundations announce changes in grant-making programs, you'll be among the first to know.

You'll penetrate the often murky world of corporate philanthropy. Find out how a new generation of CEO's is changing company giving. Chronicle readers know the secrets of winning corporate gifts now, when companies want to see real results from their donations.

We've taken an in-depth look at charitable giving by the nation's fast-growing computer companies. And you'll get annual previews of the giving plans at major foundations and corporations.

A wealth of information all in one place.

But that's not all you get in The Chronicle. Every issue brings you a package of information unmatched in the non-profit world: Details of new grants by foundations and corporations, summaries of new government regulations that affect you, an extensive calendar of meetings and workshops, deadlines on government and private funds.

You'll receive updates on major fund-raising campaigns, summaries of foundations' annual reports, changes in postal policies and rates, rulings by federal and state courts, and texts of reports and other essential documents. You'll also get the latest tax rulings -- explained clearly for the layperson, yet thoroughly for the expert.

You'll get statistics from the latest research on giving, salaries, volunteering, expenditures, and myriad other topics -- presented in easy-to-read tables and charts. You'll get summaries of the latest books and other publications on philanthropy, fund raising, and non-profit management. We'll tell you who's been promoted, who's changed jobs.

Each issue contains a special "Ideas and Resources" section that describes techniques that have worked for non-profits all across North America. It includes the "Reading List," which summarizes the best books on a particular topic, such as special events or planned giving, and "The Basics," a column offering such tips as how to thank donors with more

(Continued)

than plaques and dinners, and how to put together a sponsorship deal with a corporation.

One of our services is especially useful: Our advertisements of job openings. Each issue has several pages of ads offering professional opportunities in fund raising, non-profit management, and philanthropy.

You must be satisfied.

I believe The Chronicle of Philanthropy provides you with all the news and information you need to function effectively in this demanding field. But you don't have to take my word for it. You can try our newspaper at no risk and no cost to you.

Just mail the enclosed order form in the postage-paid envelope we've provided to start your no-risk subscription. I'll send you the next four issues to look over. If you're not satisfied, just write "cancel" on your invoice and you'll owe us nothing.

But if you are as delighted as I think you will be, you'll receive 20 additional issues (24 in all) for $67.50 . . . That's just $2.81 an issue.

And you have this additional guarantee: If you ever become dissatisfied, you can cancel anytime and we'll refund the balance of your subscription.

So send in your order today. Whether you're a fund raiser or a foundation professional, whether you serve a large institution or a small charity, you'll find The Chronicle of Philanthropy provides the news and information you need, when you need it.

At a time when information is essential for you and your organization, I think you'll find you can't afford not to subscribe.

Sincerely,

Philip W. Semas
Editor

PWS:ja

P.S. Remember: If The Chronicle of Philanthropy helps you get one grant, provides the fund-raising idea that brings in one additional gift, or leads you to the job you've always wanted, it will more than pay for itself.

1255 Twenty-Third Street, N.W. Washington, D.C. 20037

Mailer: **Cooking Light**
Key Words: **"Chocolate Eclairs!"**
Writer: **Josh Manheimer**

The Challenge

If any area of publication is crowded, it is the cooking/cuisine/epicure field.

For a publication to make an impact, especially when its dedication is to philosophy rather than to award-winning recipes, the writer has to deal in episodes which suggest uniqueness—information not paralleled by any other source.

The Implementation

The writer cleverly uses himself (writing as "herself") as surrogate for the reader. This is a potent rapport-building device and also helps make the letter both readable and credible.

Opening with an episode whose payoff is the reverse of what the reader might expect, the letter then moves in logical fashion into a "soft offer," underscored by an indented paragraph which emphasizes comparative saving.

The P.S. reinforces the opening situation as an extra touch of credibility.

Comment

The anecdote above the greeting grabs and shakes the reader because the payoff is exactly the reverse of what the reader expects. This in itself is good technique; but because it is tied to what the letter sells, it becomes an exceptional technique, with reader-appeal far beyond a straightforward, factual argument for subscribing to the magazine.

The writer reports a better than 10% gross response.

Figure 3–21. *Cooking Light*

Give Up Nothing...when you send for your Free Issue of...

COOKING LIGHT®

"Chocolate Eclairs!" my husband shouted.
"But we agreed to start eating light."

"We are!" I said with a big smile. "Friday we're having Strawberry Cheesecake."

Dear Friend,

When the doctor told my husband his cholesterol was dangerously high, he thought it meant giving up his cherished foods forever.

So when I started to dish out his old favorites like Pizza ... Pasta Primavera ... Strawberry Cheesecake ...

... he couldn't believe it!

And when I told him the pizza had only 192 calories per serving and the cheesecake hardly had any cholesterol, his face lit up like a lighthouse.

"You're wonderful!" he shouted. "But, wait a second. How ... ?

That evening I told him. Now I'd like to share my good news with you.

The secrets to dining elegantly AND nutritiously are all packed into the ground-breaking magazine of food and fitness, called COOKING LIGHT.

> Frankly, before COOKING LIGHT, to dine well AND dine "light," you had to convert recipes found in magazines like Bon Appetit. Even then, you weren't sure how they would turn out.

Now, however, that's all done for you by the home economists and registered dieticians at COOKING LIGHT. Every recipe is kitchen-tested -- and tasted -- to guarantee you're always serving your family and friends nutritious foods that look and taste absolutely divine.

> The editor tells me she's reserved a free issue in your name. To get it, just return your Invitation enclosed.

In the pages of COOKING LIGHT, you'll discover revolutionary ways to thicken sauces without using butter or heavy cream, to turn a

Clever positioning: the writer as surrogate for the reader.

(Continued)

favorite family recipe like Chicken and Dumplings into a tasty, low-cholesterol entree. How to add flavor to your soup without adding a ham hock. How to season foods sublimely -- without using salt.

From tempting appetizers to delectable desserts, COOKING LIGHT shows you how to use more nutritious ingredients in every single dish you prepare.

A healthier, happier, livelier lifestyle.

We'll also keep you posted on the most current scientific data and even turn it into practical life-enriching, life-saving guidelines you and your family can live by.

You'll find insights, facts and statistics on how lifestyle changes can add new vitality to your life and actually decrease risk of life-threatening diseases like cancer, diabetes, hypertension!

You'll also become a more informed shopper, able to read between the lines on food labels. Find the best buys in fitness equipment, videos, books. Size up all the "fitness" merchants.

To get your free sample issue ...

SEND NO MONEY. Simply return the enclosed Invitation. We'll rush your free trial issue to you. If you find the recipes and health tips as exciting as I've described and wish to sign on for a year (six bimonthly issues in all), simply honor our invoice for the low introductory price of only $8.95.

> SAVE $4.50 Please note. Others pay $13.50 on the newsstand for those same issues. You immediately save $5 or 33%!

YOUR 100% RISK-FREE GUARANTEE. If for any reason you decide the magazine is not for you, just write "No Thanks" on the bill, return it, and that's that. Keep the free issue regardless.

But please hurry, the editor can hold onto your free issue only so long before she must offer it to someone else. Avoid disappointment. Return your Invitation today!

Cordially,

Ellen de Lathouder

Ellen de Lathouder
for COOKING LIGHT

P.S. It's fun to think about the way I used to make Strawberry Cheesecake. (Compared to the COOKING LIGHT way, it had more than twice the calories per serving, more than twice the cholesterol!) And you literally cannot taste the difference!

P.P.S. We're cooking up a special HOLIDAY ENTERTAINING ISSUE this year. If you decide to stay with us, we'll send you a free copy when it comes off the press in November -- absolutely no charge! (See enclosed flyer.)

Mailer: **Eating Well**
Key Words: **"Consider this advice . . ."**
Writer: **Eugene Povskadovsky**

The Challenge

Even though nutrition is a strong buzz-word in today's health-conscious society, so much appears in the daily press and on television newscasts that a publication covering this field has a difficult task facing it. People will say, "I'm interested, but not enough to subscribe to a magazine."

The challenge, then, is twofold—first, to show the reader immediately that information in the pages of this publication is *not parallel* to information available elsewhere; and, second, to convince the reader that the magazine is, in fact, not just readable, but entertaining.

The Implementation

The first four bullets are, to any health-conscious individual, real bullets. They strike a health target with considerable force because each of them explodes a common myth.

The text of the letter promises "an entirely new kind of food magazine," and as the letter progresses, the promise is well-fulfilled. The peripheral reference to high-quality printing serves a double purpose: It shows a seriousness of purpose and also makes this appear to be a "status" publication.

Comment

With the powerful four bullets that begin this letter, any additional text runs the risk of being anticlimactic. In fact, the sampling of stories (bottom of page 2 and most of page 3) is considerably weaker than those bullets, from the viewpoint of eyebrow-lifting revelation.

What the "sampling" does is append a breadth of coverage that adds total sanity to the editorial mixture.

Figure 3–22. ***Eating Well***

The Magazine of Food & Health

EATING WELL

Dear Reader:

Consider this advice:

- Margarine is better for you than butter.
  No....margarine might cause cancer—eat olive oil!

- You can get all the vitamins you need in a balanced diet.
  No...you need lots of antioxidant vitamins to prevent heart disease and cancer—take supplements!

- The most important thing about diet is cutting out the fat.
  No...it may be more important to eat more vegetables and eat less red meat!

- Caffeine increases the risk of heart disease.
  No...caffeine is no problem—the studies were wrong!

Remember when eating well was so simple?

It doesn't seem to be simple anymore. We hear about growth hormones in beef and milk . . . about bioengineered tomatoes . . .about pesticides on fruit and in drinking water. . . about one scientific study that says a food is good for you, and another study that says the food is bad.

And there you are: you love to cook, you love to eat, you love the pleasures of enjoying a good meal with family and friends. But what should you eat? More to the point, who should you believe?

Welcome to EATING WELL, the Magazine of Food and Health. When it comes to nutrition advice and good eating, we're on your side.

Discover an entirely new kind of food magazine, an intelligent ally in these times of unprecedented change. With EATING WELL you will:

- Have the facts. We don't rush to publish the newest scare stories, the hottest miracle prescriptions, the latest rumors and ridiculous pronouncements. EATING WELL articles are carefully researched and written so that you will finish the magazine knowing more than when you began reading it, and happy about what you know.

- Have the fun. We love food! Every issue presents a wealth of tempting new recipes. Fast recipes for quick weeknight

Smashing through reader apathy with rhetorical bullets. *(Continued)* cooking. Fabulous recipes for a special weekend dinner. Healthy recipes, in which we replace the fat with more nutritious ingredients—and provide the nutrition analysis so you know what you're eating. Delicious recipes, from snacks and first courses to entrées, side dishes and desserts -- breakfast, lunch and dinner. Tested recipes—which have been tested and retested by our own Test Kitchen.

You'll discover the techniques of cooking with less fat, and in the process turn out juicy, full-flavored meat, poultry, fish and vegetable dishes. And you won't believe the desserts -- rich-tasting and tempting, without all the cream and butter.

You'll also learn how to shop smarter, ask the right questions of your doctor or dietitian, read food labels and plan meals for maximum dietary balance.

INTRODUCTORY ISSUE. If you care about the quality of the food you eat, if someone in your family needs to eat better but doesn't want to sacrifice the pleasures of good eating, we think you won't want to miss an opportunity to sample the current issue of EATING WELL.

> SEND THE ENCLOSED INVITATION FORM TODAY TO RECEIVE THE CURRENT ISSUE WE HAVE RESERVED IN YOUR NAME.
>
> I would like to invite you to be one of the first to preview EATING WELL. Please send no money now. If you continue your subscription, you will receive significant savings on future subscription orders and other special benefits of an Introductory Subscriber.

You will also be getting a food magazine quite unlike any other. Intelligent. Outspoken. A feast of beautiful photography and art. Full of common sense, new ideas and new recipes. EATING WELL recognizes that you don't have to subsist on brown rice and carrot juice to enjoy good health and longevity.

With a rare blend of clear writing, world-class photojournalism, fresh approaches to food and health, EATING WELL's outstanding team of editors and contributors will make each issue a very special reading event.

Here's a sampling of the stories you'll find:

• The New Taste of Tradition. Meet four great cooks who are committed to preserving the foods they love from their European heritage, but who are also committed to making those foods more healthy. Profiles, interviews and superb

(Continued)

recipes for dishes such as Chicken Paprikas, Cabbage Rolls, and Polenta with Mushroom Sauce.

● We Go On A Diet. It's easy for magazine editors to talk about healthy eating, but what happens when our own staff nutritionist analyzes our diet and monitors our progress? The result is a lot of handy, usable information for you about eating well in all the meanings of that phrase.

● On the Road with a Food Inspector. The scene: a factory-bakery in New York City. The crime: no one's paying attention to basic sanitation rules. The penalty ...a report and a routine warning. Are your interests as a consumer being protected by current food-safety laws?

● In Search of the Healthy English Chef. The food of England is notorious for being unhealthy and downright bad. But when we sent an intrepid writer in search of health-conscious chefs, he turned up lots of great, low-fat, local, fresh food and wrote a report you'll enjoy about the pleasures of traveling and eating in The Realm.

● Nutrition and Aging. Only now is nutrition science turning its attention to the critical subject of the role that diet plays in accelerating or slowing the aging process. Here's useful advice from the leading edge of research.

● The Low-Fat Radicals. Just when Americans were hearing messages about cutting some of the fat from their diets, along come heart-disease prophets who say we need to cut nearly all fat from our diets. Who should listen to that message? What does the ultra-low fat approach do to the enjoyment of food and of life?

● A Wide and Delightful Range of Food Stories. Simple quick breads... wonderful pastas...creamy low-fat cheesecakes...low-fat, fudgy applesauce brownies... spectacular, easy pizzas... summer salads and warm winter stews... low-fat, juicy burgers for the grill... American food, French Food, Italian Food, Asian Food: it's all in EATING WELL, it's all delicious and it's all healthy!

Judge EATING WELL for yourself. Just return the enclosed Subscription Invitation card, and we will be pleased to send the exciting Current Issue to your home.

SUBSCRIBER BENEFITS

As an Introductory Subscriber to EATING WELL, you automatically become entitled to special benefits:

LOW PRICE NOW. You can take advantage of the lowest

(Continued)

rate EATING WELL offers. Others pay a full $18.00 per year, or $3.00 per copy.

LOW PRICE LATER. As an Introductory Subscriber, you will be eligible for special low rates on gifts you may wish to purchase for friends, relatives or professional associates and on EATING WELL cookbooks.

NO-RISK GUARANTEE. Your satisfaction is always guaranteed by our full-refund policy. If you ever decide to cancel your subscription, we will send a prompt and courteous refund for all unmailed issues.

VALUABLE EDITION. EATING WELL is sure to become an important part of your permanent home library. With fine papers, expensive book-like binding and the highest standards of color printing, this is the magazine you will want to keep for years of future reference.

Send No Money Now. Simply return the enclosed Subscription Invitation in the postpaid envelope provided.

Early Postmark Needed. The number of Current Issues available is strictly limited. If we don't hear from you, we will have to reassign your reserved copy to someone else. If you love great food and value your health and vitality, we think you'll find EATING WELL must reading.

Thank you -- we look forward to having you with us for what promises to be one of the most talked-about magazines of the year.

Sincerely,

Judy Bunten

Judy Bunten
for EATING WELL

P.S. Please send the card today -- see EATING WELL for yourself. The enclosed card is all we need to secure your Current Issue and your special Introductory Subscription rate.

Ferry Road, Charlotte, Vermont 05445-9968

Mailer: **America's Civil War**

Key Words: **"You are there . . ."**

Writer: **Sheldon Seymour**

The Challenge

After 130 years, what new information could possibly surface about the Civil War? And, assuming such information did appear, who would be interested other than historians?

This publication, dedicated entirely to stories of the Civil War, deals in human interest more than in dry historical data. The challenge is to have the prospective subscribers recognize the editorial thrust and respond positively to it.

The Implementation

The writer uses "You are there!" more effectively to transport the reader back to the war years of the 1860s.

Each example plays on a well-known theme or name, so the reader does not feel the publication will be shoveling abstruse details leaving the reader with a yawn.

The text of the letter tackles head-on the typical skepticism aimed at "news after almost 130 years?" By telling the reader this publication is not for everyone before the reader has an opportunity to say, "This publication is not for me," the writer moves the reader into an elite group, which certainly enhances the possibility of subscription.

Comment

The three-word first paragraph and one-line second paragraph are as reader-involving as any opening of a subscription letter could be. The postscript is startling enough to bring those who jumped to the end without reading the letter back into the text.

Note the snob appeal of the final paragraph on page 3 and the first three paragraphs on page 4.

Figure 3–23. ***America's Civil War***

AMERICA'S CIVIL WAR

You are there!

Dear Reader,

You are there!

You're there when Admiral Farragut shouts, "Damn the torpedoes!"

You're there when the residents of Gettysburg cower in the corners of their homes, fearfully waiting to discover whether they'll be citizens of the Union or the Confederacy.

You're there to see many observers misrepresent the outcome of the battle between the USS Monitor and the Merrimack.

Ah, you're there at the very shoulder of a tough Union sergeant about to repel Robert E. Lee's last offensive north of the James River at Darbytown, Virginia. You're so close you can see the insignia on the bridle of his horse.

And you're there to see a Union raider you never heard of before, a former Illinois music teacher named Benjamin Grierson, literally dismantle 50 crucial miles of railroad and telegraph lines in Mississippi.

Where are you? In the exciting, exhilarating, colorful pages of a classic magazine unlike any other: AMERICA'S CIVIL WAR.

Should YOU Have This Extraordinary Magazine?
Read On for a Special Private Offer

It's no coincidence that I'm writing, specifically, to you. You have reason for pride, because the source from which your name came to us indicates you're both educated and thoughtful.

We cheerfully admit, AMERICA'S CIVIL WAR isn't for everyone. But it is for you, and I intend to prove that point at no risk to you whatever.

Please consider this proposition:

Six times a year AMERICA'S CIVIL WAR brings you page after page of absolutely fascinating (and absolutely factual) knowledge of the

(over, please)

Overcoming reader skepticism by making history come alive. *(Continued)*

Civil War.

I'm writing to invite you to subscribe to our much-acclaimed magazine. But I certainly don't expect you to make a commitment, even at your very low subscription rate of just $14.95 for a whole year — six big, beautiful issues — until you've sampled AMERICA'S CIVIL WAR for yourself.

Should you subscribe to AMERICA'S CIVIL WAR? I think so. But you're the one who has to be satisfied, and so I want you to examine a sample free issue before you make any commitment to subscribe.

I'm serious. No amount of description in a letter can give you the actual flavor of stepping back in time, with elegant full-color illustrations and rare photographs, to re-live those dangerous and history-making times.

NEWS After almost 130 Years? Oh, Yes...
Written Brightly and with Faithful Attention to Detail

Commentators of the time often built folklore that historians have had to unravel. The Civil War has provided tens of thousands of scholars with tens of thousands of subjects for dissection.

But only AMERICA'S CIVIL WAR gives you the true stories of the War Between the States written by accomplished historian-storytellers, so readable every article is a delight.

Our Editorial Review Board includes such distinguished names as Richard Beringer, Gerald Linderman, James Hoobler, and Joseph Suppiger. Brilliant Contributing Editors such as Albert Hemingway and Robert Collins Suhr combine vast knowledge with superb writing skills. Altogether, AMERICA'S CIVIL WAR is the blend of scholarship and easy reading you'll seldom find these days.

Beyond that, AMERICA'S CIVIL WAR is a magazine you should be getting. On a coffee table or a nightstand, it's a symbol of your own intellectual achievement as well as the regard for our nation's history every thinking American should have.

An Exciting Visual Experience Awaits You

Writing aside, every issue of AMERICA'S CIVIL WAR is an astounding archive of photographs and photorealistic paintings which makes it more than a collector's item ... it's a genuine pictorial history. Much of the art is by such renowned contemporary historical artists as Don Troiani and Tom Freeman and Keith Rocco and Rick Reeves.

-2-

(Continued)

One reason I want you to sample AMERICA'S CIVIL WAR is because of the beauty of reproduction. We're very proud of the quality of paper and perfection of color in our pages. In my many, many discussions with subscribers, I have yet to meet a single one who discards the magazine after reading. On the contrary, our back issues are themselves historical treasures.

Here is a magazine you'll be proud to show ... a magazine to enrich your life and your knowledge ... a magazine dedicated to the great tradition of excellence you and I both know is all too rare these days.

Here Is My Proposition for You:

I want to send you the current issue of AMERICA'S CIVIL WAR.

And all you have to do is say yes.

As I told you, we publish AMERICA'S CIVIL WAR six times a year. I have a copy of our latest issue, just published, waiting for you to claim it.

All you have to do is drop your Invitation Acceptance card in the mail. You don't even need a stamp.

Only after you've had the opportunity to sample the magazine that's unlike any other you've ever seen, if you think AMERICA'S CIVIL WAR is for you, then your annual subscription — five additional issues — is just **$14.95**. If you decide you don't want to subscribe to AMERICA'S CIVIL WAR, just write "cancel" on the invoice and return it, and that will be the end of the matter.

No matter what you decide, the complimentary issue is yours to keep.

My point: AMERICA'S CIVIL WAR isn't one of those mass-circulation publications you see everywhere. We ourselves know that our subscribers are among the intellectually elite, the most historically aware, the "Rolls-Royce" of subscription lists.

So I'm sure you understand that this invitation is a limited one. And we really do want you to take advantage of it.

An Episode that Makes Me Proud...

A few weeks ago I went to a dinner party at the home of a couple I didn't know well. Nor did they know of my affiliation with AMERICA'S CIVIL WAR.

(over please)

-3-

(Continued)

There, smiling up at me from the coffee table, were two recent issues of the magazine. I asked my hostess, "How do you happen to have this magazine on the table?"

Her answer thrilled me: "We've been subscribers for nearly five years, and I must tell you, this magazine has really made a difference in our lives. It's hooked us on American history. We read every issue from cover to cover. If you can imagine a magazine that's both informative and entertaining ... would you like to borrow one of these? I'll loan it to you if you'll promise to bring it back."

I can't tell you how much that statement meant to me, because it reinforced my own belief that AMERICA'S CIVIL WAR has a purpose far beyond that of the typical read-and-throw-away magazine: to be both informative and entertaining, "hooking" people on American history. (Incidentally, when my hostess discovered what my job is, I was an instant celebrity. She insisted that I sit at her right during dinner.)

Look, my friend: Nothing I tell you about AMERICA'S CIVIL WAR can possibly be as significant as what you tell you. In order to make a decision, you should have the opportunity to leaf through a copy.

And that's my invitation to you. Let me send you, at no risk whatever, the latest issue. Look it over. If I'm wrong, if AMERICA'S CIVIL WAR isn't your type of publication, no harm done. You haven't spent a dime to find out.

But if I'm right, you're in for a whole year of marvelous reading, a year of that magical blend of information and entertainment, six solid issues at a very, very low subscription price.

Take me up on my offer. You won't regret it. Thanks.

For AMERICA'S CIVIL WAR,

Roy Morris

Roy Morris, Jr., Editor

P.S. Did you know that thirty Yankees were generals in the Confederate Army? This is just one of the hundreds of fascinating facts you'll find in the pages of AMERICA'S CIVIL WAR.

-4-

Chapter 4

Collectibles

Collectibles are, really, a *non-product* because their value is not implicit, but is, rather, superimposed by an appeal which leans equally on two potent motivators—exclusivity and greed.

The success of a letter selling collectibles, then, has to convince the reader: Only you . . . only from us.

As the world of produced collectibles sophisticates itself, appeals to that world similarly must "sophisticate" themselves to have any effect in a marketplace whose competitors depend on similar claims.

Astute marketers in these sometimes troubled and always competitive waters have learned some rules of their private game. One is that a yes/no option increases response, albeit not always with a more favorable number on the bottom line. Another is that a "merchandise return" label enclosed with the original mailing (not with the merchandise, please—that's suicide) improves response. A third applies to an offer made to carefully selected lists in which the company's rejection rate—that is, refusal to send merchandise based on an individual's questionable buying-history—is low: The offer can be condensed into a double or triple postcard if no advance payment is required.

In fact, the amount of romance necessary to generate a response is tied in large part to the amount of apparent risk and to the degree of apparent bargain the buyer can expect.

So a continuity program, with each unit demanding advance payment, might be best-served by a six- or eight-page letter; a "customer loader" mailed to previous buyers as a ostensible private offer and offering inspection before payment is worth a less-expensive test.

Mailer: **Heritage House**

Key Words: **"I've reserved 'Yesterday,' just for you"**

The Challenge

Recognizing that the highest degree of response comes from prior buyers, a collectibles marketer also has to recognize a paradox: The buyer who has responded to a specific type of appeal obviously feels comfortable with that appeal, which indicates the logic of a parallel kind of letter.

Conversely, parallel letters run the risk of appearing to be the same offer, repeated. So the mailer walks a tightrope—maintaining reader-comfort level by not changing the appearance of an appeal, and maintaining reader-interest level by indicating a difference between this offer and what has been offered before.

The Implementation

One of the most innovative companies in the volatile world of collectibles is Heritage House of Nashville, Tennessee. We have included three representative letters which market three different sets of music boxes. Each of these was able to win within the "house list"—collectors who already had bought other music boxes from this producer—is an indication of the breadth of appeal possible within a narrow range of product offers.

The letter which begins "I'm truly delighted to tell you" outpulled a traditional winner, a triple postcard. The letter which begins "Three valuable free gifts" won in a competition with other letters of similar length. The letter which begins "A special memo" uses the magical word, "Charter," plus a "Yes/No" option—both tested and invariable response-increasers. This six-page letter well outpulled a similar letter in four-page length.

(Do longer letters outpull shorter letters? In continuity programs, which are a series of items, *usually;* the very word *usually* says to the professional letter writer: **test.**)

Comment 4–1

Quite properly, this letter leans heavily on *exclusivity* as its principle motivator. The first line: "I've reserved 'Yesterday,' just for you." The fifth paragraph begins: "This invitation is for you. None will be made available to stores . . . ever."

The indented paragraph at the bottom of the first page maintains the pace by offering matched registration numbers on Certificates of Authenticity.

To solidify response, early on the letter promises "valuable gifts."

Comment 4–2

This letter positions itself differently from 4–1 by immediately emphasizing the free gifts. The entire first page and part of the second page are devoted to the gifts, whose importance to both mailer and customer supersedes the importance of the item being sold. Where 4–1 was sent entirely to the "house list," the company mailed this letter to both existing buyers and to names from cold lists which had indicated a buying preference for collectibles.

This letter has no subheads, depending instead on indented paragraphs for reader-comfort.

Comment 4–3

Unlike 4–1 and 4–2, this mailing was sent entirely to non-buyers. In order for a letter of this type, which does parallel 4–2 in its emphasis of free gifts to be commercially successful, list choice has to be exquisitely careful. Mailing an offer to the public at large when the offer says, "Don't send any money now. We'll get your free gifts off to you together with 'Love Me Tender,' " unquestionably would result in a huge percentage of individuals who took the free gifts and bought nothing.

To the would-be collector or the collectible-vulnerable individual who has not yet dipped a toe into these waters, an offer of this type has to be worthy of consideration.

And it was.

Figure 4–1. Heritage House

LEJ

I've reserved "Yesterday" just for you!
Tell me yes or no right away.

No matter how many treasures you may have in your collection, I suggest you read this private invitation.

A Special Memo to a Very Special Friend!

I invite you to become a Charter Subscriber to our privately issued series of porcelain music boxes: Heritage House Classic Love Songs.

What makes this Collection extraordinary is the way it came to be. Each music box, beginning with "Yesterday," the most famous and most popular music box we ever have made available to our collectors, has been chosen as "one of the very best" --- by the collectors themselves, perhaps including you.

As you know, Heritage House is the number one source of collectible music boxes. Heritage House Classics is our Collection of the most wanted music boxes we have ever published ... in a deluxe edition lavishly adorned with pure 24-karat gold.

You have the short-term opportunity to become a Charter Subscriber. This means you can enjoy the very low charter issue direct price of just five $8.95 payments for the sublimely beautiful first edition music box, "Yesterday."

This invitation is for you. None will be made available to stores ... ever. No one except friends of Heritage House will ever be able to acquire "Yesterday" for this price --- not even galleries or museums. And that is true, too, of all other music boxes in this deluxe Collection ... the best of the very best.

The absolute "edition limit" is 9800. You know collectible art, and you know how likely it is that this very limited edition will be insufficient to equal demand.

To certify both rarity and the absolute edition limit, "Yesterday" and each subsequent music box will come to you with its individual, numbered Certificate of Authenticity. And please read this next sentence carefully:

> The number inscribed on your Certificate is yours, throughout the series. If you decide to acquire additional music boxes in the

2451 Atrium Way, Nashville, Tennessee 37210 • (615) 391-2899
A division of The Southwestern Company, publishers since 1868

"Only you" plus product glamorizing adds up to a winner. *(Continued)*

Classic Collection, each Certificate will have the identical number.

Heritage House has made it possible for you to own that number. No one else can have it, as long as you continue to collect the Classics. Think of what this may mean in years to come, if you bequeath this unique Collection. A loved one will have a perfectly matched set, verified by hand-numbered Certificates.

Valuable Gifts for You

Heritage House recognizes the historical value of each Certificate, and for this reason we have a thoughtful gift for you:

We'll send you, at no extra charge whatsoever, a handsome portfolio custom-designed to hold and display your Certificates of Authenticity. Your portfolio will have separate compartments --- a separate one for each Certificate in the series.

We have a gorgeous second gift for you: a genuine brass decorator display case will be sent at no additional charge shortly after you receive your third music box. It protects your music boxes under glass; and the shelves themselves are glass, perfect for displaying your entire Heritage House Classics Music Box Collection.

We also have a mystery gift for you. What is it? I'll never tell. I <u>can</u> assure you, this wonderful gift won't disappoint you.

Your Collection is worthy of the attention fine works of art deserve. And these gifts are the perfect complement to the music boxes themselves. The portfolio attests forever to the authenticity of your music boxes, within the strict edition limit; the display rack enables you to exhibit your Collection as a major gallery might show them.

First Edition of a Major Series

"Yesterday" begins a magnificent series of music box melodies, the "cream" of melodies most favored by our own collectors.

Others in this superb series are ...

> "Romeo and Juliet" ... "Some Enchanted Evening" ... "Love Story" ... "Love Is a Many-Splendored Thing" ... "Lara's Theme" (from "Dr. Zhivago") ... "Misty" ... "Try to Remember" ... "April Love" ... "Greensleeves" ... "As Time Goes By" ... "The Way We Were" ... "Smoke Gets In Your Eyes" ... "Feelings."

Can you imagine a more splendid collection of love songs?

(Continued)

Can you begin to imagine the pleasure you surely will enjoy from your Collection, year after year?

A very important point to consider: I'm sure you recognize the difference between a "thin" movement and a full 18-note movement. Each music box of this Collection has a full 18-note movement, flawlessly miniaturized to fit within the box.

Now you can see why this carefully chosen series is so aptly named: "Heritage House Classics." Imagine a marvelous evening --- a truly enchanted evening --- playing one after another of these immortal melodies. What a gracious and unusual way to entertain guests! What a tribute to your own good taste!

Collecting "Yesterday" assures you of an absolute priority position. You positively will have first opportunity to collect the forthcoming porcelain music boxes of the Heritage House Classics, as they are issued. Of course you're under no obligation to accept future issues, but they positively are yours if you want them.

A Triumph of the Porcelain Maker's Art

The lavish use of 24-karat gold makes "Yesterday" different from any previous Heritage House porcelain music boxes. Never before have we had so much pure gold ornamentation on a music box. Just as a fine leather-bound book uses gold ornamentation as its ultimate suggestion of opulence, so does "Yesterday" introduce a new level of splendor to music boxes by extravagant use of gold.

A gold border accents the colorful but delicate work of art by a distinguished American artist ... a quiet expression of love. (On the underside of the cover is a Heritage House emblem conceived expressly for this elegant series of music boxes, plus the title of the melody.) And more gold! A decorative gold pattern adds artistry to the sides of the box.

The backstamp is itself a work of art. In addition to the title of the series and the title of the song, the backstamp restates the absolute edition limit of 9800 and includes a musical motif "signature" unique to this series.

Every element --- the original art, the gold ornamentation, the title inside the cover, and the backstamp --- all are permanently fired into the porcelain. Your Heritage House Classics Collection should bring pleasure to the eye and the ear for many lifetimes.

Another touch of luxury: each music box is lined with rich burgundy velveteen.

Individual Works of Art

Each music box of the series is a distinctive work of art.

Forms differ. "Yesterday" is a round music box. Another

(Continued)

might be heart-shaped, or square, or oval-shaped. Each one unmistakably belongs to this Collection, but each one has its own special personality.

Too, the graceful gold ornamentation differs from music box to music box. Five distinctly different lacy designs complement the art and shape of the music box they embellish.

So what you will own is a masterful Collection of music boxes, the very best ... the most romantic ... the most celebrated songs in porcelain touched with gold-ornamented richness.

And "Yesterday" is the first! You can own it forever, for five payments of just $8.95 each. You don't pay any extra for shipping or insurance.

"Yesterday" stands alone as a work of art and music. But if you do decide to continue your Classics Collection, each forthcoming Certificate of Authenticity will have your own identical registration number (which will be entered in our permanent archive).

ONE SOLID YEAR Buyback Guarantee!

As an experienced collector, you probably can envision the sheer joy that comes from a great melody of love, cascading from a gorgeous music box. But I know you haven't yet had the opportunity to see and hear this uncommon music box. It's an opportunity you should have, before making any final decision.

Heritage House would never want you to keep an heirloom-quality work of collectible art unless you sincerely want to keep it forever. So here is our personal assurance to you:

> At any time within ONE FULL YEAR after "Yesterday" or any porcelain music box in the Classics series is in your hands, Heritage House will buy it back from you for 100% of the price you paid for it.

This means you have a whole year to display "Yesterday," to show it to friends, to listen to the gentle melody, before deciding whether you want to keep it or sell it back to us. I can't imagine what greater proof we might offer that we do want you to examine this treasure in your own home, at no risk whatever.

The Most Famous Love Song of Our Time

"Yesterday" stands at the very pinnacle of contemporary songs of love.

Certainly "Yesterday" is the most successful song John Lennon and Paul McCartney ever wrote. First played in 1965, it sold a miraculous one million copies in a single week. Within two years

(Continued)

446 different versions of "Yesterday" had been recorded, including interpretations by such diverse artists as Pat Boone, Johnny Mathis, the Big Ben Banjo Band, and the Band of Irish Guards.

The popularity of "Yesterday" is undimmed. Invariably, when an orchestra begins to play the first few bars, those present applaud.

As you'll hear when "Yesterday" reaches you, the match between the uncomplicated, sweetly memorable measures and the clear, ringing notes of your porcelain music box is strikingly unmistakable. "Yesterday" <u>is</u> a music box melody.

<u>Specially Chosen: The Classic Love Songs</u>

After "Yesterday," all your timeless favorites are here in this fabulous Collection. For example, you'll hear the familiar notes of "Some Enchanted Evening" (the song Ezio Pinza made famous) from Rogers and Hammerstein's "South Pacific."

Remember the song that won the Academy Award in 1955? It's "Love Is a Many-Splendored Thing," from the movie with William Holden and Jennifer Jones. You'll have it forever.

And when a guest says, "Play Misty for Me," that guest will hear "Misty" in its most charming form, played by a genuine 18-note imported music box movement.

You'll never tire of hearing two hauntingly beautiful melodies --- "Try to Remember" and "Greensleeves." These songs transcend time. Their serene loveliness will be as fresh a hundred years from now as they are today.

"Try to Remember" is relatively modern. It was first performed in "The Fantasticks" in 1965. "Greensleeves," on the other hand, has been played and sung for more than 400 years. In fact, Shakespeare refers to the already-traditional song in his play "The Merry Wives of Windsor."

Watch guests join in when your music box plays the first notes of "As Time Goes By." Remember who played the song in the movie "Casablanca"? Right: Dooley Wilson. It hardly seems more than 46 years since we first saw Bergman and Bogart in this film; time does go by. But not for you, because you'll have this melody forever.

<u>Don't Miss Out</u>

In all the world, only 9800 perceptive individuals will ever own "Yesterday" and the following porcelain music boxes in this limited deluxe Collection. Can you imagine the significance, in years to come, of being inside this elite group?

I have to clarify:

(Continued)

Only Charter Subscribers will have the opportunity to acquire all the other music boxes of the Heritage House Classics series. The first edition music box opens the door to a Collection far, far beyond any Heritage House ever has been able to offer before.

"Yesterday" is yours at a price so low you may think Heritage House has made a mistake: five payments of $8.95. That's all. We even pay the postage.

You have a preferred position with us, but the very low edition limit makes it necessary for me to ask you to let us know within the next 10 days if you want to take advantage of this opportunity (including your free gifts).

You don't have to send any payment now. Let your eyes and ears feast on "Yesterday." Only then, if you're truly delighted, need you send your first payment. And at any time up to one full year after "Yesterday" is in your hands, Heritage House will buy it back from you for 100% of the price you paid for it.

I'll look for your Reservation Card on my desk. It's a privilege to extend this invitation to you.

Sincerely,

Thomas Milam

Thomas Milam
President

TM:lw

P.S. Don't forget, I've personally reserved "Yesterday" for you. Please let me know either way, so if you don't want it we can release your music box to another collector. I know you don't want to miss out on your low limited edition number, so I suggest you mail your Reservation Card today or call us at 1-800-251-1520, during regular business hours, and get ready for enjoyment.

Figure 4–2. Heritage House

MELLA

Three valuable <u>free</u> gifts -- two of them MYSTERY GIFTS -- have been reserved in your name. To claim them, all you have to do is return the shipping label already addressed to you. At the same time, you'll receive -- for your review and approval -- "Love Me Tender," Heritage House's special issue in the new <u>Melodies</u> series of collector-edition, fine quality, porcelain music boxes.

You will have the opportunity -- but no obligation -- to buy this splendid music box. Whether or not you decide to buy, however, the 3 <u>free</u> gifts are yours to keep, with no strings attached.

Because this is a private offer, it can't be held open indefinitely. Please tell me "yes" or "no" right away. To avoid disappointment, send back your shipping label today!

Dear Collector:

I would like to send you 3 <u>free</u> gifts, yours to keep no matter what. Before you start thinking that there must be some catch to this, some hidden gimmick, let me tell you more about the gifts and why I want you to have them:

<u>Gift #1:</u> Your first gift is a stylish watch. It has a genuine black leather strap and an eye-catching, diamond-like stone in the dial. Keep it for yourself or give it to a friend. It's yours free.

<u>Gift #2:</u> Your mystery gift. What is it? <u>I'll</u> never tell, but I promise you this -- you'll be surprised and positively delighted with it. It is yours <u>free</u>.

<u>Gift #3:</u> And if you reply within 7 days you'll receive a <u>third "Bonus" gift</u>.

These valuable gifts are your reward from Heritage House for agreeing to take a look at a special offering. Just what does this involve?

(over, please)

11 Commerce Blvd., Palm Coast, FL 32142
A division of The Southwestern Company, publishers since 1868

A "can't miss" appeal to cold-list names.

(Continued)

It doesn't involve sending money. Not now. Not ever, unless you decide to buy. All you need to do is return the shipping label which already has your name and address on it.

We'll send both your free gifts (or all 3, if you reply in 7 days) and -- along with them -- "Love Me Tender," a special issue in the Melodies Music Box Series.

> You can't lose! You know you'll keep your designer watch and mystery gifts because they're free! And you can keep the collector-edition music box, "Love Me Tender," if you want it -- after having the chance to inspect it and listen to it.
>
> So when your music box arrives, pay special attention to "Love Me Tender." Examine it carefully. Wind it up and play it. Listen to the clear, haunting notes of this romantic melody. Admire the artistry and craftsmanship, the fineness of detail, the weight and substance. Read over the Certificate of Authenticity.
>
> Take one full month to make up your mind. If you decide you don't want to own it, no problem. Just repack it, send it back to us with the unpaid bill, and that will be the end of it. No cost to you, no obligation -- we will even pay the return postage. The free gifts are yours to keep forever as our way of saying thanks for taking a look.

Why do we go to all this trouble? Why bother sending you the music box before you decide to buy?

The answer, frankly, is that more people buy music boxes when they have a chance to see, touch and listen to them. The photograph I've enclosed -- lovely as it is -- just can't do it justice. For one thing, you can't listen to a photograph!

A photograph doesn't let you touch the music box or see how the key-wind mechanism works. Simply, it's impossible for anyone to get a feel for the sheer quality of this treasure without actually experiencing the real thing.

> Only then will you be able to see for yourself how marvelous a work of art "Love Me Tender" is. It has a precious-gem essence, with all the exquisitely polished brilliance of a Fabergé egg.

It is carefully cast out of a porcelain composed mostly of kaolin, the purest natural form of clay and the one that most closely approaches the ideal chemical formula. It is then kiln-fired at close to 2400°F for several hours to produce a classic porcelain of great strength and beauty -- porcelain that will endure for centuries.

(Continued)

Actually, nobody knows how long porcelain will last. It has been used for the very finest art pottery since the time of the Sung Dynasty in China, where it originated before the year 1000 AD. Pieces survive from that era in beautiful condition. Interestingly, the methods involved in creating porcelain ware have hardly changed at all since then.

So the music boxes of the Melodies Collection are heirs to a rich, centuries-old tradition. These music boxes are made for the ages, as heirloom-quality pieces should be.

"Love Me Tender" has been cast in an artistic heart shape. Each color is separately applied to the enchanting decoration which is then fired permanently into the porcelain. The art evokes perfectly the true spirit of love.

The art is framed in real 14-karat gold and the imported miniature key-wind movement runs like a fine watch. It contains a full 18 notes. The movement nestles beneath a layer of fine velveteen in the lid of the box. The music box is as useful as it is decorative. Mine sits on my desk table; I keep my watch and rings in it.

I could go on and on rhapsodizing about the magnificence of "Love Me Tender."

But I think you're probably beginning to get the idea - that this is truly an elegant work of art for which you'd expect to pay $75 or perhaps even more. Look through the best shops in your town, and you'll see what I mean.

As a matter of fact, you might be perfectly willing to pay a premium price for a collector's music box of this quality. But it's not necessary. Because when you accept this offer, you pay a price based on real, direct costs instead of on extravagant middle-man markups.

So the "Love Me Tender" music box is yours for -- brace yourself -- just four interest-free payments of $8.95 each. (Imagine such a low $35.80 price for a genuine porcelain music box with a superb 18-note movement!) We even pay the cost of shipping it to you. This is not a misprint. This is an all-but-unbelievable value!

"Love Me Tender" is one of those rare items that appears to be more expensive that it is. How many of those do you see these days? Isn't it almost always the opposite?

This makes "Love Me Tender" an ideal special occasion gift for someone special (if you can bear to part with it, which won't be easy) -- a gift that is so elegant, so tasteful, that it

(Continued)

compliments the giver as well as the recipient!

The beauty of this special offer is that you don't have to take my word for all this, because you have a full month after you receive it to examine the music box and decide -- and you don't pay one cent unless you want to keep "Love Me Tender."

> And my offer to you is even better: At any time within one full year, Heritage House will repurchase your "Love Me Tender" for every cent you paid for it, even including shipping costs. *Every cent!*
>
> So you absolutely can't lose, because regardless of whether you buy "Love Me Tender," the 2 (or 3, for quick reply) free gifts are yours to keep!

Remember, send no money now. Just return your shipping label* already made out in your name. We'll send "Love Me Tender" (plus your free gifts) right away. If your decision is "yes," you have 30 days to pay the first of four payments of $8.95 each. Otherwise, send back the music box (and your unpaid bill) and that will be the end of it. We'll pay the return postage. No cost, no further obligation to you -- and of course you keep the free gifts.

Don't you think you'd better act now, while this offer is still good? So, mail back your personal shipping label, we even pay the postage, and I'll look forward to hearing from you.

Sincerely,

Mark Douglas

Mark Douglas
Senior Art Curator

MD:mm

P.S. If you decide to keep "Love Me Tender," we'll add your name to our exclusive list of music box lovers, which will guarantee you the automatic privilege of examining future music boxes in the Melodies collection as they are issued -- under the same no-risk, no-obligation, 30-day trial agreement.

* Or if you prefer, call us toll-free at 1-800-829-5136, during regular business hours. Our customer service representatives will be happy to enter your reservation right away.

Figure 4–3. Heritage House

Heritage House INC.®
11 Commerce Blvd.
P.O. Box 420437
Palm Coast, FL 32142

This is a private invitation.

Please read about your free gifts!

Dear Special Friend,

I'm truly delighted to tell you that Heritage House has three free gifts for you.

Before going any further, let me assure you: Heritage House is a highly reputable affiliate of a company founded more than a century ago. And your name certainly was not chosen at random.

I'll explain:

You're on a very elite list of individuals we'd like to invite to become Heritage House collectors. And I certainly know the best way to do that is to give you a "taste" of the many benefits, gifts, and terrific buys you can anticipate.

So, yes: I have three free gifts for you. You don't have to send any money, now or ever, to enjoy them. Please read on.

These are your free gifts...

Your first gift is easy to describe. You've seen the famous $2,000 "Museum Watch." This isn't that $2,000 watch; but it's a gorgeous look-alike with a simulated diamond in its face. It's complete with a handsome black genuine leather strap. And it can be yours absolutely free!

Your second gift is well, if you knew Heritage House, you'd know what I mean by "Mystery Gift." I hope you love surprises as much as we do, because this gift is really a happy surprise.

And your third gift is for promptness. If we hear from you within the next seven days, we'll send you a second "Mystery Gift" as an Early Bird bonus!

Here's why we're so eager to send your free gifts:

Heritage House is famous in the joyous and wonderful world of music boxes. Our resources, in my opinion, are second to none.

That means our collectors can acquire marvelous music boxes

Building familiarity through the offer.

(Continued)

at a special direct price far, far below what these music boxes would cost in stores.

I want to show you an exciting music box, at no risk whatever. It's first-quality fine porcelain, with genuine 14K gold edging. The movement isn't one of those simple 12-note movements one finds in so many music boxes today; it's an imported 18-note movement.

Your music box is a collector edition. It's heart-shaped, decorated with a lovely floral design permanently fired into the porcelain, and upholstered in rich velour. You can keep your rings and jewelry in its compartment.

And the melody! Ahhh! It plays "Love Me Tender."

I've described the music box to give you a word-picture. Now, you tell me: What should a music box of this quality cost?

If you guess $75 to $100, you're perfectly safe. But not here!

That guess accurate as it is underscores the reason I'd like to show you "Love Me Tender" and welcome you as a Heritage House collector.

May I send "Love Me Tender" for your inspection?

"Love Me Tender" if you decide to acquire it is yours at the Heritage House direct collector's price, four payments of just $8.95 each.

You're reading right. There's no typographical error. Four payments of just $8.95 each.

Now, I said to start this letter, you don't have to send any money now, or ever. I sincerely mean that, and as you come to know Heritage House you'll appreciate the integrity behind this policy.

Here's what I propose to do:

Don't send any money. Just mail the enclosed Reservation Card. You don't even need a stamp.

I'll send "Love Me Tender" for your inspection. No, better than that: I'll send it for you to exhibit and play, for one full month. Of course I'll send your free gifts too (three free gifts if I hear from you within the next seven days).

At any time during that month, if you decide "Love Me

(Continued)

Tender" isn't for you, just send it back we'll pay the postage and you keep your free gifts. We'll still be friends.

And if you do want to own "Love Me Tender"...

All kinds of good things will happen!

First of all, you'll own this elegant porcelain music box for the direct price, four payments of only $8.95 each. The entire total is just $35.80.

Second, because "Love Me Tender" begins a fabulous series of music boxes called *The Melodies Collection*, you'll have the absolute right to obtain each additional music box in this Collection, as it's made available. Each one is yours, if you want it, at the special direct Heritage House price.

Third, you'll be on the Heritage House "Preferred" list for notice of private offers, most of which the general public never even sees.

Fourth, you'll own an exquisite music box, one created in the eternal medium of fine porcelain ... one with real 14k gold trim ... one with an imported 18-note musical movement ... one which plays a tune many feel is the most popular love song of the entire twentieth century ... and yes, one you can play and display with pride for many years to come.

Not just one month. ONE SOLID YEAR!

Now, the most spectacular news of all!

Let's suppose you accept my invitation. Let's suppose you get your three free gifts. Let's suppose once you've seen "Love Me Tender" you agree it's a tremendous bargain, so you agree to own it.

Now I'll tell you another benefit of being a Heritage House collector that almost no other source can begin to match:

At any time for one solid year after you have "Love Me Tender," Heritage House will buy it back for the full purchase price. I'm serious. We'll buy it back for the full purchase price, including shipping costs. Can you imagine even the most upscale gift shop or gallery making an offer such as this?

I'll tell you why:

By now you surely know we really do want you to join our family of collectors. That means we want you to be satisfied

(Continued)

not just today or tomorrow, but for as long as you're a Heritage House collector. If you aren't completely happy, we aren't completely happy.

Are you thinking of a gift for someone special?

"Love Me Tender" is the perfect gift. It combines good taste, extraordinary value, artistic gracefulness, and uniqueness.

Better yet, it's a gift of thoughtfulness and love. Compare "Love Me Tender" with anything else you might buy at this price. There simply is no comparison.

This is your opportunity. And of course you'll get your free gifts. For that matter, your wristwatch is a fabulous gift for someone, if you can bear to part with it.

And of course, whether "Love Me Tender" is for yourself or for someone else, you achieve that elevated status as a preferred Heritage House collector. You'll get early notice of other offers. As each music box in the Melodies Collection is made available, we'll send it to you on approval. You're never obligated to purchase, you always have one full month to decide, and Heritage House will buy back any music box in this series for its full issue price, at any time up to one year after you get it.

This may be your only opportunity.

Please don't put this letter aside, thinking you'll get to it later. Not only will you miss out on your Early Bird bonus gift, but you might miss out on this opportunity altogether. I doubt very much that we'll ever send you an invitation such as this again.

So right now, while the information is in your hands, mail your Reservation Card. Don't send any money now. We'll get your free gifts off to you, together with "Love Me Tender." You owe it to yourself to own this treasure!

Thanks for considering this invitation. And welcome to Heritage House!

Mark Douglas

Senior Curator

P.S. If you prefer, call our private toll-free number **1-800-829-5136.** That way you're sure to get all three free gifts.

MELLD

Mailer: Calhoun's Collectors Society
Key Words: "Cinnabar"
Writer: Herschell Gordon Lewis

The Challenge

When a company offers a new—and to many of its customers, obscure—collectibles medium, the three mandatory components of a letter are enthusiasm, stature, and exclusivity (exclusivity being the underlying motivator for most collectibles offers).

Transmitting enthusiasm is not a difficult creative task. Overcoming buyer unfamiliarity with a medium is a true challenge, because prospective buyers will not respond to an offer for a product they do not understand.

The Implementation

Beginning with a "touchstone"—a newsletter validating prior collector's plates issued by this company—the letter moves into a glorification of Chinese Cinnabar.

Cinnabar is a word most people recognize without knowing exactly what it is, so the letter also had an education job to do.

To hold the reader in a tight, word-heavy four-page letter, hand-written marginal notes keep the excitement level high.

Comment

We include this letter from one of the book's co-authors because it was the most successful collectibles letter he ever wrote.

Calhoun's Collectors Society has been gone for some years; but in the golden days of collectibles the company produced and sold many successful collector's plate series. One of these, in Cinnabar, was *The Five Perceptions of Weo Cho* (actually, the five senses).

To market this series of five plates the writer created a "lift" letter that still is quoted as the proper execution of a lift letter—to add an irresistible and apparently irrefutable dimension to the sales argument.

A caution to writers whose imagination overpowers their business judgment: The Museum of Oriental Antiquities did exist, and Ling Fu did exist. If they had not, the writer would have found another avenue to reinforce the basic message.

Figure 4–4. ***Calhoun Collector's Society***

Dear Member:

As I write this, I have at my elbow what I believe is the most authoritative commentary in plate collecting -- "The Limited Edition Plate Newsletter."

I'd like to quote you just one paragraph from that Newsletter:

> "Royal Cornwall's 1977 Bethlehem Christmas plate has been a sleeper. Best estimate of trading average puts this issue at $75. The complicated 'Creation' series has seen two issues pass into secondary trading. Plates I and II are moving at $80 each."

("Plate Price Trends" quotes the 1977 Bethlehem Christmas Plate at $85, Plate II of "The Creation" at $100!)

Why am I quoting these numbers to you?

Because our members were offered the Bethlehem plate at $24.50 and each plate in the "Creation" series at $29.50.

For the next 21 days I am keeping available for you what I believe is the most unusual, most elegant, most exciting collector's plate ever issued!

> "The Five Perceptions of Weo Cho", in Chinese Cinnabar.

Let me tell you why I hope you'll read this letter and accompanying materials carefully: as an experienced collector, you may think you've "seen it all". I know I did -- until I saw the very first collector's plate ever issued in Cinnabar.

Until I saw it, I had only a vague idea of what Cinnabar actually is. I knew it came only from the Orient, and I knew that the rich red color has been known to art collectors for centuries. What I didn't know was how difficult it is to produce a work of art with the carved Cinnabar look.

> I found out just how painstaking each step in the making of a Cinnabar plate is when I began to negotiate to obtain an allotment of this, the first limited edition plate, for our members.
>
> Many times I was ready to give up. The enormous increase of interest in Oriental art has made the small studio in which these Cinnabar plates are finished so independent that they aren't anxious to do

Calhoun Center • Minneapolis, Minnesota 55435

Building familiarity through imagination. *(Continued)*

business. The fluctuating value of the U.S. dollar made it necessary for us to post huge guarantees.

But I felt that these were plates our members should have. Now, with a guaranteed allotment for our members, I know it was worth the time and the expense.

As a member, you positively are guaranteed not just the first plate of the series "The Five Perceptions of Weo Cho" but each of the other four plates as they are issued at three-month intervals. And note this benefit of your membership in Calhoun's:

> The established issue price of Plate I, "The Sense of Touch", is $55. As a Calhoun's member you can have it for $49.50. And I personally guarantee that no matter what happens to the U.S. dollar in international trading circles, you'll be able to acquire all five plates of this extraordinary series at $49.50. Non-members pay 11% more.

If you'll take a look at the accompanying brochure we've received, I think you'll agree that this plate is an astounding buy, even at the issue price of $55. Especially in view of the official price survey published by "The Limited Edition Plate Newsletter" (I've enclosed a reprint for your interest) which reports that the secondary market value of "The Sense of Touch" has already reached the $80 level.

However, this exceptional trading interest among collector-investors is hardly surprising when you consider the extraordinary beauty of the plate. The molded sculpture is deep and ornate. The backstamp is actually hand-turned brass, with the registration number (recorded in The Museum of Oriental Antiquities) inscribed by hand. Each plate requires nine days to produce. The many layers of Chinese lacquer, the very opulence of the plate, the exotic and mysterious art, even the upholstered box, all make the Cinnabar plate a major event in the history of collectibles.

Actually below issue price for Calhoun's member only

And you, as a Calhoun's member, have first refusal rights, even though you can acquire it actually below issue price! (I imagine that it's because of our size and reputation that Calhoun's has been able to get the largest United States allotment of these plates.)

But I must have your decision within 21 days. I'm not guessing -- I know there are non-members who want these plates. Our Board of Directors has instructed that we open our membership rolls, once our members have been given the opportunity to own "The Five Perceptions of Weo Cho".

If you delay, it could mean that you won't ever have the opportunity to own this work of Oriental art, one that already is the topic of discussion in art and collector circles alike. Word has reached some of the important publications in the collectibles field, and they have begun to run stories about the Cinnabar plate. And you know what happens to the price of a collectible when collectors get wind of a "hot" issue.

> As you know, Oriental art already is in the spotlight. The timing couldn't be better. (Timothy Francis, the Oriental art expert, has told me that his own estimate of the annual increase in the value of

(Continued)

Chinese art is not 17%, as the brochure indicates, but 18.2%)

A historic plate— and perfect timing!

As you decide whether you want to own this plate at the special member price, consider that in the entire history of collector's plates there never has been a plate made of Cinnabar. This is the first edition of a milestone issue, and its importance will be felt throughout the world of collectibles.

I know that by now you needn't be reminded that when you obtain a work of art through your membership in Calhoun's you never run the risk that when you see it you might not like it. We protect our members. You can examine "The Sense of Touch", the very important first plate of "The Five Perceptions of Weo Cho", without risk.

You need send no money now. Just return the enclosed reservation form in the postage-free envelope and we'll notify you when your plate is ready to be sent to you and only then send an invoice (or process your bank charge).

Then, after you receive your first plate, take 15 days to look at it, show it, and make your decision. At any time within that period, you may return it for a full refund, including all postage. We want our members to enjoy the works of art they acquire. These could be family heirlooms for generations to come, and you must like your acquisitions or you shouldn't keep them.

In the case of "The Sense of Touch", I'm certainly willing to take the risk that you'll like it. I'd suggest that you visit a local store and inspect the collectibles they offer. Then compare anything you might see, even if it costs a hundred dollars, with this exquisite Cinnabar plate.

FREE display stand included

When you get it, display it on the stand included in the box, and I'm sure the comments you'll get will justify my own enthusiasm about this plate.

For the moment, forget about trading and investments and the sensational marketplace in limited edition plates. Instead, think of owning a Cinnabar plate, one with its own registration number permanently inscribed into a hand-turned brass back, a plate which is the very first of its type, one from an edition severely limited to 19,500.

Not all collectors have the same tastes. But just suppose each of the 4 1/2 million plate collectors (plus the thousands of new collectors being added to that total every week), wanted to own "The Sense of Touch". There would be only one plate for every 231 collectors who already exist.

Since every plate is hand-finished, I have no idea whether, in fact, there ever will be 19,500 plates. The Chinese are famous for striving for absolute perfection, but from what I've been told they aren't too reliable when it comes to actually delivering something. Our American mass-production approach hasn't reached that part of the mysterious Orient yet.

(Continued)

This is our first experience with importing from this area of the world, and only time will tell if the studio will deliver all its promises -- and its plates. But since we have the first and biggest allocation, if your reservation is processed you will be assured of being able to obtain not only this first plate, but all five of the series, at the special member price. This is a guarantee only Calhoun's Collectors Society can make.

Because of our relationship with China, the interest in Chinese arts and crafts is growing rapidly. Soon traveling exhibitions of Chinese art will be showing in this country, just as the famous King Tut exhibit did recently. Then, the demand for Cinnabar should show increases far beyond any available supply. But now you can, in effect, be "at the head of the line" and be among the first to own this new "ancient" art.

So you really have nothing to lose by sending your reservation. It costs you nothing to protect your position, since no charges will be due until your plate is ready for shipment, in two to four weeks. Then, after you have your plate, you still are under no obligation since you may return it for a full refund at any time up to 15 days after you receive it.

I want you to have this plate. I hope you won't delay in returning your reservation card. This will be the only notification you will receive from us about the Cinnabar plate, so don't miss out. If ever there were a plate worth collecting at an unbelievably low price, this is it.

Sincerely,

Stafford Calvin

Stafford Calvin
President

Don't miss out!

SC/asb

P.S. Please remember that I can protect your position only for 21 days, so don't delay in returning your reservation. After this edition is closed there never will be another plate of "The Sense of Touch" beyond the edition limit; collectors who want it then have to get it -- if they can -- from another collector, at whatever price that original collector sets.

SC

(Continued)

Figure 4–5. The Museum of Oriental Antiquities

東方博物館

THE MUSEUM OF ORIENTAL ANTIQUITIES
TAIPEI
REPUBLIC OF CHINA

Hon. Stafford R. Calvin
Calhoun's Collectors Society
One Appletree Square
Minneapolis, Minnesota U.S.A.

Honorable Sir:

It is with extraordinary pleasure that I confirm that original cinnabar plate is authorized for export to you as confirmed work of art.

Museum instructions are firm that sculpture, which we call, "The Five Perceptions of Weo Cho," cannot again be subject of reproduction in any form. Originals will be safeguarded in our vaults with individual seals to prevent re-use.

I verify to you, sir, that each plate is exported with our agreement and knowledge and that your esteemed company will be granted proportionately large share of each of the five plates in this "series". Our agreement with your most worthy Far Eastern representative has been concluded to permit me to assure you that Calhoun's Collectors Society, Ltd., will be granted prime consideration and firt position in future works of art we may be able to export.

My government assures me that there will be no delay or registration problem. I have assigned our own associate curator to inspect each plate, after brass insert is fitted to it; his personal validation, or my own will be placed with each plate. You may remove them if you like.

We regard this as important cultural venture. Cinnabar is traditionally associated with Republic of China, and I hope you will make important the fact of genuiness.

I wish you good health and fortune, sir.

Very truly,

For the Museum of Oriental Antiquities

林富

Ling Fu
Curator

RECEIVED
SRC
C.C.S. - S.R.C.
okay for distribution

Adding an extra "lift" to the sales argument.

Mailer: **U.S. Historical Society**
Key Words: **"The most dramatic moment of World War I"**
Writer: **Sheldon Seymour**

The Challenge

Translating a well-known historical event into a new medium is not only a challenge; it can result in negative mail from those who feel an image is being defiled.

To prevent such a reaction, an offer of this type has to position itself as more than an ordinary collectibles issue. It is, rather, a tribute to the original concept on which it is based.

The Implementation

Translating the famous Iwo Jima flag-raising into stained glass may well have been an inspiration, not only because of the drama color can add, but also because of the automatic stature the medium of stained glass bestows on any motif.

The issuer, The United States Historical Society, had its own image to maintain and did so through inclusion of historical data. A company with this name can and did exploit the word "official" as well as the medium of stained glass.

Comment

The reader is led to feel that not only is stained glass a logical extension of the original photograph and subsequent sculpture, but may actually be *the* logical medium for this image.

Note the "dedication" above "Dear Member." It quite directly and successfully eliminates any skepticism that might be aimed at using stained glass for commercial exploitation of this moment in history.

Figure 4–6. United States Historical Society

VIRGINIUS DABNEY
Chairman,
Advisory Committee

ROBERT H. KLINE
Chairman,
Board of Governors

UNITED STATES HISTORICAL SOCIETY®

To anyone who fought in the Great War...
To anyone whose loved one was there...
To anyone who has pride in America...
We dedicate this extraordinary work of art.

Dear Member,

The most dramatic moment of World War II now is available to you in its most artistic form --- stained glass. I want you to be among the first to have the privilege to own and display it.

I refer to the official "Iwo Jima" Stained Glass Plate.

No event in American history so forcefully or emotionally reflects our national legacy as the raising of the flag on Iwo Jima. The spectacular photograph, by Associated Press combat photographer Joe Rosenthal, symbolized the American spirit so perfectly that this image has become the most famous battle scene in all history.

This proud moment in American history has been captured in a heroic-size sculpture at the Iwo Jima Memorial. And now at last, from the talented hands of celebrated master artist Jack Woodson, the unforgettable scene is available in a single limited edition as a dramatic stained glass art plate.

This superb official United States Historical Society issue commemorates a turning point in our history in brilliant stained glass with a lustrous pewter rim.

February 19, 1945...

Let your memories drift back in time to the savage days of the Second World War. February 1945 was the critical month. The fanatic Japanese soldiers yielded ground inch by inch, preferring to die rather than surrender. American victories were bittersweet, seldom absolute.

First and Main Streets • Richmond, Virginia 23219 • (804) 648-4736 • Telex (804) 379-2638 • FAX (804) 648-0002

Waving the flag to add force to the sales appeal. *(Continued)*

Had the tide turned at last? What our gallant troops and our anxious nation needed was a sign, a symbol, a rallying-point. With one dramatic image, it appeared.

Iwo Jima was an unlikely site for that moment. The Japanese had honeycombed the island with a thousand hidden chambers, connected by miles of secret tunnels on seven different levels. The tunnels made it impossible for the Americans to mount a frontal attack because the defenders could scuttle through the tunnels and suddenly assault from another position.

From well-defended Mount Suribachi came a deadly barrage from a new Japanese weapon --- a monstrous howitzer whose gigantic shells looked like trashcans. On explosion, the shells scattered shrapnel, inflicting lethal wounds on the attacking American troops of the Fifth Marine Division.

The Marines sustained a battering that resulted in more casualties than any other battle in Marine Corps history. Still they moved ahead, doggedly fighting for each yard of ground until they reached the pinnacle of Mount Suribachi.

There, in an act that will remain forever as a magnificent testament to patriotism, five exhausted Marines and a Navy medical corpsman summoned an extra burst of strength --- and raised the Stars and Stripes. Through a miracle of fate, the photographer froze this incredible moment ... and immortalized it.

Response to the publication of this photograph was immediate and sustained. As a morale-booster to war-weary American fighting men, it was beyond comparison. As a morale-booster to our entire nation, it symbolized the determination of our troops to achieve victory over all odds.

And so it is to this day. Americans not yet born when Joe Rosenthal's camera instantly preserved this historic moment know the scene as though they were there. It was -- and is -- one of America's proudest moments, the symbol of our true national spirit.

Stained Glass ... the Link with Immortality

As an experienced collector, you know the uniqueness of stained glass.

This is art that approaches the eternal. Some of the classic stained glass masterpieces created 600 years ago are as radiant and brilliant as they were the day the medieval stained glass artisans lovingly completed them.

You know, too, the artistic significance of an original stained glass work by Jack Woodson. Alone among contemporary

(Continued)

American artists, Mr. Woodson has recaptured the classic tradition, the venerable skills of designing art for stained glass.

In his design of the official "Iwo Jima" Stained Glass Plate, he has been faithful to the original photograph. The battle-weary warriors reach to their limits to make Old Glory stand high. The flag of 1945 had 48 stars. The scarred summit of Mt. Suribachi is littered with debris and broken branches.

The artist's consummate mastery gives us a memorable orange-red sky. As light pours through the stained glass, the dimension and realism are uncannily real.

Bordering the plate are the timeless words of Admiral Chester Nimitz, commander of the United States Pacific Fleet during World War II:

"Uncommon valor was a common virtue."

No words are more appropriate for this singular event which, but for the fortunate presence and quick eye of the Associated Press photographer, could have been an unremembered footnote to history.

Deserving of Proud Display

If ever a work of art deserved display, your official "Iwo Jima" Stained Glass Plate qualifies for this honor.

Importance of subject is one gauge. On this level, Jack Woodson himself, lauded for so many of his artistic triumphs, calls this "my most significant and surely most heroic theme."

Perfection of art is another gauge. As you inspect the picture of this plate in the brochure I've enclosed, notice the perfect way the action flows with the plate shape. Notice, too, the drama of the sky ... the incredible detail Mr. Woodson has given us in such particulars as camouflage helmets, battle gear, uniforms, terrain and the flag itself.

Excellence in craftsmanship is critical in a work of collectible art. We at the Society have found a single group of artisans capable of flawless replication of Jack Woodson's stained glass art: the master craftsmen of The Stained Glass Guild, whose works grace many museums.

These gifted individuals apply 15 separate colors to the cathedral glass rounds to assure absolute fidelity to the original work. The colors then are fired, becoming fused forever with the glass. They never will fade, just as the classic stained glass windows created hundreds of years ago have endured for centuries. So will this image of Iwo Jima.

(Continued)

Only stained glass that survives multiple inspections is approved and fitted into the polished pewter rim. Each plate is hand-inscribed with its individual number. The identical number appears on the individual Certificate of Authenticity accompanying the plate.

Of course, your plate will be couched in its elegant gold-embossed cushioned presentation box. And a translucent display easel enables you to display your plate anywhere.

Benefits of Your Society Membership

You're an old friend, and you're familiar with some of the benefits of membership in the United States Historical Society. May I, though, remind you of just two?

First, the official "Iwo Jima" plate can be yours first, and yours for $125, a considerable savings from the issue price of $140.

Secondly, we value your friendship and never would want you to have a work of historical art unless you're convinced this is one you want to own forever. So after the official Iwo Jima Stained Glass Plate is in your hands, display it for one full month. Show it to friends.

I'll wager you'll want to acquire a second plate for a veteran friend or another patriot. But what if I'm wrong? You already know the answer: at any time during that month, if you decide you don't want to keep your "Iwo Jima" Stained Glass Plate, return it and we'll refund your entire purchase price. Of course, your membership will continue.

To me, the greatest benefit of membership is having the opportunity to enjoy works of art of tremendous historical value. By anyone's standard of judgment, your official "Iwo Jima" Stained Glass Plate rates as outstanding. I am honored to be able to make it available to you.

Sincerely,

Paul J. Warden

Paul J. Warden
President

P.S. In years to come, this treasured work of art will be a reminder -- perhaps to generations yet unborn -- of America's finest hour.

Mailer: **The Ghent Collection**
Key Words: **"Since the beginning of time . . ."**
Writer: **Eugene Povskadovsky**

The Challenge

This letter and the mailing of which it is part appeared during the golden era of collectibles in which anyone who had shown interest in produced collectibles was bombarded by a multiplicity of similar-looking offers.

"Man's Dream of Flight" was a continuity program. Continuity programs can be wildly successful even if the first issue represents a monetary loss, because subsequent issues represent pre-paid advertising.

The Implementation

In this instance, a series of eight plates had a remarkable buy-through average of more than six and had almost no drop-off after the second plate.

Notice the dependence on expert opinions to convince prospective buyers of the worth, uniqueness, and displayability of the porcelain plates in this series.

As is proper for an offer based on exclusivity, the response device indicated an expiration date.

Comment

"Man's Dream of Flight" is as archetypical of a collectibles letter as we have seen. It includes every basic motivator which might be aimed at the collector—exclusivity, of course; expert validation of claims; the necessity of timeliness of response; special pricing; artistic excellence; and the possibility of future value-appreciation. In concert, these arguments typified the golden age of collector's plates.

Figure 4–7. The Ghent Collection

THE GHENT COLLECTION
Bath, Ohio 44210

Dear Fellow Collector,

Since the beginning of time, all mankind has shared a dream: the dream of flight.

Only in this century has the dream come true. Man soars with the birds, speeds through the heavens like a hawk in his powerful, sleek, silvery machines.

Yet the dream of flight continues. It's part of us, forever. Who among us hasn't watched the giant jets taking off and landing, with a secret wishfulness in our hearts?

Now The Ghent Collection has commissioned master artist August Frank to immortalize Man's Dream of Flight in a series of eight limited edition plates so beautiful and so artistically perfect that just looking at them fulfills the dream. Mr. Frank takes us there, to be one with Icarus, the earliest aviator whose wax-held wings melted in the sun; with the genius Leonardo da Vinci, who invented a working helicopter 450 years ahead of his time; with the Wright Brothers, who first brought the dream to reality; with Lindbergh, the Lone Eagle, whose first solo non-stop flight across the Atlantic began The Age of Aviation; with the intrepid Barnstormers, who gave us infectious love of flying; with the supersonic Concorde whose speed still seems incredible; and with the First Man on the Moon, the ultimate flier who finally achieves what Icarus attempted --- flight into the skies, beyond the earth.

Even though we have just announced this collection and the only collectors who have seen it are reviewers who have seen "proofs", "Man's Dream of Flight" is being hailed throughout the world of collecting as an epic series, a milestone, a giant leap forward as plate collecting comes of age. Plate reviewer Phyllis Durst of the distinguished publication "Antique and Collectors Mart" said in her just-published review of "The Flight of Icarus", first edition of the series:

> "This is one of those rare plates that is worth owning for two reasons: first, because it is artistically attractive, and second, because it is a step forward in collector's plates as an art form."

(We are so pleased with Ms. Durst's review that we have obtained permission to reprint it in full. I have enclosed it for you to read.)

One of the best-known and most highly respected art consultants in the world of collectibles, Margo Lewis, told us this about "Man's Dream of Flight":

Combining many motivators to add drama and overcome apathy. *(Continued)*

"'Man's Dream of Flight' is true art. That it appears on porcelain is all to the good, because undiminished by time, it will be viewed and appreciated for centuries to come. In my opinion this is an authentic art collection on porcelain, worthy of the future."

An authentic art collection on porcelain. This is what we at The Ghent Collection strive for. In "Man's Dream of Flight" we have, the experts say, brought fine, significant art to porcelain. I'm proud to share this achievement with you and I'm anxious for you to have the brilliant first edition, "The Flight of Icarus", for permanent display in your home, office or gallery.

An unique benefit is yours because The Ghent Collection, which commissioned the original art, is offering "Man's Dream of Flight" direct to you. Because you are among the first we are notifying, actually before actual issue date (the official date is October 10), you enjoy a special benefit.

The issue price of each spectacular gold-banded plate is $37.50. That is the published, advertised price. It is the price at which dealers will sell the plate to other collectors.

But that is not what you pay. In fact, it's 27% more than your special preferred below-issue price.

Through this invitation, which is yours with the Preferred Priority Reservation Form included with this letter, your special price is $29.50 --- $8.00 below issue price.

Because you will acquire "Man's Dream of Flight" direct from The Ghent Collection, issuer of the series, this special price is guaranteed for every plate of this series.

As an experienced collector, you will appreciate yet another advantage:

As you collect this complete series, you will own your registration number within the edition limit of 19,500 worldwide. This means that each plate will have the identical registration number fired in gold into the backstamp. Your set will be perfectly matched, which can be of great significance if you decide one day to put it on the market.

What a pleasure it is for us to be able to offer you limited editions of this majesty, this artistry, at $29.50 each. Comparable plates without matched numbers, without so grandiose a theme, without original art of such excellence, sell regularly for $50 to $90. Our intention always has been to bring to our collectors works of art which have genuine merit. I think you'll agree, as you look at the pictures of the eight paintings in the descriptive brochure, that we have succeeded.

What tasteful, polished art you will own. These plates are an aesthetic delight. One can envision them as the focal point of any display, in a

(Continued)

home, an office, or for that matter an art gallery. If you acquire them to present to someone as a gift, surely they will be the finest and most prized gift he or she ever could receive.

As a first edition, "The Flight of Icarus" is doubly important. Not only does it begin the series, which adds to its distinction, it also sets a new level in limited edition plate art. August Frank has outdone himself, has created art beyond any we have seen before on porcelain.

The matched registration numbers are an obvious advantage in the future marketplace. I think that an equally important advantage is that "The Flight of Icarus" and the other plates of "Man's Dream of Flight" are limited to 19,500. You can see how the integrity of the edition is preserved: the edition limit isn't just announced; it's enforced by firing the specific number within that limit into each plate. Compare this with collector's plates that have no number at all, or those whose limit is obscure and not announced in advance.

In years to come, for those who view plates as an investment, having a worldwide limit this small should be a positive advantage. Surely this entire edition will be subscribed quickly, and the demand for plates after the edition is closed could have a profound effect on the future value of the plates.

> The low edition limit has imposed some restriction on us. We cannot permit any collector, even those to whom we're sending this priority invitation, to reserve more than two of each plate in the series.
>
> Thus, you may reserve one for yourself and one as a gift; the numbers will be consecutive within the edition limit. But we cannot honor reservations for more than two of each, in fairness to other collectors. In fact, this advantage which we have established for the early announcement of "Man's Dream of Flight" may have to be withdrawn later on, should demand exceed the number of available plates at that time.

You can see, as you study the reproductions of the sublime paintings for "Man's Dream of Flight" in the brochure, what marvelous composition and detail the artist has given us. What you can't see is the difference between each plate and the picture of the plate. There is no way the printed page can match the soft, glowing luminescence of fine porcelain. Oh, yes, this is fine first quality porcelain, by Porcelaine Etienne. The Ghent Collection would not lend its name to anything less.

As you view this series, a milestone in artistic representation of the entire history of flight, it is as though the entire panorama of dramatic history were there for you to see, over and over again.

But what if you don't agree? What if, after acquiring "The Flight of Icarus", you decide that this particular plate isn't for you?

Anyone who ever has acquired a collectible through The Ghent Collection knows about our absolute, unquestioned money-back guarantee:

(Continued)

At any time up to 30 days after you have any plate, you may return that plate for a full refund.

Are there any qualifications, any exclusions, any exceptions? None. We ask only that you return the plate undamaged, with its Certificate, in the original shipping container.

So you can see that you take not one cent of risk by entering your subscription to "Man's Dream of Flight". Rather, you automatically have these two major advantages:

1. Instead of the nationally advertised price of $37.50 for each plate, you pay only $29.50, plus shipping. You save $64 on the series.
2. You will own your registration number, which means that each plate will have the identical number. That number isn't just on the Certificate of Authenticity; it's fired permanently into the backstamp of each plate.

As you look through the brochure which shows you the eight plates of "Man's Dream of Flight", I ask that you make a private comparison of this art with any you've seen, at any price. From the moment this project was conceived, we intended to bring you art representing a new height, a new stature in limited edition plates. Have we succeeded? I'm convinced that we have, and I know that you will share my pride in the tremendous achievement accomplished by August Frank and the artisans at Porcelaine Etienne who have brought his wonderful paintings to porcelain.

You can, I know, understand my pleasure at being able to bring you limited edition plates of this quality.

Sincerely,

John Chambers

John Chambers, Director
The Ghent Collection

P.S. Please return your reservation form before the expiration date. You are among the first to whom we're sending this information (which means a lower registration number), but I'm sure you understand that in fairness to others we must ask you to send your reservation now if you're interested. We can mail only one notification to any individual collector.

Chapter 5

Product Sale

As the marketplace becomes more and more skeptical and as conventional media deliver messages of greater and greater sameness, sales letters have proved their value in motivating individuals who no longer respond to traditional advertising.

This may be because a letter walks the fine line separating "mass" media and personal communication. A letter is one-on-one, and letter-writers who deal in plurals ("those of you" and "all of you") misunderstand the advantage that exists at their fingertips.

The examples in this chapter give you an idea of the breadth of product which can be sold through direct mail. Granted, the letter may be one of many components within the mailing package; but readership studies tell us the recipient looks at the letter first. A poorly written or unconvincing letter destroys the sales power of the whole mailing, no matter how valuable, useful, dramatic, or important to the prospective buyer the offer may be.

These letters—judged by the one undeniable gauge, response—did succeed.

Mailer: **Nightingale-Conant Corp.**
Key Words: **"Dear Mental Wizard"**
Writer: **Bob Matheo**

The Challenge

Self-help on a commercial level is actually dependence on outside help. Outside help can be a source of resentment, especially if the project suggests a deficiency in an area not previously recognized as deficient by the person at whom the message is aimed.

Added to the challenge of recognizing a potential improvement is dispelling the fear of hard work needed to achieve this improvement—a double challenge when one circularizes those who have had moderate success in the work force by reaching middle management.

The Implementation

The letter both strokes and chides the reader. In four pages of easily understood text, the writer not only justifies the concept of "Mega-Memory" but makes its availability seem to be the next logical step for any logical person.

Included is justification of the training program's author, a laundry list of what the program enables the user to do, and underscoring ease of learning, even including the remarkable imperative, "Listen only once."

Comment

This letter opens with a difficult and challenging concept: stroking the reader and implying a greater potential capability, available only through a series of memory exercises.

Above the greeting is a technique called the "Johnson Box." In less proficient hands, a Johnson Box can actually suppress response by disclosing too early what the sales thrust will be. In this instance, the writer uses this box to establish rapport with the reader by recounting a common memory problem.

The opening, "Dear Mental Wizard," has an irritation potential among those who may feel the writer is making fun of them. Irritation vanishes immediately in the first two-sentence paragraph.

Notice how the writer condenses the entire offer into the first page, then moves back to validate the argument over the following pages.

Notice, too, the last sentence of the letter, which follows the proper procedure for a letter's close: Tell the reader what to do.

Figure 5–1. Nightingale/Conant

DID YOU EVER...

- Meet someone, shake hands, and forget his name the second you let go of his hand?
- Go to a store and buy a dozen things ... except the item you went for?
- Enter a room ... and forget why you went there in the first place?

Cheer up. You're not losing it. In fact, you already have memory powers beyond your wildest dreams. Read on.

Dear Mental Wizard:

You already have a photographic memory. You have the talent and ability to recall the names of 50 people you meet for the first time.

All it takes to release your talent are some simple techniques ... which you can master in about three days.

We'll let you use the training lessons for 30 DAYS -- FREE!

Just Push the Right Buttons

Why do we fail to remember things? Perhaps because we push the wrong mental button when we learn it. Or because we push the wrong mental button when we try to recall it. Or both.

To start to change all that, take the enclosed card, push out the FREE-TRIAL BUTTON, affix it to the reply portion and mail it today. We'll send you Kevin Trudeau's MEGA MEMORY -- a 16-lesson training program -- for you to use for 30 days without charge.

As you go through the lessons and perform the mental exercises, you'll wake up your brain's half-asleep neuro-transmitters ... and you'll learn to push the buttons that store new knowledge in your memory properly ... so you can retrieve it at a moment's notice.

Just as You've Seen on TV

Does the name Kevin Trudeau ring a bell? He's the host on the nation's top self-improvement TV show, "Mega Memory," and his techniques have been demonstrated on the "Tonight Show," "20/20," "That's Incredible" and the "Joe Franklin Show." Or perhaps you've read about him in a magazine or newspaper.

Turn page, please---

Nightingale-Conant Corporation
7300 North Lehigh Avenue · Chicago, Illinois 60648 · 1-708-647-0300 · 1-800-525-9000

Stroking and chiding build desire to improve. *(Continued)*

Kevin Trudeau founded the American Memory Institute, now the world's largest memory training school, after developing breakthrough training methods that go far beyond the "basic association" techniques that other so-called memory experts teach. Dr. Alex Duarte, a teacher who has worked with educationally handicapped children with dyslexia and memory problems, has checked every memory course commercially available. And he says:

> "After two hours with this genius, Kevin Trudeau, I am convinced that we have in our hands a revolutionary breakthrough in memory enhancement."

<u>A Springboard for Success</u>

There isn't a line of work in this world that you cannot do better and more profitably when your memory is improved.

Imagine giving presentations involving hundreds of facts, figures and prices <u>without looking at notes</u>. Imagine making such a presentation to 50 people or more you never met before ... and being able to address each of them by name. Imagine meeting all these people a month later ... and still knowing everyone's name!

> This is far more than a stunt for dazzling people at parties. Being able to remember people's names is one of the most useful tools in human relations. As Dale Carnegie said: "A person's name is to that person the sweetest and most important sound in any language."

Imagine recalling facts and figures that you read months ago in a trade or professional journal ... and that affect a project you're working on today.

Imagine being able to recall precisely the details of a meeting you attended ... or perhaps a conversation you overheard.

Or imagine studying for an exam for an advanced degree or a promotion ... and memorizing strings of data <u>effortlessly</u>!

Here are more things Kevin Trudeau's MEGA MEMORY program enables you to do:

- ✔ Remember instantly lists of data
- ✔ Remember travel directions
- ✔ Remember agendas, shopping lists, things to do
- ✔ Remember dates and appointments
- ✔ Remember new words, even technical and foreign
- ✔ Remember maps, charts, tables of organization
- ✔ Remember phone numbers and addresses
- ✔ Remember formulas, recipes, conversion tables

(Continued)

The Older You Get, the Harder It Is to Remember

It happens to all of us. Suddenly you can't remember an old friend's name, a colleague's phone number, or what you wanted to buy at the drugstore. No, you're not getting senile. It's just that the older we get, the more cluttered our minds become with random information. And it's hard to pull the fact we want from out of the clutter.

The truth is, YOU REMEMBER EVERYTHING -- we all do. Everything we've ever learned is stored somewhere in our memory. But it's hard to RECALL just one or two facts from the tangle of data in our minds.

Your Mental File Folders

That's where MEGA MEMORY comes in. The program teaches you how to create mental file folders for storing each new thing you learn ... and how to retrieve information from your file folders in less than a second. It's all a matter of pushing the right mental buttons.

Most people, when they can't remember something, push their THINK button. Wrong! They should push SEARCH to find the file that holds the information, then RETRIEVE to recall it. All this happens in about one-tenth of a second -- about 40 times faster than it takes to read it!

In MEGA MEMORY, Kevin Trudeau guides you through a series of exercises that train you to create mental files, to enter information into those files, and to look up and recall whatever you've stored.

No Wasted Time -- No Embarrassment

You can save precious time because you don't have to look things up. You can save yourself the embarrassment of forgetting important names. And, in today's competitive world, little things like that could just save your career as well!

Furthermore, just knowing that you have a MEGA MEMORY will boost your self-esteem and fill you with confidence. It will help you look and feel like a winner ... which, as you know, is a giant step toward being one.

Different From Any Other Audio Program

Be warned. Kevin Trudeau's MEGA MEMORY is not only different from any other memory program you may have taken. It is also different from any other audio program you've taken as well.

1. Do not listen while driving. You often do mental exercises with your eyes closed! These exercises stimulate the memory centers of the brain (like an athlete's warm-ups and stretches), conditioning you for top memory performance.

(Continued)

2. Listen only once. Each exercise leads to the next -- no repeating. For reinforcement, use your 52-page workbook.

That's it -- 16 lessons you can do in two or three days, and a MEGA MEMORY is yours! From now on, your memory keeps getting better as you exercise your "memory muscles" every day. Now you're different -- your memory improves the older you get!

Get Started Today -- While It's on Your Mind

Your tools for putting your entire brain to work are waiting. Mail the card and we'll send them to you for a FREE 30-DAY TRIAL.

Work the lessons. Do the exercises. You'll see spectacular progress even after two lessons. And long before your free trial is up, you'll know what power a MEGA MEMORY gives you. A single payment of $59.95 plus shipping and handling covers it.

If you're not convinced, however, simply return the course and the workbook without explanation ... and PAY NOTHING.

What are you waiting for? Just "push the button"!

Cordially,

Vic Conant

Vic Conant
President

P.S. FREE -- THE SECRET TO REMEMBERING THINGS YOU FORGOT. Did you ever hide something -- and forget the hiding place? Do you try to remember things from your childhood -- and fail?

Now you can retrieve "misfiled" information like that. You'll get, as an outright gift, an extra tape with the special techniques for dredging up forgotten information from your past. This 21-minute lesson, "How to Remember Everything From Your Past," is yours ABSOLUTELY FREE. You may keep it even if you decide to return the course.

The shortest distance between where you are and where you could be

Nightingale Conant

Nightingale-Conant Corporation
7300 North Lehigh Avenue · Chicago, Illinois 60648 · 1-708-647-0300 · 1-800-525-9000

1060–SL

Mailer: **The Red Cooper Family**

Key Words: **"You're one of the first"**

Writer: **Red Cooper**

The Challenge

How does one sell grapefruit by mail, especially in an era in which big, juicy grapefruit grace the produce counter in every supermarket?

A public opinion poll might show that most people think grapefruit is grapefruit. Some might guess—without passion—that pink grapefruit is somehow tastier or more patrician than yellow grapefruit. But they can get pink grapefruit in the supermarket as easily as they can get yellow grapefruit.

So the challenge: Compete by positioning this grapefruit as Olympian, beyond competition and therefore worthy of a premium price.

The Implementation

Red Cooper created the image of a "super-grapefruit," one retail stores couldn't afford to stock even if they could get them, which they can't because this is "private stock," sold only by mail.

Added to the mix is a heavy dose of exclusivity: "I paid a bunch of high-powered computer guys a lot of money for the names of people they tell me will appreciate the very best gourmet treats."

The reader feels guilty if he or she even entertains the notion that these are expensive. Repeated "money back" assurance adds both validity and comfort.

But the key to this letter's success is the inescapable conclusion: This is, after all, the King of all grapefruit!

Comment

This is one of the most famous direct response letters of the last 15 years. It has sold grapefruit to lists that previously had been unapproachable. It also is unique in that, as it is mailed each year, it generates response in which orders include a note openly crediting the letter for having stimulated the order.

The technique is deceptively casual: The writer establishes a neighborly, low-pressure, friend-to-friend relationship, carefully avoiding big words, any indication of pressure, and the "hype" one often sees in letters selling continuity programs.

We've included examples of order forms which credit the letter for the order.

Figure 5–2. Red Cooper

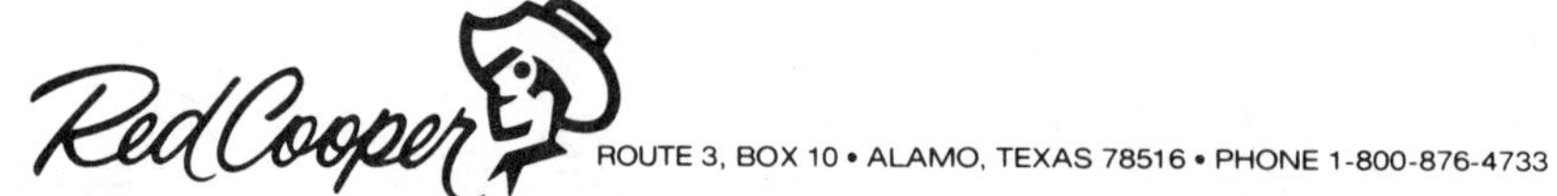

You're one of the first to enjoy this!

Good morning!

If you'll give me the next 3 1/2 minutes, in return I'll give you a treat that'll open up an unbelievable new world of eating pleasure for you. Fair enough?

A little background:

My family has been in the citrus fruit business just about forever. We've become slightly famous down here because our fruit is so much bigger and sweeter than the citrus you find in the store. When people have a special occasion, in they come to get some Red Cooper grapefruit.

Until a couple of years ago, we were perfectly content with our grapefruit. So was everybody else, and it sold like crazy. Ours always has been the biggest, sweetest, prettiest grapefruit in the neighborhood ... some say the whole country.

But then that big freeze came along. You read about it in the paper: We'd never had a bitter cold spell like that, down here where the climate is "grapefruit perfect." That freeze wiped out almost every darned grapefruit tree in south Texas. Our own gorgeous trees were frozen solid. That meant, literally, starting all over again.

What we did:

Even before the freeze we'd been experimenting with grapefruit Now, we figured, since we were starting over, why not carry those experiments as far as we could go?

I'll tell you what the experiments were:

We were trying to cross-breed a grapefruit with a big, honey-sweet orange. If we could do it, we knew we'd have the sweetest grapefruit anybody ever grew ... a grapefruit that wouldn't need sugar because it would be so sweet on its own.

Classic "Good ol' boy" letter is a masterpiece of positioning. *(Continued)*

It turned out that cross-breeding wasn't the way to go. But it led us to a discovery that - if you'll let me prove it to you - will change your taste-bud pleasures forever! Our discovery was "budding" instead of grafting. We "budded" grapefruit onto an orange tree.

Now bear in mind, when you bud you wait. And you wait. And you wait. The buds "take" or they don't. If they don't you start over. That's exactly what we did. We budded ... and we waited. And we budded again ... and we waited.

But you know what? We succeeded beyond our wildest dreams!

Understand, my friend: Budding doesn't mean a thing if the results aren't worth it. When I say we did it, I mean wow! We produced the sweetest grapefruit this side of heaven. I've been in this business all my life. I've tasted every variety of grapefruit anybody grows today. Nobody, nobody has ever produce one this sweet. We've done it! We've grown the 21st century grapefruit, and nobody else can match it.

When we got our first batch, I tried them out on my own family. They're used to the best grapefruit. But I caught them by surprise with the new ones.

First of all, the color is distinctive: It's a much richer red than even our famous Ruby Red was. Second, the sweetness is light years beyond any grapefruit they (or you) have ever tasted before. And third (what a bonus!) they're seedless, so whether you're eating them or making juice you'll have marvelous mellow flavor without the seeds.

My son said, "Dad, if I didn't see a great big grapefruit sitting in front of me I'd think I was eating a new type of sweet orange." That gave us the name: ORANGE-SWEET GRAPEFRUIT.

Why I'm writing you:

All right, why am I telling this to you?

I'll tell you why: I paid a bunch of high-powered computer guys a lot of money for the names of people they tell me will appreciate the very best gourmet treats. So if they're right about your position and lifestyle, you'll recognize and take advantage of the offer I'm about to make to you.

Understand: Our Orange-Sweet Grapefruit is just about as elite a "limited edition" fruit as anybody ever produced. Oh, sure, these are the future of grapefruit; but it'll be years and years before we send any of these to even the most upscale grocers. Anybody who wants them has to get them from us, direct.

(Continued)

That's what I invite you to do. And I'll make it worth your while, because you're the kind of person whose opinion can cause others to ask, "Where did you get these, and how can I get some?" You'll tell them. That's worth a lot to us for next year's crop.

So I have an offer I hope you can't refuse.

Your Special DIRECT offer:

Each month this winter - winter being the time when fresh grapefruit really will bring sunshine into your home - I'll send you a whole box of 15 great big Orange-Sweet Grapefruit.

I don't want any money from you now. In fact, I don't want any money until you've sampled your first shipment.

When you get them, select any four grapefruit from the box. Chill them, then put them to your personal taste test. Surprise your family for breakfast one morning ... or for that matter, as a dinner dessert, because these are so sweet they can be the most delicious (and best for you) dessert that ever graced your table. Or you might want to make some juice from one or two.

See my note in the P.S.

Only then, if you agree these are absolutely the finest and sweetest grapefruit you've ever tasted, the whole shipment is yours for just $17.98 plus a nominal shipping charge. If you don't agree just write "no, thanks" on the invoice and send back the unused fruit. We'll pay for the return shipping, and we'll still be friends.

As a preferred Red Cooper gourmet customer, you'll get a similar shipment every month through April. You don't pay for any shipment until after you've sampled it. And of course you can skip a shipment or cancel at any time.

I want to emphasize: This is the only way you or anybody can get our Orange-Sweet Grapefruit. You owe it to yourself to at least sample this wonderful new triumph in fine citrus fruit.

What a way to start the day! On those cold, bleak, overcast winter mornings you'll have some real sunshine in you life, because that's the happy effect our Orange-Sweets have!

May I have your answer quickly?

This year's crop is very limited. And bear in mind, we ship only the best of the best, just as soon as we pick them off the tree. (They'll stay fresh for weeks and weeks.) Every piece of fruit is hand-selected for size and sweetness.

(Continued)

As I told you, you're among the first to get this information. I sincerely want you to be our customer. And I intend to make it worth your while to be our customer, because I want this year's crop to be spoken for.

So please, my friend, let me hear from you right away. Really you're in a win/win situation, because if you like our fabulous Orange-Sweet Grapefruit it's yours at the direct price; if you don't, you haven't risked a cent.

Here's what you do:

Just sign the Preferred Order Card I've enclosed and drop it in the mail. Nothing else to do ... except sit back and anticipate the very best grapefruit anybody ever ate, ever, anywhere on this planet.

Really, our Orange-Sweets will change forever the way you think of grapefruit. You won't again admire any supermarket grapefruit, no matter how pretty it may look in the display ... because you'll know better. You'll realize a far sweeter, far better-tasting grapefruit can be yours.

But please, please don't wait on this. I'd hate to see you miss out. And if we don't hear from you, you won't have an opportunity to sample this spectacular 21st century grapefruit for another whole year.

You have a fantastic taste treat in store. I'm delighted to be able to make the limited-edition Orange-Sweet available to you, and I'm eager to know what you think of this "King of Grapefruit."

I'll look for your Preferred Order Card on my desk. Thanks.

Sincerely,

Red Cooper

RC/HL

For The Cooper Family

P.S. To make it even more worth your while: Take $3.00 off the cost of your first shipment. It's yours for $14.98, not $17.98 - if we hear from you within the next 15 days.

(Continued)

Figure 5–3

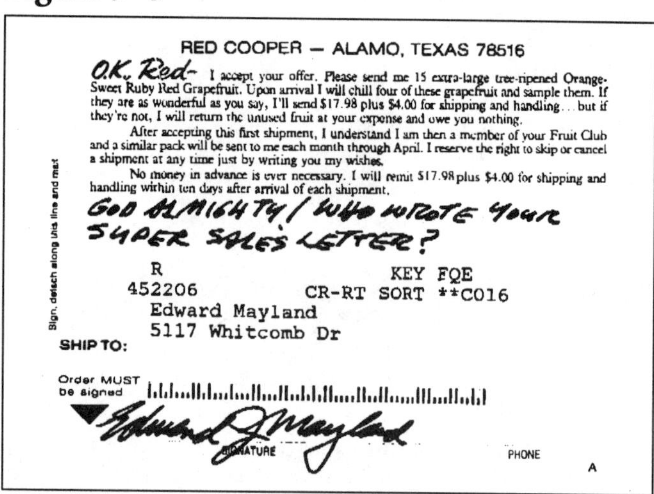

RED COOPER — ALAMO, TEXAS 78516

O.K. Red— I accept your offer. Please send me 15 extra-large tree-ripened Orange-Sweet Ruby Red Grapefruit. Upon arrival I will chill four of these grapefruit and sample them. If they are as wonderful as you say, I'll send $17.98 plus $4.00 for shipping and handling... but if they're not, I will return the unused fruit at your expense and owe you nothing.

After accepting this first shipment, I understand I am then a member of your Fruit Club and a similar pack will be sent to me each month through April. I reserve the right to skip or cancel a shipment at any time just by writing you my wishes.

No money in advance is ever necessary. I will remit $17.98 plus $4.00 for shipping and handling within ten days after arrival of each shipment.

GOD ALMIGHTY! WHO WROTE YOUR SUPER SALES LETTER?

R KEY FQE
452206 CR-RT SORT **C016
Edward Mayland
5117 Whitcomb Dr

Sign, detach along this line and mail

SHIP TO:

Order MUST be signed

Edward J Mayland

SIGNATURE PHONE A

Red Cooper order card—1.

Figure 5–4

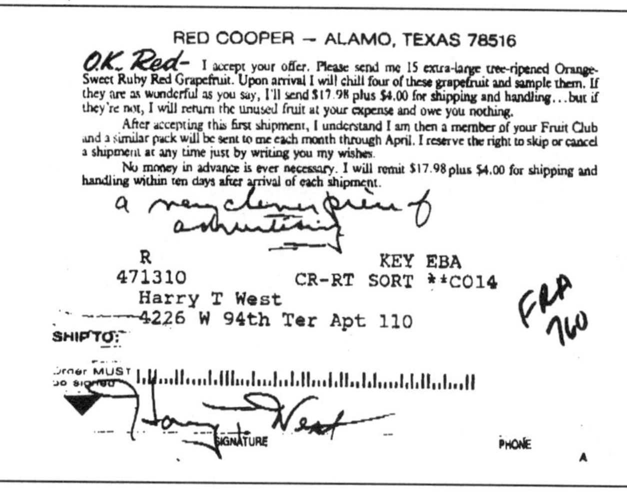

RED COOPER — ALAMO, TEXAS 78516

O.K. Red— I accept your offer. Please send me 15 extra-large tree-ripened Orange-Sweet Ruby Red Grapefruit. Upon arrival I will chill four of these grapefruit and sample them. If they are as wonderful as you say, I'll send $17.98 plus $4.00 for shipping and handling... but if they're not, I will return the unused fruit at your expense and owe you nothing.

After accepting this first shipment, I understand I am then a member of your Fruit Club and a similar pack will be sent to me each month through April. I reserve the right to skip or cancel a shipment at any time just by writing you my wishes.

No money in advance is ever necessary. I will remit $17.98 plus $4.00 for shipping and handling within ten days after arrival of each shipment.

a very clever piece of advertising

R KEY EBA
471310 CR-RT SORT **C014
Harry T West
4226 W 94th Ter Apt 110

FRA 760

SHIP TO:

Order MUST be signed

Harry T West

SIGNATURE PHONE A

Red Cooper order card—2.

Figure 5–5

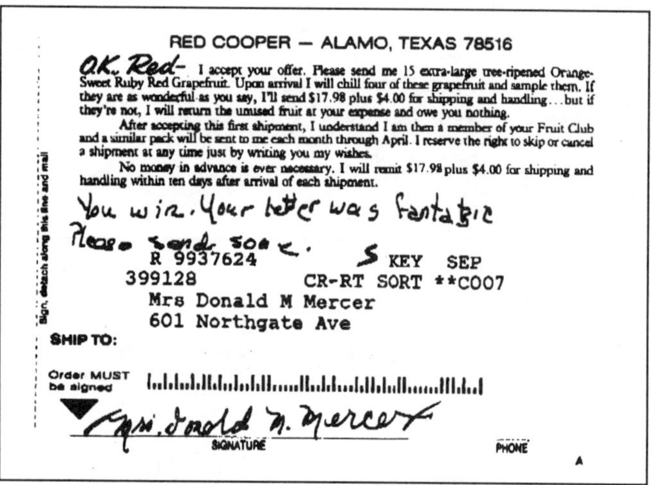

RED COOPER — ALAMO, TEXAS 78516

O.K. Red— I accept your offer. Please send me 15 extra-large tree-ripened Orange-Sweet Ruby Red Grapefruit. Upon arrival I will chill four of these grapefruit and sample them. If they are as wonderful as you say, I'll send $17.98 plus $4.00 for shipping and handling... but if they're not, I will return the unused fruit at your expense and owe you nothing.

After accepting this first shipment, I understand I am then a member of your Fruit Club and a similar pack will be sent to me each month through April. I reserve the right to skip or cancel a shipment at any time just by writing you my wishes.

No money in advance is ever necessary. I will remit $17.98 plus $4.00 for shipping and handling within ten days after arrival of each shipment.

You win. Your letter was fantastic Please send some.

R 9937624 S KEY SEP
399128 CR-RT SORT **C007
Mrs Donald M Mercer
601 Northgate Ave

Sign, detach along this line and mail

SHIP TO:

Order MUST be signed

Mrs. Donald M. Mercer

SIGNATURE PHONE A

Red Cooper order card—3.

Mailer: **Hale Indian River Groves**
Key Words: **"Please consider this"**
Writer: **John Lyle Shimek**

The Challenge

The challenge parallels that of Red Cooper in convincing a distant buyer of the value of citrus fruit ordered by mail.

The Implementation

This letter uses "membership" as a hook. Members pay 10% less than non-members.

Unlike Red Cooper, this letter offers oranges, tangelos, and/or grapefruit, giving the buyer the option of choosing the mixture.

This letter sells the concept of citrus fruit—grapefruit, oranges, and tangelos—on a level parallel to the fabled Red Cooper letter. Note the differences:

- The Red Cooper letter uses typewriter face; the Hale letter uses typeset.
- The Red Cooper letter uses a "down home" ambience; the Hale letter uses a straightforward sales tone.
- The Red Cooper letter is written to achieve an emotional tie with the reader; the Hale letter is written to achieve the reader's logical acceptance.

This letter includes a P.P.S., a device which, in less practiced hands, can detract from the power of the P.S.

As a positioning statement, the writer glorifies not just the company but the geographical area in which this citrus fruit grows. The original letter uses orange as its second color—quite logical not only because of its contrast, but also because using this color, the oranges at the top of page one are, in fact, orange.

Comment

Both this letter and the Red Cooper letter have been successful in the citrus fruit marketplace. Despite the different approaches—in presentation, tone, and character—used by these letters, each has produced exceptionally strong results, which suggests the writer does have options.

Figure 5–6. Hale Indian River Groves

HALE INDIAN RIVER GROVES

INDIAN RIVER PLAZA • WABASSO, FLORIDA 32970
(407) 589-4334

Please consider this as your once-a-year invitation to enjoy Florida's fabled Indian River citrus from November through June

as a member of

THE HALE SEASON SUPPLY CLUB

and thereby

pay 10% less than
non-members pay

Guaranteed to reach you just days from the time it's picked, in perfect condition, tree-ripe and orchard-fresh, via our own special, refrigerated through-truck delivery system.

This is a trial offer. Continue your membership only if you're delighted with your first shipment. Cancel or postpone shipments at any time you need to do so.

Your credit is good with me. I'll bill you later when your fruit is shipped.

BUT --

Please let me know your decision by November 1, so I can reserve your own personal supply of this much-in-demand citrus fruit.

Dear Member Elect:

Because your name is already on our list of those special people who have enjoyed or have inquired about our unique Indian River citrus recently --

-- I'm pleased to send you this cordial invitation to become a member of a necessarily exclusive group of citrus lovers who are entitled to enjoy the somewhat limited supply of our Indian River citrus on a regular basis.

And, because you've already experienced the unmatched taste of our citrus -- or have shown a definite interest in doing so -- you are entitled to pay 10% less for your monthly shipments than non-members pay.

YES! From November through June -- when you decide to continue your membership for a full eight months -- you save from $2.20 for a quarter bushel to $4.00 for a full bushel each month on the same fruit for which non-members gladly pay the full price.

(over, please)

Using membership as a hook for a successful continuity program. *(Continued)*

-2-

That's a total season's saving of from $17.60 to $32.00 -- enough to buy a full course dinner for one or two at a nice restaurant -- or to surprise a special child in your life with an I-Love-You gift.

Perhaps you are already familiar with our exclusive Indian River area of Florida and the fact that its fruit is recognized the world over as Florida's more superior citrus fruit.

By actual tests, it's up to 25% sweeter and far juicier than other Florida citrus, good though such citrus may be. It's rich in Vitamin C and other healthful nutrients. And it will be the high pleasure point of your breakfast -- or any other occasion you choose to treat yourself with it.

And because of its extra flavor and juiciness, it's officially and legally protected by the Pure Food Act from imitation and misbranding. This means no other Florida citrus can bask in the reflected reputation of our citrus by calling itself "Indian River".

It's the fruit everyone wants but not everyone can have. There just isn't enough of it to go around. **But you can enjoy it regularly when you send me your 10% Savings Certificate by November lst.**

Even though Indian River fruit is the best of Florida's citrus, our Indian River area produces only 20% of the total Florida crop.

So if you are one of those particular people who refuse to settle for second-best, this invitation is your once-a-year opportunity to go first-class with the extra enjoyment you'll experience with our citrus -- whether you choose our Ruby Red Grapefruit, Navel Oranges, Honeybell Tangelos, Temple Oranges or Valencias.

Why does Indian River fruit enjoy the special endorsement and protection of the U.S. Government as well as being the preferred fruit with sophisticated citrus lovers here, in Canada, in Europe -- and even in far-away Japan?

How does it earn the praise and preference of citrus lovers everywhere and of gourmet chefs in some of the most distinguished restaurants in the world?

Here in the Indian River Area of Florida, we're the beneficiaries of a lucky combination of several important things.

I've been growing and supplying fruit lovers with citrus from this region uniquely favored by Nature for 46 years now, and I still count my blessings and praise the day I chose to live and grow citrus here because:

-- Our soil is richer than that of other Florida citrus areas.

-- It contains just the right proportion of lime necessary for superior flavor.

-- Our annual rainfall of 52 inches -- plus the pure artesian water with which we irrigate our trees when they get thirsty -- contribute the extra juiciness for which our fruit is so famous.

-- The nearby Gulf Stream helps maintain an ideal growing temperature for our citrus the year around -- warmer in winter and moderate in Florida's summer sunshine.

(Continued)

-3-

All these "lucky breaks" -- plus our 46 years of honing our expertise as citrus growers -- result in the finest fruit that money can buy.

But you don't have to be a millionaire to enjoy our Indian River citrus. Far from it!

Send me the enclosed 10% Savings Certificate and you will not only enjoy this superior citrus every month of your eight-month membership. You will also pay no more than you'd pay for ordinary, run-of-the-mill supermarket grapefruit, oranges or tangelos -- plus benefiting from the greater convenience of having your fruit delivered to your door and the comforting knowledge that it is of greatly superior quality.

And, of course, you can instruct us to include more than one variety of this unsurpassed citrus in your regular shipments. We'll be happy to send you **all oranges, all grapefruit** -- or **a tasty mix of both**.

Just look at the tantalizing choices available to you during the season:

Ruby Red Seedless Grapefruit carefully hand-selected for maximum ripeness, yours from November through June. They just get sweeter and sweeter with each passing month.

Navel Oranges in November and December. They're big, some as big as grapefruit, and easy to peel -- the kind you used to find in your Christmas stocking -- only better.

Honeybell Tangelos in January. Brilliant in color and absolutely the juiciest fruit grown. So juicy you're probably safest eating them with a bib -- so delicious you'll want to revel in their flavor.

Temple Oranges in February and March. The world's finest eating orange, easy to peel, with a rich, melt-in-your-mouth flavor. Great for juicing.

Valencia Oranges in April, May and June. The last of the season and well worth the wait. The traditional orange from which your breakfast juice is made -- but you get the added bonus of its sweeter Indian River flavor.

Please review these members' privileges -- all yours when you return your 10% Savings Certificate to me. You're entitled, without question, to:

* **Cancellation privilege**. Just call or write to cancel or postpone shipments at any time.

* **Immediate Replacement**, Refund or Credit in the unlikely event that a portion of your shipment should be damaged.

(over, please)

(Continued)

-4-

* **Return Privilege**. If not delighted with your fruit, just return the unused portion and owe nothing.

* **Pay 10% less also on any purchases for yourself or others** in addition to your regular shipments -- as long as you are a Season Supply Club Member.

* **CREDIT OK**. Your credit is good with me. Send no money. We'll bill you when fruit is shipped and not before.

This is the only invitation to Season Supply Club membership you will receive this year, so it is important that you let me have your instructions just as soon as you possibly can.

I make this request because I do need time to plan the harvesting, packing and shipping schedules which will assure delivery of your first pleasure-filled carton of juicy, sweet, tree-ripened fruit in time for you to enjoy it over the Thanksgiving Holiday.

Can you please see your way clear to completing and mailing your 10% Savings Certificate promptly so I can begin treating you to the world's most wanted citrus?

Thank you for taking time to read this letter. I'll be waiting for your early reply.

Cordially,

Steve Hale, Jr.

Stephen C. Hale, Jr.
President

SH/sws

P.S.: **REMEMBER**--you save from $2.20 to $4.00 on each shipment over what non-members pay -- a total of from $17.60 to $32.00 during your membership. But this important saving is yours only if you send me your 10% Savings Certificate by November 1.

P.P.S.: Don't like filling out forms? Just call **TOLL-FREE** at **1-800-289-4253** and we'll immediately add your name to the list of discriminating people who are already enjoying my Indian River fruit regularly.

Mailer: **Hewlett Packard**
Key Words: **"Imagine a computer"**
Writer: **Stan Holden**

The Challenge

If one envisions the mail-order climate of the early 1970s, the challenge becomes obvious: Not only were lists of computer-literate individuals non-existent, but the computer itself was regarded as an exotic instrument designed for expert hands only.

This letter is one of the first to educate and simplify and has a rightful reputation as the progenitor of today's marketing of computers by mail, which we not only take for granted but no longer regard as at all unusual.

The Implementation

In the tradition of great direct response letters that introduce a genre, this text leads the reader step-by-step through the use of the computer it sells.

Page 2 delineates three areas of use—pre-recorded program cards, self-programmed cards, and pocket calculators.

To appreciate the letter and the light it casts, one does have to envision a marketplace in which a pocket calculator itself was a remarkable novelty.

Had the letter lent stronger emphasis to self-programmed cards, undoubtedly response would have been minimal because the concept was well in advance of the mass market.

Comment

This venerable letter (written a quarter of a century ago) has a logical place in any compendium of direct mail letters. In the twenty-first century, a $795 pocket "computer," with primitive technology and limited memory, is a museum piece. But if we transport our attitudes back to the early 1970s, in which the entire concept was a combination of informational re-education and salesmanship, the historical value of this letter becomes apparent.

Figure 5–7. Hewlett Packard

19310 Pruneridge Avenue · Cupertino, California 95014 · Telephone (408) 996-0100

This little card

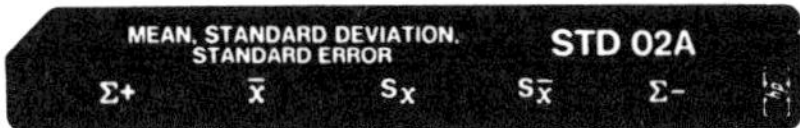

enables you to solve even extremely complex, lengthy or repetitive problems in seconds

...when you feed it through the first and only fully-programmable pocket calculator!

Introducing: The HP-65 Personal "Computer"

Imagine a "computer" that fits in your pocket! Imagine that it's no bigger than -- and looks very much like -- an ordinary pocket calculator ... but doesn't cost very much more! Now imagine this miniature marvel in your hands, as you try it out for 15 days and cut your problem-solving time down to seconds!

But why imagine? Now -- thanks to Hewlett-Packard's newest state-of-the-art technology -- there is a pocket-sized "computer" ... the HP-65!

Just like a computer, it's fully programmable. And it uses computer logic to solve even extremely complex, lengthy or repetitive problems in seconds -- anywhere, anytime -- at the touch of a few keys!

No, this personal "computer" doesn't use tiny little reels of tape or miniature keypunch cards. It uses small (approximately ½" x 3") magnetic cards. Each card can store a program -- a sequence of keystrokes -- up to 100 steps long. (And, if additional steps are needed to handle an unusually long program, you can do it in stages.)

To insert a program into the HP-65, just run a pre-recorded program card through it. All it takes is two seconds! The information from the card is duplicated in the HP-65's program memory, where it remains for as long as you leave your personal "computer" turned on.

To solve a problem, just feed in the known data by pressing a few keys on the HP-65's own keyboard. No other equipment is needed. Then start the program

(over, please)

Pioneer letter set the stage for many later computer marketers. *(Continued)* running. In seconds, the HP-65 uses computer technology to solve your problem, with up to 10-digit accuracy. And you can even program it to skip steps or to select alternate steps -- automatically -- if intermediate solutions dictate such action! It couldn't be easier ... or faster!

Actually, the HP-65 is three "answer machines" in one:

1. It operates on pre-recorded program cards (available from Hewlett-Packard) ...

2. It operates on cards you program yourself (and you don't have to learn "computer language") ...

3. It's also an advanced scientific pocket calculator (with numerous built-in functions that may be incorporated into a program or used independently).

Whichever way you use the HP-65, you'll be amazed at how much time and effort it saves you, and how it helps to reduce computational errors.

> Equally important, it enables you to handle complex, lengthy or repetitive problems that would be inconvenient, difficult or time-consuming to handle without using devices many times larger, much more expensive and nowhere near as portable as your personal "computer."

Because it operates on rechargeable batteries as well as on AC, the HP-65 can be used literally anywhere -- at a meeting, out in the field, up in a plane, down in a mine -- wherever your work takes you. It delivers the answers you need the minute you need them -- not hours or days later.

What makes the HP-65 even more incredible is that it's easy to operate! It can be used even by persons who know absolutely nothing about computers (or about calculators, for that matter). The illustrated Owner's Handbook clearly explains every detail, and the Quick Reference Guide offers a how-to-do-it summary.

Briefly, here are the three ways you can use it:

1. <u>Use it with pre-recorded program cards</u> ...

You don't need a scientific or engineering background to benefit from the HP-65's capabilities. But let's assume, for the moment, that you're involved in some project concerned with the surface area of the human body. Perhaps you're a medical technician ... a designer of apparatus for astronauts ... or a chemist working on a suntan lotion.

All you need do is take one of the pre-recorded program cards that come with the HP-65 -- the card labeled "Body Surface Area (Boyd)" -- and feed it through a slot on one side of your personal "computer." The information on the card -- the step-by-step sequence of keystrokes required to solve the problem -- is duplicated

(Continued)

in the HP-65's program memory.

Next, using the HP-65's own keyboard, feed in the height and weight of the particular body you're measuring.

Now start the program running by pushing a single key on the HP-65.

In less time than it takes to read this sentence, the answer you're seeking will appear on the HP-65's light-emitting diode (LED) display!

To calculate the surface area of a different body, just feed in that person's height and weight ... and you get the answer just as quickly.

And in case you <u>are</u> a medical technician, and you also want to find out the cardiac index (the ratio of blood pumped per unit of body surface area), simply key in the cardiac input, and the HP-65 gives you the additional answer.

Dozens of pre-recorded program cards are available ...

... and more are on the way. They're packaged in Application Pacs containing up to 40 cards, and you'll find complete information on them in the literature accompanying this letter. In addition ...

2. <u>You can create your own HP-65 program cards!</u>

No, you don't have to go to computer programming school -- or hire someone who did. You don't even have to learn "computer language," or invest in accessory hardware. All you need to write and record your own program is your HP-65, a pencil, some paper, and one of the blank program cards supplied.

Simply prepare a step-by-step sequence of the HP-65 keys you would press to solve your particular problem. If you wish, this program can include conditional tests, skips or other techniques (all of which are clearly explained in the Owner's Handbook).

Turn on the HP-65, press the appropriate keys in sequence, and run a blank card through the machine to record the program.

And that's all you do!

You may use the card again and again, whenever you need it, to cut problem-solving time down to seconds and reduce the possibility of keystroke errors. You can even edit the card, to change or delete any part of the program. Or you can erase the card and record an entirely different program on it.

(If you would rather <u>not</u> work out your own program, you may find exactly what you need among the hundreds of programs -- in a variety of fields -- in the HP-65 Users' Library. See the literature enclosed.)

By creating your own program cards, or by adapting an existing program to your

(over, please)

(Continued)

own specific needs, you greatly extend the versatility of the HP-65 while -- at the same time -- you transform it into a highly specialized, truly personal "computer."

3. <u>And you can also use the HP-65 as an advanced scientific pocket calculator</u>!

Already pre-programmed into the HP-65 are the most commonly used scientific functions. Included are log and trig functions, the constant for π, the conversion of decimal angles to degrees/minutes/seconds, the conversion of rectangular coordinates to polar coordinates (or vice versa), and numerous other functions as shown in the enclosed brochure. These built-in functions may be used independently, or incorporated into any program.

So there you have it -- the totally unique three-in-one, pocket-sized personal "computer" -- with the "super power" you need to solve just about any problem ... anywhere ... anytime!

After you read the enclosed literature, you may agree with us that the HP-65 is pretty fantastic. But only a personal trial can prove how valuable -- how indispensable -- it can be to <u>you</u>.

That's why I invite you to <u>try it for 15 days</u>!

See how it can save you hours - - or perhaps days -- of valuable time and effort, by quickly, easily and accurately solving hundreds of your complex, lengthy or repetitive problems. And see how it can free you from devices that are many times larger, much more expensive and nowhere near as portable as your personal "computer."

You might expect to pay $2,000 or more for an answer machine as incredible as the HP-65 ... but it's only $795.00 (U.S.A. only), complete with accessories as shown in the literature. And if you're not absolutely fascinated with owning and using your own pocket-sized personal "computer," return the HP-65 within 15 days for a full refund or credit!

With a product this unique, it's possible we may not be able to keep up with initial demand. Therefore, if you are interested in the HP-65, I strongly suggest you take advantage of this 15-day trial offer <u>now</u>.

Cordially,

Ray King

Ray King, General Manager
Advanced Products Division
Hewlett-Packard Company

P.S. If you send for your HP-65 now, you'll receive -- at no extra cost -- a year's subscription to the Users' Library Catalog of Contributed Programs, to greatly extend the usefulness of this personal "computer." Please see the enclosed literature for details.

RK:bn

Mailer: **Maharishi Ayur-Ved**
Key Words: **"You care about your health"**
Writer: **Carol Nelson**

The Challenge

The challenge of this mailing is extraordinary: transforming an apparent image of "fringe" operation into mainline health product supplier.

Can a product named "Maharishi Amrit Kalash" be sold by mail to those who are not members of a religious cult, to whom the name "Maharishi" does not necessarily have only positive connotations? The answer to that question clarifies the challenge.

The Implementation

We have included two "Maharishi Ayur-Ved" letters to indicate the differential in creative approach based on the specific targets.

The letters accomplish two goals: First, they respond to a request for a catalog. Second, they position the company—whose name, Maharishi Ayur-Ved, and whose principal product, Maharishi Amrit Kalash, might, without explanation, suggest a specialty product aimed at a coterie of devoted followers—as a mainline supplier of food supplements.

Comment

This letter was sent in reply to an inquiry about a catalog whose items for sale were health-oriented, rather than beauty-oriented. The letter explains some of the "Maharishi" terminology such as Rasayana, not only removing any overtone of "strangeness" but exploiting the difference.

Typically, a note accompanying a requested catalog would be brief. In this instance, a short letter would leave the catalog naked and without validated justification.

Figure 5–8. Maharishi Ayur-Ved

You care about your health. So do we.

Good Morning, My Friend!

You asked us for a catalog. Thank you. I'm about to make your request worth your while.

We want to prove that we want you as a Maharishi Ayur-Ved customer.

I'll tell you what else: We want to make it more desirable for you to be willing to experience for yourself the terrific difference between these and ordinary "health foods."

So keep in mind as you read this letter and look through the Total Health Catalog:

> As our way of showing our appreciation for your confidence, we'll give you a whopping 25% discount on any catalog items you order within the next 10 days. (More about this on page 3 of this letter.)

Discounts are always pleasant. What's even more pleasant is the realization that you're about to enjoy the benefits of total health – a concept of well-being, of both mental and physical pleasure, of contentment, of vigor and strength – developed and refined far beyond the typical health care systems with which you may be familiar.

A THOUSAND Times More Potent Than Vitamin C or E!

How dare we claim that our *Maharishi Amrit Kalash* is at least 1,000 times more powerful as a fighter against health-destroying free radicals than vitamin C or E?

I'll tell you how we dare: It's true.

A major study shows that this isn't an idle claim. (If it were, I'd never put it in writing, would I?) Respected research – not done by us but conducted under rigorously controlled conditions by The Ohio State University College of Medicine and published in the respected journal, *Pharmacology, Biochemistry and Behavior* (Vol.43, 1992) – verifies this truth.

How could any health-conscious individual settle for ordinary antioxidants after reading this news?

How could any thinking person, knowing how destructive and potentially lethal free radicals can be, not take advantage of the wonderful protection *Maharishi Amrit Kalash* offers?

(over, please)

Maharishi Ayur-Ved Products International, Inc., 1115 Elkton Drive, Suite 401, Colorado Springs, CO 80907-3535 USA
Tel. (719) 260-5500, Telex: 6976204 MAP UW, Fax: (719) 260-7400

Acknowledging strangeness and converting it to a sales point. *(Continued)*

You'd think a formulation of this strength would cost hundreds and hundreds of dollars. It doesn't. The low regular price for a full month's supply (including both the "Nectar" and the "Ambrosia") is just $89.50. And this spectacular free radical fighter is yours, right now, for 25% off its regular price. That means a month's twice-a-day supply is yours for $67.12 – just about a dollar a portion.

What's in a Name?

If we were a typical source of health food supplements, I suppose we could give our products conventional names.

We aren't a typical source. And we don't want Maharishi Ayur-Ved products confused with synthetics, nor with imitations, vitamins or minerals. Whatever you see in the Total Health Catalog you won't see in any other catalog.

And when you call us – which I hope you will, whether you order or not – you'll quickly notice another difference: Every call is answered by a helpful, knowledgeable operator, not a sales clerk. And health educators are available to answer your questions.

So when you ask for one of our *rasayanas*, you know you're getting a compound that's a step beyond... one that was perfected centuries ago. Even better, for your own peace of mind and personal benefit: Each *rasayana* is designed to achieve its effect specifically for the individual. We have rasayanas for men, for women, for midlife, for balance, and for mental clarity (if you sit all day at the computer, as I do, *Mind Plus* is a real godsend!).

As you look through the Total Health Catalog, I'd like you to note the difference separating our formulations from those you may be used to.

Yes, the names are different. But the names are just symbols of the true difference: the difference of power.

You'll see, of course, that ours is in no way a typical catalog. You won't find products you've seen before. You won't find phrases such as "Super-potent" or "More for your money" or "Unbelievable low prices" (although, truly, Maharishi Ayur-Ved Products certainly do offer you super-potency, more for your money, and unbelievable low prices).

No, what you'll find will be honest descriptions of products for which we're famous and of which we're justifiably proud.

You'll find claims which aren't just "hype"; they're true.

Maharishi Ayur-Ved Products International, Inc., 1115 Elkton Drive, Suite 401, Colorado Springs, CO 80907-3535 USA
Tel. (719) 260-5500, Telex: 6976204 MAP UW, Fax: (719) 260-7400

(Continued)

You'll find explanations of exactly how each of our formulations work... how it helps bring your mind and body back to the state of balance your mind and body deserve.

You'll find a vision of overall well-being you just won't be able to find anywhere else. And our reputation is right on the line with every item in our catalog.

A SUPER Benefit for You... Right Now.

Don't let your special Bonus Discount Certificate go to waste.

Your Certificate entitles you to a 25% discount on your entire first order. No matter how many items you order, take a big 25% off the total cost. Be sure to enclose the Certificate with your order. Or call 1-800-255-8332, Ext. 488.

When you consider that you can save a substantial amount of money by ordering direct from Maharishi Ayur-Ved Products, you'll certainly understand how valuable your extra Bonus Discount can be.

And Yet ANOTHER Benefit!

I invite you to enjoy ongoing savings, along with your ongoing good health. Each of us has only one body and one brain to work with and protect.

Many of our customers have made Maharishi Amrit Kalash a regular part of their daily lives – so many that we've established The Health and Longevity Continuity Club. I certainly hope you'll consider Membership in the Club. And to make it worthwhile for you we're offering a 20% discount on continuity orders.

Here's what I mean by "continuity orders": We'll automatically ship a supply of Maharishi Amrit Kalash to you each month.

When you're on the continuity program, we'll deduct 20% from the cost of your monthly supply of Maharishi Amrit Kalash. Every shipment. Every month. You'll have the best of both worlds – assured regular arrivals of the supplement we recommend most... and the lowest possible cost.

And that's not all. As long as you're a Club Member, we'll automatically deduct 10% from the cost of every item in the catalog, every time you order.

(over, please)

Maharishi Ayur-Ved Products International, Inc., 1115 Elkton Drive, Suite 401, Colorado Springs, CO 80907-3535 USA
Tel. (719) 260-5500, Telex: 6976204 MAP UW, Fax: (719) 260-7400

(Continued)

Take a Look. Have You Considered...?

You care about your health. You care about your vigor. You care about your longevity.

This has to be true or you wouldn't have asked for the Total Health Catalog. So, you don't have to decide that you want good health, super vigor, and a long, happy life.

What you <u>do</u> have to decide is whether the unique Maharishi Ayur-Ved formulas are for you. I hope you'll make this decision, not only because we want you to become a member of our Good Health Family, but also because the only certain way of your finding out just how marvelous you'll feel... just how big a difference in your life the catalog in your hands can make... is for you to experience the wonders of these products for yourself.

And you <u>will</u> experience the wonders of these products. We unconditionally guarantee it. If <u>for any reason</u> you aren't delighted with anything you ever get from us, just send it back within one month and we'll issue a refund or exchange, as you wish.

More great news! I have approval from Pradeep Khanna, our Director of Marketing, to offer you another special: You can have our renowned Health and Longevity Program – the complete set of seven audiotapes and Health Guides – for just $29.95. The regular price is $59.95, so you'll be saving half! (I've enclosed a Certificate for this.)

This can be a splendid "turning point" in your lifestyle. I hope you'll take advantage of it.

Thanks for giving us the opportunity to explain the philosophy behind our Total Health Catalog.

Wishing you perfect health,

John Thill

John Thill
Manager, Health Education Programs

P.S. If you're considering only ONE item for your TOTAL HEALTH, <u>*Maharishi Amrit Kalash* has to be your choice</u>. We guarantee: You <u>will</u> notice a difference, as so many thousands of others have. Be sure to use your special Discount Certificate – <u>or call our toll-free hotline at 1-800-255-8332, Ext. 488</u>.

Welcome!

Maharishi Ayur-Ved Products International, Inc., 1115 Elkton Drive, Suite 401, Colorado Springs, CO 80907-3535 USA
Tel. (719) 260-5500, Telex: 6976204 MAP UW, Fax: (719) 260-7400

Mailer: **Maharishi Ayur-Ved**
Key Words: **"Thank you for asking us"**
Writer: **Carol Nelson**

Compare this letter with the previous letter. The previous letter introduced a general line of food supplements with no overtone of gender. This letter replied to inquiries for the same catalog advertised primarily as a source of beauty aids. Notice the difference in appeal and the use of feminine terminology and examples.

Information about who is the largest group of readers is the most important and valuable bit of knowledge the writer can have. This is where database and the creative process become interlocked partners.

Figure 5–9. Maharishi Ayur-Ved

The All-Natural Way to Radiant Skin and Lustrous, Touchable Hair in Just 30 Days!

Good morning!

Thank you for asking us to send this catalog.

You're about to discover the little-known beauty secrets that women of the ancient world have passed down through the centuries. Yet few western women have rarely experienced -- or even heard about -- these rare beauty treatments.

And because you've shown such confidence in us, we'll give you a complete beauty and personal care regimen for <u>half price</u> if you order within the next 10 days. (I'll tell you more about this special offer later on.)

<u>First, a Quick Beauty Check...</u>

Take a half-second to run your fingers through your hair...

Does it feel silky and strong? Or does it feel a little coarse and brittle? Does it spring when you shake your head? Or has it lost its bounce?

Now touch your face...

Does your skin feel smooth and cool? Or is it rougher or oilier than it used to be?

When you look in the mirror...

Do you see a glowing, radiant complexion? Do you see healthy-looking hair that reflects light?

If your hair shines less than it used to ... if your skin could use a refresher ... maybe it's time to change your beauty routine.

Your mother probably told you...

Beauty is only skin deep.

Well, mother was right about a lot of things, but we now know: Lasting beauty starts much deeper than your skin. Radiant beauty <u>absolutely depends</u> on inner health as well as outer skin and hair treatment.

That's why we call our line of beauty formulas "Beauty from

Maharishi Ayur-Ved Products International, Inc., 1115 Elkton Drive, Suite 401, Colorado Springs, CO 80907-3535 USA
Tel. (719) 260-5500, Telex: 6976204 MAP UW, Fax: (719) 260-7400

Exploiting the same strangeness to sell a line of beauty products. *(Continued)*

Within." They're much more than topical beauty treatments ... they combine outer beauty treatments with inner nourishment to rejuvenate your hair and skin.

It's amazing to think about, but you'll be able to see the difference in your skin and hair in less than a month!

How does this beauty system work? Read on...

Ancient Beauty Secrets Now Verified by Modern Science...

Your mother probably didn't know about ancient cherished Ayurvedic herbs.

All natural herbal diet supplements called "Rasayanas" are the treasured beauty secrets I mentioned to you earlier in this letter.

These herbs are the all-important building blocks for our "Beauty from Within" regimen.

Our herbal formulas -- Maharishi Amrit Kalash and Ambrosia -- are powerful anti-oxidants. These ancient help restore balance to your mind and body by banishing harmful free-radicals from your system.

("Free radicals" are the destructive molecules that attack your cells and skin and contribute to premature aging.)

Because of increased air and water pollution, everyday stress, and overexposure to the sun, researchers estimate that more than 10,000 free radicals assault each one of your cells every single day and break down your body's natural defenses.

The powerful herbal formula of Amrit Kalash neutralizes the free radicals in your system.

In fact, just one gram (about a teaspoon) of Amrit Kalash is at least 1,000 times more powerful at scavenging and destroying free-radicals than Vitamins C and E.

(Don't just take our word for it. This is verified research, documented by The Ohio State University College of Medicine and published in the journal, *Pharmacology, Biochemistry and Behavior*, Vol. 43, 1992.)

While the herbs do their daily anti-oxidant scavenging, they simultaneously help bring renewed beauty to the surface of your skin and hair.

Maharishi Ayur-Ved Products International, Inc., 1115 Elkton Drive, Suite 401, Colorado Springs, CO 80907-3535 USA
Tel. (719) 260-5500, Telex: 6976204 MAP UW, Fax: (719) 260-7400

(Continued)

This is Not an "Off-the-Shelf" Beauty Solution...
This is A Beauty Solution Tailored for YOU!

Does our "Beauty from Within" program work for everyone?

Yes. But your skin and hair aren't the same as your neighbor's so the same formula may not work as well for you.

The more you know about yourself, the better our Beauty-from-Within program will bring out you natural vibrancy and radiance.

How do you determine which system is best for you individually? By choosing from three "paths" to vibrant, radiant health and beauty:

Vata, Pitta, and Kapha.

To discover which path is yours personally, take a few minutes to answer the short quiz on the enclosed card (where you'll also find valuable Discount Certificates) or turn to page 14 of your catalog (where you'll find more information on the three paths).

The highest of the three totals will tell you which personal path you'll need to balance your body's system.

One path is right for you, depending on what your body needs to be its healthiest -- and your skin its most radiant, and your hair its shiniest -- at any period of your life.

Health care for your whole family, too.

While you're browsing through our latest catalog, why not choose something for each member of your family? You'll find gum-strengthening herbal toothpaste ... sensitive-skin shaving cream (page 23) ... and a healthy alternative to peanut butter and jelly sandwiches even the kids will ask for (page 30).

Special Introductory Offer:
Try your personal Beauty from Within Starter Kit for
HALF OFF the regular price...

We want you to try our Beauty-from-Within total health system because we know it will work for you.

Choose which custom path to take toward achieving radiant

Maharishi Ayur-Ved Products International, Inc., 1115 Elkton Drive, Suite 401, Colorado Springs, CO 80907-3535 USA
Tel. (719) 260-5500, Telex: 6976204 MAP UW, Fax: (719) 260-7400

(Continued)

beauty -- Vata, Pitta, or Kapha -- and order your starter kit for just $29.95!

(If you ordered each component separately, you'd pay $60.70.)

Here's what's included:

* Herbal Day Moisturizer (to enhance radiance and luster)
* Herbal Mask (for deep cleansing and revitalization)
* Herbal Cleansing Bar (a gentle, everyday cleanser)
* Herbal Tea (to keep your system in balance and healthy)
* Herbal Churna (to season your food and nourish your spirit)
* Amrit Kalash (to create overall balance, reduce the effects of premature aging, and revive your youthful glow)

PLUS . . .

Order within ten days, and you'll receive a free sample of Raja's Cup, the powerful caffeine-free antioxidant tea. Drink it as a healthy, full-bodied alternative to your morning coffee ... and as a tasty pick-me-up throughout the day.

You'll look more radiant in 30 days ... we guarantee it!

We're happy to introduce your Beauty-from-Within Starter kit. Stick with it every day and you'll not only look younger, you'll feel younger, too. You'll have the vitality, and the radiance you may have thought you had lost forever.

We Guarantee It Or We'll Cheerfully Refund Every Cent!

We want you to be more than happy with us. If you don't notice a difference in 30 days, tell us and we'll make it right, or refund every cent.

Wishing you perfect health,

John Thill

P.S. When you try your Beauty-from-Within Starter Kit, you automatically qualify for a special discount for Charter Membership in The Health and Longevity Continuity Club: An automatic monthly supply of Maharishi Amrit Kalash. Watch your mail for this offer -- or call our toll-free hotline at 1-800-255-8332.

Maharishi Ayur-Ved Products International, Inc., 1115 Elkton Drive, Suite 401, Colorado Springs, CO 80907-3535 USA
Tel. (719) 260-5500, Telex: 6976204 MAP UW, Fax: (719) 260-7400

Mailer: Knowledge Products
Key Words: "Your mind is your biggest muscle"
Writer: Barbara Harrison

The Challenge

One hundred years ago, a series of excerpts from "The Giants of Philosophy" or "The Giants of Political Thought" would have found a willing group of targets. Those were not only kinder and gentler times; they were more literate times.

To sell audiotapes of St. Thomas Aquinas, Aristotle, Spinoza, or Schopenhauer is a heroic concept, comparable to any challenge you will find in the pages of this book.

The Implementation

The writer of this letter had the inspired notion: Get a classical education while driving your car.

Her concept, "The Audio Classics Series transforms 'downtime' into the highlight of your day," obviously matched the demographic of those at whom the letter was mailed. Our information is that this beat the previous control by a remarkable 270%.

Even though the letter sells a classical education, it uses contemporary marketing techniques. For example, the first visual is a sunburst in which we see "2 tapes for $1.00."

Comment

This letter is another example of a professional writer ignoring her own gender. The typical recipient of a letter was and is a professional male. Hence the nine philosophers shown at the bottom of each page—all men.

The first sentence, in fact, is masculine, and the staccato semi-sentences are masculine. The writer's own comment: "It's hard to make a tape about Plato sound sexy. So I infused the letter with testosterone—making the product a <u>mental workout</u> that leaves your mind fit, limber, ready for success."

Is a 6-page letter overkill? The percentile improvement over the previous control answers that question.

Figure 5–10. Knowledge Products

KNLR

PRESENTS

Ideas That Rocked The World

plus

an introductory offer that could shake yours

Dear Reader,

Your mind is your biggest "muscle." But if you don't exercise it regularly, it can get flabby. Out of shape. Old before its time.

Introducing The Audio Classics Series®: History's greatest thinkers, ideas and events on audiocassette. Simply by listening, you get a stimulating "mental workout" guaranteed to keep your wits sharp. Your mind limber. Your thinking flexible.

You are invited to try the first two cassettes for just $1.00 (a $14.95 value) -- starting with your choice of The Giants of Philosophy, The Giants of Political Thought or The World's Political Hot Spots.

It's just like having a personal trainer for your mind!

The day your introductory cassettes arrive, pop one in the player and see what happens.

Confronted with new and intriguing ideas, you'll begin to feel prodded and provoked. Stirred and inspired. Challenged. Surprised. Entertained. Educated. In fact, you may not have felt this stimulated in years!

All for just one dollar.

(over, please ...)

An inspired way to sell literary classics.

(Continued)

But that's only the beginning ...

Listen to your two introductory tapes and discover how the ideas of the past continue to shape our world today.

You will be amazed at how simple these concepts really are. How clearly they can be communicated. How colorful they become when presented by skilled narrators, professional actors, world-renowned journalists.

It's the thoroughly modern way to "read" those great books you wish you'd studied in college!

And it's so easy!

Start now with your first two tapes for just $1.00.

You're spared the dense prose of the original treatises. Each Audio Classics recording is a clear, intelligent, tightly edited presentation of the important ideas and significant quotations.

You go right to the significant material with no background courses required.

Best of all, The Audio Classics Series transforms "downtime" into the highlight of your day.

> "I drive 65 miles (one way) to college after working the midnight-to-dawn shift. Your tapes keep me wide awake and alert for the whole trip. I not only learn important things during otherwise wasted driving time, but I arrive at class with fully focused thinking ... One remaining problem: How do I shut off your contagious excitement about ideas so that I can catch some sleep?"
>
> -- Ross Barlow, Russell, PA

To receive your two tapes for just $1.00 (a $14.95 value), just tell us which of these three themes intrigues you most:

THE GIANTS OF PHILOSOPHY

Stand face to face with Plato, the first great philosopher of Western thought. You will see meaning for your own life in Plato's famous dialogues dealing with timeless issues like law and justice. Perception and reality. Death and the soul. Mind and body. Reason and passion. The nature of love.

Actor Charlton Heston, renowned for his roles in historical films, brings Plato's ancient wisdom to fresh, new life on two long-playing tapes.

(Continued)

-3-

"The Great Books continue to gather dust on my shelves, but the tapes are consumed as soon as they arrive, and then reviewed from time to time (mostly in my car.)"

-- Lewis Flagg III, Milford, MA

Future tapes in the Series will bring you into the presence of Aristotle and St. Thomas Aquinas ... Spinoza and Schopenhauer ... Kant and Kierkegaard ... Nietzsche, Dewey, Sartre and others to explore the meaning of pragmatism. Existentialism. Making choices and living with purpose. The nature of evil. Reason and perception.

Or ...

THE GIANTS OF POLITICAL THOUGHT

Cross ideological swords with men whose writings stirred our forefathers to revolution. Narrated by Craig Deitschmann, two of the most enduring documents in American history spring to life in the introductory tapes.

Tom Paine's Common Sense became the best-selling pamphlet in American history, converting thousands to the idea of independence. Six months later, Thomas Jefferson summed up the philosophy and ideas behind the American Revolution in one brilliantly worded document, The Declaration of Independence. Take a fresh look at such fundamental concepts as natural rights; government by consent; the social contract; much more.

"The tapes have reshaped my political philosophy and added to the arsenal needed to carry on an intelligent conversation or debate."

-- Jeff Wright, Dallas, TX

Engage the world's greatest thinkers in lively debate. Tapes in this Series will introduce you to political theorists whose ideas are more relevant than ever, including Thoreau, Machiavelli, Marx, Hobbes, Locke, Tocqueville and more.

Or ...

THE WORLD'S POLITICAL HOT SPOTS

Gain insight and perspective on Middle Eastern politics as you plunge headlong into one of the most volatile areas on Earth. Guided by the late Harry Reasoner, co-anchor of 60 Minutes and one of America's most distinguished journalists, you will go back 2,500 years to probe the historical, political, religious and ideological underpinnings of today's raging Middle East conflict.

(over, please ...)

(Continued)

"Knowledge Products is putting me back in touch with history. Your tapes are unique, a new way of learning ... Listening to them is the easiest and most entertaining way I've ever learned anything ... I can feel myself there! (Sometimes I take notes.) Your tapes are filling in the gaps in my sketchy historical background. Thank you for dusting off the archives."

-- James O. Roberson, Williamston, NC

Future tapes in the Series will take you behind the scenes to explore the conflicts in South Africa, Central America, Germany, Ireland, Cuba, the Philippines, the Soviet Union, China, Poland and the Eastern Bloc, and other places in the nightly news.

GET A CLASSICAL EDUCATION IN YOUR CAR!

Let's face it, most of us don't have time to read the books we'd like to on history, economics, philosophy, political theory.

But our interest in ideas remains as strong as ever.

The Audio Classics Series was created for busy professionals who profit from ideas, but don't have time to read. This unique program lets you acquire a classical education effortlessly ... simply by listening.

Since your introductory selection is just $1.00, why hesitate a moment longer? There will never be a better time to try The Audio Classics Series.

You'll become a valued participant in intelligent conversation. At times you can't anticipate, an idea will bubble to the surface ... invade your thoughts ... influence what you do and say.

Once you start listening, you'll realize how much you've learned, and how much more you'll have to contribute.

ENTERTAINING ... EXCITING ... ENLIGHTENING

Unlike ordinary recordings, The Audio Classics Series offers lively, dramatic presentations with many different actors' voices on a single tape.

Multiple voices add drama ... excitement ... entertainment. You'll feel like you are there, witness to history's most memorable moments. Key quotations from the original works are skillfully woven through the recording.

(Continued)

-5-

"I expected an abridged delivery of the text. What I got was far better: a discussion of the background and relevance of the work, plus selections from the original. I've gained enlightenment and understanding of subjects I knew very little about. I often quote ideas and concepts I've learned from listening to the tapes."

-- Thomas M. Trent, Boise, ID

The tapes are professionally scripted by historians, academicians and independent scholars who have that rare talent for making the material accessible and enjoyable.

OPEN YOUR MIND TO THE POSSIBILITIES

For a token $1.00, we will send you the first two tapes in your choice of The Giants of Philosophy or The Giants of Political Thought or The World's Political Hot Spots. In future selections in the Series, you can look forward to:

* reliving the creation and adoption of The United States Constitution (narrated by Walter Cronkite) -- from the fiery debates and back room deals in Philadelphia in 1787 to the ratification process to the Bill of Rights and Amendments we still struggle with today.

* discovering the roots of crisis and conflict in The United States at War (narrated by George C. Scott), a stirring dramatization of the political, social and economic forces behind the American Revolution through Vietnam.

* exploring The Great Economic Thinkers (narrated by Louis Rukeyser). You'll hear the ideas of Adam Smith, John Maynard Keynes, Friedrich Hayek and others ... as you explore economic ideas from 18th Century classical theory through modern-day monetarism and supply side economics.

SAVE HUNDREDS OF DOLLARS

The Audio Classics Series is the most affordable ongoing education, starting with two long-playing cassettes for just $1.00. You'll save hundreds of hours and hundreds of dollars.

Each extra long-playing cassette is up to 50% longer than the kind sold in stores. Each monthly 2-cassette album provides up to three hours of engrossing entertainment.

"Terrific! And considering the work that has obviously gone into them, a great bargain. The analysis is sound

(over, please ...)

(Continued)

and scholarly, the voice characterizations are superb, and the dramatizations give me a clear mental picture of the authors."

-- Murray Sayle, Kanagawa Ken, Japan

Tapes arrive in handsome, durable albums (two tapes per album) to keep them organized and handy in your listening library.

SAY "YES" TO THIS SPECIAL INTRODUCTORY OFFER

Give your mind an exhilarating workout. Send for your two long-playing tapes for just $1.00, plus shipping and handling.

The choice is yours: Start with The Giants of Philosophy or The Giants of Political Thought or The World's Political Hot Spots.

If you love what you hear, we will keep a steady flow of stimulating ideas coming for as long as you like, at the rate of one album (two new cassettes) a month. We'll bill your credit card just $14.95 per album, plus shipping and handling. There's no minimum purchase required and you may cancel at any time.

You know what a good workout does for your body. Now imagine what The Audio Classics Series can do for your mental prowess. Please mail the enclosed card today, or call toll-free 1-800-264-6441 right now.

To your expanded mind!

Crom Carmichael

Crom Carmichael, President

P.S. Soon after Justice Oliver Wendell Holmes retired, his legal secretary, Dean Acheson, came to read to him. Holmes chose Plato's Symposium. When Acheson asked why they should take that as their text, the Judge replied, "To improve our minds, sonny." To improve your mind, say "YES" to The Audio Classics Series 2-for-$1.00 introductory offer today.

Mailer:	**Modern Telephones**
Key Words:	**"It's 3:45 P.M."**
Writer:	**Tony Barnard**

The Challenge

In an era of super-long letters, getting response from a half-page letter is indeed a challenge.

The Implementation

Contemporary writers are disinclined to condense. This writer bucked the trend and achieved what many longer letters could not achieve—complete readership of the message. The illustration at the top of the page explains, prior to text, what the letter represents—a telephone conferencing system.

(As you can see, the letter was sent to prospects in the U.K.)

Comment

Can a U.S. writer create a message U.K. readers will accept? Why not? This brief, no-nonsense letter matches the item it is selling—a weapon to speed up business communication.

Going for the inquiry rather than the sale, a long letter probably would not have achieved the readership this one did. The writer reports that this letter well-outpulled any previous mailing for this item.

We have only one question: Mightn't a question mark at the end of the inspired overline have been in order?

Figure 5–11. Modern Telephones

It's 3:45 PM ... and a final decision is needed by 4:10 at the latest. Before you can make it, you need facts from Charles, Sidney, both Henrys and Joan.

Unfortunately . . .

Charles is poring over contracts ... Henry "one" is chin-high in dictation ... Henry "two" and Sidney are both expediting rush orders ... while Joan is frantically racing (with shoes off) toward a deadline.

So ... you simply flip 5 keys on your SPEECHMASTER for a brief three minute conference with all together (or one at a time, as you wish).

Result -- Facts obtained ... Charles, Sidney, both Henrys and Joan still rushing ahead with practically no interruption ... and your decision is made with minutes to spare.

There you have just one more problem in communications solved by a Modernphone System. For full information about solutions to all your office communication needs, just mail the post paid card above. Informative literature will reach you promptly and with no obligation, of course. Mail the card today.

Sincerely,

F.A. Boddy.
Director

Packing a super-brief letter with super-salesmanship.

Mailer: **Thompson Cigars**

Key Words: **"If I am willing to guarantee . . . Are you willing to read . . . ?"**

Writer: **John Lyle Shimek**

The Challenge

Cigar smokers tend to run on tracks. They are always willing to sample a new cigar, but only if it does not endanger their existing cigar brand.

Selling the concept this letter represents required a walking-on-eggs selling proposition in which the writer balances the appeal of a bargain coupled with a premium against a new cigar-smoking experience.

The Implementation

Recognizing the need to break an existing habit, this offer kicks the free cigars into place only after the buyer has smoked 500 of them. To soften the impact of this departure from whatever the individual may have been smoking before—including, in some cases, no cigars at all—emphasis is on $47.95 in free bonuses.

The approach is one of membership—in this case "Bonus Box Club" membership. The inclusion of a "musical calculator" is the incentive for the individual to order the first shipment of cigars.

The technique is "he-man to he-man" with phrases such as "take the bull by the horns," "getting pushed around at the cigar counter," "I have to cut my losses and cut out," and "I don't try to get a hammer-lock on my members."

Comment

The Johnson Box at the top of page 1 may overpower the attention span of some readers because it has so many numerical references. To the cigar smoker, this problem probably does not apply.

The message is a highly-convivial, me-to-you, one-cigar-lover-to-another communication.

Would the letter have been stronger without the Johnson Box on the first page? We'll never know, because of a profound edict of direct response: If it ain't broke, don't fix it.

See also Membership samples in Chapter 8. This mailing positions the offer as a "Bonus Box Club" with memberships.

Figure 5–12. Thompson Cigar Company

```
* * * * * * * * * * * * * * * * * * * * * * * * * * * *
*                                                     *
*  If I am willing -- even eager -- to send you       *
*                                                     *
*     A FREE $17.50 Piezo Electronic Lighter,         *
*                                                     *
*     50 FREE CIGARS after I've sent you five         *
*     shipments --                                    *
*                                                     *
*     -- Up to $29.50 in FREE BONUSES altogether      *
*                                                     *
*  If I am willing to guarantee you'll always         *
*  get a better cigar at a better price direct        *
*  from me here in Tampa,                             *
*                                                     *
*  If I am willing to offer you more options and      *
*  priviledges than the potentate of an emirate       *
*  to make sure you always get what you want in       *
*  a smoke,                                           *
*                                                     *
*  Are you willing to read this letter right now      *
*  and see for yourself how much you can increase     *
*  your cigar-smoking pleasure as a member of my      *
*                                                     *
*                  BONUS BOX CLUB?                    *
*                                                     *
* * * * * * * * * * * * * * * * * * * * * * * * * * * *
```

Dear Member Elect:

I know as well as you do that it doesn't take any advertising genius to give something away. But I hate to see people pushed around -- expecially at the cigar counter, and especially when they could do better somewhere else, anyway.

So I'm willing to give you -- absolutely FREE -- a $17.50 imported Piezo Electronic Lighter -- just to prove that as a member of my Bonus Box Club for more discriminating cigar smokers you don't ever have to be pushed around again.

Furthermore, after you've received 500 of the cigars of your choice -- the kind you really enjoy smoking -- I'll give

(Over, please)

"He-man to he-man," the logical pre-1990s way to sell cigars. *(Continued)*

you another 50 CIGARS FREE for staying the course, and that's the same as a 10% discount on all the cigars you've gotten so much pleasure from as a member!

> Your FREE Electronic Lighter is years ahead of any other pocket lighter on the market today. No wick. No battery. No balky, ground flint. All it ever needs is butane, which you can buy anywhere, and its tiny, almost indestructible crystals create the electric charge that gives you a quick light every time you press the thumbpiece.
>
> It's as trouble-free as the ingenuity of man can make it, and enthusiastic Electronic converts all over the country have paid $17.50 -- and often much more -- just to have this dependable, distinctive lighter. Those I've talked to say they like it better everytime they see its little lightning-bolt jet snap into action.

But you can have one FREE, yours to keep whether you decide to continue as a Bonus Box Club member or not. I'll send it to you with your first shipment of cigars -- and I'm no Indian giver. It's yours to use for thousands upon thousands of instant lights and to show with pride to smokers who are still making do with the old-fashioned kind.

Neither of us was born yesterday, and we both know nobody can stay in business very long giving away what he could just as easily be selling at a profit.

> But some of the happiest marriages I've seen in my lifetime would never have happened at all if one of the parties involved have not taken the bull by the horns and made the first smart move.

And some of the most contented cigar smokers I know would still be getting pushed around at the cigar counter, instead of smoking the kind of cigars they really wanted to smoke, if I hadn't made the first move and offered them a real worthwhile inducement like this to try the Bonus Box Club way of getting a good cigar every time.

Don't do like so many other smokers and give up in despair - because there <u>is</u> such a thing as a good cigar at a reasonable price -- even though you might have given up hope ever finding it at the stores until you got this letter. And if I thought the people who accept this offer were going to take the free lighter and then run back to the cigar store for more store-bought stogies, I'd never tempt them with something as beautiful -- and as VALUABLE -- as this lighter.

(Continued)

I'm not leading with my ace when I send you your free lighter. That's just my ante. And in order to stay in this game I have to show you a winning hand every time or the rules say you get the $17.50 ante and I have to cut my losses and cut out. I've been playing this game long enough to know I can't flash a wad and then try to bluff my way through with penny-ante smokes after that.

> In these days of sagging quality and soaring prices, and off-again-on-again shortages of everything from nails to napkins, I think you just might want to stay in this game, too. I'm betting on it.

Because if you've bought any cigars lately, you already know the one thing you can depend on is a price increase every few weeks. There are more new brands -- and more funny flavors -- than you can shake a stick at -- but no increase whatsoever in quality to go with the extra dough you have to pay for them. They still taste like they're made with cabbage leaves and last year's crop of prairie hay.

Your Bonus Box Club membership is actually your smoking security blanket. It not only guarantees you get a good cigar of your personal choice and preference it also guarantees you'll get one every time.

I don't try to get a hammer-lock on my members, either. I know how Henry Ford was willing to sell you a car in any color you wanted -- so long as it was black -- but things have come a long way since the Model T. So long as you get what you want, I'm willing to let you change your mind as often as a teen-ager in a fashion shop. For instance --

-- You can take your pick of three wrappers for your cigars -- Light Green, Medium Brown, or rich, dark Maduro. And you can let me make them for you in any one of three popular shapes. (You could spend all day and considerable money trying to do that at the cigar counter and still come away with something somebody made for somebody else's taste -- not yours).

-- You can change your choice of cigar, your choice of shape or your choice of wrapper -- any time. That's one of your membership privileges -- spelled out in advance so you'll always feel able to move freely from one kind of smoking pleasure to another.

-- You can end your membership any time -- after your first shipment of cigars or as far down the road as you want to do so -- and you can come back again after you've taken a breather with no loss of membership privileges whatsoever.

(Over, please)

(Continued)

-- AND, MOST IMPORTANT OF ALL, you can send back any box you've received -- for any reason or no reason at all -- and I'll send you a refund or give you full credit on your account, with no questions asked. If you don't like 'em you're under no obligation to keep 'em.

If I believe in my private-line, custom-made cigars enough to put a $17.50 lighter and 50 FREE CIGARS on the line and then give you enough rope to hang me with if I don't deliver, I calculate you might be game enough -- and want some good cigars bad enough -- to see if I'm talking through my hat.

You know, the man who can't control his money can't control his life, they say. And the man who can't control the kind of cigars he smokes is letting somebody else push him around, too. Most cigar smokers, I'm sorry to say, lead a hand-to-mouth existence most of the time in their search for something smokeable. They win a few -- but they lose a LOT.

As a Bonus Box Club member, all you lose is your amateur standing. You smoke the kind of superior cigars, you've been wanting to smoke, anyway, at a price that's way below what you'd pay for the same quality at the stores. You carry a Free space-age electronic lighter in your pocket that just won't quit. And I don't file and forget your membership, either. To show my appreciation for your business, you get 50 FREE CIGARS after you've received 500 as a member.

> That's up to $29.95 in FREE BONUS GIFTS for simply making sure you never get pushed around at the cigar counter again!

I'd like to send you one of these extraordinary lighters by return mail. All you need to do to own and enjoy its truly revolutionary performance is complete and mail the attached membership application. If that's pushy -- well, why not make the most of it?

Cordially,

Tom Timmins III

T. Thomas Timmins, III
Your Tampa Tobacconist

Thompson Cigar Company • 200 North Edison Avenue • Tampa, Florida 33606

Mailer: **Early Advantage**
Key Words: **"Speaking a foreign language"**
Writer: **Barbara Harrison**

The Challenge

How does one sell a $155 foreign language program to the parent of a child two to twelve years old?

The selling job is doubled because many parents regard all aspects of education as the school's job, not their own; and many others fear foreign language instruction because they feel they themselves will appear stupid to their own children.

The Implementation

This writer, through subheads, asks many of the negative questions a parent might ask, answers those questions, and verifies the answers with testimonials.

The selling argument follows a logical course, beginning with justification of the concept and concluding with a no-risk guarantee.

Comment

Big, bold subheads compartmentalize this letter to make reading easy. The "Mary R." testimonial on page 3 is inspired.

Note the P.S., an extra "kicker" which, by suggesting the parent also can begin to speak another language, not only presents a different and very effective motivator, but also unquestionably resulted in orders from adults who never would respond to a foreign language course sold on the adult level.

Figure 5–13. Early Advantage

Early Advantage®
programs for children
47 Richards Avenue
Norwalk, Conn. 06857

Speaking a foreign language is now as natural as learning to walk!

Give your child the advantage with MUZZY, the BBC's internationally-acclaimed video language course for children ages 2 to 12.

Try it RISK-FREE for 30 days!

Dear Parent,

Your child could start learning a foreign language in as little time as it takes you to read this letter!

All you need is MUZZY, the astonishing breakthrough video language course for children ages 2 to 12 from the British Broadcasting Corporation, world leaders in language education!

There's no such thing as "too young" to speak a second language. Remember the years you spent struggling over languages in school? Today even preschoolers begin speaking them spontaneously, at the touch of a VCR button. Before they can read or write!

Gone are the days of language labs, tests and study. Now even the youngest children can start speaking French or Spanish, Italian or German effortlessly with MUZZY.

> MUZZY: The BBC Language Course for Children is the award-winning program from the British Broadcasting Corporation, the world's foremost authority in language instruction. It stimulates a child's innate ability to learn languages, with spectacular results. Say "YES" and give your children the Early Advantage in school and in the world they'll grow up in.

The secret? Start early!

No one "teaches" our children English, but they all master it effortlessly. Studies in Child Language Development show that children are born with a natural ability to absorb language. Any language. This instinctive gift for languages begins to fade as children reach their teen years -- unfortunately, the age at which American schools first start teaching languages.

Now... while it's still fun for them... why not give your children the opportunity to learn a foreign language? They'll adore MUZZY today.

MZ:PI

(over, please)

Disarming objections by becoming surrogate for the parent. *(Continued)*

And thank you for the rest of their lives.

Speaking a foreign language gives your child a big advantage.

European and Asian children learn a foreign language years ahead of ours. MUZZY narrows the gap and prepares your children to compete with their accomplished international peers.

The child who is not limited to English has a distinct educational advantage. Speaking a foreign language broadens your children's horizons...trains their minds...and offers them a valuable international perspective. It makes travel more meaningful. And opens up career possibilities later on.

"Won't learning a second language confuse my preschooler?"

A child's natural language ability lets him keep the two (or more!) distinct with no difficulty. Children in bilingual homes grow up fluent in both languages. The earlier a second language is introduced, the more quickly and easily children master it.

That's the secret behind MUZZY's smashing success. You know how much they're learning, but to your little ones, fuzzy green MUZZY and the gang are just special friends who come each day to play.

> "I bought MUZZY (in French) for my daughter, who is 21 months old... she has better pronunciation of 'Bonjour,' 'Bonsoir,' and 'Merci' than I do, and I took five years of French!"
>
> -- Christopher C., Horsham, Pennsylvania

"Will MUZZY interfere with my 9-year-old's schoolwork?"

Quite the contrary! Parents tell us that MUZZY teaches their kids that learning is fun -- a lesson that carries over into their schoolwork. In fact, from what parents tell us, children involved with MUZZY become good listeners, develop excellent memories and learn to see patterns in new material -- all vital skills for academic success. When learning something new is fun from the very start, youngsters enter school with a positive attitude toward education.

"How can I teach my child French when I don't speak a word?"

You don't have to! MUZZY does it for you without "teaching." Young children don't need formal language instruction because they learn naturally...easily...intuitively...enjoyably. Simply by watching, listening and imitating, toddlers to preteens learn a foreign language by "doing what comes naturally!"

(Continued)

That's the magic of MUZZY.

The BBC Language Course for Children works beautifully without parent participation. If you can turn on the VCR, you can give your child a valuable head start.

> "My children are glued to the television and I don't mind! Please keep up the good work."
>
> -- Mary R., Rochester, Minnesota

"What if my child isn't ready for MUZZY?"

Every child is ready for MUZZY -- on his or her own terms. There's no timetable, no schedule, no syllabus to follow. Your child's own response sets the pace.

Some children want to spend time with MUZZY every day. Others are happier with an on-again, off-again, unhurried style. The Course is specifically designed to accommodate both learning styles with positive results.

One child might breeze through MUZZY in a few months, and return for "brush ups" once in a while. Another may be endlessly fascinated with the engaging characters and stories, and stay actively involved with them for years.

"Which language is easiest for my child to learn first?"

MUZZY makes them equally easy. To a child, language is natural. Even the youngest Chinese children learn to speak their language as readily as American children learn to speak English.

All things are possible when you start early.

Children use their natural "ear" for language to absorb the accent, the rhythm and the vocabulary of one language as easily as the next. And speaking a foreign language early makes it easier to learn another language later on. Parents frequently order MUZZY in another language when they see how easily their children pick up the basics of the first.

> "We are so pleased with your French language course videocassettes that we ordered last summer that now we want to order the children's Italian language course."
>
> -- Alice G., Mobile, Alabama

See impressive results. Kids start learning the very first day.

MUZZY starts working the day your BBC Language Course for Children arrives. Pop in the first videocassette and within minutes your child will be responding to cuddly MUZZY, clever Corvax, Princess Sylvia, and all the other endearing characters who bring the language to life.

(over, please)

(Continued)

Soon, you'll be wide-eyed with wonder while your child learns a foreign language he or she's never heard before.

> "All four of my children use German phrases to the astonishment of family members... It is amazing."
>
> -- Judith G., Oswego, New York

But don't take our word for how good MUZZY is -- see for yourself. You're invited to try MUZZY without risk for 30 days, in your own home.

Convenient payment plan plus our NO-RISK Guarantee.

The complete BBC Language Course for Children (4 videocassettes plus 2 audiocassettes, Storybook, Activity Book, Parents' Guide and sturdy storage portfolios) is just $159 plus shipping and handling. To get started, simply mail the enclosed order card or call toll-free: 1-800-367-4534 today. You may pay by credit card in five equal monthly installments, if you prefer.

> If you and your children are not thrilled with MUZZY, you may return it within 30 days for a prompt refund. You don't risk a penny!

But please don't wait for our schools to do the job, or you'll miss the critical "window of opportunity" that makes language learning so easy and natural.

Your child is now the perfect age for MUZZY. I urge you to send for it today.

Sincerely,

David S. Ward
Director

P.S. Special bonus for parents! While The BBC Language Course for Children was designed for ages 2-12, many parents end up speaking the language too. They pick it up simply by hearing their children chattering away with MUZZY in French, Spanish, Italian or German. Order the language of your choice by calling toll-free: 1-800-367-4534 today.

MZ:PI

Mailer: **Nature's Blooms**
Key Words: **"Use the private discount certificate"**
Writer: **Eugene Povskadovski**

The Challenge

In the crowded field of flowers by mail and phone, a new company can't just say, "We are here, too." The company must establish a competitive and comparative advantage.

The challenge is compounded by the very local nature of most flora decisions. Those who give flowers often have established a relationship with a local florist which transcends both price considerations and variety—two of the major advantages flowers-by-mail companies offer.

The third advantage—delivery to distant areas—is as competitive a facet of business as any florist, local or mail order, faces.

The Implementation

Three key words describe the implementation of this answer to the challenge. The three words appear in this line above the greeting: "Private Discount Certificate." Each of those three words combats a different aspect of competition.

Each of the subheads in this letter re-emphasizes the singularity of the company as the source.

The P.S. adds yet another benefit—a crystal candle holder—for multiple orders.

Comment

By immediately emphasizing the "private discount certificate" rather than the selection of flowers, the company positions itself differently from others whose sales thrust leans on floral beauty. This gains a competitive edge with one echelon of buyers.

The five-word second paragraph adds another dimension to the competitive position through the positive statement that these flowers are fresher than any the buyer could find elsewhere.

The entire letter underscores the difference between Nature's Blooms and other flower providers.

Figure 5–14. Nature's Blooms

Use the Private Discount Certificate I've enclosed to save a lot on your Holiday flowers!

Welcome to Nature's Blooms

A Happy Greeting from Our World of Flowers!

Before you look at the glorious flowers in this Holiday Brochure to make your choices, I want to be sure you understand the difference between these and any flowers you may have bought before.

In two words: Fresh cut.

Oh, I know everyone who sells flowers uses the word fresh. But fresh is relative... and proof is easy for us. If you order a dozen Nature's Blooms long-stem roses or a Nature's Blooms Christmas Bouquet, you never have to worry that three or four days later they'll already start to wilt.

So if, for example, you order flowers to be delivered at the beginning of the Holidays you know those flowers will still be big, bright, and beautiful for days to come. (That's especially true if you use as directed the two special Elite Chrysal food packages we enclose at no extra charge and follow our simple instructions for flower care.)

Don't compare Nature's Blooms with flowers you might get from a conventional source. This is a whole new experience—the 21st century way of assuring yourself you'll get the very freshest flowers anyone could ever buy!

Nature's Blooms ships flowers within about 48 hours after they've been cut. I don't mean 48 hours after we have them on our premises; I mean 48 hours after they've been cut. That's a big difference. Quickly, they're on their way to you or the person to whom you're sending them, including flowers imported from overseas. Nobody gets them faster than that.

And freshness is just the beginning. Please read on.

Your TERRIFIC Holiday Buy! Believe It Or Not...

"Private discount" establishes a competitive advantage. *(Continued)*

Nature's Blooms is a direct source of flowers. That should have terrific significance to you, because it means you don't have those middle-men markups you get when you go through the conventional wholesaler/retailer chain. In fact, many florists buy the same flowers at your price... then mark them up. These florists aren't doing their customers a disservice. Rather, they're assuring their customers fresh flowers. But you have the best of all prices.

And your best price is about to get even better!

I've enclosed a special Private Discount Certificate. Believe it or not, you can have the world's freshest Holiday floral assortments for even less than the incredibly low prices in your personal copy of the direct buy brochure I've enclosed.

Here's how it works:

If you order before November 15th, deduct 15% from the price of every bouquet or assortment you order. So if a bouquet is $29.00, you pay just $24.65, plus shipping. If you order the huge five-bunch assortment, our gigantic King of Christmas flowers, instead of $47.00 (one of the most sensational bargains in Holiday flowers you'll see this year), your price is just $39.95 plus shipping.

If you order between November 15th and November 25th, deduct 10% from the price of every bouquet or assortment you order. So if you order the Chinese Carnations (one of the most beautiful bouquets that ever will have graced your home), instead of the marvelously low $29.00 price you pay just $26.10 plus shipping.

If you order between November 25th and December 10th, even though we're getting close to Christmas you can deduct 5% from the price of every bouquet or assortment you order. So the magnificent $32.00 Dutch Bouquet costs you just $30.40 plus shipping.

> And these extra discounts are yours for every item you order. Send Nature's Blooms flowers to your family, your friends, your business associates... to every name on your list... and save a bundle while delighting them all.

After December 10th, for orders received up to 3 pm Eastern time December 22nd, we'll guarantee delivery on the day you specify, even December 23rd. (And don't forget the New Year as another ideal time to send flowers.) Guaranteed delivery is just one of the Nature's Blooms Guarantees I'll tell you about in a moment.

How We Ship (You'll REALLY Be Delighted!):

Flowers are our only business, and we're the best in the business... which we wouldn't be if we didn't handle your order the way you want it

(Continued)

handled. Believe me, you'll be pleased!

Let's suppose that on November 5th, you order four bouquets, all to be delivered December 23rd.

You can be absolutely 100% positive all four will be delivered December 23rd. If you want a gift card enclosed, every one will have the proper handwritten gift card you've asked for. And every one will be as fresh as any flowers ever delivered and put into a vase.

How can I be so sure? For three reasons: First, our order department is the most modern in the world of flowers. All orders are computerized, with backup to prevent problems.

Second, in our cool room every single flower has to pass an inspection... and this inspection not only takes place within just a few hours after the flower arrives, it s also just a few hours before we ship it to you.

Third, we ship every flower bouquet order by FedEx, the overnight courier service. Imagine the joy and happiness you'll create when the delivery truck pulls into a driveway (that's excitement right there!) and the uniformed driver delivers the attractive Nature's Blooms box, with each flower carefully and perfectly nestled in place.

Shipping our fresh cut flowers by FedEx assures us of being able to offer the absolute Guarantee I'm about to describe.

Your Ironclad 100% Guarantee of Satisfaction

Our Guarantee is unique in the world of flowers. We don't just guarantee the freshness of our flowers. (That's easy, because we ship your flowers within 48 hours after they ve been cut... and sometimes even quicker.) We also guarantee delivery on the day they're promised.

This means you can order early, with supreme confidence. You say it isn't for Holiday delivery, but an anniversary in November or a birthday in January? Take advantage of your early-order discount right now and rest easy, because your flowers will be delivered on the day you specify. We don't miss. (Your account won't be charged until we ship.)

And if, for any reason whatever, you aren't totally delighted, the flowers are on us, along with our sincere apologies. But obviously we don't think this will happen... and after you've sent a few Nature's Blooms flower gifts or ordered some for yourself, you won't think so either.

The Superb Difference

Your name didn't come to us by accident. This private invitation to become a Nature's Blooms customer is going out to you because we think

(Continued)

you're the kind of thoughtful, sophisticated individual who recognizes the emotional value of beautiful flowers.

I'm sure, then, that if only because of your social position, from time to time you've ordered and perhaps received flowers "long distance' either by phone or from a local florist, to be delivered by another florist in a different city.

So you're at the mercy of that second florist, who may or may not have in stock the flowers you've asked for. It's really a game of Russian Roulette.

But not when you're doing business with Nature's Blooms. We ship direct. We don't ever ship flowers that have been lying around for a couple of days. The superb difference, and I certainly hope you'll let me prove this to you, is unbelievable freshness at an unbelievable direct price.

I hope that being able to depend on an unbreakable guarantee means something to you, especially as we approach the Holiday Season. We want to be your flower company... and we sincerely want to have the opportunity to show you why getting your flowers from always-dependable Nature's Blooms makes sense for you.

So this Holiday Season, may your home be ablaze with the color only pretty flowers can add. May your family and friends admire their delightful holiday flowers and your thoughtfulness for sending such bright enviromentally friendly gifts. And may Nature's Blooms provide that Holiday loveliness for you!

With thanks for your interest,

Henri Moed

Henri Moed

P.S. Order two bouquets or more and we'll send you a genuine Mikasa Pierpont crystal candle-holder, a $12.95 value, absolutely free. Call our Order Hotline 1-800-947-9700 or fax your order direct: 305-591-6564. Operators are on hand 24 hours a day, 7 days a week.

Mailer: **Omaha Steaks International**

Key Words: **"A Private Message to a Very Special Person"**

Writer: **Herschell Gordon Lewis**

The Challenge

How does one sell filets, shipped from a distant source, for a price far higher than the gourmet section of any local supermarket or even hand-cut meat markets?

The answer lies in an obvious bit of human psychology: Anything we buy is what it is plus what we think it is. Spending more money for Omaha Steaks is just as logical as spending more money for a designer-label suit—provided the prospective buyer shares that point of view.

So the challenge is to give these steaks a proper cachet.

The Implementation

The letter brings three facets of exclusivity into sync: The first is the status bestowed on the recipient of the message, "This private invitation is going to just a handful of the millions and millions of people in America." The second is the product itself, positioned as the elite among steaks. The third is the company making the offer, which in itself adds stature to the steaks.

Instead of underscoring the expense, the letter underscores the discount from "the usual price."

In keeping with proper marketing procedures for offers based on exclusivity, this one includes an expiration date.

Comment

As of this writing, the "A Private Message to a Very Special Person" Omaha Steaks letter has been the control for about 11 years and has won a number of industry awards.

Letter 5–15a is the original letter, written in the mid-1980s. Letter 5–15b is an updated version from the year 1995. The differences are two: (1) elimination of some of the background and the "down-home" terminology; and (2) the addition of a premium.

The revised version of the letter is somewhat shorter than the original, because the company, over the years, sophisticated its image, which made some of the personal references obsolete.

Figure 5–15a. Omaha Steaks

A Private Message to a Very Special Person

Dear Friend,

This private invitation is going to just a handful of the millions and millions of people in America. You're one of that handful.

Why you?

Because we have some high-powered experts in what we call our Market Research Department. Their job is to select individuals whose lifestyles entitle them to this invitation. It's a very short list -- - and you're on it.

Why I'm Writing to You

Being on that elite list means a lot around here. It means you're someone who travels, eats in fine restaurants --- and appreciates the difference between dinner at a four-star restaurant and a hamburger on the run.

> You know, of course, it isn't unusual to pay a day's wages for a steak dinner. Fine, corn-fed beef is impossible to find in many areas. We at Omaha Steaks International know this well, because many of the most famous restaurants in the nation buy their gourmet steaks from us.

I'm writing to invite you to have those same gourmet steaks --- steaks you never on earth could get at any supermarket, steaks most restaurants can't even buy because there just aren't enough of them to go around. I want you to try some of our Special Filet Mignons, and I'm prepared to do what I have to do to convince you they're the gourmet treat of your lifetime.

In brief, so you'll know what I'm talking about:

Six (6 oz.) Omaha Steaks Filets, flash frozen, packed with dry ice, and shipped to you in our marvelous reusable container, are regularly $52.95. I've enclosed a discount check, good as cash for $23.00, which means the steaks are yours for an introductory offer price of $29.95.

Why You Should Have This Experience

You probably know that Omaha is one of the world's top meat processing centers. My family has been in this business for generations.

This original Omaha Steaks letter from the mid-1980s established the company's reputation for exclusivity and the personal touch—an image that was updated for the '90s (fig. 5–15b).

(Continued)

Back in 1917 --- almost 70 years ago --- we started separating our very best steaks from the rest. Then, as now, these steaks were a very small percent of the beef we or anyone else handled.

We sold these steaks to a couple of the swanky restaurants in Omaha. Now, bear in mind: this is right in the heart of meat-packing country, where a good restaurant could deal with anybody and try to bargain for prices way below what other restaurants paid.

> These supreme-quality steaks cost more than the restaurants had been paying. You know what? We couldn't find enough of them to satisfy the demand. Why? Because time after time, the restaurant owner told us, "My patrons say they never in their lives had a steak like this. They'll give their right arm for them."

Word got around soon enough, and before long we expanded to serve some of the great restaurants in America. We still do.

Naturally, individuals began asking for our steaks by name. That's how we began sending steaks direct, and I can tell you that our list of customers is a real Who's Who.

What Can You Expect?

First of all, our steaks look marvelous, as well they should. Line one up alongside an ordinary filet and you'd have to be blind not to see the difference in beautiful marbling, close, hand trimming and sturdy, vacuum packaging. It's like putting an elegant limousine alongside a stripped-down economy car.

But the real test "is in the eatin'." If you're serving to guests, surprise them: for the first time in their lives, they'll have steak --- with no steak-knives. They can use their butter-knives or their forks, because that's just how tender an Omaha Steaks Filet Mignon is.

When good beef is naturally aged, it turns out just that tender. The reason you'll rarely find naturally aged beef is that it takes time. There's no way around it. It requires 21 days. And during the process, the beef must be maintained at a very exact temperature. Most beef suppliers are in too much of a hurry to bother with slow and natural aging. That's why the melt-in-your mouth tenderness of these Filet Mignons will amaze you. You rarely, if ever, get such a treat.

Ah, but now the ultimate way of judging: the taste. Here's where I'm out of words, because until you've actually had one of these filets any description will seem like a lot of bragging, and after you've had one no words are necessary other than, "See?"

It's the corn feeding, along with the natural aging, that sets these steaks apart from the beef available for mass consumption through supermarkets and most butcher shops. Corn feeding beef gives the meat a wonderful interior marbling. The marbling dissolves during cooking.

(Continued)

It makes the meat sensationally juicy ... with a flavor you'll crave once you've tasted it! It's very possible that Omaha Steaks is your only dependable source for beef of this quality.

This corn-fed beef is chosen with the care you'd give to a lifetime treasure. (That's what it is, to us, because our reputation is right on the line with every single Omaha Steaks Filet Mignon.)

A GUARANTEED Steak? You're Kidding!

When I tell folks we guarantee our steaks, I often hear, "How in the world can you do that? Your customers can't return any steaks because they eat them."

Well, I certainly hope you eat them, but that doesn't affect our Guarantee.

Just about every guarantee you've ever seen includes the word "return." You have to return the merchandise, or the unused portion, or whatever, in order to get your money back. Not ours! You can keep the remaining steaks and still get your money back.

Look:

> I'm asking you to try our steaks. You didn't ask me. I know it's up to me to make this so attractive to you that you can't have an excuse not to try them! So here's my offer:
>
> Order your steaks. You'll get them in perfect condition, shipped in a container you can reuse for years, when you go on picnics or take an automobile trip or spend a day at the beach or decide to visit someone and bring the steaks with you (they'll be talking about it for weeks). I'll include a copy of our Cookbook, yours to keep. It's loaded with tips most cooks don't know about. Your steaks will be registered by actual serial number; in fact, you'll get a numbered Certificate verifying the Gold Seal of Approval.

All right, you have your steaks. Now what?

Invite someone very, very important to dinner. Or wait for a special occasion, like a birthday or an anniversary. Or just sit down to enjoy the best steak dinner of your life.

Here's my Guarantee:

> After you've had your steak dinner, whether that dinner meant grilling one of them or all of them, if you don't agree they're the dinner experience of a lifetime, we'll refund every cent you paid. And the container and Cookbook are yours to keep, regardless.

(Continued)

You know, my friend, we're here on this earth for all too short a span. One reason I admire true individuals such as you is that you know how to live --- how to get the most out of life, how to enjoy the gentle pleasures, how to build a treasure-house of experiences you never forget.

That, really, is what I'm offering you today. You may not remember what you had for dinner the day before yesterday, but I can assure you: years from now, you'll remember your first Omaha Steak.

I think you deserve this wonderful treat. I think I've proved, by sending you this exclusive private invitation, that we at Omaha Steaks believe you should have the same fantastic steak the rich and famous enjoy.

Now it's up to you. What do you think?

Do you agree you should sample Omaha Steaks, especially since you can have them at more than 43% off the usual price? Do you agree you should give me the opportunity to prove my point: that you deserve the best, and this is it? Do you agree you can't lose, since I'm taking all the risk as proof that we do want you in the select group we regard as "family" --- those who have tasted the royalty of fine steaks?

I hope you do. I want you to taste our steaks and test my Guarantee.

I'm counting on your experiencing one of the great gourmet events of your lifetime (and perhaps the lifetimes of your fortunate guests, as well). You'll never have a better opportunity.

Sincerely,

Frederick J. Simon

Frederick J. Simon

P. S. Don't wait until the expiration date on your check is on top of you. We guarantee your satisfaction. What can you lose? Call now TOLL FREE 1-800-228-9055. (In Nebraska, call COLLECT 0-402-391-3660.)

This symbol tells you that we are members of the Direct Marketing Association, the oldest and largest trade association in its field. Founded in 1917, DMA is an organization committed to finding new and better ways to make shopping by mail pleasant, convenient and satisfying for you.

MEMBER
DIRECT MARKETING ASSOCIATION
Look for this symbol when you buy direct

G2676-0585

Figure 5–15b. Omaha Steaks

Your Reply Will Really Be Appreciated!

A Private Message To a Very Special Person

Dear Friend,

This private invitation is going out to just a handful of people, yourself included. I hope you'll accept my invitation. But even if you decide not to, I want to send you a gift... ABSOLUTELY FREE.

Yes. A 4-piece "Scissors 'N Shears" set, with extra-sharp, stainless steel blades and lightweight plastic grip handles will be delivered right to your door. This versatile, must-have set can be yours... without any obligation...simply by saying you'd like to have it!

Why I'm Writing to You

I believe you're someone who travels well, eats in fine restaurants --- and appreciates the difference between dinner at a four-star restaurant and a sandwich on the run.

You know, of course, it isn't unusual to pay a day's wages for a steak dinner. Fine, cornfed beef is impossible to find in many areas. We at Omaha Steaks International® know this well, because many of the most famous restaurants in the nation buy their gourmet steaks from us.

I'm writing to invite you to have those same gourmet steaks --- steaks you never on earth could get at any supermarket, steaks most restaurants can't even buy because there just aren't enough of them to go around. I want you to try some of our Special Filet Mignons, and I'm prepared to do what I have to do to convince you they're the gourmet treat of your lifetime.

Four (6 oz.) Omaha Steaks® Filets, flash frozen, packed with dry ice, and shipped to you in our marvelous reusable container, are regularly $49.95. I've enclosed a discount certificate, good as cash for $20.00, which means the steaks are yours for an introductory offer price of $29.95, plus $6.50 for shipping and handling. And with your purchase you'll receive FREE eight of our 4 oz. Gourmet Burgers.

Three facets of exclusivity and adroit psychology ensure response. *(Continued)*

Back in 1917, my family began selling cornfed Midwestern Beef to a couple of the swanky restaurants in Omaha.

Soon word got around about the tenderness, juiciness and flavor of Omaha Steaks®. Before long we expanded to serve some of the great restaurants in America. We still do.

Naturally, individuals began asking for our steaks by name. That's how we began sending steaks direct, and I can tell you that our list of customers is a real Who's Who.

What Can You Expect?

First of all, our steaks look marvelous, as well they should. Line one up alongside an ordinary filet and you'll instantly see the difference in beautiful marbling, close, hand trimming and sturdy, vacuum packaging. It's like putting an elegant limousine alongside a stripped-down economy car.

But the real test "is in the eatin'." If you're serving to guests, surprise them: for the first time in their lives, they'll be able to slice steaks with their forks, because that's just how tender an Omaha Steaks® Filet Mignon is.

That tenderness comes from slow, natural aging. It requires 21 days. And during the process, the beef must be maintained at a very exact temperature. Most beef suppliers are in too big a hurry to bother with aging. That's why the melt-in-your-mouth tenderness of these Filets will amaze you.

Ah, but now the ultimate way of judging a steak...taste...

It's the corn feeding, along with the natural aging, that sets these steaks apart from the beef available for mass consumption through supermarkets and most butcher shops. Corn feeding beef gives the meat a wonderful interior marbling. The marbling dissolves during cooking.

It makes the meat sensationally juicy...with a flavor you'll crave once you've tasted it!

This cornfed beef is chosen with the care you'd give to a lifetime treasure. (That's what it is, to us, because our reputation is right on the line with every single Omaha Steaks® Filet Mignon.)

(Continued)

When I tell folks we guarantee our steaks, I often hear, "How in the world can you do that? Your customers can't return any steaks because they eat them."

Well, I certainly hope you eat them, but that doesn't affect our Guarantee.

Just about every guarantee you've ever seen includes the word "return." You have to return the merchandise, or the unused portion, or whatever, in order to get your money back. Not ours! You can keep the remaining steaks and still get your money back.

So order your steaks today. You'll get them in perfect condition, shipped in a container you can reuse for years, when you go on picnics or take an automobile trip or spend a day at the beach or decide to visit someone and take the steaks with you (they'll be talking about it for weeks). I'll include a copy of our Cookbook, yours to keep. It's loaded with tips most cooks don't know about. Your steaks will be registered by actual serial number; in fact, you'll get a numbered Certificate verifying the Gold Seal of Approval.

When you order, you'll have our promise...

IF YOU'RE NOT ABSOLUTELY THRILLED WITH YOUR ORDER FROM OMAHA STEAKS® - FOR ANY REASON AT ALL - WE'LL CHEERFULLY REPLACE YOUR ORDER OR REFUND YOUR MONEY, WHICHEVER YOU PREFER.

I think you deserve this wonderful treat. I think I've proved, by sending you this exclusive private invitation, that we at Omaha Steaks® believe you should have the same fantastic steak the rich and famous enjoy.

Do you agree you should sample Omaha Steaks®, especially since you can have them at more than 40% off the usual price? Do you agree you should give me the opportunity to prove my point: that you deserve the best, and this is it? Do you agree you can't lose, since I'm taking all the risk as proof that we do want you in the select group we regard as "family" -- those who have tasted the royalty of fine steaks?

I hope you do. I want you to taste our steaks and test my Guarantee.

(Continued)

I'm counting on your experiencing one of the great gourmet events of your lifetime (and the lifetimes of your fortunate guests, as well). You'll never have a better opportunity.

Sincerely,

Frederick J. Simon
President, Gourmet Division

P.S. Act now and enjoy 4 (6 oz.) Filet Mignons for the special introductory price of $29.95. Plus you'll also receive 8 of our fabulous Ground Gourmet Burgers FREE. (Sorry, only one package of Filets at this special price. But you may order a second package of 4 (6 oz.) Filet Mignons for just $39.95, and we'll send you 8 more FREE burgers, still a bargain.) Don't wait until the expiration date on your certificate is on top of you. We guarantee your satisfaction. What can you lose? Call now TOLL FREE 1-800-228-9055.

PLEASE...THIS SPECIAL OFFER IS FOR YOU AND YOU ALONE.
IF YOU ARE NOT INTERESTED, DO NOT PASS IT ON.

P.P.S. Remember, a versatile, 4-piece "Scissors 'N Shears" set will also be delivered right to your door FREE. Even if you decide not to place your order for luscious, fork-tender Omaha Steaks® right away, the set is yours FREE. If you place your order by the date shown on the enclosed insert, you will also receive a terrific travel alarm. Read about both of these great gifts on the insert included in this mailing.

This symbol tells you that we are members of the Direct Marketing Association, the oldest and largest trade association in its field. Founded in 1917, DMA is an organization committed to finding new and better ways to make shopping by mail pleasant, convenient and satisfying for you.

Look for this symbol when you buy direct

G5316-0193

Mailer: **Harrington's**

Key Words: **"Receive free gifts"**

The Challenge

How does a company not as well-known as Omaha Steaks market gourmet-quality meats competitively?

The second challenge is to educate the reader—or, rather, to *seem to* educate the reader—about the benefits of "Traditional cooking here in Vermont."

The Implementation

The letter uses two highly-professional techniques to sell boneless ham and turkey breast. The first is incentive—discount plus a free package of country bacon and wedge of cheese. The second is a cluster of testimonials.

This letter sells geography as much as it does gourmet foods. Notice the series of short, one or two sentence paragraphs. These contribute mightily to ease of readership.

Comment

Compare this letter with the Omaha Steaks letter. The terminology of the Harrington's letter is less emotional (witness the first word "Receive" instead of the more down-to-earth "get").

The letter becomes credible not only because of its plethora of specifics, but also because of the quiet multiple references to a venerable history and corporate credentials.

Figure 5–16. Harrington's

HOME OFFICE &
SMOKEHOUSES
MAIN STREET
RICHMOND, VT 05477

TELEPHONE
800-639-8114
FAX: 802-434-3166

Receive FREE gifts when you accept this invitation
to an extraordinary new dining experience.

Dear Friend:

You're someone who appreciates fine dining.

Like you, our customers are also discriminating fine food lovers. But since we couldn't find your name on our lists, I'm sending you the enclosed certificate to introduce you to the unique pleasures of Vermont's cuisine.

Traditional cooking here in Vermont preserved old English household recipes and adopted Native American ways of cooking meats. And corncob-smoked meats became a local specialty.

> For more than 100 years, Harrington's has been smoking meats over corncob and maplewood embers according to a well guarded formula that was learned directly from Native Americans.

Harrington's cob-smoked meats have been the first choice for traditional New England tables for over a century. And now you can enjoy the same superb dining pleasure in your home, at a low, introductory price and receive free gifts too!

> I invite you to use the enclosed $20 certificate toward the Harrington's Buffet Package of a 2 lb. boneless ham and a 2-1/2 lb. boneless turkey breast (both fully cooked).You have my personal, unconditional guarantee of your complete satisfaction.

Return the certificate with your order and this package of gourmet quality meats that's regularly $49.95 costs you only $29.95, a saving of over 40%!

And as our way of saying thank you for ordering, we'd like to send FREE gifts along with your order. Just check off the box on your certificate and you'll receive FREE:

> a half-pound of Harrington's delectable corncob-smoked, sliced country bacon that will spoil you for ordinary bacons and a 6 oz. wedge of aged, zesty cheddar made our way especially for us.

The 2 lb. boneless "mini" ham is fully cooked and extra lean, with the exquisite flavor of cob-smoking in every bite. Slice and serve at room temperature for buffet sandwiches, or warm and slice for a dinner entree. We doubt there will be any leftovers, but, if there are, dice and add to your favorite soup. Either way-

WITH SHOPS IN
SHELBURNE, STOWE, MANCHESTER & RICHMOND, VERMONT
GREENWICH & WESTPORT, CONNECTICUT • WELLESLEY, MASSACHUSETTS

Lots of specifics, short paragraphs, and a cluster of testimonials build credibility. *(Continued)* you'll enjoy simple culinary elegance that you'll be proud to share with family and friends.

And you'll discover the same honest goodness of Vermont old-style cooking in every savory morsel of corncob-smoked, juicy and delicate turkey breast too. The boneless turkey breast comes fully cooked and ready for carving.

Our unhurried, old-fashioned way of curing and smoking ham, bacon, and turkey is still the best way to get a captivating, natural smoky flavor that's mildly sweet and consistent from bite to bite.

After curing and smoking, a Harrington's ham or turkey breast weighs the same as it did before. Since there's no water added, or needed, you get naturally moist, succulent meat that's fork tender and supremely delicious!

We sell only through our own stores and catalog, and mail offers like this one, but not in other stores or under different labels. We won't risk our reputation. (What would our customers think who give Harrington's meats as gifts?)

If you're acquainted with Vermont pride and old-fashioned honesty, you know what I mean. Harrington's has always been a family-owned business. For us, independence is the bottom line. Independence from the pressures of "parent" corporations.

And independence lets us pay attention to the details, because quality depends on it.

Two midwestern prime meat packers select hams for us from their best grain-fed stock. We take only the hams of eight-month old pigs (up to 180 lbs.) instead of large 500 lb. hogs, so we can start off with a product that's naturally tender and savory.

Our famous, golden young turkeys come from Colorado where they're specifically bred for us and grain-fed for their tenderness and delicate texture.

In our smokehouse each ham or turkey must pass our strict inspections, or we just won't use it.

Harrington's may seem more expensive than the big name brands. Even more than those "premium" imported canned hams.

But who hasn't bought one of those brands and found not a ham, but pieces of hams packed together? Lots of fat and waste, or no uniformity in flavor or texture? And "water added," as much as 35%? The real cost per pound is staggering.

(Continued)

Many of those name-brands with the big processing plants take meats that we wouldn't hesitate to discard, and they run them through vaporized liquid smoke. In and out in 30 seconds! Yet all the while...

> up here in rural Vermont, in our smokehouse, we're still smoking only the choicest, leanest hams and turkeys slowly over corncob and maplewood embers, the same way Native Americans did!

A generation ago someone suggested to Luke Harrington that if he moved out of his old country smokehouse and into a modern plant in a city, he could "do better and do more business."

In typical Vermont manner, Luke said, "I could do more business, but I don't think I could do better."

Well, Harrington's has had to expand seven times since then, but we're still out in the country. And we still don't think we could do better. And that's what our customers tell us:

> "Your wonderful ham and smoked turkey were the best meats I have ever eaten." Nancy Ann Larson, Polson, Montana

> "Tastes like real old time HAM, not some modern day, hurry-up substitute." Edith L. Stacey, Twin Falls, Idaho

> "It was the absolutely BEST ham. Every last bite was delicious and it had the least waste of any ham I have ever eaten."
> Helen Alexander Williams, Phoenix, Arizona

That's why we still adhere to the old Native American formula and Luke's cure which uses maple syrup as a key ingredient!

We do use modern technology but only to help our Smokemaster control the formula. He applies it on a scale far greater than Native Americans or even Luke Harrington could have imagined.

Harrington's money-back guarantee of satisfaction

You can be certain each ham or turkey we ship is as perfect as nature and man can make them. Minimum fat. Trimmed to the lean. Virtually no waste. Consistent flavor, delicious, and tender throughout. A pleasure to the palate. And guaranteed.

(Continued)

Try Harrington's ham and turkey breast and ask yourself if they're simply the best you've ever had-without any reservations. If the answer is no, just tell us. There's nothing to return. Keep the free gifts and enjoy them. We'll promptly refund every cent you paid.

To enjoy the introductory, money-saving Buffet Package and the free gifts of specially aged cheddar and the best breakfast bacon available anywhere, complete the order form and return it along with the certificate. (Free gifts must ship with the Buffet Package.)

Please indicate your credit card information, or include payment for the balance of $29.95 plus $6.95 postage and handling per Buffet Package. (Limit two at this special price.)

Why not act today on this rare, limited-time opportunity? If you put it off, the expiration date could come and go without being noticed until it's too late. (See expiration date on the certificate.)

For faster service on credit card orders, call 1-800-639-8114 (ask for Ext. #3). And you'll soon be savoring the world's most superb turkey and ham.

Sincerely,

Peter Klinkenberg

Peter Klinkenberg

President

P.S. You can make certain that you'll receive FREE Harrington's delectable bacon and zesty, aged cheddar by checking off the box for these gifts on the certificate.

Mailer: **Vita-Mix Corporation**
Key Words: **"The fastest indicator"**

The Challenge

Every department store sells vacuum cleaners. Every discount store sells vacuum cleaners. How, then, can a marketer sell vacuum cleaners by mail?

In a store, an individual can test the suction power, check the weight and heft, and choose from a number of models. In the mail, only a description can sell a vacuum cleaner.

The mail marketer has another barrier: When someone comes into a store to look at vacuum cleaners, that person obviously is predisposed to consider looking at a vacuum cleaner. The mailing catches the reader unaware.

So what does an astute marketer do?

The Implementation

This letter uses multiple touchstones to justify the uniqueness of the Vita-Vac. Each employee quotes a different allergy. One suggests an asthma attack; another suggests dirt blown out the back of a typical vacuum cleaner bag; a third comments on an allergy to cigarette smoke and mold; a fourth comments on the shedding of a Norwegian Elkhound.

In concert, these semi-testimonials can generate an image overcoming automatic rejection of the idea of buying a vacuum cleaner by mail.

Comment

This letter is a classic example of generating dissatisfaction with *any* other vacuum cleaner by attacking what appears to be a ghastly error of design—"recycling dirt and even molds from the floor right back into the air!"

To avoid a negative comparison, the letter does not quote a price, although the P.S. calls for an order. The price is left to other enclosures in the mailing. As stated elsewhere, we prefer the inclusion of the price—the most dynamic element in a mailing—in the letter. But without question, this letter does an excellent job of establishing a need that didn't previously exist.

Figure 5–17. Vita Mix Corporation

Vita-Mix® Corporation
8615 Usher Road
Cleveland, Ohio 44138
(216) 235-4840 Fax: (216) 235-3726

Dear Friend:

The fastest indicator of a poorly designed vacuum cleaner is when somebody sneezes whenever you run it. You are most certainly recycling dirt and even molds from the floor right back into the air!

Some people recognize their allergies only when their symptoms disappear by using their Vita-Vacs. When the house is "Vita-Vac" clean they no longer get those fall "colds" or "sinus attacks" that were really allergies.

The other day I asked some of our employees to write about their experiences with allergies. Sharon has severe allergies and asthma and writes:

"Have you ever had a heaviness or wheezing when you laid down to sleep? Wheezing then turns to coughing, coughing into gasping for air. This is basically what happens during an asthma attack. When you're having an asthma attack it's difficult for air to get in and even more difficult for it to be expelled, which can be a frightening experience.

"It's very important to keep the house clean and free of dust and other irritants. I never used to be able to vacuum my home, or even be in the same room when someone else was vacuuming or I would start to wheeze and cough. Standard type vacuum cleaners pick up the dirt but then that dirt is blown right back out of the bag into the air. They just recycle the dust in your home when you vacuum. After using the Vita-Vac in my home for over a year, I wouldn't want to use any other vacuum because of the benefits it's given to me and my health. It has helped me to breathe easier and feel better!"

Sandy writes: "My daughter, Cynde, has an allergy to cigarette smoke and mold. We turn on the Vita-Vac and the sniffling is gone!"

Arlene writes: "Our family had a Norwegian Elkhound that would shed her coat in two layers, first the long hairs, then the furry undercoat. This seems to go on all year. Before I got my Vita-Vac my grandson would suffer with swollen eyes and restricted breathing from the time he came to visit until he left. After I got the Vita-Vac and did a thorough cleaning before he came, my grandson never had an allergy problem at our home again. Of course, 'Freyja the dog' was relegated to the garage."

Dee writes: "Many Vita-Vac owners say they cannot be without their Vita-Vacs even a few days because of their allergies."

John says: "I only recently realized that I have allergies. The discomfort was there, but I did not know what caused it."

Vita-Vac is not the most expensive vacuum on the market, but it is the most effective. There is nothing like it! Others cannot match its ability to clean your home - all without blowing dust, dirt, filth, mite residue, and other pollutants back into the air! A sure sign of a poorly designed vac is a fine layer of dust on your furniture after you vacuum. Recycling dust and dirt

Unusual touchstones overcome objections and establish credibility. *(Continued)*

with your vacuum is poor ecology - you just don't need it! That dirt is actually more injurious and dangerous than when it was laying on the floor!

To better understand the Vita-Vac's efficiency and effectiveness - before you buy one more vacuum cleaner that performs poorly - we conducted three engineering tests on five vacs. These are: 1) a reputable and expensive upright with an external bag; 2) a popular water-filled vac; 3) a top-selling cannister; 4) an expensive air-filtration vac; and 5) our Vita-Vac.

Here are the tests:
1) Each vac lifted water up a see-through plastic pipe to test for the suction power required to dig deep into the carpet for dirt.
2) Each vac filled an eight-foot weather balloon to test for the air flow required to gather quantities of dirt.
3) Each vac sucked dense, blue smoke from a smoke bomb and blew the filtered air into a closed room to test how well each vac removes ultra-fine particles from the air.

The results? Each time our Vita-Vac significantly outperformed the other four vacuums. It had the best suction, the greatest air flow, and no smoky exhaust. So whether you want the cleanest air possible when you vacuum, or the cleanest carpets and furniture - or both, Vita-Vac outperforms four of the best-selling vacuums on the market - for less money!

Why invest thousands of dollars in carpets, furniture, and draperies, and then try to protect your investment with a poorly designed vacuum cleaner that can't even keep your home looking and smelling fresh and clean? Ordinary vacs reach surface dirt. Carpets, chairs, floors, drapes, and other surfaces may look clean, but they are not! Your vac isn't effective and you get blamed for it!

Almost every home is polluted! The pollution cycle can be broken only by actually removing those contaminants from your home. The powerful Vita-Vac seals even minute particles in its bag for safe disposal. Vita-Vac makes cleaning faster, easier, and safer, all without a haze of airborne dust!

Vita-Vac is prepared to benefit you and your household. If you experience discomfort when you vacuum, or if you just want your home to be extra clean, our Vita-Vac is for you!

Best regards,

W. Grover Barnard
President

P.S. - To answer your questions, call free - 1-800-VITA-MIX (1-800-848-2649). Or order with your credit card. We ship immediately - and pay the shipping.

P.P.S. - If in 30 days you are not completely thrilled - return the Vita-Vac and I'll refund your money!

P.P.P.S. - If you have a "clean air vac," use it and then look at the area around the bag. If there is any dust, then your vac is not a clean air vac - send it back - and order a Vita-Vac.

PRINTED IN USA XLTRVV009 7/92

Mailer: **Ruth K. Westheimer, Eroscillator**
Key Words: **"Women seem to have . . ."**
Writer: **Christina Cross**

The Challenge

Even though American society has become so exposed to four-letter words and repeated references to obscenity in all media of communication (led by television newscasts), a direct mail letter which attacks the problem of women reaching orgasm can be greeted with tremendous unease.

The challenge is less one of identifying a need than it is one of having the individual overcome the classic embarrassment that any discussion of this topic with a stranger would cause.

The Implementation

The company uses a well-known "sexologist," Ruth Westheimer, as its spokesperson. Those familiar with her broadcasts and newspaper columns have no sense of shock at the explicit language of this letter.

The marketer makes the most of selling by mail, recognizing—quite rightly—that this is not the kind of product most women would buy from a retail store even if it were on display.

Comment

We end this chapter with one of the more provocative direct mail letters we've read while compiling this collection.

The subject matter is what one would expect from "Dr. Ruth." And the approach is possible only through direct mail, using a neutral legend on the envelope (in this instance, the simple return address, "R. Westheimer").

Women who might feel diffident discussing this subject even with their very close friends have no problem ordering it through the mail. Our point in including this letter is to point out that, on a one-to-one level, straight talk will outsell teasers and hints and circumlocutions.

Figure 5–18. Dr. Ruth

DR. RUTH K. WESTHEIMER

Dear Reader:

Women seem to have no problem achieving orgasms in movies and books - fantastic, multiple ones at that. The earth moves, lights flash and the walls seem to shake almost at will.

But the truth is many women have a great variety of problems when it comes to orgasms.

Some women only rarely experience orgasms. Others come close but can't quite get there. Some never experience it. In fact, most women cannot climax simply through intercourse alone but need direct clitoral stimulation

Intercourse may be great for stimulation of the man's penis but the truth is, it's rather poorly suited for stimulating the clitoris!

Please excuse me if you're not used to the direct way in which I approach this topic, but I am always frank. It's the best way to communicate.

It has been estimated that over half the women in the United States have difficulty experiencing regular orgasms. And that holds true whether they're married or single.

Yet, for most women, the solution isn't that difficult.

On radio and television and in my column I tell women to seek professional help if they're having problems experiencing orgasm. In my private practice the advice I give to women is that they have to be able to bring themselves to orgasm before they can expect to do so with a partner. Once you know how to pleasure yourself, you can teach the art to a lover.

If you want something done right...
do it yourself!

The treatment I usually recommend is simple and almost always successful. First, learn how to masturbate. Many women really don't know how to pleasure themselves so I give them instruc-

Straight talk outsells indirection.

(Continued)

tions. And for women who would benefit from it, I prescribe the use of a vibrator which almost always works.

Self pleasuring puts you in close touch with your sexuality. It allows you the time and space you need to explore your own body, to get to know it, to experiment with those sensations which are most exciting and pleasurable to you.

As you learn to masturbate, you discover exactly what fantasies turn you on, what tempo arouses you, what kind of pressure pleases you, and where you're pleased the most.

Maybe you've been told that you don't need orgasms. That's a myth - and a very damaging one. Except in the case of serious psychological problems, almost every woman can and should be able to enjoy regular, pleasurable orgasms. They feel good...and they're good for you.

- **Orgasms provide a wonderful feeling of release.**
- They can help relieve your tension and help reduce feelings of stress and irritability.
- **For many women, the vaginal and pelvic contractions which occur with orgasms help ease menstrual cramps.**
- Others say they sleep better. More restfully. Self stimulation is sometimes prescribed for insomnia.
- **Finally, increased circulation brings a healthy, attractive glow to your complexion.**

The big trick is to be able to have an orgasm when you want one. A vibrator used during masturbation will almost always give a woman an orgasm. That doesn't mean that using your fingers or running water won't work, only that vibrators are unquestionably more effective! This is very useful, particularly for women just learning how to masturbate.

Recently, I discovered a new vibrator in France called the **Eroscillator**. Actually, it is **not** a vibrator, as it oscillates rather than vibrates. But technical details are not as important to me as the fact that the Eroscillator is more comfortable to use, absolutely safe and very, very effective!

As you look at all the materials in this envelope, you'll find a copy of a recent clinical study. It compares the various types

(Continued)

3

of vibrators now available. Read it. And you'll better understand why I recommend the **Eroscillator** to my patients. You'll discover that the women who participated in the study overwhelmingly preferred the Eroscillator.

Why do women need an Eroscillator?

- **Some women simply need extra help to achieve orgasms...or want deeper, more intense orgasms.**

- Some aren't ready to explore partnerships. Others are widowed, separated or divorced and aren't currently involved with a partner.

- **Some are sexually inexperienced and use the Eroscillator to learn more about how to stimulate their own response...and how to improve their sexual skills.**

- Others have a mate but find that sometimes his timing is off and they need extra stimulation. Or they're slow to lubricate. A leading medical newsletter recently reported that "a woman of any age requires an average thirteen minutes of arousal and direct stimulation before climaxing BUT a young man takes only about three minutes between arousal and orgasm!"

- **You might be with someone who is sick or simply tired. Or your husband or lover travels and you need sexual fulfillment while he's gone.**

- Many women use the **Eroscillator** regularly - before, during or after intercourse just because they like it...and their partners like it too.

- **Some use it only when they're alone and feel sexy. There are times when they'd rather do it themselves!**

- Others say they have great sex lives but simply enjoy the added variety and experimentation it offers!

Who uses an Eroscillator?

I asked the folks who research these things to tell me. And they said that half the women purchasing the **Eroscillator** are married. The other half single. They come from a variety of economic and educational backgrounds. Half are under 35 years old. Half over. And almost 20% are over 55.

(Over Please)

(Continued)

I think it's wonderful that so many different women are using the **Eroscillator.** It's perfectly healthy and normal to want to put more enjoyment into your sex life. Pleasure was put on earth for us to enjoy. Regardless of age or whether you're married or single, virtually everyone can learn to experience regular fulfilling orgasms...and sometimes even fantastic orgasms.

The **Eroscillator** really can make your sex life better. To my way of thinking, anything that accomplishes that goal is worth its weight in gold!

Don't just dream about having sexual fulfillment!

Do something about it! You'll find complete details about this wonderful product in the various materials contained in this mailing. The product is not a cheap sex toy. It's a therapeutic sex aid manufactured in Europe to exacting standards. I believe the **Eroscillator** is the finest mechanical aid ever developed to help you achieve easier, faster, better orgasms.

It may cost more than an ordinary vibrator..but when you think about it, the cost isn't much more than you'd spend on a romantic evening out on the town. Yet it offers you the potential of a lifetime of pleasure.

Please read all the information carefully. And then decide for yourself.

One more thing. If you need to fantasize that the reason you are ordering an **Eroscillator** is because you came to see me and I told you to use one - go ahead! Imagination is the most important tool for a good sex life. The **Eroscillat**or follows close behind.

Good reading...and good sex!

Ruth K. Westheimer

Dr. Ruth K. Westheimer

P.S. When you purchase an **Eroscillator**, you do so with my personal guarantee. Use it for a full month. Follow my instructions. And, if you are dissatisfied for any reason, whatsoever, simply return it postpaid for a full refund.

Chapter 6

Books

Ever since the Book of the Month Club invented the still-potent "loaded with incentives" direct mail sale of books in the 1930s, books have been one of the cornerstones of the direct mail industry.

The category has expanded over the decades to include audio and video recordings, computer software, and CD-ROMs—all of which are the natural descendants of the Book of the Month Club, which still maintains its position of power and respect.

Selling books by mail is not easy. The prospect has no opportunity to leaf through the pages. To the aggressive and inventive writer, this is both a challenge and an opportunity because the writer not only can leaf through the book for the buyer but can avoid those less-salesworthy areas that, in a bookstore, could kill the sale.

The successful book promotion generates a high level of excitement and never abates. This is especially true for continuity programs, in which convincing someone to say "Yes" can result in the sale of dozens of books.

Reading these letters and putting ourselves in the position of someone who not only had no prior desire to buy but had no prior knowledge of what was being sold, we can ask quite logically whether the effective book-selling writer is not practicing the height of a direct mail letter-writer's art.

Mailer: **Nightingale-Conant**
Key Words: **"Do you make these common mistakes?"**
Writer: **Bob Matheo**

The Challenge

Most people need a mammoth goad in order for them to believe they need help in interpersonal relationships, leadership, and dealing with others whether suppliers, co-workers, or their children.

It is remarkably easy, when trying to tell someone he or she may not have absolute mastery over the techniques of effective interpersonal relationships, to fall into the very trap against which the letter is trying to warn the reader—causing irritation instead of acceptance.

To generate acceptance in a single mailing is, obviously, a major challenge.

The Implementation

The longest-running ad in history, for the Sherwin Cody School of English, was headed, "Do you make these mistakes in English?"

This letter, which begins, "Do you make these common mistakes in dealing with people?" has as its remarkably clever greeting, "Fellow Human Being:" It avoids annoying the reader by use of an excellent psychological ploy—If you're one, I'm one, too.

The letter uses a contemporary technique to sell a book that has been around since the 1930s. That technique, inclusion of pointed cartoons, actually uses as its sales points the techniques of persuasion taught by Dale Carnegie, author of the book itself.

Comment

Visualize this letter without the cartoons and captions. Impact would be fractional because the reader's ability to identify (on a positive level) with these situations would in turn be fragile.

The table of contents on page 6 is, in our opinion, a mixed blessing. The very first topic, "If You Want to Gather Honey, Don't Kick Over the Beehive," is a pat exercise in terminology, somewhat out of key with the straightforward approach of the letter.

The letter itself is a good example of the use of graphics to reinforce textual points, as we have seen.

Figure 6–1. Nightingale-Conant

DO YOU MAKE THESE COMMON MISTAKES IN DEALING WITH PEOPLE?

Fellow Human Being:

If to err is human, then nobody's more human than I am.

I have in my time made every mistake in the book in dealing with people.

As a young man, I tried to impress people I'd meet at cocktail parties by telling them how important I was. Needless to say, that got me absolutely nowhere. It took years before I learned that the way to impress people is to tell them how important they are, not how important I am. It took practice, but now I can do it quite naturally.

"So I said to the chairman, the way I see it, if I can have a crew of ten, I can..."

"You call yourself a dry cleaner? Look at this stain you left on my coat!"

Have you ever had a tradesman do a poor job, but been unable to get him to fix his mistake? It used to happen to me all the time.

There I'd be, screaming at the dry cleaner about the nasty stain he left on my coat. And all he'd say was that some stains won't come out. All my anger and threats got me nowhere.

I don't do that anymore. I've long since learned, if you want honey, don't kick over the beehive. In a moment I'll show you some more dumb mistakes I used to make.

I'll even show you the right way to handle these situations.

But first let me tell you how I stopped making these mistakes in the first place ... and how you too can learn better ways to deal with people WITHOUT PAYING A CENT!

THE GREATEST TEACHER OF RELATIONSHIP SKILLS

I read the best book on human relations ever written -- Dale Carnegie's "How to Win Friends and Influence People." It was

(over, please)

Psychology, friendliness, and clever graphics build rapport. *(Continued)*

-2-

written more than 50 years ago. It's still in print. Over 16-million copies have been sold.

It's a shame more people don't read it today. Dale Carnegie was the greatest teacher of relationship skills who ever lived.

The ability to persuade and deal with people, which Benjamin Franklin, Daniel Webster and Abraham Lincoln had mastered (not to mention Confucius, Buddha and Jesus Christ), had never been organized into a training program until Dale Carnegie did it back in the 1930s.

He did it after 15 years of experiment and research in the world's first "Laboratory of Human Relationships." He taught it at his famed Dale Carnegie Institute, where statesmen and captains of industry paid thousands of dollars for the training. Eventually he published it, and it became one of the greatest best sellers of all time.

> This landmark book is at last available -- updated and unabridged -- on self-teaching audiocassettes. We invite you to listen and learn from them for 30 DAYS WITHOUT CHARGE.

I guarantee that, within a week, you will stop making the kind of self-destructive mistakes I used to make.

Here's another one of my beauts. If I was in a real hurry in a restaurant, I used to say things like this. But the waiter didn't serve me any faster -- just more aggres-sively.

"We have to catch a plane right after lunch, so please serve us fast for a change."

Now I know better. Just look below to see what I'd say today in a similar situation.

And, do you know what? It really works! The Dale Carnegie principle I'm using here (and the way to use it) is described fully on Cassette 8, Side B.

"We're lucky to have this waiter. He's so fast we won't have any trouble catching our plane."

<u>An Action Program!</u>

"How to Win Friends and Influence People" will teach you dozens of techniques for persuading people -- and teach them so that you can start using them <u>at</u> <u>once</u>. This program does far more than impart knowledge ... it INSPIRES ACTION!

(next page, please)

(Continued)

-3-

It takes time to completely master all the principles (old habits are hard to break). But you can start using them right away. And you will see results -- right away!

Just think of all the people you deal with. Wouldn't it be wonderful if you could:

>> Get them to like you almost instantly?
>> Get them to do what you want?
>> Convince them that your position is correct?
>> Get them to accept or at least try your ideas?
>> Win their respect, loyalty, trust ... and even love?

All this is possible when you learn HOW TO WIN FRIENDS AND INFLUENCE PEOPLE! I'm not just talking about business associates, mind you. I'm talking about family. I'm talking about friends. But I'm also talking about total strangers you meet for the first time.

Yes, I'm talking about your clients and customers ... and all the people you'd like to have as clients and customers. I'm talking about the bosses you report to and the assistants you train. I'm talking about the bureaucrats, the suppliers and the neighbors you must deal with.

The POWER to influence people ... to make them like you ... and even to get them to change their minds CAN SOON BE YOURS!

It Works Like a Charm

Once you start using these techniques, you'll wonder how you ever got by before. Remember the nasty, aggressive way I tried to get my dry cleaner to re-clean my coat? Now I know better. I employ Principle 1 from the section on "How to Change People Without Giving Offense or Arousing Resentment" [Cassette 7, Side B]; I begin with praise and honest appreciation. And it works like a charm!

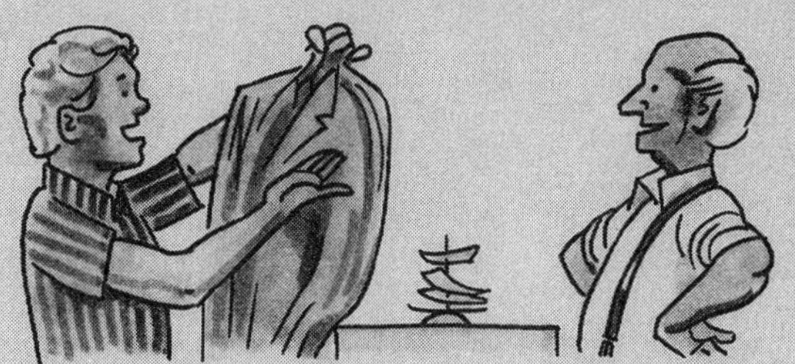

"You pressed it so beautifully, I hardly noticed the stain."

More Mistakes I Used to Make

"Three D's! You'd better apply yourself and stop goofing off!"

I used to have the notion that I could inspire my children to do better if I got angry when they failed. It didn't work, of course. But I never knew why. Now I might help them by applying Princi-

(over, please)

(Continued)

-4-

ple 3 [Cassette 8, Side A] and point out that I had the same failing when I was a child.

"I had a bad marking period when I was a boy. Then my dad showed me how to buckle down and do better!"

An artist who once worked for me was very good. But he had trouble meeting deadlines. I didn't want to fire him. But I wasn't able to get him to improve until I applied Principles 6 and 8 [Cassette 8, both sides] and Dale Carnegie's Principle 2 in "Fundamental Techniques of Handling People" [Cassette 1, Side B].

"This is the third deadline you've missed this month, Harry—you're costing us a fortune in overtime!"

"Another beautiful job, Harry—it's worth the overtime! Is there some way we can help you do work like this a little faster?"

<u>The Skill Worth More Than Any Other</u>

In his time, John D. Rockefeller was the richest man in America. He said: "The ability to deal with people is as purchasable a commodity as sugar and coffee. And I will <u>pay more for that ability</u> than for any other under the sun!"

Back in 1921, when $50 a week was considered a good salary, Charles Schwab was hired as president of U.S. Steel at $3,000 <u>a day</u>! Why? Was he a genius? Did he know more about steel than anyone else? Nonsense! Schwab admitted he had people working for him who knew more about making steel than he did. He was paid more than a million dollars a year for <u>his ability to deal with people</u>.

One of America's leading engineering colleges admits that only 15% of an engineer's financial success is due to technical knowledge ... while 85% is due to <u>skill in human engineering</u> -- the ability to lead and deal with people.

Since this is the highest priced ability under the sun, wouldn't you suppose every college in the land would offer courses in it? Well, none

(next page, please)

(Continued)

-5-

did when Dale Carnegie introduced his ideas. And, as far as I know, the subject is still given short shrift, even in prestigious business schools.

This Dale Carnegie classic is it. It's the ONE-AND-ONLY audio program created to teach the best-paid skill in the world ... the ability to deal with people!

Try It FREE for 30 Days

We are proud to be able to offer the eight cassettes plus the book in a luxurious Library Edition for a free 30-day trial. Why free? And why for 30 days?

Because most people are skeptical that spoken and printed words alone can effect such profound changes in their lives. So a free offer will ease your doubts. And 30 days is ample time to start seeing yourself change.

But don't think that 30 days is all you'll need. It's been 15 years since I first read the book. I have literally worn out my first copy, and I now have two -- one at home and one in the office. And I still turn to them as a "refresher" whenever I've been in a situation I could have handled better.

So I have no doubt that you will want to keep your program, and that you'll gladly pay the low price of $99.95.

Return It and Pay Nothing

But, if I'm wrong, you may return it. No explanations needed. Just send it back with your invoice (so we'll know not to bill you anymore) and pay nothing. You will have had 30 days of training free -- for which you'll be richer. If nothing else, you'll learn how to ask for a raise effectively [Principles 4 and 5, "Six Ways to Make People Like You," Cassette 4, Side A].

But, believe me, you'll be richer still if you stick with it longer.

As the scholars say, carpe diem! Seize the day! This offer, at this price, may not come your way again. Just mail back the card.

With warmest wishes,

Vic Conant

Vic Conant, President

(over, please)

(Continued)

-6-

P.S. At the beginning, I told of the many mistakes I made before I studied Dale Carnegie's methods. Didn't that make it easier for you to recognize your own mistakes, and want to correct them? That is just one of Dale Carnegie's 30 practical methods for winning friends and influencing people.

Here is the road you will travel in order to learn and master them all:

PART ONE

Fundamental Techniques in Handling People

1. "If You Want to Gather Honey, Don't Kick Over the Beehive"
2. The Big Secret in Dealing With People
3. "Those Who Can Do This Have the Whole World With Them. Those Who Cannot Walk a Lonely Way"

PART TWO

Six Ways to Make People Like You

1. Do This and You'll Be Welcome Anywhere
2. A Simple Way to Make a Good First Impression
3. If You Don't Do This, You Are Headed for Trouble
4. An Easy Way to Become a Good Conversationalist
5. How to Interest People
6. How to Make People Like You Instantly

PART THREE

How to Win People to Your Way of Thinking

1. You Can't Win an Argument
2. A Sure Way of Making Enemies—and How to Avoid It
3. If You're Wrong, Admit It
4. A Drop of Honey
5. The Secret of Socrates
6. The Safety Valve in Handling Complaints
7. How to Get Cooperation
8. A Formula That Will Work Wonders for You
9. What Everybody Wants
10. An Appeal That Everyone Likes
11. The Movies Do It. TV Does It. Why Don't You?
12. When Nothing Else Works, Try This

PART FOUR

Be a Leader: How to Change People Without Giving Offense or Arousing Resentment

1. If You Must Find Fault, This Is the Way to Begin
2. How to Criticize—and Not Be Hated for It
3. Talk About Your Own Mistakes First
4. No One Likes to Take Orders
5. Let the Other Person Save Face
6. How to Spur People On to Success
7. Give a Dog a Good Name
8. Make the Fault Seem Easy to Correct
9. How to Make People Glad to Do What You Want

555LR

Mailer: **Sunset Books**
Key Words: **"Now enjoy a healthier"**
Writer: **Roy Beauchamp**

The Challenge

In a glutted marketplace a book of ideas for gardening is hardly either new, an exciting development, or a publication anyone would regard as a necessity.

To initiate a receptive attitude, a letter has to say to the reader, "In the pages of the book I'm selling is a new world of pleasure for you." Information alone is not sufficient incentive to sell books.

The Implementation

The writer has loaded the letter with specifics, some of which have to connect with the reader's interests and many of which provoke a huge curiosity-response.

Examples: The subheads on page 2, written in a semi-newsletter fashion; with multiple underlinings, the letter manages to appear newsworthy as well as informative.

Comment

What a marvelous opening—"Here's to dirt."

Grammatically, the "Dear Western Gardener," greeting has a minor problem in that it ends with a semicolon instead of either a comma or a colon. We overlooked that because of the bright, reader-involving text of the letter.

Note how the writer has avoided reader eye-fatigue by interjecting occasional short paragraphs, one of which has just a single word.

The P.S. uses a device which originated in the 1990s, a "Fast Fifty" bonus. The added P.P.S. does remove some of the impact from the P.S. but justifies itself by providing a benefit-close.

Figure 6–2. Sunset

Sunset

Now enjoy a healthier, happier garden all year long...

- Choose from the 14 best climbing roses in the West! (See page 24)
- Six 30-minute garden projects with dramatic results. (Page 57)
- Bulbs, corms and tubers you should plant in February. (See page 45)
- Those easy & enchanting & ever-lasting dried flowers. (See page 87)
- Summer's peak perennials? Try the magnificent marguerites! (Page 114)
- A half-dozen ways to add sensational fragrance to your garden. (Page 268)
- The smartest and easiest ways to ward off winter's frost. (Page 206)

Preview Sunset's Western Garden Annual 1994 Absolutely FREE!

Dear Western Gardener;

Here's to dirt. Hoes. Dahlias. Tea under a tree.

Vines that dangle with juicy ripe tomatoes. Seeds in your hand. Spring. Little clippers for roses. Stalking the wild slug...

Here's to the real fun and fascination of gardening in the West--

All of it in the most useful, inspiration-filled, hands-on big-book you ever smudged with a dirty thumb:

The Premiere Edition...
Sunset's Western Garden Annual 1994
filled with the seasoned advice,
most timely information, tips and techniques
that only the editors at Sunset
could put together to cover an entire year!

Think about that.

A yearful of gardening how to's. When to's. And whys.

A month-by-month calendar for plantings, sprayings, diggings and bloomings, of fresh new ideas for gardening in your part of the West...a guide for pests and problem plants plus amazingly practical designs for dramatic and dynamic gardening.

over, please...

Powerful opening grabs, bright writing holds reader. *(Continued)*

(2)

It's all the best of Sunset Magazine's gardening articles of 1993, conveniently organized from January through December for easy reference.

More than that, it's your chance to start your library of up-to-date and complete gardening information about your region, your garden, your plants. No more having to cut out articles to save. Or hoping you can find the right information. Because it's all right here in the Premiere Edition of Sunset's Western Garden Annual series.

Best of all...you can be the first to read it, enjoy it, learn from it FREE FOR 30 DAYS!

That's right. Be our guest! This is your risk-free chance to give it a good test-run through your garden...find out why this could easily be the most practical, season-by-season book you could ever put into your library...and enjoy the special benefits of being among the first to preview this extraordinary book. (Don't miss the enclosed Free Gift Offer!)

Will it work for your garden, your style? Will it inspire you, help you with seasonal problems, keep you up (and ahead) of your planting? Is this, in fact, a book that can change the way you do your gardening?

Absolutely!

Which is why I have a brand-new, fresh and risk-free volume reserved and ready for your reply. There's no obligation except to enjoy this unique Sunset Annual--and then decide. You're sure to discover a lot of smart advice and valuable ideas no matter where you open up...

"The quickest way to destroy a climbing rose," says a noted rosarian, "is to treat it like a bush rose!"

It's right there on page 24--a fascinating story on how to tame the wild climbing rose. You'll also discover why these dainty double-flowered ramblers are at their most hearty and happy when given the right kind of direction (with ties at critical points along the way). Then we give you a chart on the 14 best of the West's climbing roses and how, exactly, you can get one going in your yard. And more, much more.

In fact, we'll tell you, month by month, the most important and fail-safe things to do in your garden so you'll know exactly what to do and when...like how to beat the budworms in July and where to mulch to your heart's content in May and why planting salvia in the fall is right.

The magic of louvered fences; now you see 'em, now you don't.

Well, why not a louvered fence for where you want light--and privacy? Or maybe for beautiful angled vines along the edge of a garden path? We show you how...

Or how about "painting" your garden with big and broad patchwork

(Continued)

(3)

plantings of perennials? (If you need some artistic inspiration, take a look at the photos on page 114!)

The Star Everlasting, frost and beans... succulents, seaside planting, new humus-based sod.

Sunset's Western Garden Annual 1994 is over 275 pages of solid advice and smart information that you'll use from one end of the year to the other. It's a timely, up-to-date look at the unique aspects of gardening in the West, at all those special challenges that make our gardening so rewarding!

So you'll get the answers you need to the immediate questions we all have...from the dangers of late frost to the delights of early beans...from the beautiful new lines of "designer" succulents to hearty seaside plantings and the perfect dried flower called Star Everlasting...

Secrets of the garden?

They're only secrets when you don't know the answers. Inside this remarkable volume, you'll catch all the high points of each season for planting and protecting, clipping and caring. You'll get the lowdown on those bugs that can really bug you...plants that love only a little water... fruit trees that will bear a healthy, bountiful and beautiful harvest every time!

Inside and outside, all around the house.

There's also a whole year's worth of advice for all those other "green" parts of your home--indoor plants and how to manage their growth...little gardens and how to make dramatic and instant changes...trellises and where they can be most effective for fostering exciting new varieties of vines...

Plus tips on building garden structures (like a handy garden work center)...sensational stairs and walkways you can make out of everything from coarse concrete to native stones...inspired decks, simple patios, classic porticos for getting your family outdoors...unique western landscaping tips for a bright, healthy and "balanced" garden...vegetable and fruit "alerts" for pests you want to side-step and produce you'd like to put on your table.

A Checklist for Every Western Garden!

Since every chapter in this beautiful volume covers one full month of the year, you can follow the progress of your garden from season to season --planning ahead, getting ready, knowing that you're always on schedule. It's the power of Sunset Magazine's gardening expertise all in one place!

Send For Your Risk Free Book, Claim Your Free Gift (no matter what!)... And Find Out If You Won $50 Instant Cash!

You've got a lot going for you when you return the enclosed Free Preview Certificate. First, if yours is among the first 50 to arrive in the mail, you'll win $50 just like that! Instantly!

over, please...

(Continued)

(4)

Second, you'll get Sunset's color-filled 275 page Western Garden Annual 1994 to read and enjoy and judge for 30 days as our guest. There's never an obligation, never any cost unless you decide to keep this volume.

The price! Just $14.95 plus shipping and handling. (You save $10.00 off the retail price!) And you'll be entitled to preview future garden books once or twice a year as they are published.

Finally, you'll receive an exciting FREE GARDEN GIFT no matter what you decide about the Annual--even if you wish to return the book, the free gift is yours! (See important information enclosed for additional details.)

If it turns out you don't wish to keep this volume, simply return it to us and that ends the matter. In fact, we've included with this mailing a postage-free merchandise label for your convenience in returning the book so there's no cost whatsoever and no hassle at any time.

Won't you take us up on this first-time-ever offer? You've got nothing to lose and everything to gain in this unique and valuable garden book!

Send for your FREE Sunset Western Garden Annual 1994 today... and make your garden the best it can be!

Cordially,

Elizabeth L. Hogan

Elizabeth L. Hogan
Editor, SUNSET BOOKS

P.S. You've never seen a book like this one from Sunset! Be the first to preview this volume as our special guest...and be among the first 50 to return the enclosed Free Preview Certificate and you'll win $50 in cash!

P.P.S. And that Free Garden Gift is yours no matter what--our thanks to you for simply previewing this new book!

Sunset Books
Menlo Park,
California 94025

Mailer: **Time-Life Books**
Key Words: **"Bull Run"**
Writer: **Paul Dexter**

The Challenge

How much Civil War will the typical individual accept as a marketable commodity?

As we may have agreed in the example of a subscription to a publication dedicated to the Civil War, the most obvious challenge is to convince the reader that anything he or she will see or read is interesting enough to justify an elective expense.

The Implementation

By incorporating a handwritten letter, ostensibly by a Civil War soldier, and including a vintage photograph of what may have been that soldier, the writer generates instant rapport with the reader.

Printing the first page in an antique effect helps to induce the desired mood. The letter quotes both specifics and generalities, with many exclamation points whose purpose obviously is to inject excitement into the text.

Comment

One needn't be a fan of history to be intrigued by the front page of this unusual letter. The writer sets a scene of high emotion rather than picking factual information from the text. The result is obvious: The letter is both readable and tantalizing.

Obviously list selection plays a strong part in the success of a project such as this. The writer points out that book buyers and history buffs constituted a large part of the mailing list but many who had shown no prior interest in the American Civil War responded because of the power of this letter.

Figure 6–3. Time-Life Books

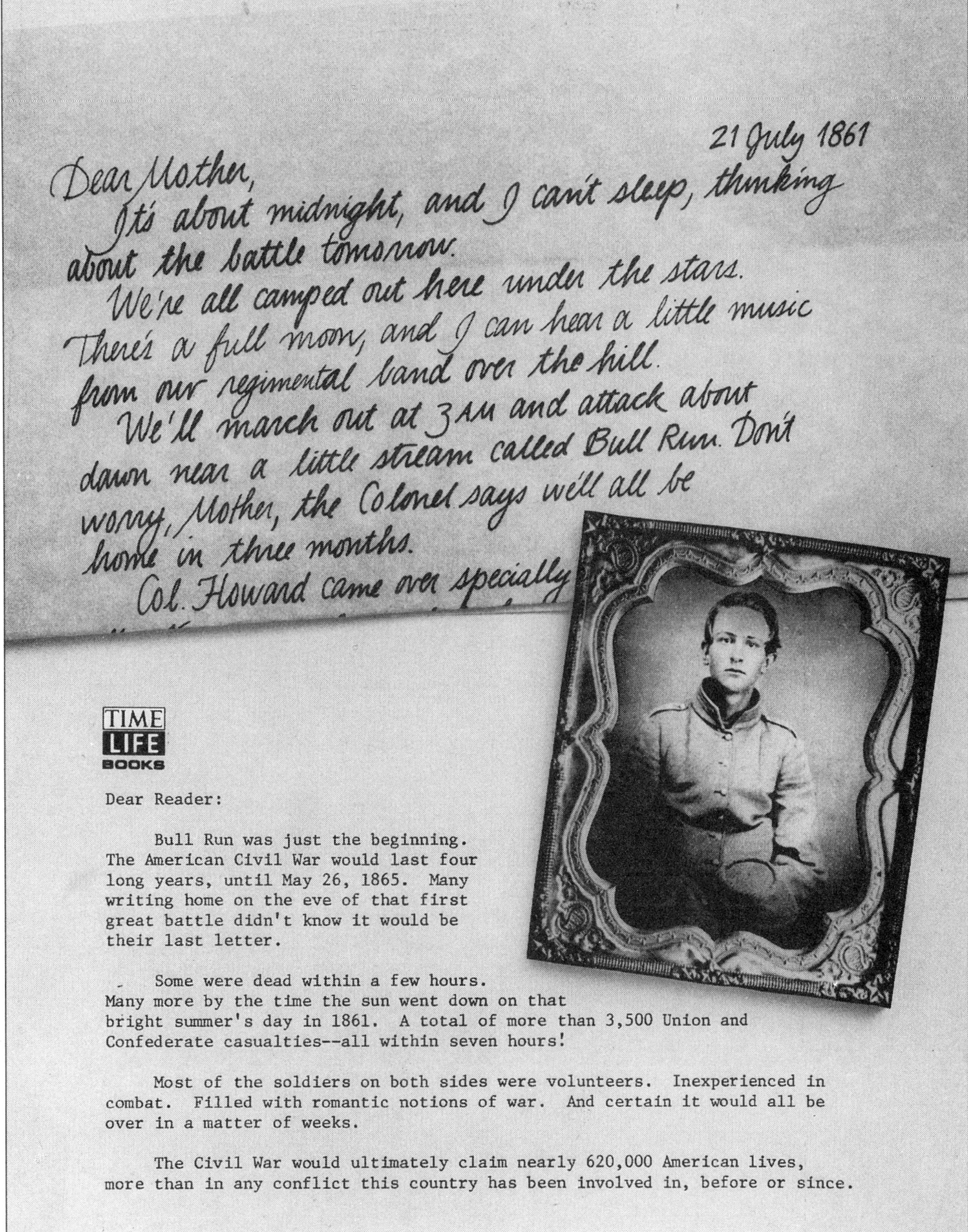

21 July 1861

Dear Mother,

It's about midnight, and I can't sleep, thinking about the battle tomorrow.

We're all camped out here under the stars. There's a full moon, and I can hear a little music from our regimental band over the hill.

We'll march out at 3 AM and attack about dawn near a little stream called Bull Run. Don't worry, Mother, the Colonel says we'll all be home in three months.

Col. Howard came over specially

TIME LIFE BOOKS

Dear Reader:

Bull Run was just the beginning. The American Civil War would last four long years, until May 26, 1865. Many writing home on the eve of that first great battle didn't know it would be their last letter.

Some were dead within a few hours. Many more by the time the sun went down on that bright summer's day in 1861. A total of more than 3,500 Union and Confederate casualties--all within seven hours!

Most of the soldiers on both sides were volunteers. Inexperienced in combat. Filled with romantic notions of war. And certain it would all be over in a matter of weeks.

The Civil War would ultimately claim nearly 620,000 American lives, more than in any conflict this country has been involved in, before or since.

Adding drama to history transforms a dry subject into high appeal. *(Continued)*

-2-

Now you can share the heroism and heartbreak through battle after battle in a handsome new series from TIME-LIFE BOOKS, entitled THE CIVIL WAR.

Every volume in this definitive home library has been meticulously researched for accuracy. Each is published in a large, richly embossed hard-cover edition abounding with eyewitness accounts and excerpts from secret diaries...awash with rare period photographs, maps, posters, charts and paintings reproduced in full-color...and--in an exciting, fast-paced narrative--many little-known, behind-the-scenes stories.

Accept First Blood for 10 days FREE
as your introduction to THE CIVIL WAR!

First Blood takes you back to the suspenseful, action-filled days between the firing on Fort Sumter and the first major battle of the war.

You'll witness the mad rush to arms as young Northerners exceed the number of volunteers requested by Lincoln. And watch as Southerners enlist in wild exaltation in every courthouse town across the Confederacy, waving goodbye to their sweethearts and boasting the names of their companies: the Tallapoosa Thrashers...Cherokee Lincoln Killers...Barbour County Yankee Hunters!

In chapter after chapter of First Blood, you'll meet the people and witness the events of this shattering period:

...tactical blunders that led to the North's first defeat

...why the Confederates counted on England and France for money and arms

...the improved "rifled" musket and its effect on traditional massed attack formations

...the "Anaconda" plan to strangle the South into submission

...Confederate spies who carried valuable information on Union troop movements.

You'll follow the savage Battle of Bull Run through all its surprising turning points...learn how an "insane" charge bought the Confederates valuable time...discover how an error of judgment altered the entire course of the campaign...and find out how the Rebels almost severed the Federals' main escape route to Washington!

Page by page, First Blood will serve as your introduction to other fine volumes in this monumental TIME-LIFE BOOKS' series.

(Continued)

-3-

A word-and-picture panorama
that covers the whole catastrophic period as never before!

The slaughter of Antietam! The terrible retreat at Shiloh! The massive campaign to take Vicksburg! The turning point at Gettysburg! The burning of Atlanta! One by one, you'll witness the battles that changed America forever!

You'll marvel at how General Lee used his famous "pincer movement" to defeat the North in the Second Battle of Bull Run...ponder the unanswered questions of the Peninsula Campaign...witness the decisive gunboat war on the Mississippi...and visit the "trysting place" where soldiers met their relatives on the other side during the long siege of Vicksburg.

And, through it all, you'll meet the leaders on both sides: General George McClellan who, early in the war, stopped within five miles of Richmond when he could have broken through the thin Confederate lines...Robert E. Lee, brilliant West Pointer and Mexican War veteran, whose answer to a tight situation was to attack even when the risks were high...Jeb Stuart, famous for his ride around the Union forces at Gettysburg...and Ulysses S. Grant, the Northern General-in-Chief who had considered himself a failure before the war.

Volume by volume, you'll relive
the whole, unbelievably savage conflict!

As you build your CIVIL WAR library, you'll find book after book reveals new and fascinating aspects of the agonizing, four-year struggle.

Rebels Resurgent takes you back to the battles of Fredericksburg and Chancellorsville. You'll endure the frustrations of the winter "Mud March"...see why a good Union plan misfired at the last moment...and marvel at the brilliant strategy that defeated overwhelming Union forces at Chancellorsville.

In War on the Frontier, you'll follow little-known conflicts west of the Mississippi...the Sand Creek massacre in Colorado Territory...the Red River Campaign...even a Rebel attack on Prescott, Arizona!

Whether it's The Bloodiest Day, in which you'll probe the mystery of Lee's "Lost Order #191" and its effect on the costly Union victory at Antietam...or Scourging the Rebels where you'll find out how Sheridan routed Confederate strongholds in the Shenandoah Valley...or The Nation Reunited with its insights into the plot to assassinate Lincoln...you'll thrill to eyewitness reports, military tactics and the sheer human drama presented in this splendid series.

A unique visual testimony!

THE CIVIL WAR brings together many rare and extraordinary war photographs

(Continued)

-4-

--including some by the renowned Mathew Brady.

You'll see a secret picture of a ship being refitted in England for the Confederacy...an actual photograph of Jefferson Davis being sworn in as Rebel president on the capitol steps in Montgomery, Alabama, on February 18, 1861... Union blockaders lying in wait off Florida...a rare early portrait of General Sherman...famous campaign landmarks and sobering shots of battlefields after combat...plus charts, tactical maps, campaign posters, engravings and full-color paintings (including a masterful canvas by Edouard Manet, the French Impressionist, depicting the Confederate ship, Alabama, being attacked by a Union warship off Cherbourg, France).

Now examine First Blood
for 10 days FREE
as your introduction to
THE CIVIL WAR!

First Blood, as you can see from the accompanying brochure, is an extraordinary book. Of course, there is only one way to truly appreciate it, and that is to see it for yourself. And you are now invited to examine a copy in your own home, FREE for 10 days.

If, at the end of that time, you wish to return it, you may do so and you will be under no further obligation. If you keep it, pay just $12.95 plus shipping and handling. You will then receive other volumes in THE CIVIL WAR series, one about every other month and always for a 10-day free examination.

As a subscriber, you keep only the volumes you want--there's no minimum number to buy--and you may cancel your subscription at any time simply by notifying us.

Start to relive the whole exciting panorama of THE CIVIL WAR...Send for First Blood by returning the enclosed postpaid order card today!

Sincerely,

Reginald Brack, Jr.
President

RB/CIL

Mailer: **Boardroom Reports Big Black Book**
Key Words: **"Where never to sit"**
Writer: **Mel Martin**

The Challenge

"Exposé" books are no novelty, nor are books which purport to tell us how to enjoy an edge over everybody we do business with or come into contact with.

Most of the best targets for a mailing such as this think they know it all, so the principle challenge is to convince them that they *don't* know it all . . . without spawning annoyance.

The Implementation

For six solid, unrelenting pages the writer beats the reader about the head and shoulders with mercilessly specific examples of how "those people" out there want to take advantage of us—and how we can turn the advantage 180 degrees so it will be in our favor.

The trick to a letter such as this is the specific page references. Without these the reader probably remains unconvinced. But by seeing that page 173 tells him or her "How to beat the minimum-stay requirements for bargain airfares," most of the automatic skepticism has to disappear.

Comment

Of all the writers represented in this book, none was more talented and none was stranger than the late Mel Martin, who, until his death in 1994, wrote irresistible and sometimes shocking letters of great length for *Boardroom Reports.*

The publisher called him the world's slowest copywriter, pointing out that he "could get stuck for a month on a letter opening."

But the results, time after time, were huge winners, and Martin can be credited with originating the technique of provocative teasers which many of his followers now use.

This 6-page letter, on analysis, is a recitation of what the reader might find in the pages of this book. The selection has multiple appeals for everyone, ranging from how to increase your tax deductions to how to beat college entrance exams to ingredients in lipstick that might cause cancer.

The letter is a reading experience on its own, and the reader hates to see it end—which has to be the ultimate compliment.

Figure 6–4. Boardroom Reports

Where never to sit in an airplane ...and the hush-hush reason why

- How to double chances of winning sweepstakes
- Vitamins that are hazardous to male potency
- Painkillers that make your headache worse
- Pay the IRS six months late...no penalty

Dear Colleague:

THE BIG BLACK BOOK is yours for 14 days free.

If it doesn't deliver everything I promised, send it back. I'm betting I couldn't pry it out of your hands if I tried.

- Standard equipment that car dealers sell as high-priced "options." Page 150
- Two famous cold remedies that make you sicker if taken together. Page 86
- What never to heat in a microwave oven. Never! Page 64
- Who sees your tax return besides the IRS. You only think it's confidential. Page 478
- Bingo is not a game of chance. Inside ways to win. Page 221
- How to get chosen as a contestant on TV game shows. Page 252
- How to substantiate tax deductions without paid bills or cancelled checks. Page 473
- How to beat the minimum-stay requirements for bargain airfares. Page 173
- How professional basketball games are fixed by NBA owners. Page 221
- Not paying taxes is a criminal offense, right? That's what they want you to think, but see page 478.

(continued...)

Merciless challenging is a marvelous reader-involvement device.

(Continued)

-2-

- If airfare is reduced before you use your ticket, the airline owes you money. But you'll never collect unless you know the secret on page 165.

- Artificial additives in natural food. Page 71

- Car waxes that should never be used on new cars. Page 157

- All computer screens give off hazardous radiation -- except for the one safe kind. Page 389

- Airlines to avoid if you're leery of flying on old jets. Page 168

- How to win radio call-in contests. (First step is to stop doing what announcer says.) Page 253

- If they assess your house at half its value, you're getting a bargain rate, right? Wrong! Their dirty secret is on page 350.

- Deductions get bigger if you move them to a different part of your tax return. Page 426

- How to beat the college entrance exams. When to guess at an answer you don't know, and when you score higher by leaving it blank. When easy answer is probably right, and when it's bound to be wrong. Page 22

- How to beat the hotel surcharge on long-distance calls. Page 306

- How to beat the IRS rule against deducting sales tax. Two big loopholes. Page 418

- Weight-loss programs that take off muscle when you think you're shedding fat. Page 72

- When not to trust the lab test results your own doctor gives you. Page 82

- When not to trust results of radon test. Do you only think your home is safe? Page 103

- When not to trust vitamin content of supermarket milk. Page 71

- How to make car warranty last longer than manufacturer intended. Page 159

- Prescription drugs without a prescription. Perfectly legal -- and you save close to 50%. Page 85

- How to get the best tables in good restaurants. Only suckers tip the head waiter. See page 178.

(continued...)

(Continued)

-3-

. Antihistamines that make your cold worse. Page 93

Did anyone ever explain all this to you before? Your accountant? Your druggist? Your travel agent? Your doctor? Your car dealer? Mine never did.

Did anybody warn you that fish oil can increase your cholesterol count? Or warn you about feeding honey to a baby? For that and lots more you may never hear in a health food store, see pages 16 and 71.

Every word comes straight from the experts -- in language you don't have to be an expert to understand.

. How to get new medicines before they're approved by the FDA. Absolutely legal and could save your life. Page 86

. Expensive tires are safer than cheap ones, right? Wrong! Some very dangerous ones carry the highest price tags. Page 160

. What insurance companies don't tell you. How to get your money back if you don't like the policy they sold you. Up to two years' premiums refunded. Secret is on page 363.

. What the government doesn't tell you. The IRS could be taping your phone calls. They don't even need a court order. Page 478

. What hospitals don't tell you. Before you write your name on anything they want you to sign, see page 79.

. What toy stores don't tell you. How those cuddly stuffed animals make children sick. Page 9

. What charities don't tell you. 90% of the money you give could be going to the fund-raisers. Before you make your next contribution, see page 380.

. What travel agents don't tell you. Cheapest days and hours to fly. You don't have to settle for the "red eye" if you're wise to these unpublicized discounts. Page 166

. What those peel-off IRS labels on your tax return say about you. Can they flag your name for an audit? Page 464

. Too much calcium is bad for your memory. Before you take any more of those diet supplements, see page 71.

. Contraceptive method to avoid if you plan on having children later. Page 44

. Pay your parents' medical bills with their money and deduct the expense on your tax return. Page 426

(continued...)

(Continued)

-4-

- Postpone your tax audit and ask the IRS for a new date. You may never hear from them again. Page 467

- When condoms prevent disease and when you only think they do. Page 44

- The secrets of non-carcinogenic tobacco. They could have been making cigarettes with it but they never did. Page 103

- The steroids that weaken your muscles. See page 51.

- How to collect real estate income tax-free. Page 411

- "Light" food means fewer calories, right? Wrong. Page 70

- Polyunsaturated means healthier, right? Wrong. Page 70

- Cash in safe deposit box when you're gone will be treated as income you were hiding from the IRS -- but not if you read page 315.

- How to read a financial statement. Where to look for the bad news they're trying to bury. Page 353

- What plastic surgeons don't tell you. One popular procedure can be life-threatening. See page 108.

- What sperm banks don't tell you. Questions to ask before you trust them for either storage or artificial insemination. Page 46

- What sushi bars don't tell you. The raw fish is probably safer than one of the exotic ingredients served with it. See page 71.

- What summer camps don't tell you. When not to take camper-to-staff ratio at face value. What to check out instead. Page 20

- Medicines that are dangerous if taken with citrus juice. Page 86

- Medicines that work better if you take less of them. Page 84

- Medicines that work differently in cold weather. Page 86

- Children's medicines that contain alcohol but don't say so on the label. Page 86

- Securities you can own without the IRS knowing it. Some are issued by the U.S. Government itself. Page 335

- Expensive home improvements that reduce resale value. Low-cost ones that increase it. Page 126

- Set up your hobby as a business -- and deduct your expenses even if you never show a profit. Legal! Page 444

(continued...)

(Continued)

-5-

. Tenant takes tax credit for renovating landlord's property. Legal! See page 415.

. Airlines will handle your baggage with special care if you know the secret on page 168.

. Air safety alert. Tipoff that flight will be hazardous and you shouldn't be aboard. Page 167

. Teflon alert. Unpublicized health hazard in non-stick cookware. See page 71.

. Pesticide alert. Supermarket fruits and vegetables are safe if washed, right? Wrong. Add one extra precaution. Page 71

. Reverse mortgage scam. Deal you make to keep living in your own home can land you in the poorhouse instead. Page 309

A grand total of 1,196 inside ways to hold your own against the airlines, the car dealers, the banks, the insurance companies...Tax strategies you never heard from your accountant.

All in plain English and straight from our nationwide intelligence network of 548 inside experts.

. Carcinogenic ingredients in lipstick. Page 118

. Fireplaces that make your home colder. Page 133

. Sunglasses that make ultraviolet rays worse. Page 99

. Eyedrops that make your eyes redder. Page 99

. Dandruff shampoos that cause dandruff. Page 113

. Paints that should never be used indoors -- never. The labels are deliberately misleading. Page 128

. When to throw out a partly used bottle of sunscreen lotion -- and the scary reason why. Page 102

. Questions you should answer on your tax return even though they're not asked. (And what can go wrong if you don't.) Page 467

. Diseases you can catch from a toilet seat. Your mother was right, but she never taught you precautions like these. Page 57

. Smoking and Alzheimer's. The last guilty secret in the tobacco business. See page 102.

. When "low-fat" means loaded with fat. Page 70

(continued...)

(Continued)

- The secret code on your Social Security card. Page 487
- What fingernail-wrapping and false nails are doing to women's real ones. Page 118
- Borrow money from your IRA. Just don't call it a loan. Page 486
- Aging parents can qualify for Medicaid and still keep assets intact for their children. Perfectly legal for nursing home care or home-care. See page 365.
- When to file for a tax refund even though they don't owe you one. (The IRS is hoping you never figure this out.) Page 460
- Beauty treatment that can transmit AIDS virus. Page 118

What they don't want you to know. 512 pages of privileged information you never expected to see in print.

Send for a copy of THE BIG BLACK BOOK at my risk. SEND NO MONEY. Look it over and see how valuable it is. If at the end of 14 days, you decide not to keep the book, simply return it without obligation.

If you decide to keep it, we'll bill you in three convenient installments of $9.99 each for a total of $29.97. That's a 40% discount off the published price of $50. There's no charge for shipping and handling.

Is it a deal? Then please mail the Free-Trial Certificate today. And many thanks.

Sincerely,

Martin Edelston
Publisher

ME:jbr

P.S. THE BIG BLACK BOOK is a tax-deductible purchase under the Tax Reform Act.

P.P.S. Important: More inside information. Get the Best Kept Secrets in America as an extra bonus when you reply promptly. Another reason why it pays to mail your order form today.

MAKES MONEY FOR YOU OR YOUR MONEY BACK
BOARDROOM CLASSICS
330 West 42 Street, New York, NY 10036

Mailer: Leisure Arts

Key Words: "In the Nick of Time"

The Challenge

How does a frequent mailer create excitement for what the woman who gets many mailings of this type—from competitors as well as from this company—might regard as just another do-it-yourself book?

The challenge is even greater when one realizes that this is a book in a series whose content remains reasonably standard year after year.

The Implementation

Among direct marketers of books, Leisure Arts enjoys a well-deserved reputation for innovation. This letter, created under the supervision of Guy Crossley, Executive Director of Marketing, and Susan Wiles, Project Creative Director, sells holiday recipes and projects. It used the inventive technique of "injecting" handwritten comments by friends of book buyers, handwritten against a white background (the letter itself was set on a pink background).

Rather than glorify the book itself, emphasis here is on the reaction the user will encounter from taking advantage of the projects in the book. As is proper for a book aimed at the active 1990s woman, equal emphasis is given to the ease and speed with which each project can be accomplished.

Comment

This letter is almost a textbook of multiple motivators, beginning with the four handwritten encomia, continuing with ongoing reassurance of professionalism without spending much time and concluding with a remarkably provocative postscript.

Short paragraphs make the letter very readable. Only one paragraph in the letter is longer than six lines: Many are one or two lines.

Figure 6–5. Leisure Arts

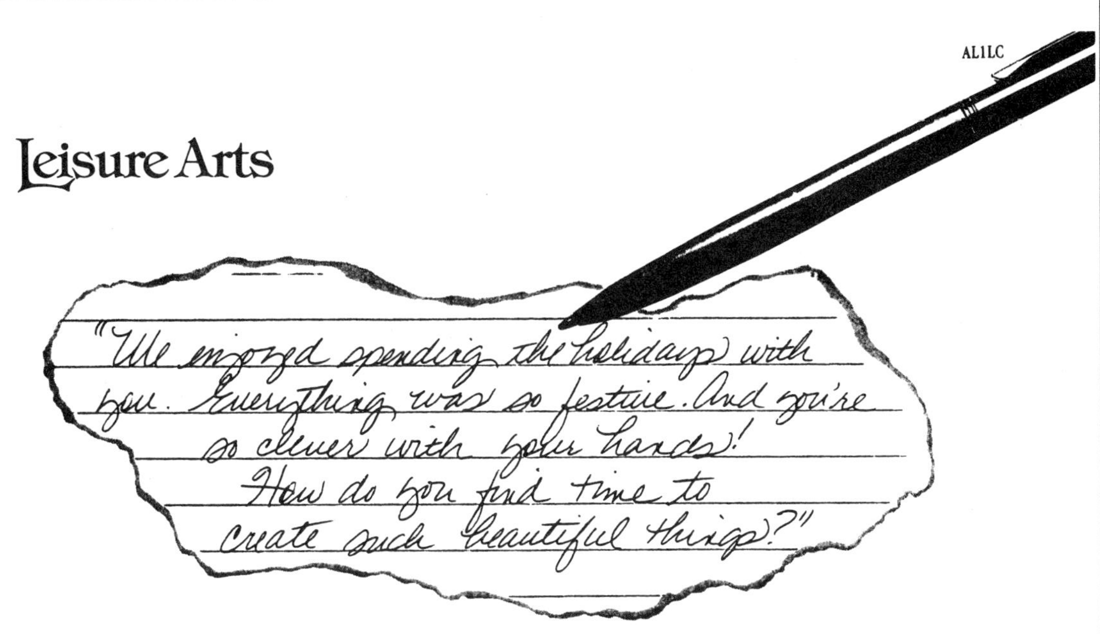

Good morning!

Thank-you notes like this are probably nothing new to you.

I'd guess you get them all the time, because you're the one who always goes the extra two miles with those special handmade cards or home-baked gifts.

Everyone looks forward to spending the holidays at your house. And you wouldn't dream of having it any other way, would you?

But your personal brand of holiday magic does take a lot of time and work, doesn't it?

A Lot of Work? Not Any More!

You know, it doesn't have to take all that time this year. I've found a way to save some extra time this year without giving up the special preparations everyone counts on.

And I want to share my discovery with you:

In the Nick of Time is the newest gem in the acclaimed Leisure Arts Memories in the Making series. This great-idea book is literally brimming over with dozens and dozens of quick-and-easy, time-saving holiday recipes and projects.

Now you can get everything on your Christmas list done in <u>less time</u> and with <u>less work</u> this year.

And that means you'll have those precious extra moments to relax and really enjoy the company of friends and family!

In this book you'll find effortless ways to create those beautiful decorations that ordinarily take hours — even days —

Repeated user benefits lift this letter out of the pile. *(Continued)* to put together. Browse through page after page of imaginative new ideas. And you can complete any one of them, with that professional look you expect from a Leisure Arts project, in just minutes!

...and how did you ever come up with those adorable teddy bear wreaths? The children were enchanted and...

Example: The precious teddy bear wreath on page 30. Who ever would have thought cuddly teddy bears would give an ordinary Christmas wreath such warmth and magic? Dress up those cute little bears in stocking caps and cheery scarves, hang the wreath on the front door, and you have an instant welcome to anyone who knocks. And you can make it in less than 20 minutes!

Or when did you last find the time to bake and trim a Gingerbread House centerpiece? You'll find one on page 52 of *In the Nick of Time*. You can't tell by looking at its detail, but it takes only about 25 minutes to create this masterpiece. (The secret: It looks just like gingerbread, but it's actually decorated cardboard topped with a snowy lace doily. You can save it and use it again, year after year!)

...the dinner napkins and napkin rings are darling. I'll cherish them and think of you every time I set our holiday table...

This year you don't have to worry about the time it takes to create those personal handmade gifts. Because *In the Nick of Time* gives you dozens of gift ideas that can be finished in a snap. They're so fast and easy, you can even start the night before Christmas ... and have them done before Santa pays his visit.

Think of the joy a basket of napkins and handmade poinsettia napkin rings will bring to someone special. (Time it'll take you to make them: just 10 minutes.)

Believe It or Not: Start to Finish in MINUTES!

And consider the wonder you'll see in the eyes of that special child who receives the reindeer basket brimming over with Nutty Maple Fudge. Time to complete: about half an hour.

See how easy this Christmas can be? You'll still enjoy giving the thoughtful handmade gifts to those very special people on your Christmas list ... and you'll still pour your love into those delicious treats you've always been famous for — but you'll

(Continued)

no longer have to spend every waking hour (and some hours stolen from your sleeptime) creating them.

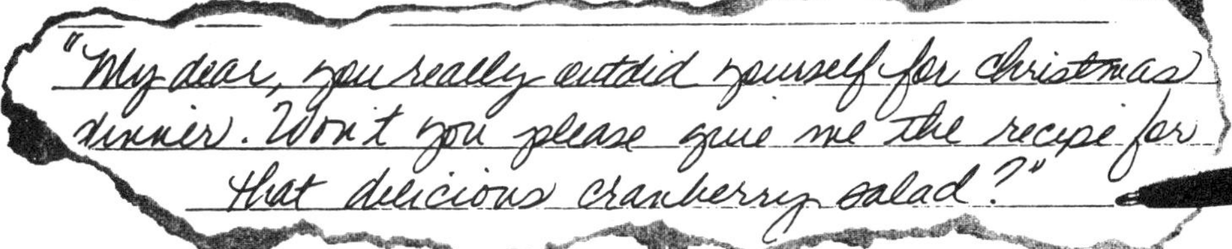

You'll find dozens of new ideas and recipes in this book — even a simple (but scrumptious) Christmas dinner with all the trimmings, but not all the effort. There are so many great ideas that take so little time to create, they fairly leap off the pages into your living room and kitchen.

These are only a few of the treasures waiting for you inside *In the Nick of Time*. And the time you'll save on just one of these projects is worth the price of this marvelous book ten times over.

Speaking of the price ... it's yours for just $14.95 — next to nothing because you're getting it direct from us. You save a full $5.00 off the regular $19.95 cover price! And because it's almost Christmas, we at Leisure Arts have some very special gifts for you, our very good friend ...

I have a surprise for you from St. Nick — a 20-page book called *Holly Jolly Iron-On Transfers* — just for agreeing to take a look at *In the Nick of Time*.

It's ready to go! Just send back the Preview Certificate and we'll brighten your season with your Iron-on Transfers (along with your personal copy of *In the Nick of Time*). You'll get a whole group of delightful holiday transfers – Santa with holly, a charming angel, a Christmas tree, a teddy bear, the phrase "Jolly Old Elf" (perfect for a sweatshirt) – eight big transfers in all.

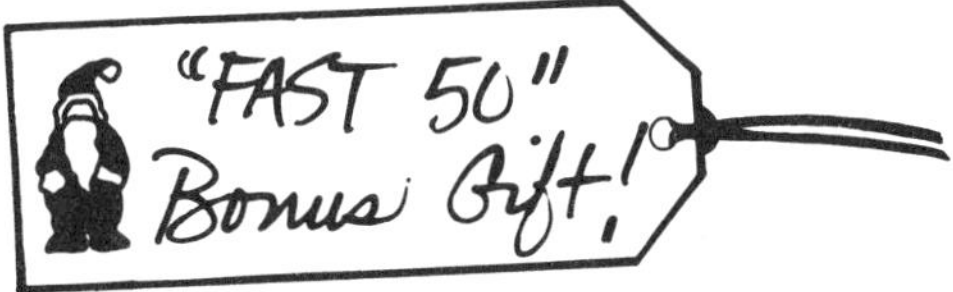

AND YOU MIGHT GET EVEN ANOTHER GIFT! If yours is among the first 50 responses to this invitation — and it's entirely

(Continued)

possible, because this is an advance notice and we aren't sending it to the general public — we'll include a <u>second</u> gift.

You'll really love this one! It's a genuine Tabletop Carriage Clock with a handsome wood finish, <u>plus</u> ...

a special Leisure Arts cross stitch design for a "decorator face" for the clock, <u>plus</u> ...

more than enough fine fabric to actually complete the design. THEY'LL <u>ALL</u> BE YOURS IF YOU'RE ONE OF THE FIRST 50 TO REPLY!

All these gifts are yours from Leisure Arts to keep, no strings attached, whether you decide to keep *In the Nick of Time* or not.

The only thing we'd like you to do is just look it over ... page through it for three full weeks. <u>Try a few of the projects</u>.

We're sure you'll be impressed with the beauty, the colors, and the <u>practicality</u> of having such a big, beautiful, useful book for just $14.95. (Remember, that's a savings of $5.00 off the $19.95 cover price!)

If, after you've had a chance to try some of the projects for yourself for 21 days, you're not convinced it's the perfect holiday companion, then just send it back. Of course, the *Holly Jolly Iron-on Transfers* book and (if you hurry) your Carriage Clock Collection are yours whatever you decide.

As you see, the risk is ours and you have nothing to lose ... except an opportunity to end forever the many hours you've been spending creating gifts. *In the Nick of Time* can be your Christmas miracle. I hope you'll take advantage of it!

I'll look for your Preview Certificate on my desk. Thanks.

For the merriest of Christmases <u>ever</u>,

Anne Childs

Anne Van Wagner Childs
Editor-in-Chief

P.S. I'll bet you can't even visualize a charming votive holder that fifteen minutes ago was a tin can. Neither could I — until I did it for myself. What a wonder this book is!

Leisure Arts, P.O. Box 56089, Little Rock, Arkansas 72215-6089

Mailer: Odysseus Editions, Inc.
Key Words: "Lefty's little library"
Writer: Herschell Gordon Lewis

The Challenge

Fly fisherman have few outside heroes. Each fisherman has his own secrets, which he is loathe to share with others. This "I have private information" syndrome underscores the challenge of marketing any book on this aspect of sportfishing.

To sell a continuity program—an entire library of books on this subject—is a major challenge, not only because of the difficulty convincing a fisherman that enough information exists to justify the library but also because of the difficulty in describing the series of books without the impression of editorial "sameness" among the books.

The Implementation

The six-page letter, signed by the only universally-recognized star of fly fishing, Bernard "Lefty" Kreh, puts an arm around the shoulder of Lefty Kreh's fellow fly fishermen, even including the classic line "if you're like I am."

The letter is written in a highly verbal fashion, paralleling a radio infomercial, with Lefty Kreh talking directly to the reader.

Comment

Sometimes a casually-conceived idea results in extraordinary response.

Originally conceived as a 4-page letter, this letter selling a series of books on fly fishing expanded to 6 pages, making possible an unusual touch: testimonials on pages 2–6.

Written in the manner of a country fly fisherman, the letter uses phrases such as, "I'm not nuts," "Now here's the deal," and "My 40 years of fly-fishing experience are right on the line."

Originally mailed as a test against an established control, this letter outpulled the control by 52%.

Figure 6–6. Lefty's Little Library of Fly Fishing

LEFTY'S LITTLE LIBRARY OF FLY FISHING

You only think you've enjoyed fly fishing up to now.
LK

Dear Fellow Fly Fisherman:

I want to send you a free book. It's a book I guarantee will have a lot more fish fighting to get at your fly. And oh, yes, a free privately-recorded audio cassette.

No. I'm not nuts. Lefty Kreh has been called a lot of things, but not nuts. Well, maybe nuts about fly fishing.

And if you're like I am, no joy is greater than picking the right fly, executing the perfect cast, and having one of those big babies grab at that fly before the second hand has gone around your watch dial even once. No despair is greater than moping over a dead line all day, being ignored by fish.

As you probably know, I've been a fanatical fly fisherman for more than 40 years. And as you might imagine, after all these years I've pretty well licked the problem of "fishless fishing." And the whole point of this letter is: You can end "fishless fishing" too.

You will know why never to strike upward when fishing a sinking line ... how to master a simple hand trick to vastly improve your casting distance ... what to do when a knot appears in your fly line and a fish is escaping . . . how to avoid forever the world's most common casting mistake . . . thousands of secrets that translate immediately into more fun and more fish.

For you: Free Book ... Free Cassette

What I propose to do is this: My techniques are packed into a series of easy-to-read books we call *Lefty's Little Library of Fly Fishing*. I want to send you the first book, free: *Lefty Kreh's Modern Fly Casting Method*.

(Please keep reading. I'm just getting started.)

DIVISION OF ODYSSEUS EDITIONS • 15 OFFICE PARK CIRCLE • P.O. BOX 530065 • BIRMINGHAM, ALABAMA 35253

Arm-around-the-shoulder "If you're like I am" approach builds rapport and confidence.

(Continued)

-2-

"One of the early books in the series, *Lefty's Little Tips*, is the most practical book on useful fly-fishing information published in over 50 years. It's hard to imagine more useful fly-fishing information packed into 160 instructional pages. The books have color pages sprinkled throughout, which gives them the feel of coffee-table editions without their size or cost." – *Fly Fisherman* magazine

---

Now here's the deal:

This book will come to you together with the second book, which you pay for after you decide you want to keep it: *Lefty's Little Tips*. I say pay, but you don't pay much. Because you'll be a Charter Member, for you that second book — and any others in my fly-fishing "library" you want to own — are only $19.95 plus a small handling/shipping charge. I'll tell you another Charter benefit in a moment. Right now, get this:

> If you mail your Charter Enrollment Form before March 31, 1994, I'll include — free, of course — an audio cassette a lot of fly fishermen would pay $50 for: *The Five Principles of Lefty Kreh's Modern Fly Casting Method.* And that cassette is yours to keep and use forever, no matter what.

I want to tell you about the audio cassette, but before I do, I want to tell you the reason I'm giving it to you. It's to make sure you'll be willing to at least take a look at the first couple of books in *Lefty's Little Library of Fly Fishing*. You owe it to your pleasure as a fly fisherman to at least do that.

If you don't like what you see, you still keep the cassette and your free book. Send back the other book (at my expense), and that will be the end of the matter. We'll still be friends.

If you do like what you see, I'll put you down for more of the books in this series, at the special direct price. I've enclosed a descriptive brochure telling you more about the other books in the series.

Five Easy Principles ... Two Easy Books

When you get the first batch of stuff from me, what I want you to do is insert that cassette into your car stereo. Play it on your way to your next fishing spot, and I guarantee you'll not only cast better, you'll do better in the one way we all keep score: number of fish you catch.

(Continued)

-3-

This cassette explains, in the clearest language I know, my five principles of fly casting. Whether you can cast a fly into a hoop from a hundred feet away or are a struggler who has trouble casting that fly fifteen feet in an unknown direction, you'll get information that will make you a better, more effective fly fisherman. I guarantee it.

Then take a look at your free first book in the series. I developed *Lefty Kreh's Modern Fly Casting Method* especially for today's graphite rods and core/coated fly lines. I have more than 120 illustrations in the book, showing you step-by-step how to make longer and more accurate casts.

You'll pay for the second book — that is, if you decide to keep it. I'm betting you will, because in this book, *Lefty's Little Tips*, are more than 175 ways to improve your fishing skills.

It took me over 40 years to assemble all these tips. You can absorb them in 40 minutes or so, then have them as part of your permanent library.

(If you want to do a friend the greatest favor any fly fisherman could do for another, loan him that book! He'll be grateful forever!)

You'll be the "Pro of the Pros" Among Fly Fishermen!

It is absolutely true that 10 percent of the fly fishermen catch 90 percent of the fish. As long as I'm making guarantees, here's another one:

My 40 years of fly-fishing experience are right on the line. I guarantee you'll catch more fish and have more fun doing it.

I'll keep sending you the books in this series at the rate of one about every other month until you have them all — the whole Library will be more than 20 books — or until you tell me to stop. When you have all the books, you'll know as much as I do — or for that matter, anybody, because the very top pros such as Dan Blanton, Gary Borger, Flip Pallot, John Randolph, Jim Teeny and Dave Whitlock have pitched in with their professional fly-fishing tips.

"The only thing little about *Lefty's Little Library* is the size of the books. At 5" X 7 1/2", these exquisitely printed and bound - sewn, not glued - hardcover editions are intended not only to command an honor spot on bookshelves, they can also be taken along on fishing excursions. Talk about gorgeous, this is it. Do we recommend the Library? Does a bear like honey?" - Gene Mueller, *The Washington Times*

(Continued)

"I think the *American Masters Fly Fishing Symposium* books are the highlight of the series. They are a stroke of genius! I congratulate you on your judgment, and on the series as a whole. Thanks." – L.D., Hicksville, New York

Each book is standard 5" x 7 1/2", printed on acid-free paper to last for centuries, bound in heavy library buckram, and illustrated in full color. It may not mean much to you that these books are sewn, not glued; it will to your descendants 100 years from now who still will be able to enjoy the books without worrying about ancient glue opening up.

I should point out a benefit: By breaking my library into "chewable" bites, I've made it easy for you to carry one or two books with you and not be loaded down. Much as I admire the "Standard Fishing Encyclopedia," for example, I'd hate to think of somebody having to lug that monster around.

You'll carry just the book relating to your fishing expedition of the day. If you're fishing for bonefish, you'll carry *Fly Fishing for Bonefish, Permit, and Tarpon*. If you're after trout, you'll put *Fly Fishing for Trout* in your vest pocket.

Now, read this extra, spectacular Charter Member benefit:

At least a couple of times a year, the Library will organize tours to the very best fly-fishing destinations on this planet — places like New Zealand, Argentina, Alaska, Christmas Island, and the Caribbean — where the big fighting fish are just waiting to do battle with you. And I'll be along on these trips as sort of your host and I hope, your fishing buddy.

I'm having Frontiers International set these up as real luxury tours, where all you have to do is enjoy the pleasures of the world's best fishing spots ... and as a Charter Member you have first crack at a super-low rate. Better than that: You'll have the right to invite one guest to come along on any fly-fishing excursion at your own special and private Charter price.

You're the Boss!

This isn't one of those deals where we get you in the door by giving away a bunch of free gifts and then keep you hooked forever.

(Continued)

Sure, I want you to own all the books in *Lefty's Little Library of Fly Fishing*. But what matters is what you want, not what I want.

So you can cancel at any time. You can return any book for every cent you paid for it. You're not obligated to buy any minimum number of books. And way, way beyond that:

> I'll buy back any book in this Library at any time up to one full year after you get it, for the total original price, provided the book is in good condition.

I'm making this offer to you for two separate reasons:

First, your name comes to me from a source that tells me you're one of us — a dedicated, sincere, good-natured, true-blue fly fisherman. This Library is for you, and that's why you're on our private list to get these books at the Charter Member price.

Second, these books aren't available in bookstores. For that matter, right now they aren't available to anybody except those on our Preferred List who are getting this Charter Invitation. I need your answer so I'll know how many books to print for a general (and probably considerably more expensive) offer later on.

You Don't Say!

You say you don't think you can improve your fly-fishing skills?

You say even Lefty Kreh can't show you how to cast farther and straighter?

You say you don't know why if you went out today, on the same stretch of water with me, I'd catch more fish than you?

You say, "Show me!"?

Okay.

"Lefty, I wanted to personally let you know how much I am enjoying being a member of your Little Library series. The information is refreshing as well as captivating and I gotta admit, at times, I feel I am being personally tutored. What a great feeling." – J.P., Murrysville, Pennsylvania

---

(Continued)

"The books are really well done, great photos, and nicely bound. Keep up the good work." – L.W., Seattle, Washington

---

I'll show you, if you'll let me. And I really think you should let me show you, for two reasons: First, I'm taking all the risk. If what you get doesn't please you, keep your audio cassette and first book — they're absolutely free. Send back the other book and don't pay a dime.

Second, think of why fly fishing is so enjoyable ... and how easy it will be to make it far more enjoyable. My Library is available to you right now, at the special Charter rate. We've struck some electronic curbs in our name selections, which means this may probably be your only opportunity to sample *Lefty's Little Library of Fly Fishing* at this price.

I'm keeping this charter offer open for you until March 31, 1994. You don't pay anything until and unless you're satisfied. Whether you decide to keep any of the books or not, the audio cassette and first book are yours with our compliments. And you'll be invited to all the private luxury world-wide fly-fishing excursions.

How about it? Are you with me? Great! Thanks!

For Better Fly Fishing,

Lefty

Bernard "Lefty" Kreh

P.S. If I hear from you within the next ten days I have yet another free gift for you — a full-function calculator (so you can translate pounds into kilos, or vice-versa, when weighing all the fish you catch). I'll send it to you with your second book — yours to keep.

Mailer: **Secrets of Successful Direct Mail**
Key Words: **"I was in a meeting once"**
Writer: **Jack Walsh**

The Challenge

Selling a book of direct marketing to professional practitioners of direct marketing can easily be compared with sticking one's head in a lion's mouth.

The challenge of a project such as this is to have the reader conclude that, yes, the book does offer intelligence even the most accomplished professional may not be able to match.

The Implementation

In an unusual move, the writer of this letter—one of the better known professional direct response writers—adds his own name and address as the letterhead.

The author of the book avoids self-aggrandizement by having his name at the top of the "lift" note, a secondary enclosure.

The basic letter is written "insider-to-insider" with many name droppings and personal references, bringing the reader into the "insider" orbit.

Comment

Not often does the direct response writer have the opportunity to sign the letter he writes. This was such an opportunity, because the book was one whose prime targets would know the name not only of the author, but of the person who wrote this letter.

To an outsider, some of the text would be as impenetrable as "Yes, we have no bananas"; to those in the business, the targets of this letter, the names dropped in this letter are pure gold.

We also are including the lift note which accompanied the basic letter. The note was signed by Richard Benson, perhaps the best-known and most respected direct marketing consultant; but our information is that the writer of the basic letter wrote this as well.

Figure 6–7. John P. Walsh, Inc.

John P. Walsh, Inc.
35 EAST 38TH STREET/SUITE 6-J
NEW YORK, NEW YORK 10016
(212) 697-3900

Dear Reader:

I was in a meeting once with Linda Wells, who is another direct mail writer, and a prospective client whom Dick Benson had introduced us to.

"Don't get me wrong," said the prospective client at one point, "I agree with 90% of what Benson says."

"That's not bad," I said. "It means you're only wrong 10% of the time."

He hired Linda.

If you find only humor in the incident, you miss my point. The words fell from my lips without thinking, as if I were commenting on the weather or what day of the week it was.

Indeed, disagreeing with Dick is, to me, like saying it's raining when the sun is blinding or that Labor Day falls on Thursdays.

That is up until today.

For now he's gone and done perhaps the first dumb thing in his life.

He's written a book.

> Telling anyone who'll part with $19.95
> everything he knows! Blabbing about
> secrets that others have paid him
> thousands to share with them!

Secrets gleaned from decades in the direct mail business.

As a co-founder of American Heritage.

As co-owner of the world's two largest newsletters, Contest News-Letter and University of California, Berkeley, Wellness Letter.

As the launch architect of Smithsonian, New York, Southern

Selling to professionals using the "insider-to-insider" approach. *(Continued)*

Living and Psychology Today.

As top-level advisor to Ogilvy & Mather, R.L. Polk & Co.; Young & Rubicam; Interpublic; the Richard Viguerie Company.

As consultant to Time Inc., Dow Jones, 3-M, Hearst Magazines, Children's Television Workshop, Knapp Communications, INA, Johnson & Johnson, Avon, three different catalog houses, World Book -- even the IRS!

In fact, he calls his book Secrets of Successful Direct Mail. Over 40 years of wisdom in just 176 pages!

So who needs to hire him now?

> Actually, owning the book is probably better than having him on retainer. Because it's exhaustive and crystal-clear, so you won't have to wait for him to get off the phone with another client to get your answer. (Not to mention the money you save on flights to Skidaway Island.)

Just the first chapter alone -- only two pages long -- is worth many times the price of admission. It's called "Benson's Rules of Thumb."

Thirty-one of them, of which he says, "...ignore any of these at your peril."

The value of a two-time buyer ... sweepstakes ... credit offers ... yes-no and token order forms ... memberships vs. subscriptions ... premiums vs. cash discounts ... long vs. short copy ... half-price vs. full-price introductory offers ... two premiums vs. one ... predicting final mail results....

And, as they say, much, much more.

As free-lance writer Hank Burnett points out in the Foreword, Dick can be "brutally frank." Even about his own mistakes. Two in particular I urge you to study closely: How not to sell cameras by mail and how not to run a book club.

This second is especially worth heeding because it illustrates one of his shibboleths that goes something like: If you look around (and you always should) and no one is doing your idea -- maybe there's a lesson in the observation, itself.

Whatever you do, however, do pay particular attention to Chapter 15.

(Continued)

It starts with a discussion of what's always the most crucial dynamic in analyzing mail campaigns and is often the most overlooked one. It is the "bogey" -- the maximum allowable cost of acquisition of a new buyer.

Nor is anything more compelling than his explanation for rejecting the popular premise that an acceptable list test can be pyramided only five times in the next usage.

If you're a specialist in renewals, you may consider writing Dick a blistering letter after you read, "I don't believe copy and format on renewal efforts has any effect...." But the urge will no doubt fade after you read why.

And because the subject of renewal is the be-all and end-all in so many of our businesses, I'll cite one more of his tenets on the topic: "I believe advance renewals are 50% incremental; i.e., you wouldn't have received those orders in the normal course of the renewal series."

If you hire, are -- or have even the remotest plans to someday become -- a consultant, you have to own Secrets of Successful Direct Mail. Why? Because of a chapter that is the tautest, most lucid explanation of "What Does a Consultant Do?" you're ever likely to read.

> And speaking of reading, in his book Dick discusses the one book that has had the most influence on his professional thinking. Read Dick's book and you may not have to read the other. But I'll bet you'll want to.

You won't get through Page 1 before you're aware that Dick's an iconoclast of the first water. (He has a plaque given him by a client inscribed, "To the world's most direct mail consultant.")

But he is not a destroyer of sacred cows simply to be a maverick. For as he says in his summation, "The biggest failure in the practice of direct mail is the preponderance of preconceived mind-sets."

Among the most offensive, as you'll see, is the predisposition of marketers to make premiums compatible instead of desirable. If you're selling records, goes the errant thinking, give away a record cleaner instead of a proved people-mover like a watch. If you're selling cookbooks, forget about a highly coveted calculator and give away a spice chart.

Dick's book is bound to start a lot of direct mail people thinking as they perhaps never have before. Differently, more deeply, more productively.

And I certainly hope that among these people there will be you. Which takes me, and I sincerely hope you, to the enclosed Order Form. For at least three reasons:

1. Returning it is, in all likelihood, the only way you'll ever be able to see this definitive book. It will not be sold in retail stores. (Maybe in college bookstores as a text, but nowhere else.)

2. Return the Form and you'll pay just $19.95 plus shipping and handling.

3. You've got nothing to lose. You can get all your money back if, in your opinion, you don't make money through Secrets of Successful Direct Mail.

Perhaps you'll agree, these three reasons are sufficient for trying the book ... but take my word for it, you'll find hundreds more after it arrives.

No, don't take my word for it. Take, instead, that of the Chairman of Boardroom Reports, Inc., Marty Edelston, as he phrased it on the Order Form.

Thank you for reading my letter and I do hope Dick hears from you in just a day or two.

Sincerely,

Jack Walsh

P.S. There's a writer in the business whom you may have heard of named Bill Jayme. After reading the manuscript, he wrote Dick saying: "If Lee Iacocca had sold magazines, insurance, cookbooks, records, financial services, wines and Polar expeditions instead of just cars, this is the book he might have written -- an American success story as inspiring and as instructive as the Ten Commandments."

If you won't take my word or Marty's, how about Bill's?

(Continued)

Figure 6–8. Dick Benson lift letter

RICHARD V. BENSON
4 BAYWOOD LANE
THE LANDINGS, SKIDAWAY ISLAND
SAVANNAH, GEORGIA 31411
(912) 598-1051

Dear Colleague:

Some day I may be able to teach Jack Walsh to write.

His letter which (I hope) you just read misses several important points:

First, my book deals with only one small part of advertising, direct mail. Not "direct response." Direct mail.

And within this tightly defined discipline, there is no one who can't learn from the book, if the person wants to.

From beginner to boardmember. Fulfillment people, printers, computer whizzes, art directors, numbers-crunchers (especially numbers-crunchers), product managers, circulation executives, letter-shop operators, editors, even writers (except, perhaps, Jack).

Something else I hope may give you reason to return the Order Form is that I'm a great believer in giving back some of the bounty life has given us.

> Accordingly, all the net proceeds from the sale of Secrets of Successful Direct Mail will be donated to the Education Fund of the Direct Marketing Association.

I wouldn't have written the book in the first place if I wasn't dedicated to the ideals of sharing and educating.

And I hope one further reason you buy the book is the realistic anticipation of your earning more money through it than even the Education Fund will realize.

Sincerely,

Richard V. Benson

Using professional reputation to increase response.

Mailer: **Childcraft Supplement Service**

Key Words: **"Bam!"**

Writer: **Jeff Strouse**

The Challenge

How does one interest a parent in a book about outer space, aimed at the child?

The problem is dual—creating the desire to even consider a book and to bring into orbit this particular book.

The Implementation

The writer uses three clever devices to assure reader-interest. The first is multiple handwriting in the letter which both personalizes and eases the weight of the sales argument.

The second is the popularizing of the educational aspect of this book. A parent might not respond to a recitation of planetary and galactic terminology but will respond to familiar names such as "Big Bear" and "Little Dipper."

The third is the true/false mini-test which replaces the P.S. on the letter and which certainly will pique a parent's interest—perhaps even to the point of sharing these questions with the child.

Comment

Does handwriting in a letter increase readership? If you agree that it does, you implicitly agree that increased readership translates into increased response.

This letter uses handwriting lavishly and also uses devices such as marginal notes, brackets, arrows, check marks, and hand-underlining, all in the second color (blue).

Instead of using a P.S., this letter has a boxed group of five questions designed to give the reader a taste of what he or she will find in the book.

Note that the handwriting is not "calligraphic." Rather, it parallels the handwriting of the signature—which it quite properly should.

Figure 6–9. Childcraft Supplements

THE CHILDCRAFT SUPPLEMENT SERVICE
POST OFFICE BOX 182265
CHATTANOOGA, TN 37422-7265

Ready to blast off?

You and your children are about to take a fun-filled, fascinating, fantastic voyage through outer space ...

Dear *Childcraft* Owner,

Bam!

That's the sound of a meteorite smashing into the moon.

With almost no atmosphere to protect itself, the moon is defenseless against these flying rocks which create gigantic dents called craters.

Now, in an exciting new book, the editors of *Childcraft* bring to life the magic and mystery of outer space.

This *Childcraft* supplement opens your children's minds to the wonders of the universe. It's titled ...

A Look into Space

... and as promised when you bought your *Childcraft* set, you're automatically entitled to preview this supplement for 15 days free!

Each year, *Childcraft* interviews over 25,000 customers like you to determine which topics will enlighten and entertain their children the most. The editors of *Childcraft* -- together with experts in child development and education -- then create a new supplement that will make a lasting impact on your children's intellectual growth.

I'm not surprised an overwhelming majority of parents selected such an exciting topic as *A Look into Space* for this year's *Childcraft* supplement. As a parent myself, I know from first-hand experience that kids learn more when they're having fun!

From the dark mysteries of black holes that stalk the universe, gobbling up all matter in their path ... to the sudden bursts of exploding stars in distant

(over, please)

An "explosive" opening and three devices—multiple handwriting, the use of familiar terminology, and a mini-test—increase response. *(Continued)*

– 2 –

galaxies thousands of light years away ... *A Look into Space* takes your children on spectacular adventures that will thrill them!

> If you and your children aren't absolutely fascinated with this new book, you may return it within the 15-day preview period and owe absolutely nothing.
>
> But I'm convinced that when you see your children's genuine looks of excitement as they explore the universe, you'll want to keep it.

I cherish the memory!

I happily remember the first time I shared a book on the stars and outer space with my daughter. Alyssa and I grabbed a couple of pillows from the couch and spread out on the family room rug, taking turns reading to one another.

We asked each other questions about the Big Bear, Little Dipper, shooting stars, and the sun. With each page, Alyssa's enthusiasm and curiosity grew. She found the universe fascinating, a new frontier to discover and enjoy.

When you give your children *A Look into Space*, you'll be doing much more than encouraging an active interest in the universe.

You'll be promoting a lifelong love of learning!

✓ Your children will develop stronger reading skills — When kids view reading as a fun, enjoyable activity, their reading skills improve naturally. This captivating volume guides your children on an incredible journey through outer space that leaves them eager to venture deeper into the exciting world of science!

✓ Build vocabulary skills — *A Look into Space* teaches your children how to pronounce and define words like *orbit, gravity, atmosphere,* and *meteor*. Your children also learn how to recognize and name planets, comets, constellations, and galaxies.

✓ Stimulate "scientific curiosity" — *A Look into Space* sparks your children's interest in science by actively involving them in a way no textbook can compare. Easy-to-do activities help your children discover the excitement of invention. They'll develop sharp, inquisitive minds buzzing with bright ideas for class projects and science fairs!

Makes learning an adventure — and fun, too!

✓ Fire the imagination — Eye-popping illustrations portray breathtaking wonders of the sky. Your children get a fascinating look at comets, supernovas, superclusters, pulsars, quasars, red giants, white dwarfs, and other oddities of outer space.

With *A Look into Space*, learning becomes a sheer joy! No child will want this wonderful trip to end! Punchy sentences and short, snappy examples

——→

(Continued)

– 3 –

make it fun and easy to read, while riddles, rhymes, myths and experiments add to your children's learning adventure.

What better way to show your kids how much you care!

Together, you and your children will ...

Helps forge motivated, confident, responsible adults!

Meet space heroes and terrific role models -- such as Galileo, Copernicus, Isaac Newton, Albert Einstein, Jules Verne, Mae Jemison, and Maria Mitchell -- who will help you instill enduring values in your children.

Probe the secrets of the Solar System, to discover how asteroids may be used to build future colonies, what destructive forces may have caused the dinosaurs to become extinct 65 million years ago, and why scientists believe sunspots triggered the Little Ice Age in the late 1600s. *A Look into Space* stimulates your children's curiosity and encourages them to learn more about the mysteries of the universe.

View the universe through the eyes of ancient astronomers -- including the Egyptians, Greeks, Maya, Inca and Navajo -- who charted the stars to decide when to plant crops. Your children will see how science is applied to everyday life -- then and now.

Great for science class!

If you're like most parents I know, you worry about the effect television is having on your children.

Research shows that the average child between the ages of three and ten watches over 30 hours of television each week. From birth to age 18, a period when they're developing 80% of their adult intellect, children spend 15,000 hours watching television -- compared to spending only 11,000 hours in the classroom.

What can compete with television and help your children develop the reading and learning skills necessary to succeed in school and in life?

Childcraft supplements can!

These thought-provoking books educate *and* entertain, using a child-tested format that makes learning fun and easy!

They're written at a primary grade level and bring to life the key subjects your children study in school. They promote the strong reading habits and attitudes toward learning that are so important in today's complex world.

As a parent, I can't think of a better way to inspire your children than with this year's *Childcraft* supplement ... *A Look into Space.*

(please turn the page)

(Continued)

-4-

Soon you'll automatically receive your copy of *A Look into Space* for a 15-day free preview without cost or commitment.

Your children will never forget this lasting gift!

When it arrives, open the carton and share the book with your children. Sit down and watch their excitement grow with every turn of the page.

If, after this 15-day free adventure, you aren't completely satisfied for any reason, just return the volume and owe nothing. *Childcraft* will even refund your return postage upon request. Otherwise, you're entitled to keep *A Look into Space* for the low *Childcraft* owner's price of just $17.95, plus $3.45 shipping and handling.

No-risk, 15-day free preview

Should you decide to cancel this supplement in advance by writing "cancel" on the enclosed card and mailing it back, your children will miss out on the benefits of *A Look into Space*. But, as the recent purchaser of a *Childcraft* set, you'll automatically receive an advance announcement about the next supplement, which you're also entitled to preview for 15 days free at no risk or obligation.

Please take advantage of *Childcraft's* free examination privilege. Keep an eye out for the mail. In a few weeks, you and your children will be taking off on a learning adventure that will last a lifetime!

Sincerely,

Robert Martin

RM:js
CA 3153

Robert Martin
President

P.S. Please sit down with your children and take this brief quiz. It may surprise you...

Science Fact ... Or Science Fiction?

1. Each year, the moon drifts 2.5 cm away from the Earth. _ True _ False
2. A large sun flare releases enough energy to supply a big city with electricity for 200 million years. _ True _ False
3. Pluto is the smallest planet, yet it takes the longest to travel around the sun -- 248 Earth years. _ True _ False
4. Living in weightlessness makes you taller. _ True _ False
5. The impact of an asteroid crashing into a planet could equal the explosiveness of ten atomic bombs. _ True _ False

Believe it or not, these statements are all true! Your children will make many other exciting discoveries in the latest *Childcraft* supplement, *A Look into Space* -- yours to preview absolutely free for 15 days!

Mailer: **American Psychiatric Press**
Key Words: **"I'm not surprised"**
Writer: **Kate Petranech**

The Challenge

How does one sell a book to psychiatrists in private practice and teachers of psychiatry in medical schools?

This has to be one of the most negative, most resistant groups of potential buyers, even when the publisher is a Press sharing its specialty.

The Implementation

Typically, a letter written within the publishing house would describe the text without adding color or flavor. This writer took a different approach, paralleling the technique of selling consumer books. She reports: "It demonstrates how lively you-oriented copy works as well with so-called 'professionals' as it does with the rest of the world. It puts the lie to notions like 'our market is different' . . . and 'that kind of approach is fine for consumers, but it would never work with doctors.' "

Obviously, the envelope had issued a challenge—three questions. The letter makes instant reference to those questions and cleverly avoids answering any of them until the second page.

The letter does indeed give the lie to the concept that doctors will not read longer letters and does so by dealing almost entirely in specifics rather than in loose rhetoric which would turn off a professional in this field.

Comment

To understand the opening, one has to know that the envelope copy ("How would you answer these three questions?" listing three psychiatric problems) pushes the reader forward into the sales argument. The questions are exquisitely chosen to hurl down a professional gauntlet before the professional reader. By offering concepts with which even the highly educated psychiatrist might not be completely familiar, the writer justifies this offer.

Figure 6–10. American Psychiatric Press

Dear Colleague:

I'm not surprised -- though I am pleased -- that you opened an envelope offering answers inside.

(And I promise those answers shortly.)

After all, looking for answers to questions is what you do every day.

Thumbing through the DSM-III-R. Consulting with colleagues. Cogitating between appointments.

Looking for the approach, the diagnosis, the treatment plan that will bring relief to the people you see.

If this is your experience, I believe you will want to add three new references to your list of resources:

The Clinical Interview Using DSM-III-R

DSM-III-R Casebook: A Learning Companion to the Diagnostic and Statistical Manual of Mental Disorders, Third Edition, Revised, and

Problems in Differential Diagnosis: From DSM-III to DSM-III-R in Clinical Practice

You can order these volumes today by completing and mailing the accompanying order form. Or, for faster service call the Press toll-free at 1-800-368-5777.

Don't let me mislead you. These books don't hold the answers to the hundreds of questions you confront each day. Those answers must still come from you.

But these resources will help you find the answers faster, as well as help you do a better job interviewing and diagnosing the people who come under your care.

Now, if you'll turn the page, we'll get to those questions.

1400 K Street, N.W., Washington, DC 20005 • (202) 682-6268 • FAX (202) 789-2648
London Office • 17 Belgrave Square • London, England, SW1X 8PG

The use of a consumer technique—asking enticing questions—sells to this group of professionals.

(Continued)

1. Which is better ... open-ended or close-ended questions for a person with borderline personality disorder?

Such an individual usually talks in a more genuine way if you ask open-ended questions. So take that approach.

This is the kind of practical, useful recommendations you'll get in The Clinical Interview Using DSM-III-R.

Use the book to develop, or fine-tune your interviewing style by exploring the process inside out ... and then seeing that process at work in actual clinical situations.

This major reference will assist you in countless ways. For example, do you

... have trouble establishing rapport with some patients?

This book will demonstrate how subtle changes in questioning technique can help you build intimacy.

... wish you did a better job at information gathering?

This book will help you to get the data you need by dealing more effectively with complaints .. overcoming resistance ... melting defenses.

You'll learn the four steps in assessing mental status. And the seven-point checklist for making a diagnosis.

This is not, however, a theoretical volume. Far from it. Each point is illustrated with an example and actual dialogue so you feel as though you're sitting in on a session. This text offers you page after page of tips and cues. For example:

> ... when diagnosing beginning dementia, look for signs of perplexity or suspiciousness. And use only short questions when interviewing... because the patient may not remember long ones.

2. How would you diagnose a modern-day Lady Macbeth?

Our "Lady Macbeth" is actually a 14 year old girl who has fears about germs, superstitions, anxiety about certain words and thoughts ... and must repeatedly wash her hands.

(Continued)

Is she suffering from obsessive-compulsive disorder? Or obsessive-compulsive personality disorder?

The former ... according to the DSM-III-R Casebook.

Obsessive-compulsive disorder features true obsessions and compulsions ... and also involves major depression.

Personality disorder, on the other hand, features such personality traits as perfectionism, indecisiveness, and restricted ability to express warm and tender emotions.

Lady Macbeth may be easy for you to diagnose. But what about the more complicated disorders -- such as the borderline personality -- where the symptoms aren't straightforward?

The Casebook will give you a chance to explore both types in 250 fascinating vignettes -- drawn from actual clinical situations -- and covering every mental disorder in DSM-III-R.

By reading brief histories of Tiny Tina ... Anna O. ... and Comrade Yen, you'll learn how to recognize and diagnose

... anxiety disorders in children
... conversion disorders
... and recurrent depression, respectively.

The Casebook will also give you the opportunity to see rare mental disorders such as -- Trichotillomania, a Disorder of Impulse Control Not Elsewhere Classified, and a new entity in the DSM-III-R ... thereby adding to your store of knowledge.

3. What's your interviewing style ... smorgasbord, checklist or canine?

Smorgasbord ... you aren't guided by a specific hypothesis but believe instead that a variety of areas should be "sampled."

Checklist ... you start with a preconceived idea of what's important.

Canine ... you "sniff" around for potentially vital data until you find a "bone."

Problems in Differential Diagnosis will teach you how to blend these techniques for multi-axial diagnosis. Demonstrate how to apply differential diagnosis to the most complex clinical problem.

(Continued)

And perhaps most important, this text will help you absorb automatically the changes in DSM-III-R by focusing not on the manual but rather on the syndrome ... as you do in your own clinical setting. For example, you'll learn about

- -- a new classification, organic anxiety syndrome ... and how it differs from functional anxiety disorder
- -- ten new, specific syndromes for substance-induced organic mental disorders ... and learn why they were added
- -- the role of "negative" symptoms in diagnosing schizophrenia
- -- new criterion in diagnosing agoraphobia
- -- new time restriction in diagnosing hypochondriasis
- -- the distinction between personality traits and personality disorders

ALL NEW IN DSM-III-R

Order one or more of these volumes today. As I mentioned at the start of this letter, you can order via the form enclosed. (We pay the postage.) Or if you want faster service call us toll free at 1-800-368-5777.

No Risk Guarantee

We're so certain you will value these books, we're prepared to make this guarantee.

Order the books today. When they arrive, look them over carefully. If after reviewing the references you find one or more is not useful to you, return it to us within 15 days with a request for credit. We'll cancel your order. Refund your money. And consider the matter closed.

With this guarantee ... why not order all three new titles for your personal library? Today.

Sincerely yours,

Carol C. Nadelson M.D.

Carol C. Nadelson, M.D.
Editor-in-Chief
American Psychiatric Press, Inc.

P.S. These new volumes also come highly recommended for library reference and teaching textbooks. See for yourself. Order today.

Mailer: **Rodale Books**

Key Words: **"Trigger miracles free"**

Writer: **Josh Manheimer**

The Challenge

Popularizing self-help medicine is a tricky proposition. Many try to do this but run afoul of the reader's own experiences. This results from a poor choice of examples or from explanations the reader might regard as outlandish.

To penetrate the reader's skepticism, both concept and example have to be more than provocative . . . they have to be convincing.

The Implementation

The letter uses the tested method of multiple teasers (How do you soothe itching with plain tea? Which vitamin slows down aging? When should you choose a sauna over a steambath?) plus highlighting.

The front page of the letter could not be more readable. It says to the reader, "I'm not going to be pedantic and I'm not going to be obscure. I'm going to be easy-reading."

The text begins in high-gear and the technique of short paragraphs pulls the reader to six full pages of anecdotes, examples, and salesmanship.

Comment

This letter, represented as the most successful package in the history of the Rodale Book Division, has three openings. The first is a semi-Johnson Box at the top of the page. The second is the instant reader-grabber, "QUICK!" Shirley shouted. "Grab the coffeepot!" And the third, after the "Dear Reader" greeting, is the first sentence of the actual letter.

A word about highlighting: Some writers have found that, although highlighting does lead the reader's eye, non-highlighted text is overlooked. Is this a problem? To the professional direct response writer, the only problem is lack of response.

Figure 6–11. Rodale Press

Trigger Miracles FREE - for 21 days!

* Your neighbor's child comes down with mysterious warts. The parents are baffled and afraid it may be serious. Quietly, you pull them aside and reveal how an allergy specialist can trigger the child's natural immune system. Several days later, the warts drop off and you're a hero! That night, you thank God you read PAGE 39.

* You wake up with a toothache. Before calling a doctor, you wisely put an ice cube on your hand. In seconds the pain subsides -- thanks to the timeless natural remedy you learned on PAGE 42.

* Your friends suggest a dark little ethnic restaurant. You are wary, but go along. Later, everyone gets sick -- except you. All because you read on PAGE 226 which foods to avoid while traveling.

"QUICK!" Shirley shouted. "Grab the coffee pot!"

Dear Reader,

I looked at her like she was crazy.

Our friend Bob was having a severe asthma attack right in front of our eyes ...

... and Shirley wants a cup of coffee!

Pushing me aside, she grabbed the coffee and forced Bob to drink. "This should do the trick," she said ...

In seconds Bob was breathing easier.

Seeing my amazement, Shirley laughed and explained, "I just learned how caffeine can provide instant relief for asthma. It triggers the body's natural immune system."

Powerful, down-to-earth examples convince the skeptical reader. *(Continued)*

"Did you know that by using simple trigger techniques you can ...

"Repair the damage from heart disease!"

"Ease arthritis!"

"Relieve migraine headaches!"

"Prevent cancer!"

"Lose weight forever!"

"Eradicate colds ...!"

"It's all here," she said, pulling something from her bookshelf. "Have a look."

Oh no, I thought, not some dense medical text book.

But to my pleasant surprise ...

... there in plain English was a collection of mankind's instant health cures, many of them passed down through the ages ...

... ancient Chinese herbal remedies next to the latest laser technology ...

Technology not yet available in this country!

As I thumbed through the pages, I saw remedies, antidotes, treatments, therapies, relief ... you could apply at once!

Things my doctor never told me!

* How do you soothe itching with plain tea? Stop vomiting with Coke syrup? Prevent swimmer's ear with white vinegar? There in Everyday Health Tips were the natural and inexpensive home remedies on PAGE 121.

* What is absolutely the most soothing thing you can do for hemorrhoids? Hard to believe, but there was the most simple cure on PAGE 35.

* Which vitamin slows down aging? Which vitamin sharpens your memory and helps you sleep? It was all clearly spelled out on PAGE 100.

* What is the most dangerous room in your house? Goodness! There was the startling information on PAGE 116.

* You should sit up when you wake up, right? Wrong! What should you do? PAGE 14 was chock full of advice no one ever told me on how to ease back pain.

* The bathroom medicine cabinet is the best place to store medicine, right? Wrong! It's the worst. There were the facts on PAGE 120.

* Diarrhea? These common drinks may be the best for you. See PAGE 21.

2

(Continued)

* Which of your friends can be helped by having skin removed from behind his ears, grafted onto his face and fine-sanded? PAGE 36.

* Travelers: How do you drag a spare tire out of a car trunk, stuff a briefcase into an airplane's overhead compartment -- without back pain? For latest techniques, read PAGE 14.

* When should you choose a sauna over a steambath? When is it best you choose neither. PAGE 17.

* An ancient Oriental treatment better than acupuncture? Yes! PAGE 17 tells you why so few have heard of it.

As I leafed through this remarkable publication, I grew more excited.

Bob was not our only friend with health problems.

Here on PAGE 26 was a way I could help my sister Gladys with her eye problem. PAGE 72 offered new hope for my nephew with his bad heart. PAGE 24 gave surprising new advice for my husband's allergies.

Whom could you help?

Did you know ...?

* Moles can turn into skin cancer. PAGE 40 tells you the warning signs and the 100 percent solution if you catch the symptoms early.

* You could be swallowing air instead of breathing it. For the side effects and how to stop, see PAGE 18.

* Gas pains? These seemingly healthy foods may be the cause. See PAGE 18 for fast relief.

* 5 steps that conquer constipation every time. PAGE 20.

* The 10 best foods for zinc. PAGE 110.

* Regulate your blood pressure with fruits and vegetables. PAGE 71.

* The vitamins you should be taking to fight off aging ... cancer ... cataracts ... respiratory disease ... bleeding gums ... infertility. PAGE 100.

"Where did all this come from?" I asked Shirley.

"Rodale Press," she replied. "You know them. They publish Prevention and Organic Gardening magazines."

"Some time ago the folks at Rodale realized there was no one place you could turn for instant home remedies.

"So, with their vast resources, Rodale assigned a team of researchers to gather together the most effective health tips currently known to mankind.

"Finally, after years of research, here is the fruit of their labor. Instantly, you can get your hands on over 2,000 trigger methods ... hints ... tips -- all bound within the covers of one over-sized, illustrated volume. 3

(Continued)

"It is the most important book they've ever published!"

I nodded my head, fascinated ... and read on.

There was everything from avoiding colds ... to removing molds.

* What are the 3 factors that determine if you will catch someone else's cold? How do you "short-circuit" just one to remain healthy? PAGE 2.

* You should turn on your air conditioner in the summer, right? No! A brief burst of mold contamination can lie hidden inside the filter. How to clean it? PAGE 25.

* Can eyeglasses give you a facial rash? Yes. PAGE 24.

* How do you prevent the crippling deformities of arthritis? PAGE 22.

* The 3 factors that make an exercise program successful? (Otherwise, don't bother.) PAGE 260.

There were dozens of helpful "do's! ..."

* Why you should get up at the same time every morning -- no matter how badly you've slept! PAGE 28.

* Why you should take fewer showers. PAGE 37.

* Why you should take faster showers. PAGE 37.

* Why you should garden in the evening. PAGE 25.

* When you should drink more water than your thirst calls for. PAGE 45.

And the most eye-opening "don'ts ..."

* Why you should not read in the bathroom. PAGE 21.

* Why you should not use a wash rag when treating poison ivy (or poison oak)! PAGE 25.

* Who should not use soap anywhere but under the arms and on the genitals. PAGE 37.

* The absolute worst time for your body to do paperwork or read? PAGE 26.

* Over-the-counter corn-removal medications? No! Soaking and sand-paper for corns? No! An easy way to avoid them? Yes! PAGE 46.

If you have questions, the easy-to-grasp explanations spell out all the answers clearly.

* What is "palming?" PAGE 27.

* What is a better alternative to eyedrops? PAGE 26.

* What is the secret to healing cuts twice as fast? PAGE 32.

4

* What is the "S" stance? How can it help an aching back? PAGE 12.

(Continued)

* How can a canvas-covered device filled with a mixture of sand and silicone help you? See PAGE 16.

If you have a specific problem, the handy index takes you right to the solution.

* Prostate problems? Sex may be the best prevention. PAGE 52.

* Athlete's foot? First, dust with cornstarch inside your shoes. Then turn to PAGE 47 for the key to picking perfect socks.

* Age spots? Lighten them. PAGE 40.

* Gastric ulcer or duodenal ulcer? What not to do! PAGE 19.

* Blister? Sterilize a sewing needle with 70 percent isopropyl alcohol. Clean the blister with antiseptic. Make small holes to release fluid. Final critical step -- PAGE 47.

* When should you skip the above advice and rush immediately to your doctor? PAGE 47.

See through myths ... and shibboleths.

* Sneezing into a tissue prevents colds, right? Wrong! PAGE 2 explains why.

* You should cut a "V" in the center of an ingrown toenail, right? Wrong, again. PAGE 49 tells you what does work.

* "Unscented" products have no scent? Sorry. Many are masked with a chemical that can cause allergic reactions. PAGE 24.

* You accidently knock out a tooth. Should you wrap it in a tissue and drive right to a dentist? No. First, put it back inside your mouth. Then get in your car. PAGE 43.

* If your gums are pink and clean, are you okay? Not necessarily. Hidden bacteria can eat away at the bone supporting the tooth. Stop it cold. PAGE 43.

How do you know ...?

* Is the same sales clerk selecting the best pair of shoes for you? Six critical things to watch for. PAGE 48.

* Which is really better? Chocolate or carob? Sugar or honey? PAGE 67 has some surprises in store for you.

* Your friend has painful swelling in her big toe. You tell her it's because she eats too many sardines. She looks at you like you're Marcus Welby, M.D. Quietly, you thank PAGE 48.

When I finally put the book down, I was afraid to ask Shirley my next question.

"What does a book like this cost? It must be outrageous."

Shirley laughed and said, "Believe it or not ...

5

(Continued)

"You get to sample it free for 21 days."

"How?" I asked.

"Easy," Shirley replied, "mail in your Free Trial Certificate. When the book arrives, pour yourself a cup of tea, sit down, and thumb through it. You're encouraged to try out several of the instant trigger health hints and see how well they work.

"Only then, if you decide to keep your personal volume, do you pay in three low, easy monthly installments."

You and I know, a visit to the doctor can really cost. Just one tip from Everyday Health Tips could pay for itself many times over.

"Remember, don't send them any money now," Shirley added.

"And if for any reason you do wish to return the book, Rodale will gladly pay the return postage. (A return shipping label is enclosed in this package. Just affix it to the box the book comes in. And that's that.)

"And ... I almost forgot ..." Shirley said.

"You also get a free Special Report prepared exclusively for you by the much-respected Division of Health Services at Rodale.

"It's a breakthrough study you won't find in any store.

"Inside, Rodale health experts reveal for you the miracles of the high seas. Miracles that have kept the Greenland Eskimos free from heart disease, cancer, arthritis, diabetes, and headaches!

"The advice alone is worth hundreds. And they give it to you as a free gift, which is yours whether you keep Everyday Health Tips or not!"

When Shirley was done, you can bet I sent for both books immediately. You feel better just knowing that instantly, you can get your hands on over 2,000 trigger methods ... hints ... tips -- whenever you (or your friends!) need one.

Cordially,

Kathi Fry

Kathi Fry

P.S. About Bob, the friend I mentioned at the start of this letter. He's all better thanks to Shirley's instant remedy.

Whom will you help save with over 2,000 instant trigger cures at your fingertips?

P.P.S. Because only so many copies of Rodale's free Special Report can be prepared at one time, first-come must be first-served.

Therefore, to avoid any chance of delay, return your Free Trial Certificate by
6 the earliest possible postmark. Thanks! K.F.

B9005

Mailer: **Nightingale-Conant**
Key Words: **"Complete mind/body approach to weight loss"**
Writer: **Barbara Harrison**

The Challenge

At least 100 percent of those interested in weight-loss programs have experienced negative results with other weight-loss programs. Thus they are at once hopeful and dubious.

Overcoming this complicated state of mind, which dictates caution, requires more than exhortation. The challenge, then, is to cause the reader to think, "This isn't just another of those programs."

The Implementation

As many of the exhibits in this book have shown, the communicator who is part writer and part psychologist knows that people do not want to buy books. They want to buy what the books represent.

This letter sells permanent weight loss—the result of the book—rather than the text itself. The writer points out: "It takes a weird, none-too-concrete notion (losing weight by bringing your mind and body into balance) and makes it seem easy, do-able, and enjoyable."

The first paragraph dismisses both the family doctor and diet books as well as "the most exclusive health spas." The result is an impression that if the reader wants this information she gets it only in the pages of this book.

Comment

The original of this letter was printed on bright yellow paper to maximize eye-appeal and to minimize the impression of actually being a letter.

By suggesting that the "science" of mind/body approach to weight-loss has been in use for more than 6,000 years, the writer walks a dangerous tightrope. Yet, the danger diminishes paragraph by paragraph as the text explains not only why this approach differs from "standard" weight-reduction plans, but also quietly dismisses other programs.

Quite properly, the offer includes a free 30-day "audition"—an inspired word.

Figure 6–12. Nightingale-Conant

Bring your mind and body into balance and say goodbye to weight problems forever!

In just 30 days, see the slender, healthy you come shining through!

Try it FREE!

Dear friend,

This remarkable "new" weight-loss method is as old as time. But your doctor probably won't mention it. Diet books don't discuss it. And the most exclusive health spas would quickly put themselves out of business if they revealed its amazing power.

Used for more than 6,000 years, the Science of Natural Health Care, or Ayur-Veda, can put you in tune with your body's needs. Without discomfort or denial, it helps correct the imbalances that cause weight problems in the first place.

Dr. Deepak Chopra, M.D., a practicing endocrinologist and world leader in the field of mind/body medicine, shows you how effortless and natural permanent weight loss can be.

As an added benefit, you will also experience renewed self-confidence along the path to self-discovery.

Try THE COMPLETE MIND/BODY APPROACH TO WEIGHT LOSS FREE for 30 days. Listen...learn...look forward to a future filled with perfect health and bliss. Keep it if you love it, and say goodbye to weight problems forever.

For all the millions of men and women who have endured endless diets, or lost and regained the same pounds year after year...THE COMPLETE MIND/BODY APPROACH TO WEIGHT LOSS puts permanent weight loss within easy reach.

Simply by listening, you can harness your own inner

Nightingale-Conant
7300 North Lehigh Avenue
Niles, IL 60714

Selling results instead of content gives big lift to response. *(Continued)* intelligence to bring your mind and body into perfect balance. "teach" your body to convert food into positive energy instead of fat!

This remarkable weight-loss technique is not about creating a new you, but about discovering the hidden you deep inside.

Where diet programs have failed you in the past, THE COMPLETE MIND/BODY APPROACH TO WEIGHT LOSS can work miracles. Dr. Chopra shows you:

How to use food to influence the mind/body connection.

Which foods tone the digestive canal.

The lessons revealed in Nature's own packaging.

How massage can help rid your body of impurities.

How to alter your metabolism by up to 25% with spices.

Where counting calories and measuring mouthfuls have led to frustration and disappointment in the past, you will find that THE COMPLETE MIND/BODY APPROACH TO WEIGHT LOSS can bring lifelong freedom from obesity. Discover, for example:

A natural method for dissolving cellulite.

Foods that bring you back to your ideal weight without calorie-counting or restrictive routines.

How you can know, moment by moment, what your body needs in order to create ideal digestion, proper metabolism and perfect balance.

When standing on the scale has led to shame and dismay, Dr. Chopra helps you get in touch with your body's inner intelligence through THE COMPLETE MIND/BODY APPROACH TO WEIGHT LOSS.

A balanced mind and body are within your reach!

In addition to losing weight (whether you have 100 pounds to go or that last stubborn 10)...

The principles in THE COMPLETE MIND/BODY APPROACH TO WEIGHT LOSS will also fill you with energy...improve your digestion... strengthen your resistance to disease...boost your physical endurance...and infuse you with a feeling of bliss.

No wonder modern medicine is turning back to the lessons of the past!

(Continued)

Dr. Chopra distills the teachings of 6 centuries and guides you effortlessly through THE COMPLETE MIND/BODY APPROACH TO WEIGHT LOSS. Listen as you drive to work. Unwind with the audiocassettes at the end of the day. Listen with headphones as you walk.

It's like having a personal trainer design an effective weight-loss program just for you.

As Dr. Chopra guides you, step by step, you will make amazing discoveries about your body and mind. Listen as he reveals...

How to keep your skin toned and firm as you lose weight, to prevent sagging and wrinkling.

Why you really are what you eat.

Which foods distort your natural sensation of hunger and give rise to misleading signals that can cause you to overeat.

The Ayurvedic cure for snacking.

Why reducing calories is the least effective way to lose weight.

The three most common exercise mistakes people make.

How to alter your satiety threshold – the point at which your body feels full.

To gain the maximum benefit from this program...

Use the richly detailed 58-page spiral-bound Workbook included with your audiocassettes. The Workbook supplements Dr. Chopra's practical recommendations and helps you apply what you learn with ease.

The Workbook includes Dr. Chopra's Satisfaction Meter™ to assess your true level of hunger...charts to help you determine your body type...guidance in doing Ayurvedic massage to speed weight loss...checklist for Body Intelligence Techniques... illustrated yoga exercises and much more.

Won't you try THE COMPLETE MIND/BODY APPROACH TO WEIGHT LOSS free for 30 days?

(Continued)

To achieve permanent weight loss effortlessly...

Send no money now. Simply say "yes" and we'll rush you THE COMPLETE MIND/BODY APPROACH TO WEIGHT LOSS right away. The entire program is yours to audition for 30 days, absolutely free. Don't miss this chance to change your body and your life without risking a cent.

Be inspired by Dr. Chopra's patient teaching, his brilliant clarity, his firm foundation in both Western medicine and ancient Eastern philosophy.

Be motivated by the effortless ease of this remarkable program, and how naturally it fits into your life.

Be reassured by your FREE 30-DAY AUDITION — enough time to listen to all four audiocassettes and begin to follow the action plan outlined in the spiral-bound Workbook.

And if you wish to continue your journey until your ideal weight is achieved...

You may keep THE COMPLETE MIND/BODY APPROACH TO WEIGHT LOSS for just $49.95, a tiny fraction of the cost of other weight-loss programs. Use it again and again for guidance and direction along your road to self-improvement.

To a balanced, blissful you!

Vic Conant

Vic Conant
President

P.S. With THE COMPLETE MIND/BODY APPROACH TO WEIGHT LOSS you will receive Dr. Chopra's unique Satisfaction Meter™. Use it to assess your true level of hunger, and determine when to eat and when to stop. So much simpler than following a rigid diet! So much more effective than weight-loss programs that rely on strict rules instead of your own inner intelligence.

I urge you to send for it FREE without delay!

Mailer: The Legal Classics Library
Key Words: "Our trustees and editorial advisory board"
Writer: Jack Walsh

The Challenge

The challenge faced by this series of books is similar to the challenge faced by the series just described and is even more profound in that peripheral readership—non-lawyers—is not sought out at all.

Adding to the problems a program like this might face is the paucity of well-known titles, the inclusion of works which lawyers probably had studied in school (draining the entertainment factor away), and the unrelievedly serious nature of the editorial content.

The Implementation

Unlike popularly oriented series, this program aims itself solely at lawyers and does so with a comprehensive, straightforward exposition of the components of this continuity series followed by a status appeal based on the production of the books.

By offering a one-year repurchase guarantee, the offer bypasses the recipient's fear of being trapped in an endless program.

The "Dear Counselor" opening leaves no doubt—this letter is aimed solely at the legal profession.

The writer immediately identifies himself (J.D., *Juris Doctor*) as a fellow barrister. But there the rhetorical tie to the legal profession ends. The letter is far more readable than one would expect of a message selling books about the law to lawyers. The writer uses contractions, indented paragraphs, and quotations—all devices usually reserved for the rest of us.

Comment

As you read this letter, you probably would not have noticed, had we not called attention to it, that nowhere does the writer tell the reader what each book costs. This may be because the letter was part of a price test (the sample in our hands shows, on the response device, an introductory price of $24.50 for the first book and $49.00 for subsequent books).

We prefer a direct mention of cost, especially to a reader as literal-minded as the typical lawyer. Letters for this kind of offer often quote the price up-front, in the first paragraph of the first page. Stating price early in the letter reinforces price testing, and the different prices can be dropped in without difficulty. But understand, our preference is opinion. The results of this letter are indisputable fact.

Figure 6–13. The Legal Classics Library

L-A

The LEGAL CLASSICS LIBRARY

LESLIE B. ADAMS, JR.,M.A.,J.D.,LL.D.
Publisher

Our Trustees and Editorial Advisory Board

Cordially Invite You

To Become a Member of

THE LEGAL CLASSICS LIBRARY

A Collection of the Great Books in the Law

Bound in Genuine Top-Grain Leather

With the First Volume,

Oliver Wendell Holmes, Jr.'s

THE COMMON LAW & OTHER WRITINGS

Offered at Half Price

To Attorneys Joining the Library at This Time

All Volumes Are Offered Under an Unconditional

One-Year Repurchase Guarantee

Dear Counselor:

I feel obliged to caution you that - if a growing number of our colleagues is any indication - the invitation above could become habit forming. In a most beneficial way, of course!

For many are now subscribing to become owners of a unique, privately printed collection of the greatest legal books of all time, in exact replicas of the famous - and exceedingly rare - originals.

THE LEGAL CLASSICS LIBRARY

And this letter is your invitation to join their select number. Any by way of introduction, to own your leather-bound edition of the celebrated The Common Law & Other Writings, by Oliver Wendell Holmes, Jr., at half price.

"I'm one of you" plus status sell specialized continuity program. *(Continued)*

- 2 -

Unless you have seen an actual volume from this extraordinary private library - in a friend's collection, or at our booth at a recent convention - it is hard to visualize its breathtaking beauty and enduring quality.

The same time-consuming craft skills, the same luxurious materials lavished on the finest books of the Eighteenth and Nineteenth centuries have been devoted to this Library. Each volume is sumptuously hand-bound in carefully selected genuine top-grain leather, the spine richly tooled in genuine 22-karat gold. With the fine papers and ink, the gilded leaves and elegant endpapers, the effect is a literal treasure of the bookmaker's art - an heirloom volume that will last for generations to come.

> So confident are we of the Library's quality and enduring value that we offer each selection to you for acquisition under this extraordinary warranty:
>
> For an entire year after you have taken possession, we guarantee to repurchase any book in good condition at exactly the same price you paid for it! Just send it back - no explanation required - and our check will be in the mail. No ifs, ands, or buts.

After you've had a chance to savor the Holmes selection, you'll receive your second and subsequent volumes in the Library for your consideration every six weeks or so (occasionally late delivery of gold or imported leather may cause a slight delay). Each volume will become an important addition to your library.

Each volume in The Legal Classics Library is unique in format. Unlike uniform, mass-printed editions, no two volumes are exactly the same. Yet, together, they are designed to comprise a complete and harmonious collection on your shelves.

Each exactly replicates the best available specimen copy of the famous original - usually the first edition - and is faithful in every respect - size, type, illustrations. Nothing is omitted. You'll enjoy the satisfaction of holding in your hands a perfect, almost uncanny recreation of the very volume generations of attorneys before you cherished and consulted. (And never fear if the original languages of some titles elude you; an authoritative translation will accompany all non-English selections.)

Thus, these are practical volumes to which you can refer, for as Sir William Osler observed, "the higher education so much needed today is not given in the school, it is not to be bought in the market place, but it has to be wrought out in each one of us for himself; it

(Continued)

is the silent influence of character on character and in no way more potent than in the contemplation of the lives of the great and good of the past, in no way more than in 'the touch divine of noble natures gone.'" Gone today are the great nobles in the development of the law - Coke and Kent, for example - but their truths, and their errors, are still available to instruct us.

> And the endorsement of the Library by many leading institutions and educators underscores the relevance of the classical literature to the modern attorney.

These are bold statements. But if I'm right (and I think I am), The Legal Classics Library will be a significant and proud possession, one that you'll display prominently, but even more important, one that you'll refer to repeatedly.

And one that will appreciate in value to you emotionally ... and perhaps monetarily. For it is impossible to contemplate the series we aspire to without being aware of a trend that was perhaps best summed up in an article in Money magazine not too long ago:

> "In economic terms, good books are a decreasing commodity facing increasing demand as ... more people are attracted to collecting."

And shouldn't this be particularly true of an extraordinary library of the great classics of the law?

And soul-satisfying it is today to read the very words of the great masters of the law as first set down decades or even centuries ago. And to feel a part of the noble "apostolic succession" of attorneys to which Osler so feelingly referred!

That succession is never more happily exemplified than in the celebrated work we have selected as the premier volume in the Library, Holmes' The Common Law & Other Writings. For the first time ever, all the books published by Holmes during his lifetime are here presented in exact facsimile in one binding: his landmark opus, The Common Law, along with his Collected Legal Papers and Speeches.

Speaking of selection, let me tell you how we are going to choose the books that will be included in your collection, as selectivity is the key to any great library. What are the great books in law? To answer that question, I am pleased to consult with a number of scholars who have enthusiastically agreed to serve with me on the Editorial Advisory Board. And I must admit that their enthusiasm is contagious!

I felt myself the most fortunate of men when these extraordinarily gifted and incredibly busy attorneys agreed to serve. While you may

(Continued)

not know them all personally, I'd be surprised if you did not know most of them by name:

> Neill H. Alford, Jr., Esq., LL.B., J.S.D., Percy Brown Jr. Professor of Law, University of Virginia.
>
> Thomas G. Barnes, Esq., D.Phil., Professor of History and Law, University of California at Berkeley.
>
> Yale Kamisar, Esq., LL.B., LL.D., Henry K. Ransom Professor of Law, University of Michigan.
>
> Roy M. Mersky, J.D., M.A.L.S., Hyde Centennial Professor of Law and Director of Research, Tarlton Law Library, The University of Texas at Austin.
>
> L. Ray Patterson, Esq., LL.B., Pope Brock Professor of Law, University of Georgia, School of Law.
>
> Peter Gonville Stein, Esq., M.A., LL.B., Ph.D., F.B.A., Regius Professor of Civil Law in the University of Cambridge, and Fellow of Queens' College, Cambridge.
>
> Calvin Woodard, Esq., LL.B., Ph.D., Doherty Professor of Law, University of Virginia.
>
> Charles Alan Wright, Esq., LL.B., William B. Bates Professor of Law for the Administration of Justice, University of Texas.

I certainly feel, and I suspect you'll agree, that it is a major compliment to the concept and integrity of The Legal Classics Library that these experts - all busy professionals - are willing to take so active a part in assuring its success.

After Justice Holmes, the titles and authors the Board had definitely decided upon are equally distinguished. These include, of course, the towering peaks of legal literature - without which any respectable library would be incomplete. (And they also include some very rare and intriguing lesser-known works that will add spice to your collection.) Among the classics you can look forward to are:

> The work most influential in the development of the common law - particularly in North America - Sir William Blackstone's Commentaries on the Laws of England. Our edition will be an exact facsimile of the very famous - and very rare - first four-volume edition of 1765-1769. Nor could we go long without publishing the work of Holmes' distinguished successor on the bench of the Supreme Court of the United States, Benjamin N. Cardozo.

(Continued)

- 5 -

Our plan on Cardozo, like Holmes, is to present in one volume all the books Cardozo published in his lifetime: The Nature of the Judicial Process (1921); The Growth of the Law (1924); The Paradoxes of Legal Science (1928); and Law and Literature (1931).

Sir Henry Sumner Maine's Ancient Law is important in that it is likely the most durable work of jurisprudence in the English language after Blackstone. In masterful fashion, Maine explores the origins and development of primitive law (just to partially cover the book's wide-ranging subject matter).

And surely it would be impossible to structure the collection we're contemplating without The Federalist of Alexander Hamilton, John Jay, and James Madison. These insightful documents have been called "the greatest individual contribution to the adoption of the government of the United States." The Federalist remains today a classic commentary on American constitutional law and the principles of government generally.

Another book we'll likely publish early on is Montesquieu's L'Esprit des lois. Variously described as "one of the most important books ever written," and "the greatest book of the French Eighteenth century," Montesquieu's magnum opus was of significant influence upon the framers of our Constitution, who adopted a great part of his teachings, especially with respect to the balance of power. The Spirit of Laws has a remarkable freshness even today. Especially today?

As you can see from these few examples, the riches that await you are prodigious as is our task in selecting among them. Names that come to mind - all of them in preparation or under consideration - include:

Brandeis...Coke...Littleton...Glanvil...Wellman...
Fortescue...Hand...Pound...Frank...Pollock...Maitland...
Grotius...Story...Hale...Bracton...Thayer...Langdell...
Marshall...Wigmore...Salmon...Kent...Plato...Thomas
Aquinas...Austin...

The more I name, the more that come to mind. If you have a favorite, please drop me a note when you return the enclosed Enrollment Form. Our Editorial Advisory Board will give your suggestion its closest attention.

Once a title has finally been approved for publication by the Board, the work really starts. First, the work of finding the finest

(Continued)

- 6 -

copy of it extant. Or even just a copy, for many of these books are very, very rare, even virtually unobtainable.

Our editors literally traverse the globe to locate the specific edition selected by the Board as being the best original edition for reproduction and inclusion in the Library. They visit the Bodleian Library at Oxford, the Library of Congress, the rare legal book collections at Cambridge, Harvard, Yale, and Columbia, the British Museum...wherever necessary to find the very best edition for our purposes.

The result: a collection like no other. The most complete library of all the best editions of the world's legal classics assembled in one convenient accessible place - your home or office! A standard against which any subsequent effort - in the unlikely event it were attempted - would be measured. To complement the preeminence of these titles, the physical appearance of your Library will be as impressive as its scope.

When you slip the book out of its customized shipping case, rub the back of its deeply embossed 22-karat gold spine. Then breathe in the rich aroma of its genuine top-grain leather binding. Luxurious!

The volumes feature ribs across the spine, called "hubs," a characteristic of fine European library bindings. The special French joints permit your volume to lie flat at whatever page you open it to - for easy, "no hands" reading. The cover boards bulk to an uncommon 123 points. And unseen, but essential to long life, is the tough all-cotton-ply thread used to sew the book's signatures together.

Design and manufacture of the Library, including the critical hand-binding process, is under the personal supervision of a team of some of the world's foremost fine-edition specialists.

The top-grain leather bindings range from Indian goatskin to pigskin to buffalo calf to cowhide - whatever is deemed appropriate to the particular volume and to the collection as a whole. All will create a rich panoply through varying textures and colors. (We believe conforming, matched sets of books belong in supermarkets with other packaged goods.)

All three sides of the leaves are gilded to give them extra - and elegant - protection from light, moisture, and dust.

Papers for the text and the faithfully-reproduced original illustrations are selected from the finest grades available, chosen for their low acidity or in most cases

(Continued)

- 7 -

completely acid-free content. This is a Library designed to last for generations, and beyond.

Endleaves are handsomely decorated with marbleized papers. No two volumes will be the same.

For ease of reference, each book contains a permanent silk ribbon marker in a color complementing the leather binding.

Every selection is delivered with an authoritative booklet, "Notes from the Editors," describing the book's history and significance.

To summarize the guarantees of Membership:

1. The first title, Oliver Wendell Holmes, Jr.'s, The Common Law & Other Writings, is yours at a 50 percent savings, with membership.

2. Every volume in the Library will be delivered under a one-year Repurchase Guarantee that assures you we will buy it back as long as it is in good condition any time within twelve months of purchase for exactly what you paid for it.

3. Your Library will be complete and comprehensive, including all the premier writings in the history of law, as selected by our distinguished Editorial Advisory Board with the help of interested members.

4. All books will be bound with the finest genuine leather, of value comparable to fine editions selling at retail at far higher prices.

5. Each selection will be accompanied by an authoritative pamphlet, "Notes from the Editors," describing the book's history and significance to the profession.

6. Of special importance, there is no commitment on your part to buy a minimum number of books; you may quit anytime you wish...and our repurchase warranty is binding for an entire year.

All of which is designed to assure you that returning the Enrollment Form exposes you to no risk whatsoever.

(Continued)

- 8 -

To take advantage of this opportunity to begin your own collection of the great books in the legal tradition, please mail the Enrollment Form today.

Sincerely,

Leslie B. Adams, Jr.

Leslie B. Adams, Jr.
Publisher

P.S. I noted in the Times recently that a London dealer had purchased at Sotheby's a rare first edition of Blackstone's Commentaries on the Laws of England for $10,000 - a record for a legal book. It should be gratifying to know that your facsimile copy of that pioneer legal work will be faithful to the famous original in every detail.

That it, and other volumes in your Legal Classics Library, may also appreciate in value over the years may also be of interest. But certainly not the primary reason for collecting them. That, as our Members assure us again and again, derives from the enduring satisfaction of owning these splendid volumes, reading them at leisure, feasting one's eyes on the shelves they adorn. And - quite pardonably - showing them off to colleagues, family, and friends.

And with the Repurchase Guarantee, you are assured the books will not decrease in value for an entire year, at least. Don't you wish you could buy stocks under such an arrangement?

Division of GRYPHON EDITIONS

Printed in the U.S.A.

Chapter 7

Financial Services and Investments

Writing an effective investment or credit card letter is one of the more difficult challenges for the professional letter-writer. The principal reason: rampant skepticism, the marketer's curse of the last decade of the twentieth century, with even more dismal prospects for the first two decades of the twenty-first century.

This skepticism isn't the fault of letter-writers; rather, it's the fault of too-easy mass communications. Every single day we have conflicting points of view by broadcast talk show hosts (for example, consecutively on the same station or network an "I'm always right" liberal and an "I'm always right" conservative); by competing television commercials (consecutive commercials for different makes of automobile or competing fast food restaurants, each with identical claims), and by government pronouncements (semi-factual attacks by each party upon the other, with confusing analyses by "experts"). All have led to a passive rejection of almost any promise made by a previously unknown source.

Financial mailings bear the brunt of this latter-day skepticism because, more than any other appeal, they necessarily must depend on *greed* as their basic motivator.

The problem is compounded by growing dependence on database, which results in the best target being the most likely to get a mailing from a financial competitor.

Mailer: Invesco Funds Group
Key Words: "This may be the 375th letter"
Writer: Sheldon Seymour

The Challenge

Most investors take one of two polarized viewpoints toward solicitation: (a) I already have the best broker/investment counselor in the world; (b) none of you know what you're talking about.

Overlaid onto both attitudes is the *bete noir* of direct response—apathy.

The Implementation

The letter tackles both major typical objections head-on. While doing so, it also brightly disengages the apathy-generating mechanism.

Shorter than the typical investment letter, this one-pager begins with a free gift, acknowledges the recipient's position, and strokes the recipient's ego with the statement, "This may be the 375th letter you've had this year suggesting ways to invest" . . . and makes an apparently mild, non-threatening offer.

Comment

Note the convivial terminology:

- "No surprise—investors like you get the most mail."
- "Your obligation? Zero. Zip."
- "While I have your attention, a 15-second commercial."

The letter ends with the single word, "Thanks!" which many writers report adds measurable response. We have heard of no test of a mailing with and without the word "thanks," but we certainly do know it doesn't hurt.

Figure 7–1. Invesco Funds Group

P.O. Box 173706
Denver, Colorado 80217-3706

THE #1 FAMILY OF FUNDS
HAS A FREE GIFT FOR YOU... *(No strings attached)*

Dear Fellow Investor,

This may be the 375th letter you've had this year suggesting ways to invest. No surprise—investors like you get the most mail.

My proposition is different.

All I want today is to tell you a little bit about one of our top, no-load mutual funds (Financial Industrial Income Fund) and get your okay to send you a free six-month subscription to *Kiplinger's Personal Finance Magazine*. That's the authoritative and very readable publication which used to be called *Changing Times*. Or, if you prefer, we'll send you Kiplinger's acclaimed 448-page financial guidebook, *Watch Your Money Grow*.

Your obligation? Zero. Zip. Oh, I'll enclose a pamphlet, "Making the Right Investment Moves." And I'm counting on this pamphlet—which is *loaded* with bright and logical investment strategies— to help you with your investment decisions. But even if you don't send in the reply card, you'll know who we are—so we're still ahead.

While I have your attention, a 15-second commercial:

We want you to know about a company with an unassailable 61-year track record. And, while past performance is no guarantee of future results, Lipper Analytical Services ranked our Financial Industrial Income Fund *Number 1* among *all* equity income funds for the most recent 30- and 25-year periods ended December 31,1992. *Money* Magazine also ranked our family of no-load funds Number 1 among 25 leading fund families for overall investment performance. Some funds pay a modest distribution fee.

End of commercial. But, I hope, the beginning of your interest in what INVESCO might do for you.

For INVESCO Funds Group,

Dan J. Hesser
President and CEO

P.S. I do want you to have your free *Kiplinger's* subscription, or Kiplinger's 448-page financial guidebook, *Watch Your Money Grow*. Drop the enclosed card in the mail or call us toll-free at 1-800-525-8085. Thanks!

INVESCO's Financial Funds ranked number one in *Money* Magazine's August 1992 issue among 25 major fund groups for total fund family asset-weighted performance for various two year periods during the past six years ended 4/30/92. For the 30-, 25-, 10-, 5-, 1-year, and 3-month periods ending 12/31/92, Financial Industrial Income Fund was ranked among all equity income funds by Lipper Analytical Services as #1 out of 9, #1 out of 11, #2 out of 19, #2 out of 40, #68 out of 69, and #8 out of 74, respectively. Total return assumes reinvestment of dividend and capital gain distributions. Investment return and principal value will fluctuate so that, when redeemed, an investor's shares may be worth more or less than their original cost. For more complete information, including management fees and expenses, call or write for a free prospectus. Read it carefully before you invest or send money. INVESCO Funds Group, Inc., Distributor.

Overcoming apathy by attacking objections and skepticism head-on.

Mailer: Barclay Card
Key Words: "Being a full time student"
Writer: Andy Owen

The Challenge

This letter, a successful promotion in the United Kingdom, shows how universal the problems of financial promotion can be.

Identifying a problem common to a vertical-interest group, and convincing members of that group that the solution is at hand requires a combination of motivators. Rejection of any one of those motivators means rejection of the offer.

The Implementation

The writer depends on exclusivity and greed as the two principal motivators for this letter, aimed at students. These motivators would translate perfectly for use in any industrialized country. This letter indicates how, except for spelling of words such as "cheque," "favourite," and "travelling," force-communication from the U.K. parallels that of the U.S.

On a single sheet, the communication both describes and shows the combination of benefits, and it does so without losing the touch of high personalization.

Comment

A generation ago, no financial institution would allow the phrase, "It's tough." The gradual introduction of verbalisms, which has become standard in the U.S. since the late 1970s, now is universal throughout the English-speaking world.

And why not? This is exactly what today's marketer should do—communicate within the reader's experiential acceptance level, not the writer's.

Notice how the letter follows a classic pattern: Identifying a problem, sympathizing with the problem, and then providing a solution to the problem.

Figure 7–2. The Barclay Bank

A FREE BARCLAYCARD FOR STUDENTS.

BARCLAYCARD

05920 D 1

Miss H Jones
9 Robert Street
Glynneath
NEATH
West Glamorgan
SA11 5EG

Dear Miss Jones,

Being a full time student these days is extremely hard work; a lot is expected of you. And you have to become pretty much financially independent as well.

It's tough. No doubt about that. However, not as tough as it may first look, because help is at hand.

Student Barclaycard is specially designed to address your financial worries and to provide help and assistance when you require it most.

> Maybe your grant cheque is late, or you need to purchase that important book; no problem - Barclaycard is there, just when you need it. You can use your card to pay for almost anything - dining out, music and video purchases, travel tickets - Barclaycard is accepted wherever you see the VISA sign.

Issued **completely free** to students, Barclaycard offers a number of attractive benefits :-

* A choice of free gift upon acceptance of your application.
* Acceptance of your card in over 10 million outlets worldwide.
* The convenience and ease of purchasing, with added security of Barclaycard Purchase Cover.
* A competitive interest rate of 1.65% per month. Our lowest for 15 years.
* Ideal money management tool, with detailed monthly statements to enable you to plan your budget sensibly.
* Up to 8 weeks interest free credit.

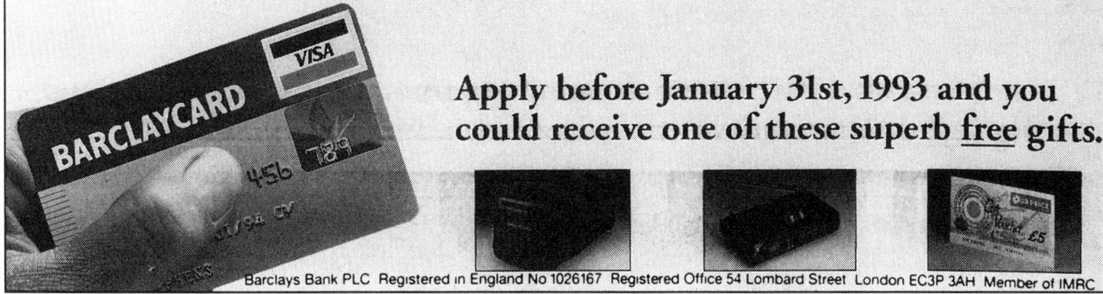

Barclays Bank PLC Registered in England No 1026167 Registered Office 54 Lombard Street London EC3P 3AH Member of IMRC

Using the classic formula and communicating at the reader's level of experience make this letter a winner. *(Continued)*

* **Barclaycard Travel Accident Insurance, giving you automatic cover of up to £50,000.**

These are just a few of the many benefits of being a Barclaycard holder - there are others too!

Gone are the days when you have to queue outside a box office for tickets to see your favourite artists in concert. Now, all you have to do, is pick up the phone and book the tickets on your Barclaycard. It's simple, easy, convenient and, a whole lot warmer!

When you feel the urge to spread your wings a little, Barclaycard is an ideal travelling companion, right from booking to return. Wherever you are in the world, immediate help and assistance are always on hand should you need it, with Barclaycard International Rescue. This is a <u>free</u> service, available 24 hours a day.

Furthermore, if your Barclaycard is lost or stolen whilst on holiday, we can advance you cash in local currency, usually within 24 hours of your call, to enable you to continue your holiday without worry.

> **All in all, an attractive package, specifically tailored and ideally suited for <u>you</u> and your current lifestyle. And remember, Barclaycard is issued <u>free</u> to students.**

To apply for a Barclaycard couldn't be simpler. The enclosed brochure, which gives you further information on the many benefits available, contains a simple application form.

Just complete the form and return it to us. No stamp is needed.

Once your application is approved, your Barclaycard will quickly be on its way to you and you'll soon be enjoying its broad range of complimentary benefits and services.

We look forward to receiving your application form.

Yours sincerely,

Mark Duckworth,
Manager, Barclaycard.

PS Don't forget to let us know your choice of <u>free</u> gift.

Mailer: **Comerica Bank**
Key Words: **"Who needs another credit card?"**
Writer: **Richard Goldrosen**

The Challenge

The first sentence of the letter mirrors the challenge: "Who needs another credit card?"

In reality, most of the best prospects for a credit card don't need another credit card. So the challenge of any mailing of this type (a number of which appear in this chapter) is to leap above the automatic rejection that has the recipient saying, "Ho-hum, another credit card offer."

The Implementation

This letter, like other successful financial mailings, immediately acknowledges and attacks the reader's skepticism. The first sentence "Who needs another credit card?" has to be a question the best prospects will be asking, because the best prospects don't need another credit card.

By taking the position of "surrogate" for the reader, the writer literally becomes the reader; so when the writer dispels the skepticism, the reader goes along.

Comment

Much as we admire this mailing, one negative: We are unalterably opposed to asterisks. On the other hand, some financial institutions are unalterably opposed to removing asterisks. We, subject to a lawyer's friendly interpretation, would reposition the statement following each asterisk, using the simple device of parentheses. Parentheses serve two purposes: First, they do not break up the reading flow; second, by their very nature, they subordinate whatever statement is inside the parentheses.

Is the phrase, "please call" in the final paragraph as potent as the single word, "call"? Two points of view here: One says politeness works. Another says telling the reader what to do works better. It's an unanswerable question until and unless some brave financial institution decides to test the word "please."

Figure 7–3. Comerica Bank

ComericA

Comerica Bank-Midwest, N.A.

Pre-Approved!

No
Annual Fee
12.4% APR*
Up to $10,000
credit line

Mr. Sample A. Sample
123 Anystreet
City, State Zip

Dear Mr. Sample:

"Who needs another credit card?"

You may very well be asking yourself that question right now. Especially if you're already using a credit card that provides refunds, car rebates or frequent flyer miles.

Why are we writing you today? Because the Comerica MasterCard is not just another credit card. The difference between those other cards and ours is simple:

- 12.4% variable rate APR*
- No annual fee
- Up to $10,000 in pre-approved credit**

Now, the other cards you carry have their place, and they provide a valuable service, such as rebates, refunds or air miles--at a price. All those extras add up when it comes time to pay the bill--especially if you carry monthly balances on those cards.

We recommend you enjoy the best of both worlds - keep using your other cards for the benefits they provide, but transfer your high-interest balances to the Comerica card. You'll continue to enjoy the extra services they offer while paying much less in interest for any balances you maintain. We'll even send you personalized checks to make transferring as easy as possible.

Unlike other credit cards that focus on giving you rebates, refunds and frequent flyer miles, we simply give you the added savings and extra purchasing power you deserve.

To accept your pre-approved Comerica credit card, please complete and mail your Acceptance Certificate today. Or, if you wish, please call 1-800-292-1300 to RSVP by phone. In either case, your new Comerica card will be rushed to you.

Sincerely,

P. K. Chatterjee
Senior Vice President

P.S. Please respond by May 12, 1994 to take advantage of this low, 12.4% variable rate, no annual fee opportunity. You're already pre-approved, so please respond today.

* Your Annual Percentage Rate, which may vary quarterly, is determined by adding 6.4% to the Comerica Bank Prime Lending Rate.

** The minimum line available is $1,000, the maximum is $10,000. The amount of your credit line will be based on your annual income.

Asking the reader's own obvious question disarms negative attitudes.

Mailer: Colonial National Bank

Key Words: "It's amazing"

The Challenge

As we explore the competitive nature of credit card mailings, the standard challenge becomes so clear we sometimes wonder how *any* of these mailings can succeed.

Those that do succeed somehow have to separate themselves from the mélange of others, avoiding the gray sameness that infects so many financial mailings.

The Implementation

In the early 1970s a shrewd marketer named Joseph Sugarman developed a winning approach to force-communication. Typical was an opening sentence of no more than two to three words. The technique persists to this day—as well it should, because a brief opening is non-threatening to the reader.

With the constraints of a financial mailing such as this one, in which the "applicant information" and the "transfer request" are attached to the letter, a brief opening is not only comfortable; it's very welcome.

In keeping with contemporary credit card mailings to business people, this one attaches the application so the communication becomes a single unit. (In reality, this simplifies the lettershop process of personalization.)

Comment

This letter uses contractions and straightforward rhetoric to make its point. Only if you envision the same letter with typical arm's-length bank rhetoric can you really appreciate how this letter connects with its target.

Figure 7–4. Colonial National Bank

If you're not saving money with a low 12.9% variable APR, and no annual fee, it's time to ask yourself why.

Colonial National Bank USA

Dear Herschell G Lewis:

It's amazing. People will search high and low to get the best mortgage and car loan rates possible. Yet they're still willing to pay 16% or more on their credit card balances.

Frankly, I think it's about time someone offered you a better deal.

That's why I am inviting you to request the Colonial National VISA® GOLD Card with a low 12.9% variable APR -- a rate that's far below the national average -- no annual fee and a credit line up to $5,000.

It's your opportunity to say good-bye to high-rate cards with hefty monthly finance charges. You are now pre-approved for an account that gives you one of the lowest rates in America. Plus, you can take advantage of these two money-saving features:

1) Save Hundreds Of Dollars With Our Transfer 'n Save℠ Service. Move your balances from any higher-rate credit cards -- from banks, department stores, or any other cards -- to your new 12.9% variable APR Colonial National account, and you could easily save $150 or more a year! Just fill out the Transfer 'n Save Authorization Request above. We'll handle all the details, with no transfer fee of any kind.

2) You Pay No Annual Fee. This is not a limited-time offer or trial period. You simply pay no annual fee with this Colonial National VISA GOLD Card.

(over, please)

A brief opening is welcome and creates receptivity for the message. *(Continued)*

It's easy to see how this VISA GOLD Card could save you hundreds of dollars on the purchases you've just made. But this card offers you more than savings. Because it's a Colonial National VISA GOLD Card, it gives you an exclusive array of prestigious benefits and features:

- Accepted At Over 11 Million Locations Around The World -- over three times the acceptance of a $75 a year American Express® Gold Card.

- An Interest-Free Grace Period Of At Least 25 Days on purchases when you pay your full balance each month.

- VISA GOLD Purchase Security And Extended Protection Program® protects most retail purchases against covered damage or theft for 90 days and extends manufacturers' U.S. warranties of 3 years or less -- at no cost to you.

- Exclusive Package Of Colonial National VISA GOLD Card Services: Including free Auto Rental Collision/Loss Damage Insurance, free $500,000 Travel Accident Insurance, instant cash advances at thousands of Automated Teller Machines (ATMs) nationwide, and much more.

Take a minute right now to complete your Pre-Approved Status Invitation. You'll immediately save with this no annual fee offer. That's like awarding yourself a bonus of $30 to $75.

Then transfer balances from your other higher-rate credit cards to save on interest charges. Don't keep giving your money to a credit card that charges higher rates and annual fees. Save it for yourself. Mail your Pre-Approved Status Invitation today.

Sincerely,

Robert Marshall

Robert Marshall
President

(Continued)

Credit Card Division

P.S. Money is tight enough these days without paying hefty finance charges on your credit card balances. So request your Colonial National VISA GOLD Card -- with its extremely low 12.9% variable APR, no annual fee, and money-saving Transfer 'n Save Service -- to save on finance charges on <u>all</u> your higher-rate credit cards. Just complete and mail your Pre-Approved Status Invitation before the expiration date. And start saving money A.S.A.P.!

TERMS OF PRE-APPROVED OFFER

I request a Colonial National Bank USA VISA® GOLD Card account upon acceptance of my request in Delaware. I agree to be bound by the terms and conditions of the Cardholder Agreement mailed with my Card, including the provision therein that the Cardholder Agreement and my account will be governed by Delaware and Federal law. I agree that my signature as applicant or co-applicant means I agree to pay all amounts charged to my account by the applicant, any co-applicant and/or any person authorized by either to use my account. My Pre-Approved Status Invitation must be completed, signed, and received at your processing center by the date shown on the Invitation. I must be of legal age. You must be able to verify the accuracy of all information I provide. You may obtain reports, now or in the future, from the credit bureau(s) of your choice. If I ask, I will be given the name and address of any bureau providing a report. I understand that my pre-approved status means that I may be assigned an initial credit line of $100 to the maximum line amount shown on my Pre-Approved Status Invitation, depending upon my creditworthiness and income, and that if there has been a recent significant adverse change in my creditworthiness, such as a bankruptcy filing or charge-off, you may be unable to open an account for me. I must have a minimum annual household income of $30,000 to qualify for a VISA GOLD Card account and for the maximum credit line stated. If I don't qualify for a Gold account, you may open a regular Card account for me on the same terms as in the DISCLOSURES. I understand that cash advances may be limited to a portion of my credit line, and that balance transfers and cash advances may be unavailable in connection with certain regular Card accounts having credit lines below the maximum line stated. This offer is non-transferrable and cannot be accepted if I reside in ME, provide only a P.O. Box or foreign address, am a current Colonial National cardholder, or have another Colonial National credit card application in process.

DISCLOSURES

Annual Fee	None.
Annual Percentage Rate (APR)	12.9%.
Variable Rate Information	The APR may vary. The rate will be a 6.65% spread above the highest U.S. Prime Rate published in The Wall Street Journal on the third Tuesday of the month preceding the calendar month in which the billing cycle closes.
Grace Period for Repayment of Purchases	You have at least 25 days from the statement closing date, if the new balance is paid in full each month, before a finance charge is imposed.
Minimum Finance Charge	$.50 (on purchases in any billing cycle that a finance charge is due).
Method of Computing the Balance for Purchases	Average daily balance (including new purchases).
Cash Advance Fee, Late Fee* and Overlimit Fee*	Cash advance fee: 2% of amount of advance but not less than $2 or more than $10. Late fee and Overlimit fee: $10 - $15.

*These fees vary in amount from state to state.

Residents of Illinois may contact the Illinois Commissioner of Banks and Trust Companies for comparative information on interest rates, charges, fees and grace periods at State of Illinois — CIP, P.O. Box 10181, Springfield, IL 62791 or 1-800-634-5452.

WISCONSIN RESIDENTS ONLY: Wisconsin law provides that no agreement, court order or individual statement applying to marital property will affect a creditor's interest unless prior to the time credit is granted, the creditor is provided with a copy of the agreement, court order or statement, or has actual knowledge of any adverse provision.

(Continued)

Pre-Approved Status Invitation

Pay less interest to your credit card.

❑ YES! Send me the Colonial National VISA® GOLD Card at the terms indicated below:

Low Variable APR: 12.9%
Annual Fee: FREE
Credit Line Up To: $5,000
Reply Deadline: 06/30/94

Herschell G Lewis
340 N Fig Tree Ln
Plantation FL 33317-2561

Applicant Information (Please Print)

Birth Date ____ / ____ / ____ Social Security # ____ - ____ - ____

Annual Income† $ ____ (Including any Co-Applicant) Home Phone (____) ____

Employer ____ Bus. Phone (____) ____

Mother's Maiden Name ____ (For Your Security)

Co-Applicant Information

Full Name ____ Social Security # ____ - ____ - ____

WOULD YOU LIKE CASH IMMEDIATELY?

Upon approval of this request, please send me a check for (even-dollar amounts only): $ ____

I (we, if any co-applicant) have read and agree to the TERMS OF PRE-APPROVED OFFER and DISCLOSURES on the reverse side. $30,000 minimum annual household income required for a Gold Card and for the maximum credit line stated.

Applicant Signature X ____ **Date** ____ / ____ / ____

Co-Applicant Signature (if any) X ____ **Date** ____ / ____ / ____

†Alimony, child support or separate maintenance need not be disclosed unless you want us to rely on it for repayment.

H170322374 1683 3

Save on the purchases you've already made.

❑ YES! I want to save money with Transfer 'n Save℠, your special bill consolidation service.

Transfer 'n Save lets you quickly and easily transfer balances from your high-rate credit cards to your new, low 12.9% variable APR, no annual fee Colonial National account. There's no transfer fee of any kind, and the balances you transfer are treated like a purchase, so you can get an interest-free grace period of at least 25 days. Simply complete the Authorization Request below, then sit back and enjoy the savings — we'll do all the paperwork for you.

TRANSFER 'N SAVE℠ AUTHORIZATION REQUEST

Yes! Upon approval of this request, I want to transfer the exact amount(s) below on the credit card account(s) listed below as a purchase to my new Colonial National Bank USA account.

(PLEASE PRINT)

Card Issuer ____	Card Issuer ____
Payment Address ____	Payment Address ____
City ____ State ____ Zip ____	City ____ State ____ Zip ____
Complete Account # ____	Complete Account # ____
Exact Amount To Pay $ ____ . ____	Exact Amount To Pay $ ____ . ____

H170322374 Signature **X** ____

Mailer: **VISA**

Key Words: **"An Exclusive Family Advantage"**

The Challenge

Putting an individual's name on a credit card—as the issuer of the card—is a novelty. But is it a welcome novelty? Or does the recipient feel patronized?

Part of the challenge is one of production: The personalization must not look forced or artificial.

The Implementation

Oddly, this letter does not identify any specific financial institution. The reason undoubtedly was to underscore the statement in the letter, with your family name on it right where you'd expect to see a bank's name.

The percentage of readership had to be extraordinarily high because the card itself, printed in standard Visa colors, showed through a second window on the envelope, as though it were an actual credit card.

No letter in this entire collection reiterates the recipient's name so often within such a short communication. (Only the first side of the letter has been computer personalized.) Contemporary technology makes customizing of both sides practical, and as equipment to do this becomes standard, the personalized face and pre-printed back will give way to total personalization.

Comment

The inclusion of this letter foretells a technique unknown in the 1970s, common in the 1990s, and undoubtedly prevalent in the 2010s. That technique is the combination of database influence on product and creative execution, and total personalization of product and creative execution.

The first sentence, "Did you know that experts estimate we have over 183,277 people in the U.S. with the name Lewis?" has a double-personalization unquestionably based on a list company's simple total. If the name were Grzltwicz, which might have a total of 12 names, the sponsor of this card probably would have moved on to another.

To the recipient, the medium is the message, so the writer's job is not as difficult as it would be without this hook. Still, take nothing away from this writer, who maximized the use of personalization.

Figure 7–5. Lewis Card

THE LEWIS
FAMILY LEAGUE

AN EXCLUSIVE FAMILY ADVANTAGE
The No-Annual-Fee Lewis FamilyCard® Visa®,
a line of personal credit up to $25,000, with an initial reduced Annual Percentage Rate (APR) of 9.9% on balance transfers.†

RVIV-F
Margo E. Lewis
340 N. Fig Tree Ln.
Fort Lauderdale, FL 33317-2561

This may be the only chance you have to join.

Dear Margo E. Lewis:

Did you know that experts estimate we have over 183,277 people in the U.S. with the name Lewis?

That's a lot of people. More than enough to make something good happen. That's what the LEWIS FAMILY LEAGUE is all about.

In a moment I'll tell you about the Lewis Family History Report and your Gift Certificate. But first let me explain the big advantage.

It's the NO-ANNUAL-FEE Lewis FamilyCard Visa card.

As of today, you have 30 days to request your own Lewis FamilyCard Visa with your family name on it, right where you'd expect to see a bank's name. Just complete the enclosed short-form request and mail it in the enclosed postage-paid envelope.

Members of the LEWIS FAMILY LEAGUE carry our FamilyCard Visa wherever they go. And talk about prestige—wow!

Your Lewis FamilyCard Visa is the ultimate in financial identification.

It's the ultimate in subtle one-upmanship with friends and business associates.

It's the ultimate conversation piece at Lewis family gatherings. Guaranteed! Everyone—third cousins included!—will want to know how you got your FamilyCard Visa and how they can get one.

AND THERE'S SOMETHING MORE:

Your FamilyCard Visa is easily one of the most economical, powerful, versatile, and convenient credit cards in the world. It runs rings around most other cards. Family name aside, your new FamilyCard Visa is pure good business.

So even though you probably already have other cards, it makes sense to switch over to the Lewis FamilyCard Visa. Just look at the advantages:

- 9.9% INITIAL APR on balance transfers and cash advances as soon as you receive your FamilyCard Visa. This means you can pay off other high-rate bills with your new Visa for a limited time at this super-low rate and save money. You will be sent Preferred Access Checks® along with your card that draw on your Visa credit line instead of your checking account. Use your Preferred Access Checks like personal checks to pay off other accounts, or use them to make purchases.

(over, please)

Call 1-800-764-3422 For The One Card That Recognizes You By Name.

The No-Annual-Fee Lewis FamilyCard Visa
With Your Personal Credit Line Up To $25,000.
Call 1-800-764-3422. TDD Users, Call: 1-800-833-6262.

Print your name as you would like it to appear on card. Please print clearly in ink.

Social Security # – – Birth date / /

Mother's maiden name (for security purposes)

Monthly housing payment $ | Do you: Own home Rent

Home phone ( ) | Your annual salary $

Business phone ( ) | Other income + $

Employer Years there | Total household income $

Position | Source of other income*

Check all credit cards you currently hold: MasterCard® Visa® American Express®

▲ Detach here

Please complete only if you have moved or changed employers in the last three years.

Previous address

City State ZIP

Previous employer or school

Position Years there

To request a card for a friend or relative

Name of authorized user Relationship

If address below is not your current home address, please provide correct address.

RVIV-F 8B EG-293 4652
Margo E. Lewis
340 N. Fig Tree Ln.
Fort Lauderdale, FL 33317-2561

Signature Date / /

MY SIGNATURE ABOVE MEANS THAT I AGREE TO THE CONDITIONS ON THE REVERSE SIDE OF THIS FORM.
*Alimony, child support, or separate maintenance income need not be revealed if you do not wish it considered as a basis for repayment.

Personalization and customization give this letter rapport-building power.

(Continued)

- <u>NO ANNUAL FEE</u>. This makes you a guaranteed winner the moment your new FamilyCard Visa account opens.
- <u>COMPETITIVE FIXED APR ON PURCHASES</u>. You pay an APR of only 16.9% on purchases.
- <u>HIGHER LINES OF CREDIT</u>. Your FamilyCard Visa has a line of credit up to $25,000.
- <u>SUPPLEMENTAL RENTAL CAR COLLISION COVERAGE</u> up to $15,000 is automatically yours when you use your Visa card to rent a car.* Save on the high cost of supplemental collision coverage.
- <u>EXCEPTIONAL CUSTOMER SERVICE</u>. The FamilyCard Visa is issued by one of the largest credit card companies in the world. Customer Service Representatives are on duty 24 hours a day, 365 days a year. Requests for credit line increases are answered within 30 minutes.
- <u>FREE EXTRAS</u>. Extra cards are free for anyone you want to have access to your account. Credit Card Registration for all your credit cards, a valuable service in case of loss or theft, is also yours at no additional cost.
- <u>YOUR TWO BONUS GIFTS</u>

Mail your request immediately to qualify for the following two bonus gifts upon approval. (Allow 6-8 weeks from receipt of card for delivery.)

A FAMILY HISTORY research report, with crest, printed on parchment-style paper. Suitable for framing, the Family History Report links you and family firmly to your roots. Visiting family members are sure to want to read it.

$5.00 GIFT CERTIFICATE good toward any item from the Catalog of Heraldry. You will see a wide variety of clothing, jewelry, and home accessories with your family name and crest. These are super gifts for all occasions.

The opportunity is in your hands.

Please take a moment now to complete and mail your request. For even faster service, call 1-800-764-3422. We'll take your request over the phone in just a few minutes.

Sincerely,

James E. Carrington
Executive Vice President

P.S. As you can understand, this special invitation has to have a deadline. If you delay beyond 30 days, I can't guarantee that the No-Annual-Fee FamilyCard Visa and two bonus gifts will still be available. Now is the time to take care of this. Mail your request form or call 1-800-764-3422 today.

*Certain restrictions apply to these and other benefits as described in the benefits brochures sent to you shortly after your account is opened.
Visa is a federally registered service mark of Visa U.S.A. Inc., used pursuant to license.
MasterCard® is a federally registered service mark of MasterCard International, Inc., used pursuant to license.

Printed on recycled paper

C11/94AOO1

†Annual Fee	$0
Annual Percentage Rate (APR)	16.9% for purchases.
Grace Period for Repayment of Balance for Purchases	At least 25 days from Statement Closing Date.
Method of Computing the Balance for Purchases	Average Daily Balance (including new transactions).
Transaction Fees for Cash Advances and Fees for Paying Late or Exceeding the Credit Limit	Transaction fee for bank and ATM cash advances: 2% of each cash advance ($2 minimum, $25 maximum). Transaction fee for Preferred Access Checks cash advances: 1% of each cash advance ($2 minimum, $10 maximum). Late-payment fee: $15. Over-the-credit-limit fee: $15.
Transaction Fees for Purchases	Transaction fee for the purchase of wire transfers, money orders, bets, lottery tickets, and casino gaming chips: 2% of each such purchase ($2 minimum, $25 maximum).

†APR for cash advances is 9.9% through your first six statement closing dates, commencing the month after your account is opened, and will be 16.9% thereafter (will apply to both new and outstanding cash advance balances).

Transaction fees for first two specially designated Preferred Access Checks will be waived.

The information in this application is accurate as of 10/94. For more current information, please call (800) 764-3422.

—CONDITIONS—

I have read this application, and everything I have stated in it is true. I authorize the issuing bank to check my credit, employment history, or any other information and to report to others such information and credit experience with me. I understand that the acceptance or use of any card issued will be subject to the terms of this application and the Credit Card Agreement that will be sent with the card, and I agree to be responsible for all charges incurred according to such terms. I am at least 18 years of age.

This account is issued and administered by MBNA America Bank, N.A.

A 9-2611-94A

Mailer: **Shawmut Bank**

Key Words: **"I invite you to upgrade"**

Writer: **Christina Cross**

The Challenge

Upgrading a credit card means increasing the cost of that card. In the mid-1990s many upgrades are offered for no additional fee. When this letter was mailed (early 1980s), all upgrades—and all credit cards, for that matter—were subject to an annual fee. So selling an upgrade required a combination of obvious benefit and obvious stature.

The Implementation

By avoiding an immediate increase in cost (the additional fee is not called for until the next annual payment, but the upgrade becomes effective immediately), this letter makes a positive impulse reaction both possible and logical.

Note the comparative chart in the upper right corner. Including the chart, which shows clearly a comparative advantage, makes the sales argument in the letter self-validating.

Comment

Just in case the "Sample A. Sample" is unclear, this is the name most commonly used for printer's samples of a mailing (most recently, "Jonathan A. Extralongname" has joined Sample A. Sample as different name lengths integrated into the middle of a line can skew paragraph lengths).

This letter gets to its point immediately. Why? Because the bank needn't worry about the target individual opening the letter, since he or she already is a bank customer. That pre-existing relationship demands both a straightforward exposition and a quick explanation that the subject of the letter is benefit, not complaint.

Figure 7–6. Shawmut Bank

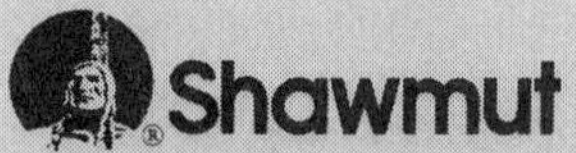

Compare Annual Fees and Annual Percentage Rates – you'll see that Shawmut Gold Mastercard® card costs you less!

Gold Card Issuer	Annual Fee	APR*
Shawmut Bank	**$36**	**15.84% (v)**
Bank of New England	$42	17.92%
Bank of Boston	$45	17.40%
Chase Manhattan Bank	$50	16.50%
State Street Bank	$50	16.99% (v)
Citibank	$50	16.80%
American Express	$75	American Express Card does not offer the flexibility of payment options.

**Annual Percentage Rates advertised as of September 30, 1989. Shawmut's current variable rate of 15.84% is the lowest possible rate under our current Gold MasterCard agreement. (v)=variable rate.*

Sample A. Sample
123 Somewhere St.
Anywhere, USA 99999

Dear Sample,

I invite you to upgrade your current Shawmut MasterCard or VISA® to the card we reserve for our most highly-regarded customers:

The Shawmut Gold MasterCard.

Through your ongoing Shawmut card membership, you've established a special relationship with us. The Shawmut Gold MasterCard reflects that distinctive relationship. It says you're someone exceptional.

The Gold MasterCard gives you all the advantages of your present card, plus a new level of financial freedom and security.

You'll take advantage of a credit line increased to $0000

And, if you act now, you can carry a Gold MasterCard for your current regular MasterCard or VISA fee. Your $24 regular card fee is all you pay until your next scheduled annual fee payment. And then, the annual fee is just $36.

When you carry this extraordinary card, you can count on a wide array of travel services and benefits. Consider:

- Free emergency card replacement -- normally within 48 hours or less -- if your card is lost or stolen while you're travelling.

Validating the sales argument with a chart "proves" both stature and benefit. *(Continued)* o Need Cash? Get instant access to your credit line -- up to $350 a day, any hour of the day, at any CIRRUS® Machine nationally. Or get an emergency cash advance from any MasterCard banking office around the world.

o The entire MasterAssist™ family of services, including:

<u>MasterRental</u>™: Complete car rental insurance covering collision, damage, vandalism, theft, fire, and loss of personal belongings.

<u>MasterAssist/Medical</u>™: Emergency travel medical expenses and assistance.

<u>MasterTrip</u>™: Emergency cash and assistance to replace lost or stolen travel tickets and documents.

<u>MasterLegal</u>™: Legal referrals and assistance covering legal fees while you travel.

The Shawmut Gold MasterCard is like having a protective umbrella whenever you travel.

You can enjoy all these new benefits soon. So send us your Gold MasterCard request right away.

Sincerely,

Karen O. Beach

Karen O. Beach
Vice President

P.S. You deserve this card, and we want you to have it. But hurry. To take advantage of this offer, you must return your Acceptance Certificate no later than December 29, 1989.

Mailer: British Airways Chase Card

Key Words: "Earn up to 11,000"

The Challenge

Tying a credit card to an airline is something of a conceit. The typical member of the "British Airways Executive Club©" is in no need of an additional credit card and undoubtedly has frequent flyer miles already in place.

So an offer such as this one has many facets of the "I'm not interested" reaction to overcome.

The Implementation

Printed on good paper, in keeping with the image of the airline, the letter achieves the impression of one-to-one personalization despite the hobble imposed on it (see "Comment," following).

The indented bullets seize the eye quickly so that specific benefits receive immediate attention.

Comment

We're including this letter because it exemplifies what the writer faces when a company imposes conditions on the technique of writing.

Our position, inalterably, is that asterisks and footnotes have no place in a direct response message. This one has five within a one-page letter—perhaps a record for this length. We suggest that you read the letter, asking yourself each time the reading flow is interrupted by a footnote or a registration or service mark, whether the letter might have gained strength each time one of these was either excluded or explained in a separate enclosure.

This is especially true of the double asterisk which appears not once, but twice after the word pre-approved, telling the reader unmistakably that pre-approved is conditional.

Our point: Don't blame the writer unless the writer was the source.

Figure 7–7. Chase/British Airways

BRITISH AIRWAYS

Herschell G. Lewis
340 N. Fig Tree Ln.
Plantation, FL 33317-2561

Earn up to 11,000 bonus miles. And no annual fee your first year*. With your preapproved Chase/British Airways Gold Visa card.**

Dear Herschell G. Lewis:

As a valued member of British Airways Executive Club® frequent flyer program, you've been preapproved** for the Chase/British Airways Gold Visa card, with **no annual fee your first year***.

With this newest benefit of Executive Club membership, you can earn Executive Club miles every time you make a credit card purchase. Add those miles to the miles **you earn every time you fly on British Airways, USAir and Alaska Airlines** and you can fly free faster than ever.

What's more, **you can redeem your miles for free flights on British Airways as well as on USAir, American Airlines® or Alaska Airlines.** You'll have hundreds of destinations to choose from - not just overseas but right here in the United States, Canada, Mexico and the Caribbean.

With your new Chase/British Airways Gold Visa card, you'll get one Executive Club mile for every dollar you charge. Plus...

- You'll get **4,000 bonus miles** just for accepting the card[1].
- Charge your first $1,000 and Chase will match those 1,000 miles with an additional **1,000 bonus miles.**
- Fly round-trip transatlantic on British Airways between 6/15/94 and 9/10/94 and you'll receive **6,000 additional bonus miles.**

That adds up to 11,000 bonus miles - more than half of what you need for your first free domestic travel award.

So simply return your Preapproved Acceptance Certificate today or to apply by phone, call 1-800-292-2212[2]. And earn Executive Club miles faster than ever for free flights in the U.S. and around the world.

Cordially,

Robert A. Heaney
President
The Chase Manhattan Bank (USA)

David Charlton
Vice President, Marketing
British Airways Plc

P.S. Here's one more great reason to accept your Chase/British Airways Gold Visa card: As a new cardmember, $500 will be automatically credited to your new account if you fly in First Class or Club World℠ (Business Class) on your next round-trip transatlantic flight on British Airways from 6/15/94 through 9/10/94[3].

* See Credit Disclosures on back of Acceptance Certificate.
** See terms of Preapproved Offer on back of Acceptance Certificate.
[1] Mileage bonus will appear on your statement after your first credit card purchase.
[2] Monday - Friday, 8 a.m. - 8 p.m. Eastern Time.
[3] The $500 credit will be applied automatically to your Chase/British Airways Visa account and will appear in the Chase billing statement upon completion of your round-trip transatlantic flight on British Airways.
American Airlines is a registered trademark of American Airlines, Inc.

7131 13A-018870

Did personalization and eye-catching presentation overcome devices that interrupt the reading flow? *(Continued)*

LOOK AT ALL THE WAYS YOU CAN EARN BRITISH AIRWAYS EXECUTIVE CLUB MILES.

MILES FOR BUYING

Get one mile for every dollar you spend when you use your Chase/British Airways Gold Visa card to:

- Purchase everyday items
- Buy airline tickets
- Pay for hotel stays and car rentals

MILES FOR FLYING

Fly British Airways, USAir, USAir Express, the USAir Shuttle, Alaska Airlines and Horizon Air

EVEN MORE MILES

- Stay overnight at participating British Airways Executive Club hotel partners
- Rent a car from Hertz[2,3]

PLUS, YOU CAN ADD MILES EVEN FASTER WHEN YOU:

- Get up to **4 additional credit cards** at no extra charge for other family members. Purchases made with those cards also earn you miles.
- Set up a Household Account in the British Airways Executive Club, and combine the mileage activity of household members into one account.
- Take advantage of Executive Club's unique Mileage Booster option, which allows you to add 5,000 miles to your account for a fee of just $100.[1]

ENJOY A WORLD OF FREE TRAVEL AWARDS.

Free round-trip tickets on British Airways can take you virtually anywhere in the world. And free round-trip tickets on USAir, USAir Express, the USAir Shuttle, American Airlines, Alaska Airlines and Horizon Air can take you to places such as:

Atlanta	Chicago	Des Moines	Indianapolis	Miami	Pittsburgh
Baltimore	Columbus	Ft. Lauderdale	Little Rock	New Orleans	San Francisco
Boston	Dallas/Ft. Worth	Honolulu	Los Angeles	New York	Sarasota
Charlotte	Denver	Houston	Louisville	Philadelphia	Tulsa

20,000 MILES = ONE FREE DOMESTIC ROUND-TRIP TICKET[2]

40,000 MILES = ONE FREE INTERNATIONAL ROUND-TRIP TICKET[2]

***NO BLACKOUT PERIODS* FOR BRITISH AIRWAYS TRANSATLANTIC FLIGHT AWARDS.[2]**

ANNUAL FEE	VARIABLE APR FOR PURCHASES
$65* (waived for your first year)	Now 16.15%*

[1]A minimum of 35,000 miles is required in order to purchase miles through the Mileage Booster option.
[2]For full rules and regulations of the Executive Club please call British Airways Executive Club Member Services at 1-800-955-2748.
[3]Certain restrictions apply. Hertz rental must be in conjunction with a British Airways flight.
*Please refer to Credit Disclosures on back of application.

CBA-LTRB-G2-5/94

Mailer: Bank Atlantic
Key Words: "This authentic 100 Intis Bank note"
Writer: Carl Bloom

The Challenge

Crashing through the clutter of unsolicited loan offers is a challenge so formidable that few combatants can qualify.

The Implementation

This is one of those few.

Inclusion of a bank note (although almost no one who gets this has any idea what the value of the bank note might be) generates a sure winner, at least from a readership point of view.

Adding to the impact of the bank note is the boxed, bold-faced statement, "You could have $50,000!"

Comment

This letter is a perfect illustration of how an inexpensive "freemium" can lift readership and intensify the impact of what otherwise might have been a mundane, standard home equity loan mailing.

Many undoubtedly felt obligated to respond because any gift whose worth (or lack of worth) cannot immediately be determined generates guilt if one does *not* respond.

Figure 7–8. BankAtlantic

BankAtlantic
A Federal Savings Bank
1750 East Sunrise Boulevard
Fort Lauderdale, Florida 33304

March 3, 1995

Mr. Lewis, You Could Have $50,000!

Mr. Herschell Lewis
340 N. Fig Tree Lane
Fort Lauderdale, FL 33317

Dear Mr. Lewis:

This authentic 100 Intis banknote from Peru is a great collector's item. But if you need real American money *now* to buy the things you deserve, you can get it quickly!

If you had $50,000 right now, what would you do with it? Build a garage, add a pool, buy a new car or boat, repay holiday expenses, pay for education, start a business? Well according to county records, you *could* possibly have up to $50,000 available to you right now. Your untapped resource is the **equity built up in your home**, which can help you buy almost anything you need.

... And Save Money

You can **cut your monthly bills** by getting rid of those outrageous store and credit card charges. Combine all your bills into one manageable monthly payment -- at a much lower interest rate! And **reduce your taxes...** interest on most other forms of borrowing are no longer deductible on your Federal Taxes; but interest you pay on equity loans may be 100% deductible for you!

$0 Closing Costs

Save All Closing Costs! You WON'T PAY ANY CLOSING COSTS for lines of credit or equity loans from $2,500 up to $50,000 -- this could save you up to $350.

And whatever your personal style of money management, BankAtlantic has the plan to suit you. With our flexible equity line of credit, you can have some cash now and then draw more money whenever you need it... or, choose a traditional fixed-rate, fixed term equity loan and lock in today's rates... or, if you only have a smaller amount of equity available, ask about our special "100% Equity" program.

So if you need real American money for any worthwhile purpose, act now. Call our Home Equity Hotline at 1-800-351-7799 to find out how much cash can be available to you. Or simply drop the Equity Action Card in the mail, and we'll rush you more information. The equity in your home is a resource that can help you have a better life.

Sincerely,

Anthony Figlio
Senior Vice President

P.S. If you activate your equity line with at least $2,500, you'll get a 1/2% discount on your interest rate until September 20, 1995... so act today and take advantage of this special offer!

Offer good for loans of less than $50,000. 1/2% discount and/or no closing cost offers do not apply to the 100% equity program. The 100% equity program applies to all equity loans up to $20,000 in which the loan to value exceeds 80%. Current variable loan APR is 10.5% as of 1/25/95; but can vary depending on time of application. APR for 100% Equity Loan is 12% as of 1/25/95. Maximum APR will not exceed 18%. Rates are subject to change. Property and flood insurance may be required. Borrowing Power based on an estimate of current value. Application and approval are necessary to calculate actual amounts. Consult your tax advisor regarding the deductibility of interest. Prime plus 1 1/2 is valid until September 20, 1995. Thereafter it reverts back to Prime plus 2.

A "freemium" that generates guilt and response. *(Continued)*

BANCO CENTRAL de RESERVA del PERU
B6528994F
100
26 DE JUNIO DE 1987
PRESIDENTE
DIRECTOR
GERENTE GENERAL
CIEN INTIS
RAMON CASTILLA
B6528994F
100
100

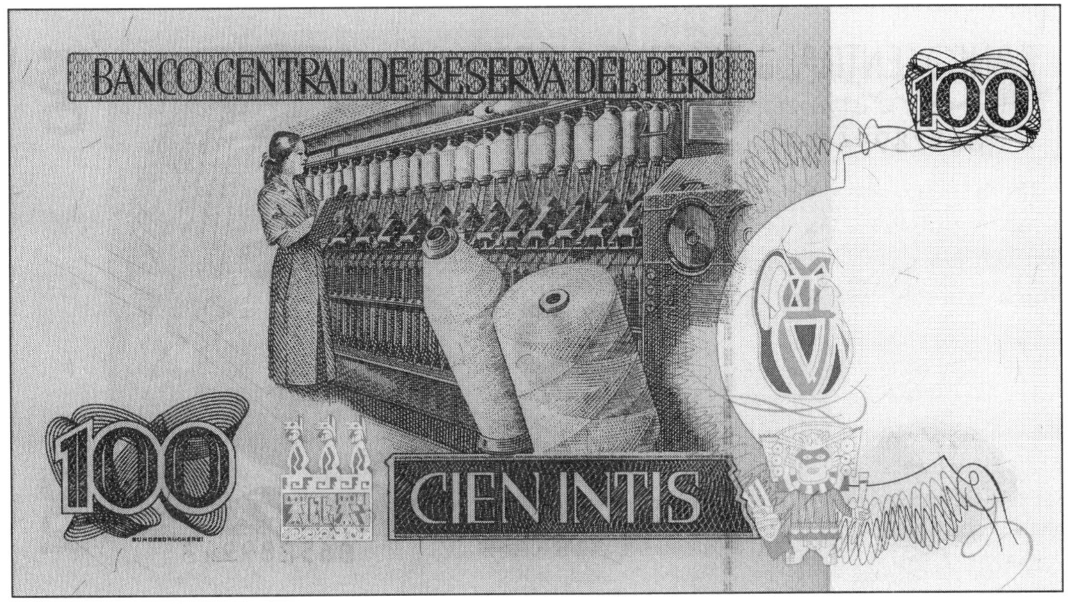
BANCO CENTRAL DE RESERVA DEL PERU
100
100
CIEN INTIS

Mailer: **Household Finance**

Key Words: **"Bills . . . Bills . . . Bills"**

The Challenge

In an era of dense credit card usage, this company faced a tough challenge: convincing people to use a line of credit rather than the implicit credit of conventional cards.

Increasing the challenge was the demographic of the group to whom this mailing was sent—people who had no prior direct financial experience with this company.

The Implementation

The check portion of this letter was visible through the window of the envelope, prompting the recipient to open it. Once open, it became apparent that this was, in fact, an actual check (as opposed to a voucher, an application, or an "Acceptance Form").

A mailing of this type would have been impossible in pre-computer personalization days. With the benefit of the computer and multiple fonts, some of which replicate handwriting, both personalization and excitement became absolute.

Comment

The success of this mailing was proved by an unprecedented percentage of response, considerably beyond that of contemporary mailings which did not use this device.

Had the check portion not been an actual check, much of the impact would have been dissipated. The ease of use unquestionably was a factor in the outcome of this mailing.

Figure 7–9. Household Finance Corporation

HFC
1355 Roswell Rd.
Suite 125
Marietta GA 30062

Account Opener 374170
325201-252458187CRLB7066259577-4000V12.90 4301203741705

Household Bank, f.s.b.
Bloomingdale, Illinois 60108
70-7001
2719

Feb. 8, 1995

Pay to the order of Sample A. Sample Amount: $3,100.00

Three Thousand One Hundred Dollars and no cents**

VOID VOID VOID VOID

Sample A. Sample
Johnson & Quin, Inc.
7460 North Lehigh Avenue
Niles, IL 60714-4099

By endorsing the back of this check you accept our offer and agree to the terms, Form 903GA(01/95)

AUTHORIZED SIGNATURE

NOT VALID AFTER: March 31, 1995

0190044336 271970011 32520137417030

SIGN BACK AND DETACH HERE

Household Finance Corporation
1355 Roswell Rd.
Suite 125
Marietta, GA 30062
(404) 973-4060

Bills ... Bills ... Bills!

Those are the words most folks are repeating this time of year, Sample A. Sample.

But you don't have to.

Relief from a pile of bills is as close as the check at the top of this letter. As you can see, **Sample A. Sample**, your name is already on it.

I'll state it directly: This check is a real check. Take it to your bank and deposit it. You'll walk out of that bank with $3,100 more in your account. Then pay off those bills, "consolidating" them into one convenient monthly payment instead of four or five.

But that's not all. Because we know everyone can use some extra cash after the holidays you're pre-approved for a line of credit of $4,000.

It's as easy as taking this check to the bank, **Sample A. Sample!**

Depositing this check activates your HFC revolving line of credit. It can give you the type of financial freedom many people never can achieve ... because the money is there for you to spend on anything you like. And spend it again and again. Because as you pay back the principal, you automatically add that amount back into your account.

Once you deposit this check, we'll send you a book of personalized checks. This gives you maximum financial flexibility. If you see something you like at one of those "after the holidays" sales, you can go ahead and buy it ... and save money, because you'll enjoy those low sale prices that won't be available later on.

So gather up the bills from your holiday shopping and use this check and your line of credit to consolidate them. That is, get rid of them by paying them all off with your HFC revolving line of credit and replacing them with one convenient monthly payment to HFC. Let your HFC revolving line of credit clear off that deskload of bills.

Congratulations on your new line of credit. Enjoy it!

Sincerely,

Mark Shepherd, Vice President

P.S. Just one request: If you're going to take advantage of this check and your new line of credit, you'll need to deposit the check before March 15, 1995. Thanks.

* Initial disclosure of Variable Rate: The offer is Prime + 12.90%. The rate and payments may vary monthly with the Prime Rate. As of February 1, 1995, the Prime Rate was 8.5%, the monthly periodic rate was 1.783% (the ANNUAL PERCENTAGE RATE was 21.4%). Because this information may have changed after the above date, contact your HFC office for further information. The Account Agreement found on the back contains a full explanation of the terms and conditions of your HFC Personal Credit Line Account, including minimum payments and any annual fees which may apply.

07-9092 Form 903GA(01/95)

Impressive personalization coupled with ease of use created a winner. *(Continued)*

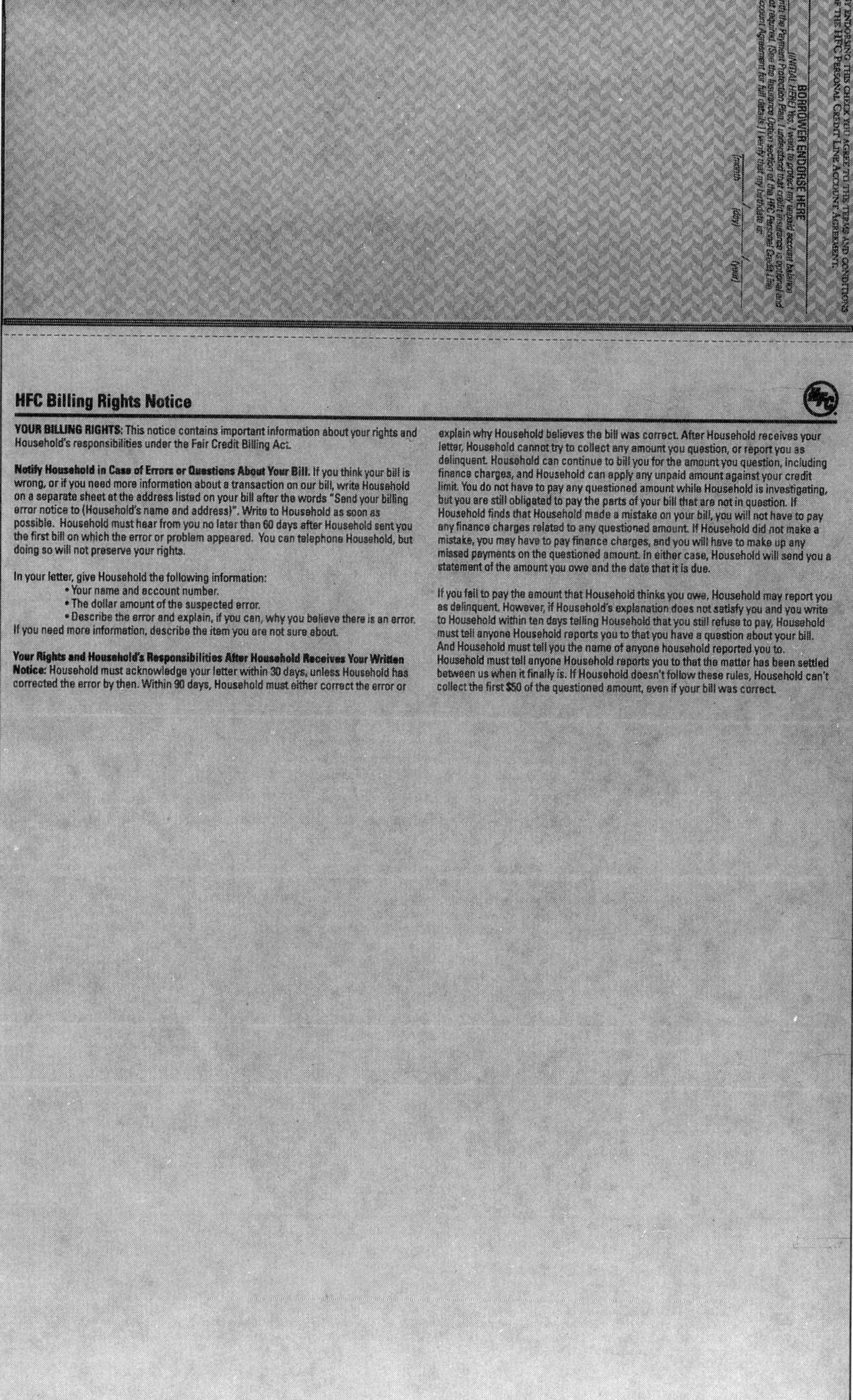

BY ENDORSING THIS CHECK YOU AGREE TO THE TERMS AND CONDITIONS OF THE HFC PERSONAL CREDIT LINE ACCOUNT AGREEMENT.

BORROWER ENDORSE HERE

_______ (INITIAL HERE) Yes, I want to protect my unpaid account balance with the Payment Protection Plan. I understand that credit insurance is optional and not required. (See the Insurance Option section of the HFC Personal Credit Line Account Agreement for full details.) I verify that my birthdate is: ____/____/____ (month) (day) (year)

HFC Billing Rights Notice

YOUR BILLING RIGHTS: This notice contains important information about your rights and Household's responsibilities under the Fair Credit Billing Act.

Notify Household in Case of Errors or Questions About Your Bill. If you think your bill is wrong, or if you need more information about a transaction on our bill, write Household on a separate sheet at the address listed on your bill after the words "Send your billing error notice to (Household's name and address)". Write to Household as soon as possible. Household must hear from you no later than 60 days after Household sent you the first bill on which the error or problem appeared. You can telephone Household, but doing so will not preserve your rights.

In your letter, give Household the following information:

- Your name and account number.
- The dollar amount of the suspected error.
- Describe the error and explain, if you can, why you believe there is an error.

If you need more information, describe the item you are not sure about.

Your Rights and Household's Responsibilities After Household Receives Your Written Notice: Household must acknowledge your letter within 30 days, unless Household has corrected the error by then. Within 90 days, Household must either correct the error or explain why Household believes the bill was correct. After Household receives your letter, Household cannot try to collect any amount you question, or report you as delinquent. Household can continue to bill you for the amount you question, including finance charges, and Household can apply any unpaid amount against your credit limit. You do not have to pay any questioned amount while Household is investigating, but you are still obligated to pay the parts of your bill that are not in question. If Household finds that Household made a mistake on your bill, you will not have to pay any finance charges related to any questioned amount. If Household did not make a mistake, you may have to pay finance charges, and you will have to make up any missed payments on the questioned amount. In either case, Household will send you a statement of the amount you owe and the date that it is due.

If you fail to pay the amount that Household thinks you owe, Household may report you as delinquent. However, if Household's explanation does not satisfy you and you write to Household within ten days telling Household that you still refuse to pay, Household must tell anyone Household reports you to that you have a question about your bill. And Household must tell you the name of anyone household reported you to. Household must tell anyone Household reports you to that the matter has been settled between us when it finally is. If Household doesn't follow these rules, Household can't collect the first $50 of the questioned amount, even if your bill was correct.

C41-195

Chapter 8

Memberships

Of the five great motivators (fear, exclusivity, greed, guilt, and need for approval), and the two "soft" motivators (convenience and pleasure), the one mandatory for a membership is exclusivity.

Regardless of the worth of the membership itself—such as rescue when one's car breaks down on the highway or discounts for hotel rooms or travel—without exclusivity, all we have is a straightforward offer to do business.

The concept of making available an opportunity others cannot have becomes increasingly valuable as contemporary society devolves into groupings of units instead of individuals.

This is why we sell by mail "Clubs" that really are not clubs at all and "Memberships" that really are either subscriptions or goods for sale.

Exclusivity works, and our prediction, as we move into a computerized universe, is that it will continue to work for a good many years to come.

Mailer: **The Good Sam Club**
Key Words: **"Want to know how . . ."**
Writer: **Tony Barnard**

The Challenge

This excellent letter, which dates from the antediluvian year 1980, is an early example of a membership communication which has considerable text before the greeting.

Suggesting to an experienced RV traveler that this organization could eliminate mistakes of judgment in campground choice—and doing it not only without irritating the recipient but with an overtone of "good friend" benefit—was, at the time, an extraordinary challenge.

The Implementation

The letter opens with benefit-laden questions of club members. But, then, after the greeting, the narrative uses others as surrogates for a standard RV owner problem.

Rather than specify single inclusions, the letter deals in extensive benefits, with emphasis on uniqueness. The reader is made to feel that no other source will have this information base.

Comment

To "cold lists," the letter probably would have been stronger without the preface, opening simply with "The trip was a disaster for RVers Bob and Helen Wallace." But this letter is to *existing* members, and projecting a new benefit is a logical beginning.

Thus, when the reader does come to the "disaster" he or she already knows how to avoid that disaster.

Postscript: Through good fortune, we have been able to get a more recent "Good Sam" mailing. Compare the mid-1990s approach, which is a far more action-oriented appeal based on a sure-fire contemporary motivator: "You've been paying too much."

Figure 8–1. The Good Sam Club

Want to know how to beat the tightening energy squeeze? Learn where and how to get GUARANTEED DISCOUNTS at thousands of campgrounds & service centers across the country? Like to benefit from a whole new way of rating coast-to-coast campgrounds, service centers, and tourist attractions that helps you plan your trips with mistake-free confidence?

It's all there - plus a good deal MORE - in the ALL-NEW 1980 Trailer Life RV Campground & Services Directory.

And it's yours, as a Good Sam Club Member at nearly 40% OFF the regular price... IF you accept this exclusive PRE-PUBLICATION offer now.

Dear Good Samer:

The trip was a disaster for RVers Bob and Helen Wallace.

With their perky-tailed beagle, Scruff, they'd eagerly set forth for the fun park they'd discovered last year.

Bob could already feel the trout tugging his new graphite rod. Helen was mentally practicing her square dance steps. And Scruff was all apanting at the prospect of scampering off the playing field with a snatched baseball or two.

Two days, 800 miles, 90 gallons of gas later -- the Wallace's dreams were dashed.

(please turn)

An early example of a potent device—the acceptance-building overline. *(Continued)*

The park was closed.

Worse, it took them another day and a half to find a campground they liked that would accept their pet.

You see, Bob and Helen made that classic mistake too many RVers do. They relied on an old out-of-date directory.

The point is that in just one short year, there may be a 20% or more turnover among the nation's 12,000 private campgrounds. Old ones closing without warning. New ones, with spanking fresh facilities waiting to be tried, opening - perhaps close to you.

In these days of shrinking gas and soaring costs, you can't afford to plan your RV trips with outdated directories. Especially not this coming year when things may be even worse.

> That's why it's so important - essential even - that you act NOW to reserve your copy of the all-new up-to-date 1980 Trailer Life RV Campground & Services Directory.
>
> To make it easy, we've reduced the cost by nearly 40% to Good Sam Club members only. But to take advantage of the saving, you must act quickly.

Let me tell you why this new directory is such a great buy...

First off, it's not a revision. Not an "update." Every one of the 22,000 listings has been newly created from scratch! It's been a mammoth job for our field representatives. But they've done it -- individually reviewed each one of the 12,000 private campgrounds...8,000 public campgrounds...and 2,000 service listings nationwide.

From Alaska to Maine, from Canada to Central America, you'll know for sure which campgrounds are open - and which have gas or LP-gas.

And getting there will be easier than ever before. We've tightened up the directions to make them crystal clear. To save you getting lost and wasting gas along the way.

THEN THERE'S THE BIG EXTRA BONUS FOR GOOD SAMERS LIKE YOU:

> Thousands of listings - many of them new - of Good Sam Discount locations... where you'll receive a full 10% OFF on full overnight rates at parks, on accessories at RV service centers, and at major tourist attractions across the land. (Your savings here will repay the low cost of your Directory many times over!)
>
> And remember - Your Good Sam Discount is GUARANTEED at every SAMpark and Commercial Member campground listed in the 1980 Directory.

(Continued)

But the best news of all for you is this...

Our whole new rating system! Gone is the limited 1-4 scale. Now - for the first time - the Directory rates every campground, every RV center, every tourist attraction all the way from 1 to 10...based not just on total facilities, recreation programs and such - but on "overall impression." There's no separate rating chart to refer to, no cross references required. Right at the end of each listing, you'll find our 1 to 10 rating choice - based not on guesswork or hearsay, but on the experience and "feel" of campers like you.

IN ADDITION, you'll be told in advance whether the parking spaces are grassy or paved. And what both the minimum and maximum site rentals will cost. PLUS...you're given the correct, current phone number of all locations, to make it easier arranging for reservations ahead.

The new Directory features go on and on...

An entire front of book section is built around better RVing in the 80's - beginning with how to RV happily on less energy. You'll get useful, money-saving tips on making the most of gas, LP-gas, water, and electricity.

Another practical feature covers staying on the road trouble-free -- including a complete pre-trip checklist for safety and certainty...plus basic how-to's on maintenance you can handle in emergencies yourself.

PLUS -- Special tips on how to have a great campground stay...fishing afield...favorite recipes for cooking in and a fun eating out guide. Rules of the road nationwide...a full-color two page map of the U.S. with handy mileage chart showing distances between major cities...where to get free travel information and consumer assistance in every state. Local TV channels and reception ratings and CB channel logs are also part of the listing section. And more and more.

You get the idea. The all-new 1980 Trailer Life Campground & Services Directory is, quite simply, the most complete, most accurate, most useful how-to and money-saving guide ever published for active RVers like you.

Here's the deal:

The Directory will be off press mid-December and rushed to you then. In appreciation for your advance reservation now, we'll give you a full $2.50 discount OFF the regular $8.95 price.

IN ADDITION, we'll deduct the $1.50 charge for postage and handling others will pay.

In short - you pay not $8.95 plus $1.50, or $10.45 -- but only $6.45 complete. Total savings to you? $4.00!!

(Continued)

But to realize this big saving, you must order before November 1.

So, do it. Try the new 1980 Trailer Life Directory. Try it with this no-questions-asked guarantee: if not satisfied in every way with this big benefit-packed 1400-page Directory...if not convinced it will save you many times its low, low cost...then simply return it and say, "no thanks." Your money will be refunded promptly in full.

The important thing is to act NOW. Simply return the enclosed Pre-Publication Discount Card in the postage-paid envelope provided.

Every RVing day of 1980, you'll be thankful you did!

Best regards,

Susan Bray

Executive Director
Good Sam Club

P.S. In the past 2 years alone, the U.S. government has forced over 10,000 billboards and campground signs off the highways. More than ever before, you need our Directory to find the way. This Pre-Publication offer expires November 1. Be sure to get your members-only discount order in today!

P.P.S. Remember - if the Directory fails to save you at least 10 times its cost in discounts and gas miles saved over the coming year, you may still return the Directory 12 months later for your money back in full! Hurry - Order NOW.

Mailer: Good Sam Club

Key Words: "Estimated savings"

The Challenge

In the years since the first "Good Sam" mailing was sent to members, the techniques of member-motivation have increasingly switched to specifics—specifics tied to money-saving.

In this instance, the club is marketing not a travel guide but insurance, one of the most competitive areas they possibly could have chosen. The truth of this is obvious when one considers that undoubtedly every recipient already had insurance coverage.

The Implementation

Using sentence structures which parallel speech is a technique not only perfected in the 1990s, but accepted by 1990s readers.

The letter, totally in the present tense, takes the huge rubber stamp-effect overline, massages it, and uses it as an underpinning for description of other benefits not related to cost. Such a letter would not have been possible in 1980, not only because comparative figures were not available, but also because the total power of comparisons had not yet been recognized.

Comment

Calling this "VIP Insurance" was an inspired concept for which credit should go to the marketing department rather than the creative department. But the creative team deserves credit for relentless hammering at the dollar savings, which, we are told, produced results beyond original expectations.

Figure 8–2. Good Sam Insurance

Good Morning,

Suppose I were to tell you that because you're a Good Samer, you're about to save $226.06 a year -- or even more, maybe much more?

Okay. I'm telling you.

We're constantly looking for benefits for Good Samers. This one is a benefit you'll really appreciate! We've arranged for Good Sam VIP RV/Car/Tow-Vehicle insurance coverage for members who are in an area in which our computer says we can really offer a competitive rate. (Congratulations.) So I'm safe in predicting that you'll probably save a big chunk of money.

On average, we've found Good Samers who switch to VIP coverage save $226.06 a year. But you might save a heck of a lot more than that. Some of the 160,000 Good Samers who have switched to VIP are pocketing $300.00 to $500.00 a year they otherwise would be overpaying for insurance coverage.

I'll tell you why this is possible: The combination of our terrific "clout" -- after all, we have some 900,000 members -- and the kind of people who constitute our membership give us position with one of the nation's top insurance carriers, National General Insurance Company. In my opinion nobody can beat this deal.

I should point out, too, that this is custom coverage. If you weren't a Good Samer, we wouldn't offer VIP coverage to you no matter where you live or whom you know.

You travel. You know how Murphy's law applies: Trouble comes only when it's most inconvenient.

Most of us grew up with the notion of a local insurance agent. But that was when we didn't drive so much and so far. Believe me, I've concluded a local agent is nothing more than a costly middleman and isn't much help when you're a thousand miles from home, with another car's bumper stuck into your RV's rear end.

What is a help and a comfort . . . what does let you drive with an untroubled mind . . . is a huge network of more than 4,000 claims representatives, throughout the United States and Canada.

Promise of extraordinary "VIP" benefits is an irresistible hook. *(Continued)*

And the network never sleeps. It never goes on vacation. No matter where you are, no matter what hour of the day it is, help is right there for you in any emergency, 24 hours a day, every single day of the year.

In fact, because these folks have an unmatched background in RVs, they can settle smaller claims right over the phone. No hassle. No "Get three estimates and we'll let you know."

VIP understands such RV "standards" as antennas, awnings, built-ins, water systems, and auxiliary power sources. Try explaining these to an adjuster whose background is limited to automobiles.

And you might have your golf clubs in the trunk of your car, but you can have a whole wardrobe in your RV. VIP protects your personal belongings in the RV automatically, up to $1,500.00.

To get a to-the-penny exact quote, use the Free VIP Quote Form. The questions are simple and you don't have to look up any statistics. Completing that Form is a matter of about 3 1/2 minutes.

VIP starts off with low rates. Now take a look at some of the discounts available to our members in almost every state:

-Over age 50? In most states you automatically get at least a 10% lower base premium.
-Safe, mature driver of a low mileage vehicle? In most states you automatically get a 15% lower premium.
-Insuring more than one vehicle? In most states you automatically get up to a 15% lower premium.
-And when you've driven three years with no at-fault accidents, VIP gives you another 5% lower premium. Note, please: I didn't say "no accidents"; I said "no at-fault accidents." VIP recognizes the difference when an accident isn't your fault.

160,000 Good Samers already have taken advantage of VIP coverage. Please do check around for competitive coverage. I think you'll quickly understand why VIP is the only plan we think is qualified to get our absolute endorsement.

For The Good Sam Club,

Sue Bray

P.S. Your location means you probably do qualify for a very favorable rate. Just complete the simplified Good Sam VIP Quote Form or call the toll-free VIP hotline -- **1-800-VIP-AUTO.**

Mailer: **September Days Club**
Key Words: **"A short time ago . . ."**
Writer: **Hugh C. Chewning**

The Challenge

Anyone who has sold anything to seniors knows the automatic challenge that pertains to any offer. Convincing this group of people, who very rightly are both suspicious and cynical when analyzing an offer to save money, that *this* offer really will save money.

The Implementation

This letter, whose personalization admittedly is primitive and not state-of-the-art, has (according to the writer) cut the cost of member acquisitions by one-third and has remained the unbeaten control for more than four years. The thrust of this membership is tied to the word "Days," because the sponsor is "over 1,300 participating Days Inns, Hotels, Suites, and Daystops," and members get discounts at these hotels and also for purchases of ancillary items negotiated for "members" by the club.

Comment

The over-fifty age group knows very well what the word *September* means. Some might regard this as talking down, but most will regard it as a selective word with a positive spin.

Are you bothered by the obviously mismatched personalized greeting and paragraphs?

Curiously, the very lack of integration of the personalized elements into the letter draws the eye to those elements. Had they been set in the same typeface as the letter proper, the reader might slide past them.

This message is unusual in that it is a 3-page letter. Most writers deliver letters in multiples of two, avoiding a blank panel. In this case, the length seems to be just right.

Figure 8–3. The September Days Club

P.O. BOX 4001, HARLAN, IOWA 51593-4165
Kenneth Mitchell, General Manager

MR. SAMPLE A. SAMPLE
123 MAIN STREET
ANYTOWN, US 99999

DEAR MR. SAMPLE,

A short time ago, my wife and I took a 3 day vacation. I did some fishing while Betty caught up on her reading.

Two months earlier, we took ten days off and drove down to Orlando to meet our children at Disney World®.

Between these two trips we saved $408 on lodging and meals.

Can you imagine a better way to end a perfect trip than having your hotel bill cut almost in half? Now, we're planning to use the money we saved to pay for our next trip.

MR. SAMPLE, YOU CAN ENJOY THESE SAME BENEFITS BY USING THE SPECIAL SEPTEMBER DAYS CLUB MEMBERSHIP CARD I'VE ENCLOSED.

Don't take a chance on losing it. Remove your card now and put it in your wallet or another safe place.

Your membership card saves you up to 50% at over 1,300 participating Days Inns®, Hotels®, Suites® and Daystops®.

Plus, as a Club Member, you will receive big discounts on meals, gifts, admission to theme parks, car rentals, travel packages, and much more -- beginning today! Let me explain.

The September Days Club® is a national discount travel club. Since we started the Club in 1974, it has become the largest travel club of its type -- with over a quarter million members.

We use our large size -- and the fact that we limit our membership to people age 50 and over -- to get you the best deals. Here's what membership brings you:

* Up to 50% off at over 1,300 participating Days Inns, Hotels, Suites and Daystops

* Our "members-only" September Days Club News travel magazine

* Up to 50% off admission to participating theme parks, attractions and museums

Clever appeal to a difficult group of readers. *(Continued)*

Page 2

* Exciting travel packages at up to 40% savings

* Your "members-only" toll-free number to call the Club's full-service travel agency from the convenience of your home

* Substantial discounts on Alamo® car rentals

Plus you'll save another 10% off meals and 10% off gifts at our participating restaurants and gift shops. And when your children or grandchildren travel with you, they eat free at many of our properties.

To take advantage of your benefits and start saving on your next trip, just fill in your pre-approved Membership Acceptance Form and return it to me today in the postage-free envelope I've enclosed.

As soon as I receive your completed Acceptance Form, I'll send your Member Benefits Kit and your permanent membership card, and start your subscription to our quarterly <u>News</u> travel magazine.

In the meantime, use your temporary membership card and begin enjoying your September Days Club savings now!

And remember, when you join, your spouse becomes a Member <u>absolutely free</u>. You'll both save at least 15% -- and as much as 50% -- <u>every night</u> you stay at Days Inns, Hotels, Suites and Daystops.

Your room will have a king, queen or two double beds. You'll always have a full bath with both a shower and tub. A direct dial phone -- with free local calls in many areas -- will be near your bed.

You'll also have a color TV -- many with cable and free movie channels -- and independent climate control so you can adjust your room's heat and air conditioner to the temperature you like.

Many of our hotels offer suites and efficiency units complete with all electric kitchens and dishwashers. And most have swimming pools.

For your service and security, a trained and professional manager will be standing by to help you 24 hours of every day.

The pictures I've enclosed show why our hotels are rated so highly. What they don't show are your additional savings.

As a September Days Club Member, you'll <u>save up to 50% off admissions to participating theme parks, museums and attractions.</u> Big

(Continued)

Page 3

attractions like NBC's Television Tour in California, and Florida's Silver Springs.

You also get substantial savings on travel packages and car rentals plus the best available rates on cruises, airline travel and tours. And you'll be given a special "members-only" toll-free telephone number for our full-service travel agency.

Our Club travel consultants -- known for their efficiency and courtesy -- will be standing by to offer you the best savings on your travel needs. All from the convenience of your home or while traveling.

Additionally, you'll save on medicines, vitamins, travel, health and personal insurance and receive a FREE subscription to our "members-only" magazine!

Your "members-only" travel News magazine is full of fascinating stories, travel advice and spectacular photography.

Each issue shows you places to go and hints on how to get there and is packed with tour schedules, coupons, and even bigger discounts on Days rooms in selected cities.

MR. SAMPLE, AS A SEPTEMBER DAYS CLUB MEMBER, YOU CAN TRAVEL MORE FOR LESS MONEY!

You have my Money Back Guarantee. If your membership doesn't save you money every time you travel -- or if you become dissatisfied for any other reason -- you get a full refund on the remaining portion of your membership. No questions asked.

When you join, your spouse automatically becomes a Club Member -- free. Plus you get three bonus coupons valued at $15 -- more than the cost of membership -- if you return your Acceptance Form within the next ten days.

Your first year introductory membership is only $5 -- a 58% savings off our annual renewal dues of twelve dollars. Plus when you join, your spouse automatically becomes a Club Member -- free!

So why wait? Fill in your pre-approved Membership Acceptance Form and return it to me today in the postage-free envelope I've enclosed.

Sincerely,

Ken Mitchell

Kenneth Mitchell
General Manager

P.S. Return your completed Acceptance Form within the next ten days and I'll send you three bonus coupons good for $15 in additional savings -- that's more than the cost of membership. Fill in your pre-approved Membership Acceptance Form and return it to me today.

Mailer: **Civil War Trust**
Key Words: **"If you've ever toured . . ."**
Writer: **Tom McCormick**

The Challenge

If someone were to ask *you* if you might be interested in membership in an organization dedicated to the study of the Civil War, what might your reaction be?

You've just explained the challenge underlying this letter, which not only tackles the issue head-on, but turns the reader's casual interest (as a reader) into aggressive interest (as a prospective member).

The Implementation

Here we have a classic membership mailing. The top of the letter points out that the recipient has been "selected," not "invited"—and not for "Membership," but for "Charter Membership."

This letter might have been included with fund-raising mailings because the Civil War Trust is a not-for-profit organization. We include it here because it is an excellent example of an upscale membership offer, and the proof is (according to the writer) that it has been the control since the Trust's launch.

Comment

This letter walks a fine line between the intellectual and the emotional, and it does so with remarkable success. Had the letter limited itself to an intellectual description, reader-involvement would have been limited; but as written, the reader feels honored to share in the Civil War Trust.

Figure 8–4. The Civil War Trust

FROM THE NATIONAL HEADQUARTERS OF
THE CIVIL WAR TRUST:

I am pleased to advise you that
you have been selected for

CHARTER MEMBERSHIP

in The Civil War Trust, and are thus entitled
to all related rights and privileges upon your
acceptance of this nomination.

EDGAR M. ANDREWS, III
Executive Vice-President

Dear Charter Member Elect:

If you've ever toured any of our Civil War battlefields -- places like Manassas, Harpers Ferry, and Antietam -- you will surely recall the special feeling these places evoke.

Even if one's knowledge of our Civil War is a bit rusty, few of us can walk these fields and woodlands without being somehow stirred.

For the land we stand upon is part of that crucible in which the America we know today was forged. At places like Chancellorsville and Vicksburg, young Americans of courage and conviction clashed and died for their ideals during our nation's most formative struggle.

North or south, these battlefields are truly hallowed ground.

Yet, as you read this, the vast majority of them lie vulnerable to the worst forms of misuse. For owing to financial and jurisdictional limitations, our government can do little to protect the majority of these national treasures.

As a result, there's virtually nothing to prevent some 85% of our most historic Civil War sites from being engulfed or covered over with tourist attractions, urban sprawl, industry, or worse.

In fact, since most lie near key highways and, thus, in the very path of development, we could well lose many within just the next few years!

That's why your Charter Membership in The Civil War Trust...<u>a private non-profit society formed at the suggestion of the U.S. Secretary of the</u>

(over, please)

An upscale membership offer that balances appeals to intellect and emotion with unusual skill—and success. *(Continued)*

Interior...is so urgently important.

For if we're to save these living links with our heritage, we'll need to represent a formidable legion of Americans who stand foursquare for their rescue and preservation.

Hence our pressing need for you to accept your appointment to Charter Membership in The Civil War Trust. I'll explain how your doing so will add power to our national campaign in just a moment.

Right now, though, I want to give you just a few examples of the places we're striving to save so you can better understand the kinds of dangers that threaten so many of our most historic battle sites.

At BENTONVILLE, North Carolina, where in 1865 nearly 100,000 men collided in combat when Confederate General Joe Johnston struck at Sherman's invading forces, a mere 90 acres of their 6,000-acre battleground are protected today. And the breastworks still standing from that time now face destruction to make way for livestock.

At STONES RIVER in Tennessee, site of one of the war's deadliest blunders where in January 1863, Southern troops sought to scare off some Union infantry with a hasty charge, only to spark a melee costing 23,000 casualties -- this battleground is today menaced by a super highway sure to bring with it layers of intrusive development.

At GETTYSBURG, our premier military park in Pennsylvania, the boundaries of this place which saw nearly 50,000 American casualties are becoming ever more crowded by commercial sprawl, with a huge shopping mall now in the offing. Worse yet, a private landowner is actually planning a camping facility on the very grounds of this national historic site.

At HARPERS FERRY, West Virginia, where Stonewall Jackson overran the Union garrison, thus clearing his way to the epic 1862 battle at Antietam, a development planned for this tract has fortunately been dropped...making its rescue still possible, *if* the needed funds can be found in time.

At THE WILDERNESS in Virginia, where May 5th and 6th of 1864 saw Robert E. Lee's Confederate army engage U.S. Grant's forces in two days of savage fighting under utterly appalling conditions, the acreage upon which the battle's most pivotal action occurred is now planned for a housing subdivision.

As you can see, even the most sacred of our Civil War battlefields are today being thoughtlessly endangered both from within and without.

On the one hand, privately owned tracts that are actually part of these special lands are often at the mercy of local economic pressures and market forces.

(Continued)

However, the most common menace to our historic Civil War sites is the crush of housing tracts, strip malls, and tourist magnets pressing ever closer around them -- threatening the now-peaceful hush of their consecrated ground with torrents of blare, bedlam, and blinding neon.

Regardless of the specific perils, though, there is still time to save and preserve most of these gloried places.

And with our Civil War Trust as the leading force in this formidable mission, we can indeed accomplish it with the backing of enough caring citizens!

That's why your role as a Charter Member of the Trust -- and your clearly stated support for its objectives -- are so important.

You see, it's around those Americans chosen for this distinctive role that we are building a citizen-alliance...a national membership whose resolve and weight of numbers will give us the influence needed to win essential funding from private foundations and corporate sponsors.

For the combined voices of Americans united in a worthwhile cause carries greater sway with these potential supporters than you likely imagine.

Once granted the necessary dollars, and backed by throngs of steadfast members, The Civil War Trust can quickly expand its drive to rescue historic Civil War battle sites across the land.

Working hand-in-hand with community preservationists, the Trust has already begun its drive to preserve these living shrines at places like Mill Springs and South Mountain.

Our approach is simple and fair.

Wherever key battlegrounds lie vulnerable to development or other forms of intrusion, our strategy is to help concerned local groups buy the land outright or, if more appropriate, assure its protection by easement.

In this way, the Trust plans to safeguard an entire network of America's most historic Civil War sites.

After that, our goal is to preserve these venerable places so they may serve the generations to come as living, teaching memorials of the conflict that shaped our nation, its freedoms, and its values.

It is with all this in mind that the officers of The Civil War Trust have selected you for the status of Charter Member -- to take your place among those Americans chosen to compose an exemplary cadre around which we can build the truly national membership essential to our success.

Please understand that agreeing to your selection does not obligate you to help directly with Trust projects. While we may welcome such offers, we look to our Charter Members mainly to generate awareness of the

(over, please)

(Continued)

Trust's mission through their normal business and civic contacts.

In return for your support, The Civil War Trust will accord you several exclusive benefits, including the following.

A free annual subscription to CIVIL WAR CHRONICLES! Highly graphic and historically revealing, this colorful quarterly is an endless treasury of little-known facts and personal memoirs about battles and camp life during the Civil War.

Exclusive discounts on Civil War Trust productions! Your Charter Membership will also bring you special opportunities for substantial savings on books, videotapes, and similar Civil War-related items sanctioned by the Trust as they become available.

A year of the CIVIL WAR LANDSCAPE! The Civil War Trust's official publication, this newsletter reports to you quarterly on projects of the Trust, and advises you of special membership events and on-site seminars.

Yet I'm sure the benefit you'll value most will be your unique role in helping to build the national membership so vital to the Trust in saving those battlefields from which the United States of today emerged.

In closing, I must ask that you not delay in accepting your designation as a Charter Member of The Civil War Trust. For as you have seen, it's vital that we build the citizen-support needed for our crusade quickly if we're to spare many of America's most historic sites from the bulldozer.

So be sure to return the enclosed Charter Membership Acceptance form as quickly as you can. Today if possible.

Finally, on behalf of the officers and staff of The Civil War Trust, allow me to welcome you to the distinctive ranks of our Charter Membership.

Sincerely,

Edgar M. Andrews, III
Executive Vice-President

P.S. As a special gesture of thanks for getting your acceptance of Charter Membership to us right away, while we're especially needful of it, we will send you an exclusive videotape featuring vivid reenactments of major Civil War battles -- with narration by none other than Bruce Catton, author of today's most respected Civil War histories!

To be absolutely sure of receiving yours, though, you must hurry. For quantities are limited.

TMLP

Mailer: **American Automobile Association**
Key Words: **"If you believe as I do" and "Hurry!"**

The Challenge

At one time the American Automobile Association had the field of auto travel protection to itself. In recent years, a number of competitors have begun to offer similar coverage, often at a highly discounted rate in order to wean drivers away from the AAA.

The challenge is dual: to hold off competition and to generate action from those who belong to no motor club.

The Implementation

We've included two letters for Automobile Club membership to give you an idea of the variety of creative approaches available even within a narrow offer.

Each letter makes the same basic offer. The only visible difference seems to be 50¢ for the second membership ($11.00 vs. $11.50). But the presentation and the appeal of each letter in no way parallels the other until, in mid-letter, each writer lists specific benefits.

Comment

The first letter (8–5) is more dispassionate than the second in that it often refers to "Members" instead of staying with "you." The second letter (8–6) is written the way the writer might speak, with paragraph lead-ins such as "Now do you understand what this means?" and "Oh," and "I'll tell you what else."

So we can conclude that each letter will appeal to some who might not respond to the other.

Figure 8–5. American Automobile Association

501 Centerville Road
Warwick, RI 02886-4390
(401) 732-5000

If you believe as I do
that nothing is better than FREE,
don't miss out on this remarkable AAA Membership offer!

Dear Motorist,

No matter how many offers you may have seen from AAA over the years -- I assure you, this is the one to act on. And quickly. Because you only have 10 days to cash in on all we're offering to you -- right now -- absolutely FREE.

During this special limited time membership offer you'll receive:

- A $6.00 savings off the regular membership dues.
- A Second Membership for half-price...(An additional savings of $11.00).
- A FREE trial period to make use of selected AAA benefits...
- A FULL One-Year Money-Back GUARANTEE!
- A FREE Bonus Gift with payment...an AAA welcome special!

Enclosed are your Temporary Membership Cards...along with special NO CHARGE VOUCHERS...made out to you and another member of your household so you can have the benefit of AAA's renowned Emergency Road Service -- the very next time you have a problem. Even today, if necessary...

Simply present your Temporary Membership Card and your NO CHARGE VOUCHER to the AAA Service Professional who comes to your aid. It will be honored until the expiration date shown on the temporary card (allowing time for your permanent Membership Card to arrive). And entitling you to:

- FREE Roadside Service
- FREE Battery Boosts
- FREE Flat Tire Changes
- FREE Delivery of Gas
- FREE Towing to Safety*

(continued)

*The average cost of a tow in the local area is between $35.00 and $45.00.

Offices: Barrington • Cranston • Fitchburg • Greenville • Middletown • Narragansett • Providence • South Attleboro • Swansea • Warwick • Woonsocket • Worcester

Straightforward, no-nonsense listing of member benefits. *(Continued)*

2

This 24-hour-a-day service protects you and your spouse against the worry, expense...and yes, the danger that so often accompanies emergencies on the road.

In addition to Emergency Road Service, there are many additional benefits -- many of which you may not even associate with AAA Membership -- now available to you as part of our best offer ever:

FREE AAA Maps, TourBooks®, and TRIPTIKS®

Whether you are planning a weekend drive...or cross-country tour...stop by the nearest AAA office for FREE AAA maps, TourBooks, and one of our famous TRIPTIKS.

These spiral-bound maps will guide you through every mile of your trip, highlighting the most fuel-efficient or scenic route (whichever you prefer). Plus, they'll guide you around road construction, alert you to speed traps and advise you of road conditions.

FREE AAA Travel Agency Services

AAA also maintains a full service Travel Agency to help you plan your trips. Our trained Travel Consultants will make all your reservations -- in many cases, at special low rates you won't believe. And you'll receive discounts on vacations, cruises and tours anywhere in the world!

FREE $150,000.00 Travel Accident Insurance

When you purchase your airplane, motorcoach, train or cruise tickets through the AAA Travel Agency, you are automatically protected with $150,000.00 in travel accident insurance.

This is in addition to the round-the-clock protection you have under AAA's Personal Accident Policy. It covers you anywhere in the world for specific injuries, accidental dismemberment and death.

Fee-FREE AAA/American Express® Travelers Cheques

To safeguard your money when you travel, AAA offers American Express Travelers Cheques with no service charge whatsoever. You save $10.00 on every $1,000.00 worth of travelers cheques you purchase (That's the average bank charge in our area). And there's no limit on how many travelers cheques you can get.

Guaranteed Hotel Rates -- Or We'll Pay The Difference

Included in your free AAA TourBooks are hotel and motel rates guaranteed to AAA members. If you're ever charged more than the published guaranteed rate, just send us a copy of the bill and we'll reimburse the difference. That's a promise.

(Continued)

3

Approved Auto Repair Services

As a Member of AAA, you can count on quality repair work at any AAA Approved Auto Repair facility. Each facility has agreed, by contract, to give AAA members a limited guarantee of 90 days or 4,000 miles, whichever comes first. The garage also has agreed to abide by the decision of AAA's experts in resolving any dispute between a member and the facility.

Low-Cost AAA Financing

Members can save time and money with Club arranged financing. Both new and late model used cars as well as trucks, boats, campers and camping trailers can be financed at low annual rates. Your money is usually available within 24 hours.

AAA/Visa Credit Card with
Charge Guard® Credit Card Protection

The AAA/VISA credit card program is an exceptional value which combines increased savings with greater convenience. Now Club members have all the advantages of a regular VISA card, plus a host of special AAA features and benefits, including no first year annual fee, automatic AAA annual membership renewal, $150,000 air/travel insurance and much more. And, you can shield yourself from liability should your AAA/VISA or other credit cards be lost or stolen with AAA Charge Guard credit card protection. This service would cost you $15 to $20 a year, however, it is FREE with your AAA membership.

Money-Saving Discounts
on Avis and Hertz Car Rentals

Your AAA membership entitles you to special member-only discounts on both Avis and Hertz Car Rentals all across the country.

FREE $5,000 Bail Bond/$1,000 Arrest Bond Protection

Your permanent Membership Card is also a Get-Out-Of-Jail-Free Card. If you're arrested for a minor traffic violation, it provides a $1,000 Guaranteed Arrest Bond good in most states. For more serious traffic violations, there's also a $5,000 Bail Bond. Both are provided by National Surety Corporation and are FREE with your AAA membership.

And There's More...

Your AAA membership also includes: a full year's subscription to the Club's newspaper, AUTO CLUB NEWS...AAA's Legislative Representation...passport photos...International Driving Permits ...camping directories...maps...plus free quotes on auto, home and life insurance and much more!

(continued)

(Continued)

4

So Many Benefits...So Many Extras

All the AAA services I've mentioned...including FREE Emergency Road Service...can be yours. Join now...and we'll waive the entrance fee of $6.00 on your membership. Better still, under this special offer, a second driver in your household can join with you and get a whole year of membership at Half-Price.

If You Don't Agree It's Worth Every Cent,
We'll Refund Your Money

You are guaranteed complete satisfaction or you can return your Membership Card at anytime during the first year -- even on the 364th day -- and receive a full refund.

So put your AAA Membership Card in your wallet. Return your Reply Form today. There's nothing to lose.

Nearly 32,000,000 American motorists have already discovered that AAA can reduce their driving headaches and hassles. Why not discover it for yourself? Especially now with the tremendous savings you can realize. Don't let this limited-time offer slip away. Return your Reply Form now.

Sincerely,

Richard O. Cox

Richard O. Cox
Director of Membership Services

P.S. If for any reason you're not comfortable accepting this invitation to join AAA -- THE BEST OFFER WE'VE EVER MADE TO ANYONE, with $6.00 off your first year fee, a Half-Price Membership for a second family member and a FULL one-year, money-back GUARANTEE -- please write and let me know why. I'd personally like to know your thinking.

Figure 8–6. American Automobile Association

Hurry! You have just 10 days to get all these Free Gifts.

Dear Worcester County Motorist,

I'm holding a fistful of good things for you. They're yours if I hear from you within the next 10 days; otherwise they can be lost forever.

Just one of your gifts is an elegant full-color USA wall map, suitable for framing. It's a full 24" x 37" and loaded with the kind of travel tips for which the American Automobile Association is famous.

That's the beginning. Here's part two:

We've waived your New Member fee. (As you know, Membership is $35 a year; new Members also pay a $10 enrollment fee. For the next 10 days you start out as though you've been a Member before -- no New Member fee for you.)

I'm just getting started! Join within the next 10 days and we'll issue a second Membership for half the normal dues. So if you want to include your spouse or another driver in your household, it's only $11.50 instead of the usual $23.00.

Why is AAA giving you all these? (And we're not even close to halfway through the benefits.) Because we think you're the kind of driver we want as a Member. Your name wasn't chosen at random.

When do benefits start? TODAY.

Part three is the pair of Temporary Membership Cards I've enclosed. One is for you and the other is for your spouse or another driver in your household. Detach those cards. Mail back the New Member Information Data Card. Start carrying your

(Next page, please)

Offices: Barrington • Cranston • Fitchburg • Greenville • Middletown • Narragansett • Providence • Raynham • South Attleboro • Swansea • Warwick • Woonsocket • Worcester

Informality adds appeal to a strong offer.

(Continued)

- 2 -

Temporary Membership Cards right now. (They're good until your permanent cards arrive.) I'll tell you why:

Your car can't tell you when it might break down or blow a tire or run out of gas. It could be an hour from now. Your Temporary Membership Cards can save you a lot of aggravation -- and maybe a lot of money. Do you know how much a typical tow to the nearest local authorized service station will cost you without the card? An average of $35 to $45; and on the road, a tow easily can cost more than $100.

It has happened. We have many, many reports of Members who needed their cards the very first day they had them. They used their cards to...

-- start a car with a dead battery...
-- get roadside service...
-- change a flat tire...
-- get some gasoline for an empty tank...
-- get a tow to safety.

You know how much you'll pay, as a AAA Master Member, for all this protection? Nothing. Zero. Zip. Every one of them is part of your AAA Membership.

And, you get this HOST of other FREE benefits:

Now, part four. This will take some time, because your Membership includes so many benefits.

Your permanent Membership Card can literally save you if you're arrested for a traffic violation. It provides a $1,000 Guaranteed Arrest Bond good in most states. If you have the misfortune to be involved in a more serious violation, you also have a $5,000 Bail Bond.

Do you understand what this means? It means instead of frantically wiring for money and having to sit there until the money comes, your AAA Membership is your "Stay Out of Jail Free" Card. If you use this once in your lifetime, you're ahead.

Now, let's suppose you're planning a trip -- a trip to anywhere in the country. Stop by the nearest AAA office (there's one near you) and pick up free maps, TourBooks, camping directories, and a unique "TripTik" only AAA can offer you.

(Your TripTik is literally a customized spiral-bound map book. Your maps will be spiral-bound so they'll lie flat while you're driving; tell us whether you want a scenic route or the fastest way, and the roads will be highlighted...avoiding construction and alerting you to areas of "special enforcement.")

When you're planning a trip, call the full-service AAA Travel Agency. The Agency not only will make all your reservations, whether plane, train, cruise, tour, hotels -- often at rates far

(Continued)

- 3 -

lower than you might have known about -- but also will protect you automatically with $150,000 in travel accident insurance. You can also get special access to passport photos and International Driving Permits.

Incidentally, as a AAA Member you're entitled to special discounts on Hertz car rentals anywhere in the U.S. And your TourBook tells you the special AAA rates for hotels and motels. If any of these hotels or motels charges more than the guaranteed rate in your TourBook, send us a copy of the bill and AAA will rebate the difference.

What else? Well, you get fee-FREE American Express Travelers Cheques. (If you want $1,000 worth, you've saved $10 right there.) You get repairs guaranteed for 90 days or 4,000 miles at any AAA-Approved Auto Repair facility. You get $500 car theft protection.

More? You bet you get more!

I'm just getting my second wind. (See? I told you describing all the benefits of Membership would take some time.)

Here's one you didn't expect: You get special <u>exclusive</u> AAA discounts at a whole batch of popular attractions and theme parks, as well as discount tickets for movies and other local entertainment activities. Believe me, what you can save from this benefit alone could pay for your Membership ten times over.

You're eligible to apply for a AAA/VISA Credit Card. You know how much the fee is for this card for the first year? Nothing. And on top of that, your Card can be registered for Charge Guard protection, so if you lose your Card or somebody steals it, we notify the issuing bank and you aren't on the hook for illegal use of your Card.

Have you heard about AAA's wide range of Financial Services? With your AAA membership you'll get low cost Auto Financing, Home Mortgages and Equity Loans. Also, you can save thousands of dollars with AAA's Car Buying and Pricing Services - and it's hassle-free. In addition, you'll get free favorable quotes for all your auto, home and life insurance needs.

Oh, then you'll get a full year's subscription to the Club's publication. And I should mention you get the power of AAA's legislative representation. We're your voice -- a much-needed voice -- not only in Washington but in state legislatures and in the ongoing battle against nuisance motoring laws. Believe me, when your AAA speaks out, bureaucrats listen.

When you drive, why not drive without worry?

Do you know what the BIGGEST benefit of your AAA membership is?

<u>Peace of mind</u>.

(continued)

(Continued)

- 4 -

With your AAA membership, you know you won't be gouged by some unscrupulous service station. You know you won't be on the hook for an outrageous towing bill because your car broke down at 2 a.m., 20 miles from home. And you know you won't spend the night in jail waiting for enough money to bail you out.

I'll tell you what else you'll know:

You'll know you can depend on the biggest, most reputable, longest-established, and most member-responsive automobile club in the world. That AAA Card can be your best friend when trouble hits, and its value never stops even when you're just shopping, planning a trip, or considering any of the many services not directly related to driving.

The ULTIMATE Guarantee: Your Money Back.

A Guarantee is only as good as the organization issuing it. In this case, your AAA stands behind this Guarantee:

> If for any reason, at any time during your first year, you decide AAA Membership isn't for you, just tell us so. We'll cancel your Membership and refund 100% of your dues.

Really, though, I don't think that will happen. I think getting Membership for just $35 (that's all these benefits for less than 68¢ a week) with no new member $10 enrollment fee...and getting a second Card for someone else in your family for just $11.50, half the usual dues...this has to be the bargain of the year.

But all the benefits of this offer are yours for just the next 10 days. So right now, while this is fresh in your mind, mail back your New Member Information Data Card. The benefits of your Temporary Membership Cards then begin this very day.

Welcome to Peace-of-Mind driving. You deserve it.

For AAA,

Richard D. Cox

Director of Membership Services

P.S. As soon as your Membership is processed, we'll send your Permanent Membership Cards and your big, beautiful U.S. Wall Map. Meanwhile, use your Temporary Cards for immediate driving protection. And, oh, yes -- feel free to affix the AAA emblem to your rear bumper. Thanks for joining us!

Mailer: **North American Hunting Club**
Key Words: **"The purpose of this letter"**
Writer: **Christina Cross**

The Challenge

Will hunters join a club because it offers them a shoulder patch, a magazine, a bumper sticker, and some ephemeral benefits?

Hunters are less clannish than those who might be invited to membership in more social activities. This is because hunting is, by its very nature, not a "mass participation" sport. So a membership has to respect the hunter's psychology while offering benefits outside the periphery of that psychology.

The Implementation

The letter uses two tested 1990s techniques—a rubber stamp and handwriting—to bring the reader into the text. Exclusivity is emphasized to a high point.

Terminology is carefully edited to reassure the reader that the greeting—"Dear Fellow Hunter"—is a fact and that the signatory *is* a fellow hunter.

Comment

Few letters in this collection exploit exclusivity as thoroughly as this one. Notice that the first sentence, in about three lines, underscores exclusivity in a number of ways. (Especially impressive is that the reader isn't just invited to membership; he is invited to "full" membership.)

The second paragraph is a potent reinforcer, as is the paragraph opposite the emblem on page 2.

The finishing touch to this offer is its "impulse" emphasis in which the nominee need not send any money in order to accept the invitation.

Figure 8–7. North American Hunting Club

I need to hear from you within the next 2 weeks. Please read this now - and act on it. Thanks.

Dear Fellow Hunter,

The purpose of this letter is to invite you to full membership in the prestigious North American Hunting Club (NAHC), with maximum privileges. (I've enclosed your official Membership Card.)

Your nomination to membership hasn't been accidental. If you'll give me the next 3½ minutes, I'll make it worth your while.

Your Member Shoulder Patch, bumper sticker, and complete Membership Kit are here at Club headquarters, waiting for your okay so we can ship them to you.

Once you've activated your Membership and returned your Field Test Registration Form, your name automatically goes onto the preferred list as an NAHC Field Tester. Field Testers are just what the name implies: You can get equipment, gear, clothing, a firearm, a scope, a bow -- all types of outdoor gear -- for testing.

And you keep anything you test, in exchange for a report on how it works and how you like it.

(As a Member you'll also have access to Field Test results reported in the Club magazine by other members. These candid, unbiased, field-tested reports are private, for our members only.)

Why NAHC Membership is exclusive:

I want to point out, strongly:

Membership is by invitation only. The Club is specifically inviting you -- not a neighbor, not a friend. The invitation is for you, because we think you're our kind of person.

I don't think we're wrong. Our Membership is comprised of thoughtful, aware, alert hunters. We really do think that describes you. So before I go any further: Congratulations on

Over please...

A heavy emphasis on exclusivity and a potent offer make this a strong rapport-builder. *(Continued)*

being invited to join this exclusive Club.

You may have seen this shoulder patch and wondered how to get one for yourself. There's only one way: <u>Only</u> Club members are authorized to wear this emblem. Only Club members can display the bumper sticker I've enclosed.

But those are just symbols. Far more significant: Club members are recognized not only by the Club, but by equipment manufacturers, outfitters, and hunting locales, as deserving of special opportunities and discounts.

A few more benefits of membership:

Hang onto your hunting cap, because you're about to acquire a list of benefits non-members don't even see.

First of all, as I told you, you'll be eligible to be a Club Field Tester. On your request, we'll send you an official enrollment form. You tell us what type of hunting you enjoy and equipment you're interested in testing ... and your name then goes on the list.

When your turn comes up, you'll get a product to test. It could be a firearm. It may be camping gear. It may be a bow, arrows, a knife, a decoy, a hunting vest, a telescope, a sight ... who knows? You'll try out your product, send us your Field Test Report for publication, and keep the product for your trouble. (Sometimes you'll get an item up to a year before it's available to the public.)

Want a new gun? You can enter to win one. Regularly, your Club gives away gear and guns, at random, to lucky Members.

Want a free Big Game Hunt? Your Club gives away dozens of free hunts every year (more than 300 so far, worth close to half a million dollars).

Have a hunting photo you want to have published? Your club's national magazine, *North American Hunter*, is looking for photos and articles from Members. In fact, the magazine is willing to rewrite a story if the content is worth telling. I'll tell you, seeing your photo or your "byline" on an article in the magazine is a real thrill!

Your private Club magazine - jam-packed with the information <u>you</u> want.

I'm just getting started! Read on.

-2-

(Continued)

One of the big benefits of Membership is the exclusive Club magazine, *North American Hunter*. I say "exclusive" because you won't find it on newsstands. It's strictly for Members.

But beyond that, you'll see special offers in the pages of *North American Hunter* they just don't make anywhere else. There are discounts you never knew existed before. You'll see bargains you never could find anywhere else ... because they're strictly for NAHC Members. In fact, Member-to-Member bargains are an extra benefit of your Membership!

(Typical examples: A Member offers firearms and bowhunting equipment to other Members at an impossibly low 5% over cost. A taxidermist Member offers a big discount to other Members. There's a stack of these in every issue.)

North American Hunter also has a section of "Swap Hunts." For example, one Member might offer to swap a fall deer hunt in Ohio for an elk or bear hunt elsewhere.

And the magazine also has a "Meeting Place" section where Members can trade or sell everything from guns to wooded acreage. Every issue is loaded with more than a hundred pages of pure adventure.

In every issue, you'll get a terrific bonus -- *Keeping Track*, the Club's confidential newsletter section. It'll be bound right into your issue of *North American Hunter*, and it gives you additional access to more benefits, discounts, and Club news.

I want to send your Official Membership Kit ... right now.

As soon as you mail back your Invitation Certificate, I'll get your Official Membership Kit off to you, pronto.

Take a look at the back of your Membership Card. You'll see a space for a Validation Sticker. That Sticker will be in your Kit. It will have the key piece of information, your personal, permanent membership number. Just affix the Sticker on your Membership Card and you're set for a whole year of benefits.

We'll include an <u>extra</u> entry form for the current Gear and Gun Giveaway, so you'll have a double chance to win, going in.

We'll send you some handy coupons enabling you to get outfitter or guide information and the newest edition of the Club's "Approved Outfitters and Guides" book, compiled from fellow members' experiences, which gives you information on

-3-

Over please...

(Continued)

hundreds of professionals in the U.S. and Canada.

Once you're a full Member - and it's your decision now, because from our point of view you're pre-approved - you'll share in the wealth of information, bargains, and special opportunities no other Club in the world can offer you. I promise: You'll be as enthusiastic about being a Member as we are about having you!

Don't send any dues now ... not one dime!

All I want from you right now is your acceptance. Don't send any money now.

(After you get your Official Membership Kit, that's when your first year's dues are due. They're just $1 a month. That includes everything, all the benefits I've described ... including the Club magazine which alone is equivalent to "public" magazines with a cover price of $3.95 per issue.)

So right now, while this message is in your hands, detach your Invitation Certificate and send it back. You don't even need a stamp: Just use the postage-paid envelope I've provided.

Okay, that's my story. Or rather, it's the beginning of my story, because a whole new world of hunting enjoyment is about to open up for you. You're joining the most prestigious, most reputable, most helpful hunting organization in the world.

If ever, during the first full year of your Membership, you aren't completely delighted with the benefits that are yours, tell us so and we'll refund every cent of your dues. You must be satisfied. Your Club absolutely guarantees it, and that's a guarantee you can take to the bank!

It's a pleasure for me to issue this personal invitation, on behalf of the North American Hunting Club. Thanks for reading this. And welcome to the beginning of a full year of Member benefits!

Good hunting!

For the Membership Committee,

Bill Miller

Bill Miller
Executive Director

P.S. To take advantage of this invitation, please mail back your Invitation Certificate within the next 14 days. I'm holding your Membership open for you until then. Don't miss out.

-4-

Chapter 9

Business-to-Business

Three theories exist for the most effective way to reach a business person by mail.

The first theory is the safest: Tell the prospective buyer, with no embellishment, no "b.s.," no hype, and a minimum number of adjectives exactly what the offer is.

The second theory is that unless the writer is able to dazzle the reader, the communication will never get past the receptionist.

The third story is that since the same individual who reads business mail also reads personal mail, business communications should parallel personal communications.

Each theory carries within it some seeds of validity; each, depending on the target, is flawed.

To executives who joined the workforce in the 1945–1965 period, the business ethic decries hype. Typically, this type of business buyer wants facts undiluted by puffery.

To business buyers who joined the workforce between 1965 and 1985, "corporate think" and office politics often enter into a buying decision. Good salesmanship suggests penetration of both skepticism and fear of making a mistake. The writer does this by superimposing enthusiasm which, the writer hopes, will be contagious.

The business buyer who joined the workforce after 1985 is the product of the MTV generation, responding to showmanship as much as to hard information. In fact, to some, information is not digestible unless it is swathed in glitz.

The other component to this complex mixture is that nasty appendage, the "mail room." More and more companies—including, believe it or not, some advertising agencies—actually instruct their mail rooms to discard communications which obviously are third class mail or appeals to do business. The mail room clerks, usually the youngest people aboard the corporate ship, become filters. No, they become first editors, deciding which pieces get delivered and which don't.

Recognizing the difference between *theory* and *tested fact,* we certainly do not want to suggest a blanket reaction based on age. We do suggest that each creative team make a concerted effort to determine who their targets are. (This may be an impossible charge. In some mainline computer companies the executives are in their early twenties and the mail room clerks are in their sixties.)

The most successful business mailings reported to us seem to follow the obvious middle ground: A provocative opening and hard fact with a light coating of romance.

Mailer: **Cooperative Marketing Concepts, Inc.**
Key Words: **"I'll tell you what we'll bet . . ."**
Writer: **Christina Cross**

The Challenge

Add to the list of highly-competitive industries: telemarketing. A company in this business is hampered by the mechanical/electronic limitations—all have similar equipment, all have similar technology, and all have similar (specifically limited) function.

The challenge, then, for every telemarketing company, is to break out of the pack.

The Implementation

Two facets of inducement position Cooperative Marketing Concepts uniquely. The first is the offer of a round-trip ticket to Memphis—an offer different enough from any competitor to warrant attention. The writer recognized this immediately and put that offer in a handwritten overline.

The second is the group of seven parallels, called "Deadly Sins," each of which pinpoints a problem every in-house telemarketing operation faces every day.

Heads have to nod "yes" to at least some of these points.

Comment

Had this letter begun, "Do you need additional telemarketing help?" it probably would not have had any impact—not only because the automatic answer to this type of question is "no," but also because it is a naked plea for business. As structured, with an immediate reference (after the handwritten overline which offers a free trip) to "Seven Deadly Sins," the reader is drawn into the letter.

Within the text are enough specifics to satisfy any Chief Financial Officer, Office Manager, Director of Telemarketing, or any other executive to whom this mailing might be routed.

Good Concept-CP1

Figure 9–1. Cooperative Marketing Concepts, Inc.

I'll tell you what we'll bet: a free round-trip airplane ticket to beautiful Memphis.

Good Morning!

What'll you bet you won't ever again have to worry about THE SEVEN DEADLY SINS OF YOUR TELEMARKETING OPERATION?

You know those Seven Deadly Sins, of course, and if you're in business you've experienced all seven at one time or another:

Deadly Sin #1 -
A caller hangs up because all your toll-free lines are too busy, too long.

Deadly Sin #2 -
You lose an order because your operator can't answer a relatively simple question about what you're selling. Then you lose a bonus order because your operator doesn't upsell.

Deadly Sin #3 -
Staffing for nights and weekends costs more than the value of orders coming in.

Deadly Sin #4 -
An outside telemarketing company assigns ignorant or semi-literate operators to answer your 800 number, and you lose orders because they don't capture basic information.

Deadly Sin #5 -
Two employees call in sick, and the resulting shifts make lunchtime a call-answering disaster.

Deadly Sin #6 -
Your telemarketing department is so noisy, overloaded, and inefficient that implementing any new idea or program is next to impossible.

Deadly Sin #7 -
You don't have anyone conducting ongoing training or upgrading of your telemarketing programs, and no one maximizing your telemarketing opportunities and always planning, planning, planning ahead.

Why am I rubbing salt into these all-too-common wounds? Because I'm in a position to tell you flatly and absolutely: You don't have to put up with a single one of those deadly sins.

We've done it enough times for me to be able to make you a promise I know we can keep: At last you have a source of inbound and outbound telemarketing as reliable, accurate, and enthusiastic as the best person

(over, please)

6000 POPLAR AVE. • SUITE 300 • MEMPHIS, TN 38119 • TEL: (901) 683-5210 • FAX: (901) 681-0711

Listing the reader's problems and concerns—and offering solutions—make this letter stand out from competitors *(Continued)* on your own staff can be. In fact, I can promise you if we're handling your calls, no customer we speak to will know we aren't right there on your premises.

MCI, Federal Express, MasterCard, and a host of smaller accounts have used us. Sometimes we'll handle it all, because we do have 120 inbound/outbound lines. Sometimes we'll handle just a portion, or the overflow. Sometimes we're called on to train in-house telemarketers, or set up controls.

I want you to fly to Memphis for a day – as our guest, of course – so you can see what a state-of-the-art telemarketing center looks like.

I'm confident, too, that we can show you how CMC not only represents smooth-running efficiency, but also a considerable dollar savings. Aside from our commitment to helping you end your thorniest, nastiest telemarketing problems, we'll literally make you an offer you can't refuse.

Example of an offer you can't refuse: If you call me in the next 30 days, I'm prepared to give you the first month – up to 5,000 minutes – free. Yes, free. I figure if we can't prove our value to you, you should take that free month and then walk away.

But I'm not really gambling. We've assembled our S.M.A.R.T. Call Center with the exquisite precision of a fine Swiss watch ... and that's exactly how it runs.

(S.M.A.R.T. stands for Strategic Marketing Applications and Resources for Telecommunications. You don't need us to just answer the phone, mindlessly. We're marketers, 100% bottom-line oriented.)

Take a look at your calendar. Pick a day within the next month. Jot it down on the enclosed Business Reply Card or give me a call, and I'll send you your ticket to Memphis. If it isn't the most profitable day, relative to your telemarketing operation or plans, you've ever spent, I'll buy lunch. (I'll buy lunch anyway.)

Every day could be costing you money, needlessly. Let us hear from you. We're ready, willing, and 100% able to put our S.M.A.R.T.s to work for you.

For Cooperative Marketing Concepts,

Matthew Ellenthal

Matthew Ellenthal
Vice President, Business Development

P.S. I'm serious. We're budgeted for your visit ... and I promise, if you'll budget the time – just one day – it'll be time well spent.

Mailer: **Graphic Service**

Key Words: **"You're one in a million"**

Writer: **John Yeck**

The Challenge

To appreciate this challenge, one has to move back in time—perhaps half a century.

Who cares if the telephone company has mis-listed a number, other than the organization or individual whose number has been mis-listed?

It doesn't happen often, but when it does a year can pass before anyone corrects the number. So the challenge in this instance was to convince those who got this letter—undoubtedly clients and prospects of an advertising agency—to enter in a business directory the proper phone number.

The Implementation

The original of this letter is lost in history. We are grateful to one of the titans of direct marketing creativity, John Yeck, for resurrecting it from his personal file.

The letter is written as a narrative, without the slightest indication of heat or anger. That's why the reader is deep in the letter, caught up in the narrative, before discovering in the next-to-last paragraph what the purpose is: The phone company has mis-listed the number.

Realizing this, realizing that two generations have passed since this letter was written, and realizing that it dates from a time when no formal training in direct marketing or business letter writing existed, how would you—with today's intensive knowledge in force-communication—have structured a letter instructing your clients or customer to change the listed phone number for your organization?

Comment

The letter is so old it dates from days when telephone numbers had six digits. The benefit of seeing a letter of this type is the realization it gives us that powerful communication, on an informal basis, is not a recent invention.

Figure 9–2. Graphic Service

GRAPHIC SERVICE
846 South Main
Dayton, Ohio

"You're one in a million," said the Telephone Company.

We blushed prettily . . . . then stopped. Wasn't this the same Company that gave us a fast bit of number changing not long ago?

Still, that sounded nice. "Thanks," we said tentatively.

"The Ohio Bell Telephone Company is one of the world's outstanding financial organizations," the Company boomed. "It pays dividends to millions of stockholders. It utilizes the world's most advanced technical knowledge in its subsidiary, Western Electric. It has plush-lined restrooms for its female employees. It is a dream come true."

We wondered what this had to do with us. "Continue," we said.

"Our publishing ventures are classics in their field," said the C., its vest buttons popping. "We publish directories at the drop of a hat, with millions of names in little two-point type. Such things as listing "Yeck and Yeck" and "Graphic Service," both with the same new telephone number, are pie. We do everything through channels, and verbal orders don't go. We have more complicated systems for answering questions than the Army, and in our great publishing ventures, we have less than three errors per thousand listings."

"Nice," we said, "but when we have one error in a thousand some kill-joy wants to know 'why.' What's this long speech to us?"

"You're one in a million," said the Telephone Company.

We began to feel faint.

"Look," the Company continued quietly, "we gave the quick shuffle to your 'Yeck and Yeck' listing and it didn't get in the new book at all. And Graphic Service's number change must have stuck to the bottom of some printer's beer glass, for it reads Fulton 8211, not 1166. Think how absolutely and utterly unique this makes your organization. Only three people in a thousand get any errors at all, and you get two . . .

"You're one in a million."

That's us.

John and Bill Yeck

P.S. Honestly, we're not proud. We'd rather be common, ordinary people with our name in the book. But, since we're not, would you mind writing it in? That's right . . . Fulton 1166 . . . call it often.

The right tone of informality can produce the right response.

Mailer: **Advertising 7**
Key Words: **"Sabe usted"**
Writer: **John Lyle Shimek**

The Challenge

Suppose you were asked to mount an appeal to advertisers—the most difficult target any marketer could select—the purpose of which is to interest those advertisers in marketing to Hispanics in their own language.

Making a positive out of a circumstance many people in business think is antithetical to the "American way," and doing so on an apparently dispassionate business level, is the challenge this letter faced.

The Implementation

One runs into a potential roadblock—ethnic rejection of the very concept. In one sentence, a sentence not even in the English language, the writer dissolves a roadblock.

Notice that the writer does not duck the ethnic issue:

> The patronizing "Let 'em learn English" attitude has not worked out as a viable marketing plan, and will not do so in the future.

What makes this communication superior, in addition to its straightforward confrontation of what may be a hidden prejudice, is the inclusion of professional terminology such as "viable marketing plan," "tapping this market," and "responsive media."

The P.S., which translates the first sentence, is unassailable.

Comment

The heavy reverse at the top of the page is, in a word, inspired.

How did *you* react to that reverse heading? Didn't you immediately look to see if the letter itself was in English? And did you then lose any antagonism, realizing that the letter was not "assumptive"?

Had this been written in formal, stilted English—the English one would expect from someone for whom English is a second language—rapport would have been impossible. By phrases such as "let-em-learn-English" and contracted words, this problem is not only avoided, it becomes, in fact, an asset.

Figure 9–3. Advertising 7

¿SABE USTED QUE MILLONES DE DOLARES LE ESPERAN EN EL MERCADO HISPANO DE ESTE PAIS?

July 27, 1994

Mr. Jack Calderon, Marketing Vice President
Group Technologies Corp.
10901 Malcolm McKinley Drive
Tampa, FL 33612

Dear Mr. Calderon:

If you decided you didn't care to read the above sentence written in a "foreign" language - or if you needed a translator to understand it, you will get some idea of how 25 million Spanish speaking people in this country feel when they see your ads in English.

"The myth was that down the road everyone will speak English and we don't need to do anything in Spanish", says a member of a Miami advertising agency. "That was the credo of many corporations 15 or 20 years ago."

It hasn't happened.

The patronizing "let-'em-learn-English" attitude has not worked out as a viable marketing plan, and will not do so in the future.

Today, 88% of U.S. Hispanics speak Spanish only, while 45% are bilingual.

The rapidly growing Spanish market must be reached in Spanish, and advertisers - with the courtesy and consideration to advertise in Spanish - are more likely to sell their products to the Spanish speaking market.

In 1980, according to the U.S. Census Bureau, there were 16 million Hispanics in the U.S., with a purchasing power of $52.9 billion after income tax. Hispanic purchasing power hit $189 billion in 1993 and is expected to exceed $200 billion in 1994.

An imaginative P.S. that "translates" into strong response.

(Continued)

Page 2

It is no surprise, then, that tapping this market can be very lucrative. What is surprising is that so few advertisers and their agencies are taking advantage of the opportunities that are ready for the taking in this market.

If you think it's time you and your clients looked into the possibilities of advertising in Spanish, but have hesitated because you didn't have a Spanish marketing department or staff members who speak the language -

- YOU DON'T NEED TO GO TO THE CONSIDERABLE EXPENSE OF SETTING UP A NEW DEPARTMENT AND HIRING ADDITIONAL PERMANENT PERSONNEL.

For now, you can draw on the talents, experience and expertise of **ADVERTISING 7, INC.** - a 20-year old Tampa agency with a completely bilingual staff and long experience in preparing and placing Spanish language advertising in the responsive media.

ADVERTISING 7 can handle all of your Spanish language advertising needs. They welcome a collect call from you - **813-251-8520** - or an appointment to meet you personally to discuss the possibility of helping you to get your share of the expanding Spanish speaking market.

Cordially,

J. Laino
President

P.S. That first sentence says, "Are you aware that millions of dollars await you in the Hispanic market in this country?" It's not a fact to be ignored in any language.

ADVERTISING 7

ADVERTISING • MARKETING • PUBLIC RELATIONS
• SPANISH MARKET SPECIALISTS •

324 South Hyde Park, Suite 275 • Tampa, Florida 33606 • 813-251-8520 • Fax: 813-254-1109

Mailer: **Alpha Software Corporation**

Key Words: **"My name is Richard Rabins"**

Writers: **Karl Freitag, Bob Hebeisen**

The Challenge

One look at one week's mail illustrates the challenge to any business person: In that week's mail will be X number of offers from computer software companies.

So no novelty exists, and to a business executive, very little difference exists among the various software packages, even though some may be sales-related, some may be operations-related, some may be pure computer enhancement, and some may not be related to business at all.

Getting attention in such an overcrowded marketplace is half the challenge; translating attention, once gained, into action, is the other half.

The Implementation

The overline at once enlists the reader in the writer's psychological army.

Had the personalization been in favor of the reader instead of the writer, this would have been just another solicitation to do business.

The letter is written conversationally, which in itself differentiates it from the regrettable quantity of business letters that wear a monocle and spats and seem to have been written by someone wearing formal attire.

Comment

What an impressive rapport-builder! The overline is in red. What lifts it above the conventional letter of this type becomes obvious if you envision the line as only "I need your help!"

The first sentence reinforces the delightful tone: "I'm in a bit of a dilemma." Again, envision this line without "a bit of." Look at the third paragraph, which begins "My problem is this: we're a little late to the Windows game." Here's another soft rapport-enhancer. If the writer had been late instead of *a little* late, the effect would not have been as complete.

What follows in this letter is a high-powered sales argument for a computer software program which clarifies what's for sale to even the barely literate computer user.

Although we usually do not endorse a P.P.S., in this instance we can't object to it. Had the writer included an additional set of numbers in the original P.S., the result would have been confusion.

Figure 9–4. Alpha Five

My Name is Richard Rabins and I Need Your Help!

***If You Help Spread the Word about Alpha Five,
Our Revolutionary New Windows Database,
I'll Let You Have Alpha Five for only $99.95 (SRP $495),
plus FREE Software Worth Nearly $170!***

Dear Friend,

I'm in a bit of a dilemma.

We're the makers of Alpha Four, the best-selling DOS end-user database in the world. Now, with the release of new Alpha Five, we have the best Windows database on the market.

My problem is this: we're a little late to the Windows game. So I need your help to spread the word that new Alpha Five for Windows is really the only database on the market that actually ***delivers*** on the promise of power and ease of use. In fact, David Kalman, Editor in Chief of DBMS Magazine said *"Alpha Five has the most clever, intuitive, and productive graphical interface implementation of any end-user database package I've seen."* (DBMS Magazine, Sept. '94)

The fact is, all the giant software conglomerates claim their Windows databases are easy to use. But if you've tried Paradox, Access or any of the other big-name Windows databases, you've already discovered how misleading those claims can be. Those so-called easy-to-use databases come with a steep learning curve and require lots of complex programming.

Well, no more! With Alpha Five for Windows, **you** can easily create powerful, sophisticated, customized Windows database solutions for your business or personal projects. That's because Alpha Five was built from the ground up to be an easy-to-use, results-oriented database.

That means you can create your own customized solutions quickly and easily. If you handle invoicing for your business, now you can get paid faster. If you manage the mailing list for your association or club, now you can make the entire process lightning fast and almost automatic. If you create applications for other people to use, you can get the job done much more quickly and easily.

You Can Be Up and Running in Half an Hour!

This is not an exaggeration! You can literally lay out powerful applications that really work in just minutes. Without being a computer expert, you can easily create impressive data entry forms with pick lists, sub-forms, radio buttons, graphic files, embedded scrolling browses, rich text, and more. You'll be astounded at the sophistication of the database solutions you can create. All the tools you need are right there for you on-screen.

In addition, there are time-saving point & click learning aides (called "Genies") to guide you through key tasks like creating databases, designing reports, and running searches. There's also Bubble help describing each button and On-line context-sensitive help you can browse through at any time. But, don't be fooled by Alpha Five's ease of use.

Getting attention and translating that attention into action with a friendly, but businesslike, tone.

(Continued)

There's Absolutely No Compromise in Power

Our 800,000 DOS users tell us that the heart of any database application is data entry. After all, if data is not entered accurately or consistently, nothing else matters. Well, Alpha Five is the best data entry workhorse you can buy. It's packed full of powerful field rules (over 45 rules in all) that speed up data entry and eliminate data entry errors.

For example, to make sure data is always entered correctly, you can easily define field rules that allow only the correct kind of data to be entered into your database. For example, you can specify that...

- **A field only accepts one type of character (letters or numbers).** For example, set up a phone number field as a numbers-only field and no one can enter letters into that field. Ever.

- **A field automatically pops up a "pick list" of pre-defined choices you can enter with a click.** Imagine having an alphabetized list of all your clients' files pop up every time you get to the customer field on your invoices. This is a major time-saver.

- **A field checks the credit card number you just entered against a file of "invalid" numbers.**

- **A field automatically capitalizes the first letters of name fields, even for exceptions like "O'Hara" and "MacMillan".**

- **A field depletes "live" inventory on hand** when orders are placed and automatically restores inventory when an order is cancelled, too.

- **A field performs any calculation (using over 140 functions) automatically.**

If you're starting to get excited, I don't blame you. Here's something else that's important:

Alpha Five is a State-Of-The Art "Relational" Database

Relational databases are the most powerful kind of database, because they let you link together multiple databases into a "set", and access all the data simultaneously. Alpha Five's powerful set editor even recommends which fields to link and does the set-up work for you! Sophisticated features like referential integrity are taken care of automatically. Now if you're using your customer database and you need verify something in your inventory database, no problem. With Alpha Five, you can view as many databases on your screen as your memory will allow.

Plus, with Alpha Five's multi-session data entry, you can work on two or more records in the same database at the same time. You can open up to 30 sessions on a single machine. For example, if you are making changes to one customer's record and you are interrupted by a phone call from another customer...no problem! You can open a second session to handle your second customer's information.

There's so much more! For example, most other Windows databases only do mail merges with external word processors. Alpha Five does that too. But why bother? You can use Alpha Five's powerful built-in Form Letter Editor to easily create great-looking, personalized mass mailings without leaving the program. Your form letters can even include embedded reports and variable paragraphs.

With just a click of the right mouse button you can access the properties editor box to assign fonts, colors, sizes and backgrounds to any object on your form or report. You can add logos, borders, and graphic images.

(Continued)

And Wait Until You See the Output You Produce!

Talk about impressive! When they see logos, fancy borders, eye-grabbing fonts and special effects like drop shadows, images and colors, people will swear you brought in a high-priced desktop publishing expert to design your reports for you. And, it's so easy! You can quickly and easily set up reports, letters, labels or anything else right from Alpha Five's drag & drop toolbar.

That's the beauty of Alpha Five. Everything is specifically designed to be as easy as possible. Even complex reports with snaking columns and embedded sub-reports are a snap. Try doing that in Access!

Best of All, You'll Never Run out of Power!

Plus, if you want that extra level of control, you'll have the programming power of Xbasic™, the simplest, easiest flavor of the popular BASIC language. David Kalman, Editor-in-Chief of DBMS Magazine, said of Xbasic, *"Alpha Software deserves kudos for its Xbase language implementation -- trademarked as 'Xbasic.' (Why didn't somebody think of that before ?) As users become more comfortable with Alpha Five for Windows, they can extend its power by writing Xbasic scripts."*

Alpha Five really is the best of both worlds. If you're a business person, you can easily automate any project or function without programming. And, if you're a database consultant, an MIS manager, or a "power-user", you can use powerful Xbasic to make highly refined applications.

Either way...

...What you'll appreciate most is how easy it is to get things done -- and get them done your way!

If you're not using a database yet, Alpha Five will make your life massively easier and save you hours by computerizing any task or project. For the first time, all your mission-critical information will be at your fingertips.

If you're using a DOS database, now is the time to step up to the added power and ease-of-use of Windows for a great price.

If you're running a Windows database and you're frustrated by all the complex programming it takes to get anything done, now you can *easily* do infinitely more than you ever dreamed possible.

And, if you're a professional programmer, you can create ultra-powerful, custom applications in a fraction of the time it takes in other Windows databases.

By the way, you can easily import the information you've been storing in other programs without re-keying. That goes for whether you're currently storing your data in a word processor, spreadsheet, DOS database, Windows database, or even a mainframe application.

Here's all you get:

1. **New Alpha Five for Windows** - It runs flawlessly on any 386DX or faster PC (Windows 3.1 or better, 8Mb of RAM required.)
2. **The "Getting Started" booklet & Complete Tutorial** - Gets you up and running fast. (It may be all the documentation you'll ever need!)
3. **The Easy Alpha Five Users Guide.** Written in plain-English (not "computerese") that answers any question you might have.
4. **The Xbasic Guide.**
5. **30 Days To "Test Drive" Alpha Five RISK-FREE.** Take a month to use Alpha Five on your own computer and automate any task you desire. Then decide. If you're not 100% satisfied, just send it back for a refund.
6. **A Valuable FREE Software Bonus** - More about that in a few moments.

(Continued)

Everything I just mentioned is yours for only $99.95! How can we possibly offer you a world-class database like Alpha Five for $99.95? Our goal is to make Alpha Five the #1 end-user database, and we need your help in spreading the word. So we're making this offer completely irresistible.

Get Alpha Five for just $99.95
And Use It Risk-FREE for 30 Days!

Go ahead. Use Alpha Five in your business for 30 days without risk. Watch routine tasks become automatic. And, see how even the most complex tasks are fast and easy. If you don't think Alpha Five is easily worth TEN TIMES what we're asking, return everything for a fast, courteous refund of the product price. No questions asked.

To order Alpha Five with your credit card, call toll-FREE

1-800-666-9339

Or fill in the enclosed reservation card, place it in the postage-free envelope I've provided and drop it into your nearest mailbox. Or to save time, you can fax the completed order card to 1-800-432-5744.

Respond within 30 days and I'll include not one, but TWO free gifts. **Bravo!** is an extraordinarily powerful Windows presentation graphics package that makes stunning slides, printed presentations, overheads, and on-screen animated multimedia presentations quickly and easily. And, we'll also send you **WinDelete**, a safe and simple Windows Un-installer, that will easily free up hard disk space and improve Windows' speed and efficiency. These programs sell for a combined value of $170, but they're yours absolutely FREE while supplies last as a special thank you for acting promptly.

Sincerely,

Richard Rabins
Co-Chairman

P.S. Add 6 professionally designed **Alpha Five Applications** to help run your business for just $24.95 additional. With the Alpha Five Application 6-Pack, you get state-of-the-art, ready-to-use business applications for mail list management, invoicing, purchase orders, accounts payable, employee records and contact management. Add it up. You get all the powerful applications above for less than $5 each! Plus, pick up **Alpha Five's Productivity Pack** for only $19.95, and you'll have ready-to-use form templates at your fingertips. There are 24 productivity aids in all, including a Conference Room Scheduler, an Inventory Listing, an Investment Analysis and many more. All 24 are yours for just $19.95!

P.P.S. We've found a way for you to save even more money! Order the **Alpha Five Power Bundle** for only $139.95. You'll get Alpha Five for Windows, the **Application 6-Pack** and the **Productivity Pack** described above, **Bravo!, WinDelete**, plus FREE SHIPPING! That's a savings of $400 off the retail price of these products! Please see the enclosed brochure for more details.

Mailer: **South Florida Business Journal**
Key Words: **"I am reminded of the old story"**

The Challenge

Opening with an anecdote can win the writer or reader . . . or it can drive away the reader who might otherwise respond positively to a straightforward presentation.

Especially vulnerable to reader-annoyance are the first-person anecdotes describing a circumstance to which the reader was not privy and about which the reader does not care.

Add to this the purpose of the mailing—to sell a subscription to a business publication, one of which the reader is not a current subscriber (suggesting no prior interest)—and we have a considerable challenge.

The Implementation

This writer not only avoids the first-person trap, but quotes an anecdote so well-known that the reader feels comfortable with it even before coming to the punch line.

Yes, tying the anecdote to a trial subscription requires a mild stretch of the reader's understanding. But it is perfect.

The busy business executive appreciates the many short paragraphs in this two-page letter. Five of the paragraphs are one-liners; thirteen are two-liners.

Comment

Delivering information in chewable bites is smart marketing in the impatient late 1990s.

We admire this writer because this letter is atypical and atypical creative approaches often run into the standard corporate roadblock: "This isn't the kind of letter our readers will appreciate."

Exactly. This letter is not going to the publication's readers, but to those who, to this point, have resisted becoming readers.

Figure 9–5. ***South Florida Business Journal***

SOUTH FLORIDA
BUSINESS JOURNAL

1050 Lee Wagener Blvd. Suite 302
Ft. Lauderdale, FL 33315
305-359-2100 FAX 305-359-2135

Dear South Florida Business Person:

I am reminded of the old story about a little boy who walked into a candy store and asked for a pistachio ice cream cone. When the owner told him it would cost a dime, the boy said that the store across the street only charged a nickel.

"So why don't you buy it there?" asked the owner.

"Because they are out of pistachio," replied the boy.

"Well," said the owner, "if I was out of pistachio, I'd charge a nickel, too."

The point is: when you've got it - whether it's ice cream or information - you're in a better position than your competitors to capitalize on business opportunities.

And information is what the South Florida Business Journal is all about because it concentrates solely on what's happening in business in the tri-county area.

What are the latest developments in business?
Who's selling what in real estate?
What are the trends in the financial area?

You can't put a price tag on news like this. News that could perhaps give you a head start on your competitors. But I'd like you to try it for free with no cost or obligation.

I'd like to send you five weeks of the South Florida Business Journal - absolutely free - no strings attached! It's up to you to decide how helpful it is to have the must-know details of the business world delivered to your desk every week. For example...

How businesses are finding new ways to generate profits in these tough times.
(Use this knowledge to improve your own business.)

People on the move up the corporate ladder or changing companies.
(These are people you should know about.)

A familiar, pertinent anecdote leads the reader easily to the offer. *(Continued)*

The latest big real estate transactions.
(Is something happening that will impact your business?)

New incorporations in the area, with names, addresses and top officials.
(There could be some great sales leads here!)

This is the kind of information you'll get every week, information that will give you a better handle on what's happening today and tomorrow.

The Business Journal's reporting is timely, lively, on-target with no punches pulled.

Think about it! Just one news item you may have missed...one listing the local papers didn't carry...could have an impact on your business.

But don't take my word for it. Find out for yourself - without risking a cent - by accepting this special free trial offer.

I have reserved a FREE five-week trial to the South Florida Business Journal in your name. To receive it, simply return the enclosed **FREE TRIAL RESERVATION CARD.** Read it...use it...compare it with your other sources of local business news.

If you agree that it's just what you need to keep up to date and one step ahead of your competitors, then you will be entitled to receive a full one-year subscription, 52 additional weeks, for a payment of only $55.

If you decide that the Business Journal is not for you, the free issues are yours to keep with our compliments.

The bottom line: you risk nothing by accepting our free five-week trial. But you could gain a valuable new tool in today's tough, competitive business arena.

So give us a try by mailing the **FREE TRIAL RESERVATION CARD** today.

Cordially,

Judy W. Kelner

Judy Kelner
Publisher

P.S. To start receiving the South Florida Business Journal even faster, call today to activate your free trial: 305-359-2100.

1050 Lee Wagener Blvd. Suite 302
Ft. Lauderdale, FL 33315
305-359-2100 FAX 305-359-2135

Mailer: **Official Airline Guides**
Key Words: **"Are you borrowing someone else's copy"**

The Challenge

The biggest challenge, marketing an airline guide, is convincing anyone that such a publication fills a need. Even with a $20 discount, the cost is still $66 a year—hardly an impulse buy for many business travelers.

Adding to the challenge is the realization that most business travelers are once-removed from making the airline reservation. This usually is handled by a subordinate or by a travel agency.

The challenge of this letter is to convince the recipient that this publication is necessary.

The Implementation

The Johnson Box at the top of this letter combines two sales arguments, either one of which might penetrate. The first line penetrates lack of need and the second line penetrates delay.

The actual selling copy, justifying the need for the Guide, does not begin until midway down the page. The three bullets reflect circumstances known to every business traveler, regardless of the technique that traveler might use to book a flight.

Comment

It never hurts to tie exclusivity into an offer. The writer of this letter obviously understands this concept, as you can see in the first sentence: "You've been selected to receive a very exclusive discount."

Transparent? Yes. Effective? To some readers, yes. But that isn't core of this letter's effectiveness. Rather, it's the combined three bullets beneath "How many times have you heard:"

The question of whether to begin with the discount or with the challenge can be answered only by testing one against the other. Would this letter have been more of an immediate "grabber" had it opened with the "How many times have you heard" episode? You decide . . . before adapting this technique to your own next mailing.

Figure 9–6. Official Airline Guides

OAG® Official Airline Guides
a division of REED TRAVEL GROUP

2000 Clearwater Drive Oak Brook, Illinois 60521

Are you borrowing someone else's copy?
Get your own ... and save $20!

Dear Business Traveler,

You've been selected to receive a very exclusive discount.

$20 off 12 monthly issues of The OAG® Pocket Flight Guide® and 1,000 miles in the frequent flyer program of your choice!

This is the one pocket flight guide that gives you instant access to over 100,000 direct and connecting flights. It covers over 130 airlines, 570 cities, all in one handy book. It's the authority thousands of business travelers trust.

*Now you can subscribe for **$20** less ... but **only** when you respond to this offer.*

Since you travel, you need this Guide!

How many times have you heard:

- "The meeting's moved up three hours. Can you make it?"
- "Sorry, we overbooked your flight."
- "This is the office. A new opportunity's come up, but you've got to get back in town *right away!*"

That's when you need The OAG Pocket Flight Guide. It lets you review all your options, *including connecting flights.*

Last minute changes? NO PROBLEM. Save time by selecting a connecting flight ... save money by avoiding overnight layovers.

This is the time to get the Pocket Flight Guide. By using the enclosed voucher, your subscription will cost only $66 for 12 monthly copies. If you choose, we will bill you. There's no telling when we'll repeat this special $20 savings offer.

PLUS, if you say "YES" before this special offer expires, you'll earn 1,000 miles in the frequent flyer program of your choice. We will credit your choice of one of the following frequent flyer programs with 1,000 miles when we receive your paid order: American Airlines®, America West, Continental, Delta Air Lines, Northwest, TWA or United Airlines.

To find out more about the Pocket Flight Guide take a look at the enclosed brochure. But, don't delay sending in your reply! (If you prefer, you can call us TOLL FREE at 1-800-DIAL-OAG.)

See you at the airport!

Dennis J. Flavin
Vice President Product Sales

P.S. Not sure? Check "maybe" on the enclosed reply card. We'll send you the very next issue FREE, plus an issue of *Frequent Flyer* magazine. There's NO OBLIGATION to continue. But, we're betting you won't want to be without an up-to-date copy every month. If you decide to continue receiving the Pocket Flight Guide you'll save $20 off the regular subscription price of $86 and, we'll credit your chosen frequent flyer program account with 1,000 miles as soon as we receive payment– it's our special "thank you."

Challenging reader objections highlights benefits.

Chapter 10

Personal Services and Insurance

"I don't need it."

"I've made out all these years without it."

"I don't know who you are, so if I decide to have somebody provide this for me it'll be somebody I know."

Selling a service is difficult enough when the salesperson is head-to-head with the prospect, able to blunt and respond to objections. Recognizing the additional penalty imposed on a written communication—trying to outguess the recipient's attitude—too many letter-writers become strident, letting enthusiasm (necessary) degenerate into hyperbole (deadly in this Age of Skepticism).

The letters we have selected for this section successfully maintain enthusiasm without sacrificing dignity. The necessity for this is obvious when one compares the written word with the spoken word: Would you buy from a salesperson who loses dignity because of the heat of enthusiasm?

Mailer: **Transamerica Insurance**
Key Words: **"We'll pay you back"**
Writer: **Sheldon Seymour**

The Challenge

The challenge is obvious to anyone who has either sold or bought insurance by mail: Those who are most interested in switching their auto insurance are those who are least desirable as policyholders.

So the insurance company not only has to counter the waste which follows attraction of useless leads, but also has to attract useful leads. This almost parallels a chemical compound which kills weeds while it nourishes flowers.

The Implementation

This letter uses two effective contemporary techniques—a rubber stamp and handwriting. Also effective is the greeting, which immediately establishes exclusivity in the mind of the person reading the letter—"Dear Careful Driver." This letter cleverly inverts the sales argument by stating flatly, ". . . we'll pay you to continue to drive safely."

Page 2 of the letter reestablishes the exclusivity factor. Page 3 quietly denigrates competitors. The P.S. of the letter introduces a benefit the reader may not have thought of, but it is one that same reader immediately recognizes as possible.

Comment

As readers of this book know by now, the authors embrace both rubber stamps and handwriting as contemporary attention-getters.

We aren't the only ones who endorse these concepts, and as a result, many letters have begun to appear using both techniques. Some seem to make the decision, "Let's use a rubber stamp and handwriting," without carrying the implementation of that decision onto a professional level.

This letter achieves high professionalism in its use of both procedures.

Notice the handwriting on page 2 which accomplishes two goals: It adds exclusivity and forces the skimmer, who may not have read the previous several paragraphs, to go back to see what it was that caused "why not?" to be written.

Figure 10–1. Transamerica Insurance Group

Transamerica
Insurance Group

NEW! Especially for Good Drivers in Virginia

Transamerica Premier Insurance Company

P.O. Box 19644 • Irvine, CA 92713

We'll pay you back for being a good driver. You bet we will!

Dear Careful Driver:

I have an extraordinary proposal for you.

If you accept my proposal --- and continue to drive safely --- Transamerica Premier Insurance Company, a subsidiary of one of America's most reliable corporations, will make it worth your while in a way we both understand:

A cash reward for you!

You're one of a relative handful of Virginia safe drivers I'm inviting to participate in our Good Driver Reward Policy. Here's how it works:

> When you have this remarkable policy, we'll pay you to continue to drive safely.
>
> If you remain a Transamerica Premier Good Driver Reward Policyholder and maintain a claim-free record for three years, we'll give you a Reward Refund of 25% of your first six month's premium.

An example of how your Reward Refund would work:

Suppose your premium for the first six months you were insured with us was $275. 25% of $275 is $68.75. That can be your first Reward Refund.

> Once you receive your Good Driver Reward, every six months you'll get a good driver refund of 25% of your premium from three years before, as long as you drive claim-free as a Transamerica Premier policyholder.

(What is claim-free? It's driving without a reported loss other than towing, regardless of fault.)

(over, please)

Contemporary presentation and a strong opening build exclusivity and strengthen the sales argument. *(Continued)*

Why Doesn't Your Present Insurance Company Do This?

At last, you get the Reward you deserve for driving claim-free with Transamerica Premier.

Most companies don't reward their good drivers. We don't agree ... so we've done something about it.

Are you a safe driver? Keep driving the way you've been driving, and we're going to do something for you.

If you drive claim-free as a Transamerica Premier Policyholder, you enjoy the benefits. As a claim-free driver, you're entitled to more than congratulations. You're entitled to a reward, and that's exactly what Transamerica Premier will give you ... plus other benefits described in the brochure I've enclosed.

exclusivity → This offer is for you. There's no point showing it to your neighbor.

Why not? Because your neighbor may not qualify.

At Last: Real Rewards for Good Drivers!

Transamerica Premier's Good Driver Reward policy is worth your attention, just as any opportunity to save money is worth your attention.

I can understand your asking, "What's the catch?" In fact, about half the executives sitting around our conference table asked that same question when I first described this Policy and asked for the Board's approval to offer it to you. "What's the catch? Where's the rest of it, the fine print?"

My friend, there isn't any catch and there isn't any fine print. This policy is yours direct from Transamerica Premier. If you think a company our size would risk its reputation by giving you an insurance policy filled with doubletalk, then you wouldn't take advantage of this offer no matter what I said.

Here's what I propose to do:

> As soon as we have your application approved with your payment, I'll send your policy off to you.
>
> When you get it, look it over and compare. Transamerica Premier has loaded this policy with "good driver benefits." Good driver --- that's you. Insurance company recognizing you're a good driver --- that's us.

-2-

(Continued)

I'm proud to be able to bring you the coverage you choose and the benefits you deserve because you drive safely. So when I tell you, "We make safe driving worth your while," I mean it!

Why Transamerica Premier Should Be Your Choice

Let's suppose you <u>don't</u> drive claim-free as our policyholder, over the next few years. Have you lost anything?

Certainly not. You've been covered by a big, reputable, nationally responsible insurer, a company that handles claims with the speed, efficiency, and compassion you're looking for.

After all, your Good Driver Reward Policy isn't our only type of coverage. Thousands and thousands of motorists in other states are enjoying the security of Transamerica Premier coverage <u>without</u> the Good Driver Reward. We aren't offering them this extra benefit, and even without it they see the superiority of Transamerica Premier's auto insurance.

So if you have a claim we won't give you a hard time. You won't qualify for the Good Driver Reward, but because you're a Transamerica Premier policyholder the clock starts running right away ... which means if, after you've had a claim, you then drive claim-free for the next three years as our policyholder, you'll then qualify for the Good Driver Reward.

Now do you see why you can't lose? If you drive without having a claim for three years with us (and if you've been driving claim-free for the past several years odds are you will) you're automatically entitled to your Good Driver Reward. If you have a claim, you don't have to worry about the company behind the policy.

What You Should Think About

Unlike some insurance companies, Transamerica Premier lets you be the boss. You tell us, for example, how big a deductible amount you want on your collision insurance. The most popular deductible choices are $100, $250, $500, and $1,000. (Obviously, a $500 deductible policy costs less than a $250 deductible.)

Chances are you won't need this next benefit because you're a good driver, but it's comforting to know: If you're arrested, your policy pays up to $250 for bail bonds.

What Transamerica Premier has done is try to make this coverage as attractive as we possibly can make it, for the drivers we want most: drivers who don't have accidents and who do pay attention to what's going on around them when they're behind the wheel.

—3—

(Continued)

Phone Us or Mail the Request for Quote

You can enter the information in the simplified "Request for Quotation" form. Or, if you want fast action and an immediate cost quotation, call our toll-free phone:

1-800-446-0400

I suggest that for convenience --- and a direct comparison of what Transamerica Premier Insurance Company gives you --- you have your present policy available when you call, although it isn't mandatory. Trained insurance people (not just telephone operators) man the toll-free phones weekdays from 9 a.m. to 9 p.m. Eastern time.

Now It's Up to You

The decision is yours --- just as the Good Driver Reward Refund can be yours.

After all, without your Good Driver Reward you could drive for a lifetime claim-free and have nothing to show for it.

Many drivers do just that. You no longer have to. I'm pleased to be the one making it possible for you to get the break you deserve on auto insurance rates.

For continued safe driving,

David Madigan

David P. Madigan, Vice President

P.S. At the very least, call for answers to any questions you may have. Over a period of time your good driving record could help pay for your vacation each year!

—4—

Mailer: **The Financial Advantage Company**
Key Words: **"Yes, you can go to college"**
Writer: **Christina Cross**

The Challenge

As a student approaches his or her high school senior year, information about scholarships seems to pour out of the heavens onto the student and his/her parents.

Accompanying that deluge is an outpouring of horror stories about the time involved in applying for scholarships, the unfairness on the part of those who award them, and the competition from hundreds of thousands of students seeking the same awards.

Convincing a student or parent of the worth of a scholarship search and placement program means overcoming either ignorance or skepticism, either of which is a formidable marketing opponent.

The Implementation

The writer carefully establishes a foundation for the claim made in the overline. The overline says, "Yes you can go to college" followed by a handwritten "And we'll show you how!"

Had the letter immediately launched into a promise, the reader's skepticism would not diminish. Instead, this letter begins with a premise the reader accepts in light of the claim: ". . . millions of dollars in scholarship money will go unclaimed."

The first page is computer personalized, the other three pages standardized.

The letter appears to be personalized because of the repeated use of the student's first name (no, the co-author is not a high-school student; the company reprinted this for purposes of inclusion in this book).

Comment

On the very first page of this letter, the writer faces—and faces down—all major objections, skeptical reactions, and reasons for delay.

Notice the dynamite exploding from the first two sentences under the subhead "Read This ABSOLUTE Guarantee: Suppose someone said to you 'If you don't qualify for at least $100 in financial aid, I'll give you $100.' Somebody just did."

This guarantee, a classic of straightforward promise without any exceptions or conditions, is a delightful variation from many of the "guarantees" we've seen.

Figure 10–2. The Financial Advantage Company

THE FINANCIAL ADVANTAGE COMPANY

Larry Richter
PRESIDENT

FINANCIAL ADVANTAGE PROGRAMS • INTERNATIONAL SERVICES

Herschell Gordon Lewis
Box 15725
Plantation, FL 33318

Yes, you can go to college.

And we'll show you how!

Dear Herschell,

Urgent Memo: To the family of a High School Senior:

Astonishing but 100 percent true information -----

This year, millions of dollars in scholarship money will go unclaimed. Why? Because nobody asks for the funds in these "hidden" scholarships. YOU can have some of this money.

Scholarships are established, then lie there unclaimed. This happens throughout the United States. Other sources of student-aid money are publicized somewhat, but not to the high school seniors who specifically qualify to get that money.

Herschell, you know what happens?

Deserving high school graduates who could benefit both socially and financially from a college education never get to college at all. They never do realize the potential they have. It's a shame. But it's an absolute fact.

I propose to make it possible for you to go to college, Herschell, helped by scholarship money. In fact, I guarantee it. Our name, TFAC, stands for **THE FINANCIAL ADVANTAGE COMPANY.** And I propose to give you a real financial advantage.

I'll describe three different ways to "Transform Your Future". You may be interested in one, two, or all three. Each of them can literally change your life, so please read on.

Here's the first way to transform your future:

How Much Help Can You Get?

Herschell, I state flatly and re-emphasize: You --- and every student who uses our program --- will get financial aid.

Lock Box 640073 · El Paso, Texas 79904
915-751-2676 · telefax 915-751-5150
24-hr. hotline: 1-800-733-TFAC (8322)

Using a straightforward, unconditional promise to explode objections and gain reader acceptance. *(Continued)*

The average grant through TFAC's Advantage Program last year was about $1200. That goes a long way toward helping pay tuition and expenses. (Of course, some applicants got much more.)

You may have heard of "computerized scholarship matching services" and "private scholarship sources". Don't put TFAC in that category. It's like comparing the Wright Brothers' first plane with a 747. "Private scholarship sources" are just the beginning. How about government programs? How about campus based student aid programs? How about state and federal grants many deserving students never even heard of?

Read This ABSOLUTE Guarantee

Suppose somebody said to you, "If you don't qualify for at least $100 in financial aid, I'll give you $100."

Somebody just did.

Please don't miss a word of this. It's in writing, which means the post office will jump on us if we don't live up to it. You know we mean it:

> TFAC will provide the name and address of the financial aid sources for which you're qualified, based on the information you send us on our official questionnaire.
>
> Your total fee is $89 if you reply within the next 15 days. If you don't qualify for at least $100 in financial aid, TFAC will refund every cent of your $89 . . . and give you a $100 U. S. Savings Bond to help pay your college costs.

Forget the idea of "information" or "being considered for aid". We guarantee you'll be able to get financial aid. Forget writing for generalized lists of money sources. We'll send you money sources tailored for your circumstances.

BE AWARE

You or your parents will receive (or may have already) a number of preprinted letters from "scholarship sources" offering financial assistance for college. Their form of financial assistance normally guarantees to provide from "five" to "ten" financial aid sources. They offer no guarantee of financial aid (e. g., grants, scholarships, money, etc . .).

As you and I both realize there is a big difference between "a list of five to ten financial aid sources" and "guaranteed financial aid". What do you want for your college needs: "a list" or "guaranteed financial aid"? A good high school guidance counselor can provide you with "a list of five to ten financial aid sources": however, he cannot provide "guaranteed financial aid".

TFAC will provide you "guaranteed financial aid" or your money back plus a $100 U. S. Savings Bond.

How Can TFAC Offer Such a STRONG Guarantee?

Whereas most "scholarship sources" have access to a data base of 4 to 8 billion dollars in financial aid; TFAC's data base has more than 28 billion dollars in available financial aid.

(Continued)

Our data base is 3 to 7 times larger than the average "scholarship sources" data base. That's why TFAC can "guarantee financial aid" and others can only provide "lists".

How to Get Started

I've enclosed a Preliminary Application Form. It asks just a few questions. It isn't your Guaranteed Financial Assistance Questionnaire; this form is just to give us basic information. (I'll tell you in a moment about the Questionnaire I did enclose . . . a different advantage.)

The TFAC Guaranteed Financial Assistance Program costs $109. That's very low for this service. But send back the Preliminary Application Form within the next 15 days and your total fee is $89.

As soon as we have your Preliminary Application Form, we'll get your Questionnaire off to you. Fill it out carefully. You can answer every question without requiring any outside references, because all the questions are about you and your family. (Plan to spend 20 to 30 minutes entering the information on the questionnaire, when you get it.)

Mail that Guaranteed Financial Assistance Questionnaire back to us and within two to three weeks you'll get specific financial aid availabilities you specifically qualify for and can get.

How Can You Possibly Lose?

Now, let's suppose you do this. Your family sends the Preliminary Application Form and $89.

What if nothing happens? What if you don't qualify for at least $100 in aid?

Then we'll not only refund your $89, we'll send you a $100 U. S. Savings Bond as part of our guarantee. That's how sure we are you'll qualify for financial assistance.

BUT PLEASE UNDERSTAND:

I'm not suggesting that $100 is all you'll qualify for. It's entirely possible you'll qualify for thousands of dollars in aid, on an ongoing basis. $100 is just the floor under the TFAC program, so you're assured of getting something for your time.

Here's the Second Way to "Transform Your Future"

The yellow sheet I've enclosed is your College Selection Questionnaire. That is, it's yours if you want it.

This is a separate service. You don't have to combine it with the Scholarship Service, although many do.

This Questionnaire asks 14 questions. Based on your answers to those questions, the computer matches you with colleges and universities that fit you.

You'll get a spiral-bound, full-scale "College Selection and Advanced Placement Report" listing all the colleges with the

(Continued)

characteristics you've chosen, plus current tuition fees, room and board costs, out-of-state fees, admission requirements, average SAT scores needed for admission (remember this ingredient for a moment), sports, majors available, special programs --- every scrap of useful information about every school matching your personal profile.

Example: Suppose you want only private colleges, located in big cities, offering a degree in business, with a strong intercollegiate tennis program. Your Advanced Placement Report will list every school matching this requirement, plus other schools with near-identical characteristics.

You'd expect this invaluable long, thorough, personalized college Selector-Report to cost $100 or more. No. It's $59.00. And for the next 15 days it costs $49. Counseling costing hundreds of dollars might not match you with the right college, the way your personalized Report does.

Here's the Third Way to "Transform Your Future"

One more component: Some colleges --- perhaps including the one you most want to attend --- insist on an SAT score above a minimum number.

Here's the problem you may face: Many, many good students "choke" when they take the SATs. They score far lower than their intelligence and learning ability should have them scoring.

Even the brightest student can benefit from a knowledge of how to take the SATs. If you're interested in raising your SAT score, you'll want our "SAT TEST BUSTERS" --- an actual SAT test, analysis telling you what you should review. You'll also get test-taking tips for raising your overall score . . . before you take the test for real.

TFAC's SAT Test-Busters package is $109.00. It's yours for $89, if you order it within the next 15 days. You save $20.

So consider:

Right now, you hold in your hands the key to your future. Will you and your family start moving toward the college education which can lift you up among the elite and wealthy? Or will you do nothing? It's up to you. But I certainly hope you do choose the path that will change your life forever . . . for the better!

For the Financial Advantage Company,

Larry Richter

Larry Richter
President

P. S. A BONUS FOR YOU: If you decide to really take your destiny in hand, with the Guaranteed Financial Assistance Program, the College Selection and Advanced Placement Report, and the SAT Test Busters, all three are yours --- for the next 15 days only --- for $195. That's $32 less than the special low prices individually and $82 less than the regular cost! Use the Special Private Discount Certificate I've enclosed!

Mailer: Gold Lotto Australia
Key Words: "Dear Friend in America"

The Challenge

The United States is glutted with lotteries. Why would anyone bypass his or her own state lottery in favor of a lottery in a country 10,000 miles away?

What a challenge!

The Implementation

Most Americans are Australophiles. The disarming first two paragraphs create a happy and receptive mood.

This letter shows what the successful marriage of proper list selection and knowing how to appeal to those lists can work. The lists were subscribers to lottery-oriented publications. The letter exploits this vertical field of interest directly. To a novice, one who has no knowledge of how lotteries work, the letter would be almost incomprehensible; but outsiders are not logical prey for this offer, nor was the offer mailed to such individuals.

Most Lotto players want to have total control over their bets; at the same time, they have no idea how to enter the Australian Lotto. This letter covers both circumstances.

Comment

Would this letter make any sense to someone who had no prior lottery experience? The question is academic. More to the point, the letter exploits those areas in which the Australian lottery is superior to various American lotteries, making that point not academically, but dynamically.

The perfect P.S. makes its point without the heavy-handed approach so many writers might employ. Those writers would say, "One of our big winners was Ken Mathis of Georgia who won [whatever number of dollars]." This one lets the reader draw the conclusion: "If you're in Dalton, Georgia, you might see Ken Mathis looking over one of his shopping centers. Know how he got rich? Right."

Figure 10–3. Gold Lotto Australia

I L A

International Lottery Agents

42 Bundall Road, (B1) Gold Coast, Queensland, 4217 Australia.
Telephone Australia (075) 38 3977 International 61 75 38 3977
Correspondence to P.O. Box 5649, Gold Coast, Qld, 4217 Australia.

Dear Friend in America:

Good morning!

(Or as we say it here in Australia, "G'day!")

Your name is on a very special list, and that's why I'm contacting you. I think you'll be interested in winning a share of the $6 million handed out every week in Australia's Gold Lotto. And this is your opportunity.

I've enclosed some official entry forms. Think for a moment: What are your lucky numbers? (If your lucky numbers have let you down lately, our computer can pick some new ones for you.) Keep those numbers in mind while you consider this:

For $39 you can play for 10 whole weeks. That gives you 70 --- yes, seventy --- chances to win.

Do Americans win? And how they do! Sometimes they win big, sometimes they win less, and sometimes they don't win. But compare this to some of the lotteries in the U.S. and elsewhere:

> Each game in Gold Lotto gives you one chance in 214 of winning a prize. That's darned good. (The New York lottery gives you one chance in 466.)

If you play a full "wheel" you're automatically playing from 7 to 462 games each week. Each game has its own set of winners, so you can see how strong your chances are. When the six winning numbers appear in your selections, you're absolutely guaranteed of winning the jackpot first prize! Wouldn't it be lovely if you were the sole winner of the Special Super Draw and won over $5 million, tax-free? If you do, we'll fly you over --- all expenses paid. (Of course we'd introduce you to our international tax consultant who can advise you on the best way of investing your millions.)

One other point: I read in a California newspaper about a $4 million winner there. The winner didn't know about it, never claimed the prize ... and lost it forever. That can't happen with us. The "A" in I.L.A. stands for "Agents." We'll be your watchdog so you can't accidentally miss out.

Look over the exciting private information I've enclosed. You can mail your entry or phone our toll-free number:
1-800-CASH-WIN. In Nevada, call 702-795-2399.
Our perky operators will take your calls from 9 am to 11pm Eastern time.

Good luck, my friend. You deserve it.

From Australia,

Terry E. Morris, President
INTERNATIONAL LOTTERY AGENTS

P.S. If you're in Dalton, Georgia, you might see Ken Mathis looking over one of his new shopping centers. Know how he got rich? Right!

Financial Success — the Reward of Persistence.

A "perfect P.S." is a strong wrap-up to a strong sales appeal.

Mailer: TRW Credentials Service

Key Words: "I'm sure it's no news to you"

The Challenge

An individual's credit is sacrosanct. Any comment about one's credit position, indelicately presented, can result in powerful antagonism—exactly the reverse of what the communication intends.

At the same time, most people don't regard their credit position as a cause of positive action. That is, few will consider spending money to either investigate or shore up their reputations among outsiders whose identity they may not know.

The Implementation

Elsewhere in this text we mentioned the great motivators of our time—fear, greed, guilt, exclusivity, and need for approval.

The power of fear is undiminished in the late 1990s. What has changed is the type of fear that initiates a reader response. Jaded readers of the daily press and viewers of the nightly crime scene on televised newscasts have gradually become numbed to the concept that they might be the next victim of burglary or assault. But suggest to someone—especially someone with a credit card—that the individual's credit report might include some negative information, and you bring a new level of fear bubbling to the surface.

The letter uses a contemporary technique of having the response device attached to the bottom of the second page.

Comment

Accomplished letter-writers long have known the technique of starting with a problem and then easing the reader's mind by supplying the solution to that problem. This letter does just that. The first paragraph strokes the reader. The second and third paragraphs frighten the reader. The fourth paragraph and beyond supply the solution to that fear, and the second page explains the conditions of that solution.

Attaching the "Charter Membership Certificate" to page 2 of the letter enables the mailer to personalize that certificate.

Figure 10–4. TRW Credentials

11000063

TRW CREDENTIALS.
SERVICE

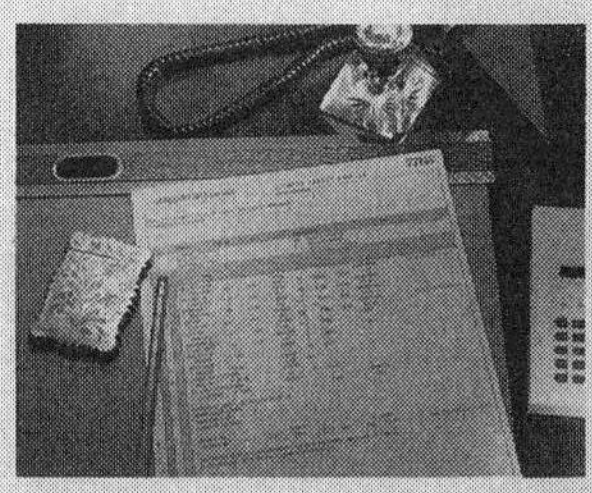

Gene Spinelli
909 3rd Av.
New York, NY 10022

Dear Gene Spinelli:

I'm sure it's no news to you, Gene Spinelli, that your present financial status places you far above the average in terms of means, influence, and credit resources.

What if negative information were to enter your credit report? Would you find out about it in time?

Or would your first inkling of a problem be an embarrassing credit refusal of an important mortgage, credit line, or loan?

Introducing TRW CREDENTIALS* service. Now, let America's foremost credit reporting service keep WATCH over your credit status.

TRW CREDENTIALS service was created to help you guard your vital credit status.

It starts with Credit WATCH -- our exclusive service that notifies you automatically should negative information ever enter your credit report. Your credit status is monitored from the moment your membership is activated. In the event that negative information enters your report, you'll be notified by first class mail -- so you can take the appropriate action.

CREDENTIALS* gives you constant access to your TRW* credit report. You'll receive a copy of your credit report for your personal review. You'll see the precise information many credit grantors look at when they make their decisions. And you can request free copies as often as you wish.

You're notified when anyone receives copies of your TRW credit files. With CREDENTIALS, you're no longer in the dark about what goes on with your TRW credit files. When anyone receives a copy of your credit files for any reason, you'll know about it -- and know who's receiving it.

Make the best impression whenever you apply.

When you join TRW CREDENTIALS service, you'll have the opportunity to complete your own personal Financial Profile form. This form, designed in an easy-to-read, standard credit application format, lets you provide your complete and unique background and financial information and acts as a supplement to the financial history contained in your TRW credit report.

Apply for credit more conveniently -- even by telephone! Because it also acts as an all-purpose credit application, your Financial Profile also allows you to apply for credit at thousands of participating credit grantor locations just by giving your CREDENTIALS membership number and PASSCODE. It's the easiest way possible to access credit sources.

(continued)

A strong appeal to fear and putting the solution right at hand ensures a strong response. *(Continued)*

Letter w/ uniqe serial # for special gift. Simply call to activate

11000063

good pull power

<u>Take advantage of credit opportunities -- and save.</u> Your TRW CREDENTIALS membership gives you instant recognition at participating banks and stores. So you can shop for the best terms -- then use your PASSCODE to apply. And by monitoring your credit status through CREDENTIALS Credit WATCH, you may even qualify for preferred terms offered by some credit grantors.

<u>You benefit from 24-hour-a-day credit card protection.</u> As a TRW CREDENTIALS member, you're protected should your credit cards ever be lost or stolen. One toll-free phone call is all it takes to protect you from liability and get replacements.

<u>Here's how to enroll.</u>

To become a TRW CREDENTIALS member, simply fill out and return the attached order form. We'll rush you a Membership Activation Kit to complete. Once we receive it, you'll be enrolled in TRW Credit WATCH, receive your credit report and Financial Profile for review, and we'll enroll you in our Automatic Notification and credit card protection services. We'll also send you your membership card and PASSCODE.

<u>Your membership is pre-approved at the
Charter Member's fee -- and is entirely risk-free.</u>

The cost for a Charter Membership in TRW CREDENTIALS is less than $4.20 a month -- and includes all the benefits described above. (Or you may choose TRW CREDENTIALS service without Credit WATCH for less than $3 a month.)

Even more important, as a Charter Member you're entitled to an unprecedented guarantee. If you are dissatisfied for any reason during the first six months of your membership, you may cancel and get a full refund.

Return the enclosed Pre-Approved Membership Certificate to start your membership. Or call toll-free, 1-800-426-2900, 24 hours a day, 7 days a week, with your VISA® or MasterCard®.

Sincerely,

Mel Wellerstein

Mel Wellerstein
Vice President and General Manager

P.S. Credit WATCH will begin the moment your membership is activated. Monitor your valuable credit status -- mail the reply form, or call now.

TRW CREDENTIALS.
SERVICE

TRW Credit WATCH service has been reserved for:

G7099K
Gene Spinelli
909 3rd Av.
New York, NY 10022

To order, mail this certificate today, or call toll-free 1-800-426-2900.

CHARTER MEMBERSHIP CERTIFICATE TRW

☐ **YES,** enroll me in TRW Credit WATCH and enter my membership in TRW CREDENTIALS service. I understand that I will receive notification whenever negative information enters my TRW credit report, and that as soon as I return my completed Membership Activation Kit, I will receive a copy of my TRW credit report, my Financial Profile that allows me to apply for credit conveniently, my membership card, and credit card protection. I will also receive notification whenever anyone receives copies of my TRW credit files. Enclosed find my check for the amount of $50.

☐ I prefer to enroll in TRW CREDENTIALS service *without TRW Credit WATCH* protecti[on]. My check for $35 is enclosed. I understand I will receive all the TRW CREDENTIALS benefits stated above *except for* notification whenever negative information enters my TRW credit report. (Make check payable to TRW Credentials service.)

Please bill my: ☐ VISA® ☐ MasterCard®

Credit Card Number ____________ Expires __/__ Date

Your Signature ____________ 2900

Mailer: **The Mutual Assurance Company**
Key Words: **"I'm thrilled to offer this to you"**
Writer: **Sheldon Seymour**

The Challenge

Selling insurance by mail is challenge enough. Selling a totally new concept in homeowners insurance magnifies the challenge geometrically.

This is not an easy concept. Shortly into the letter, the writer says, "May I explain?" What follows will either make the challenge unbeatable or wash it away.

The Implementation

One cannot imagine a clearer way of presenting this novel concept in homeowners insurance. While explaining single-payment coverage, the writer also manages, with great economy of words, to explode disbelief.

The overline is not particularly dynamic and seems to be the result of determination to include an overline, but the P.S.—a thoroughly tested appeal to exclusivity—is both proper and safe.

Comment

"What if . . ." is an ideal way to begin a letter, because it combines two reader-involvement devices: the question, which, unless grotesquely misused, *has* to involve the reader; and the non-threatening teaser. The non-threatening teaser differs from teasers which throw the reader into a new problem, by allowing the reader to believe he or she is simply observing a circumstance . . . while actually being drawn into a circumstance.

So "what if" used as professionally as this writer has used it is a happy solution for a writer selling a service the reader might quickly reject if that service were presented through straight exposition.

Figure 10–5. The Mutual Assurance Company

The Green Tree Group

I'm thrilled to offer this to you!

Dear Preferred Homeowner,

What if...

...what if you could make a single payment to cover your homeowners insurance...

...then get back every dime should you or the company ever cancel your policy?

You say such coverage just doesn't exist? For most homeowners, you'd be right: It doesn't. For you, I certainly do have news that should be both exciting and profitable.

May I explain?

The Green Tree name is not only one of the most respected in the world of insurance; it's also one of the oldest, going back more than 200 years (founded 1784). Many companies grow old in their attitudes, but The Green Tree always has been a leader, an innovator. And nothing proves this as much as the offer I have for you today. Please read on.

I invite you to take advantage of this exclusive Green Tree Perpetual Homeowners Insurance offer. My offer to you makes it possible for you to make a single up-front deposit. You don't pay annual premiums.

TWO big benefits — one of them a "minor miracle"!

The "miracle" is this: Should you cancel your policy (or should The Green Tree cancel it, for that matter) you get back every cent. Every cent. That holds true no matter how many claims you may have filed. Has any insurance company ever extended an offer like that to you?

The second benefit: If you don't want to put up your entire deposit, The Green Tree enables you to finance it. Not only are any interest payments tax-deductible, but again you get back the entire amount you've deposited on cancelation of your policy.

Now, obviously, your up-front deposit has to be larger than a single annual premium would be. That's why we give you the option of either making a lump-sum deposit or taking advantage of the special home equity financing program available to you. By spreading out your deposit payments, you'll probably save a considerable amount of money from what you're now paying for non-refundable coverage.

Continued. . .

Reader-involvement devices draw the reader into the circumstances of the sale. *(Continued)*

That's the second benefit: Whether you pay in one lump sum or finance your deposit over a period of time, your deposit is always guaranteed refundable. That's true regardless of the number of your claims or how big your claims might be.

Speaking of claims...

We've had more than two centuries to learn how to cut through the red tape that may have infuriated you in the past. These words are typical of comments we get from our policyholders:

> "I've never seen such a response from an insurance company in all my life. I can't really do justice to how pleased I am with The Green Tree. They bent over backwards to help us. They understand what service is all about."

If you're considering us, you should know America's leading insurance analyst, A.M. Best Company, ranks The Green Tree A+ (Superior) for reliability and quality of service — the highest rating Best gives.

Really, I can't think of a single reason why you shouldn't get an instant quote. You can, right now, by calling our toll-free number: 800-468-8733.

I don't have to tell you that you have everything to gain and nothing to lose by phoning us. This could be your biggest money saver of the year! Do call. Thanks.

For The Green Tree

David P. Madigan
Senior Vice President

P.S. We didn't choose your name by accident. Your neighbor probably didn't get this invitation. The sooner you call **800-468-8733**, the sooner you'll be turning an expense into an asset.

Mailer: **Advanced Financial Services**

Key Words: **"Can you believe"**

Writer: **Herschell Gordon Lewis**

The Challenge

Presenting an argument in favor of a home equity loan is easy enough when contacting those who have expressed an interest in such a loan. A "cold" contact is a very different matter.

This introductory type of letter has three objectives: initiate or sell the concept of a loan, demonstrate its value, and establish or confirm the logic of dealing with the company making this contact.

The Implementation

Should a "door-opener" run four pages? Normally, no. But consider the challenge. The letter serves three separate purposes: initiating the concept of a loan, proving the value of the loan, and confirming the logic of dealing with AFS.

The letter must get attention quickly and hold it since the contact is unsolicited. To add to the challenge, the implementation must communicate some rather complex ideas in a reasonably thorough manner to overcome the reader's natural skepticism.

To hold attention, this letter, innovative for its time (early 1980s), included handwriting within the letter, subheads, and short, staccato paragraphs. Subsequently it literally became a template for communications of this type.

Comment

At the time this letter was first mailed, the question of whether a four-page letter could generate enough additional response to justify the additional cost did not have a definitive answer.

This letter provided the answer and, although repeatedly attacked by challenges, remained the control for years. The writer believes this is because of the combination of two motivators—exclusivity and greed.

Note the stated expiration date in handwriting on page four. Our opinion: All exclusivity-based offers should have an expiration date.

Figure 10–6. Advanced Financial Services

46 Amaral Street East Providence RI 02915 1-800-333-3004

"Can you believe this company wants to loan me money because I haven't been applying for a loan?"

"Come on, you're kidding."

"No. I'm serious. And they're serious."

You bet we're serious.

And we're talking about you.

Dear Good-Credit Homeowner:

Did you ever wonder how a financial company decides whether or not to lend money to someone?

I'm about to tell you. And it's *good news* for you.

You're Already Conditionally Approved

The source from which your name came suggests to us you're an excellent credit risk. We could be wrong. But we don't think we are.

So we've already given conditional approval for a loan to you, from $10,000 to $100,000.

Yes, we know you haven't been looking for a loan. That, in fact, is one reason for your preferred position with us. Of course you aren't desperate for money.

But have you considered....

A week from now you can be driving a new car.

A week from now your new swimming pool can be in the ground.

A week from now you can be arguing with a real estate salesperson about the price of that beach cottage you've been thinking about...and you'll be ready to pay cash for it, which improves your bargaining power.

A week from now you can be enjoying the view from the top of the Eiffel Tower.

A week from now you can be admiring all those new appliances,

Powerful combination of exclusivity, greed, and ease of response. *(Continued)*

for your about-to-be-remodeled kitchen.

Do you know where to go to get this money? *Nowhere!* Your telephone makes the trip for you.

One Toll-Free Phone Call. No Office Visits.

Wasting your time sitting in a waiting room isn't exactly the most delightful way to spend a day. You've done enough of that, and certainly you don't have to put up with sitting and waiting.

We're the applicant, not you.

So here's our proposition to you:

You don't have to come in — at all.

Instead, call our toll-free number (any time during the business day) – 1-800-333-3004.

The entire transaction can be by phone. And the call to apply for your Home Equity Loan takes less than 10 minutes. If you'd rather have us call you, drop the Preferred Approval Card in the mail and we'll do it.

What's a Home Equity Loan?
And Why Does It Make Sense For You?

I'll explain a little more why we think it makes sense for you to establish a business relationship with us:

First of all, if you've been able to follow the twistings and turnings of the tax laws, you know you can't deduct the interest you pay on a lot of loans – car loans, for example.

> But even if you use the money from us to buy a car, your interest is *100% deductible.*

That's because you're a homeowner, and we're talking about a "Home Equity Loan." You're using the equity you've built in your home as the basis for the loan. (Equity is the difference between the current market value of your home and the amount you still owe on any mortgages. I'll explain this on the next page.)

Can you use $10,000? $25,000? $50,000? $100,000? It's possible. Your equity enables you to borrow money. How much money? Your phone call of less than 10 minutes will answer that question.

(Continued)

Now, second of all: Because your loan is secured by the equity in your home, you can borrow money from Advanced Financial Services at rates considerably lower than you'd pay for other types of loans.

As an example: Right now, a lot of mortgage companies are insisting on a "floating" rate in which you never know how much interest you'll be paying six months from now. Advanced will give you a *fixed rate loan starting as low as 12.25%* You choose the repayment time, from 12 to 240 months.

The difference in total payments could be thousands of dollars. The difference between this and the standard, cold-blooded "everybody who qualifies gets the same take-it-or-leave-it loan" is beyond description.

Tens of thousands of others, who may want this loan, at this rate, can't get it.

We think you can.

How It Works

I said you can handle everything by phone, in less than 10 minutes. Why not test me?

Lift your phone and call our toll-free number. To repeat: It's 1-800-333-3004.

We'll want to know the amount of your mortgage and the approximate market value of your home. I'll tell you why:

The equity in your home is the difference between the market value — what you think your home would bring if you put it up for sale and waited for a logical buyer — and how much you still owe. In general, that's the amount you can borrow over the phone.

If you'd rather have us call you, mail the Preferred Approval Card.

I don't have a lot to say about how this works, because there isn't a lot to do. It isn't as though we never heard of you before. Just tell our representative who picks up the phone that you're interested in a Home Equity Loan. Mention this letter.

I promise you a fast decision. You may have applied for a loan and then waited for weeks, even a month, waiting for a group of bankers to meet and give you a decision. Not with Advanced

(Continued)

Financial. Oh, certainly every loan is subject to credit approval; but I must tell you, I really don't anticipate any problems.

And that's all there is to it. Oh, one more thing: you do have to come in to pick up the check It'll be waiting for you at the Advanced Financial office nearest you.

Take a Look Around You.

Is your car starting to cost you money because of niggling repairs? Has it been too long since you had a decent vacation? For that matter, can your home use some improvements?

Human nature suggests waiting. Wait until the car won't run at all. Wait until your doctor forces you to take a vacation. Wait until the paint is blistering off your house or a tiny leak becomes a major problem. What I'm offering you today is a fresher look. You don't have to wait. For once you can put your own comfort first. Isn't it about time?

Here's what I'll do:

I'll hold these exact terms open for you, for the next 15 days If I don't hear from you by then I'll assume you're not interested.

A month from now this country's entire economic picture could change. Advanced Financial might not be able to come remotely close to the truly advantageous terms I'm offering you today. Then we're both losers.

I hope you'll take me up on my "10-minute offer." Believe me, we've done everything humanly possible to prove to you that we want you as a customer. Call us and let us show you we really do mean it.

Sincerely,

Robert Lewis

Robert Lewis
Vice President

RL/aa

P.S. Much as I'd like to, I can only guarantee your preferred position for 15 days Call us in the next day or two. It'll take 10 minutes — or less.

Connect

Mailer: **Colonial Penn**

Key Words: **"When you take responsibilities"**

The Challenge

Of all the types of insurance sold by mail, the most difficult is life insurance because it doesn't deliver an immediate benefit. Unlike auto insurance or homeowners insurance, in which the prospect realizes a claim could develop tomorrow (and, in fact, without which the individual may not be able to legally drive, or close on a home), life insurance often is regarded as a weak option until the individual can no longer qualify for it.

The Implementation

What a classic first paragraph! By referring to rumble seats, radio serials, and Studebakers, the writer immediately positions this letter as an appeal to the mature readership.

By using "we" instead of "you" the letter avoids a "preachy" tone and makes its point without using a rhetorical sledge hammer.

Some of the stroking may seem to be heavy-handed. That may be because the overline is both assumptive and typewritten. Nonetheless, the letter maintains a rapid pace.

Comment

The professionalism behind this copywriting is apparent throughout the letter. Aside from the nostalgia, the letter becomes a quick guide for those who only read the underlined segments. The two subheads perfectly divide the text and the reader follows the logic.

Notice the $1 followed by eleven zeros on page 2. The amount would have been the same without the last two zeros, but the effect would not have been as powerful. Many readers won't be able to translate all those zeros into one billion dollars . . . but they'll certainly be impressed.

Figure 10–7. Colonial Penn

Colonial Penn Life Insurance Company • 1818 Market Street • Philadelphia, Pennsylvania 19181

When you take responsibilities as seriously as you do, it's good to know you can help take care of this big one for as little as 23¢ a day!

Dear Friend,

If you can remember rumble seats, radio serials or Studebakers, you probably also remember that our families went through some rather difficult times when we were growing up. We saw that our folks had to work pretty hard for a dollar. Or, when things were really rough, we went without.

As a result, we learned responsibility early--and the lesson stuck. And I'm sure you still take pride in managing to pay your own bills each month--no matter how high they grow.

But as careful as you are to pay your own way today, you could--without realizing it--be leaving a large financial burden to the people you care about most. Because unfortunately--

your loved ones will probably face some pretty substantial costs once you're gone--<u>costs that are probably far higher today than you could ever begin to suspect</u>.

That's why I've had the enclosed Guidelines and Recommendation prepared for you personally. To tell you all about these costs and the outstanding whole life insurance plan that helps you take care of them <u>for as little as $6.95 per unit per month</u>...or even less when you choose to pay annually.

<u>YOUR ACCEPTANCE GUARANTEED</u>

You see, if you are age qualified, this valuable life insurance protection is yours for the asking--because of a two-year limited benefit period. Simply complete the enrollment form and return it with your first premium to increase your life insurance estate. So you won't be leaving your family to struggle someday with your unpaid bills.

Your cash benefit will be paid direct to the beneficiary you name. They'll collect this money quickly--when they need it most, even if it takes weeks or months to settle the rest of your estate.

What's more, if your death results from an accident before age 85, <u>your benefit will automatically double</u>. And that additional money can be very important to a family faced with a sudden loss.

Also, because you're getting permanent whole life insurance, you'll have these two other important advantages as well--

(over, please)

Clever use of graphic devices and an appeal to nostalgia help focus the appeal to this letter's target.

(Continued)

1. Your protection will last for the rest of your life. Unlike some term life insurance, your coverage won't run out on you--ever. Your benefit won't decrease simply because you grow older, although it is limited in the first two years. And regardless of your age or health, your protection can never be cancelled as long as you pay your premiums.

2. Your insurance can provide an emergency fund for you. Over the years, your coverage builds cash value -- money you can borrow against for any reason.

But to see the valuable features and guarantees you get, please review your Guidelines carefully. You'll discover, for example, how a two-year limited benefit period makes guaranteed acceptance possible and that once you've enrolled, your rate can never go up. Your Benefit Chart has complete information on costs, benefits, limitations and exclusions.

In brief, we think you'll find that this is exactly the kind of protection you'd expect from Colonial Penn--the people who specialize in providing solid, affordable life insurance for mature Americans.

Colonial Penn Life Insurance Company has received the "A" (EXCELLENT) rating from the A.M. Best Company. This is an indication of our soundness, permanence and financial stability. A.M. Best is a highly respected and impartial insurance statistical and financial reporting organization.

Today, Colonial Penn has over $1,000,000,000.00 of life insurance in force.

And it's another excellent reason for following the Recommendation and using this whole life insurance to help take care of your own final bills.

RETURN YOUR ENROLLMENT TODAY!

It just takes a minute to complete and return your enrollment. And you won't risk a cent. Because you're protected by this 30-day money-back guarantee--

> If you're not 100% satisfied with this insurance, simply return your Certificate of Insurance within 30 days of receiving it and your money will be refunded immediately.

So please act at once. This way you'll help take care of your responsibilities as quickly as possible. And since your benefit is based on your age, you'll be sure to get the highest amount of this coverage for your money--guaranteed for the rest of your life.

Sincerely yours,

Richard G. Petitt

Richard G. Petitt
President

P.S. If you have any questions about this valuable protection, just call us TOLL FREE at 1-800-282-2517.

Mailer: **Travel Smart**
Key Words: **"The hotel desk clerk . . ."**

The Challenge

Discounts have lost their novelty. This is because such a plethora of sources seems to be offering them, in every field from subscriptions to computer software.

Compounding the challenge and the difficulty of solving it is the number of disappointments that have been publicized when recipients respond to this type of offer, only to find that it is not as represented.

The Implementation

This letter opens with examples of money-saving, first for a hotel room and second, immediately after the "Dear Traveler" opening, for airfare.

Although the letter sells a publication, we are including it in this chapter because the publication presents itself as a personal service.

Power stems from the use of verbalisms such as, "Here's where your 'smarts' begin"; "O.K. but what's the catch?"; and "You get first pick." As you read the letter you can sense the text being spoken rather than written. This is a sure sign of copywriting talent.

Comment

The writer certainly knows how to write within the experiential background of the typical traveler. The letter is loaded with specifics. Most impressive of all those specifics is the promise—and delivery—of four actual phone numbers within the text of this letter.

The publication positions itself as both knowledgeable and incorruptible: "No advertising means no whitewash and no baloney!" Exposition such as this, apparently straightforward, gives a heavy ring of truth which, coupled to the actual examples, makes this a superior piece of letter-writing.

Figure 10–8. Travel Smart

(5B)

THE HOTEL DESK CLERK SAYS THE PRICE OF THE ROOM IS $124. BUT YOU'LL END UP PAYING MUCH LESS. WHY? BECAUSE YOU'RE A SMARTER TRAVELER.

. . . AND HERE'S WHERE YOUR "SMARTS" BEGIN:

(1) You're about to receive a **FREE** copy of an acclaimed $16.95 book that can save you $$ THOUSANDS on air travel!

(2) You'll get right now, in the letter you're holding, four phone numbers for INSTANT SAVINGS on air fares, hotel rooms and car rentals!

(3) Then, throughout the year ahead, your monthly issues of the TRAVEL SMART newsletter will continue to lead you to fabulous travel at exceptional savings -- or you don't pay a penny!

Dear Traveler:

Like every avid traveler, you love discoveries.

EXCEPT the kind where you discover that the folks in the next cabin are sailing along for about 30% less than YOU paid! Or the person buckled-in next to you paid 55% less for the airline ticket! Or the couple down the hall are getting a free rental car with their hotel room ... and guess who isn't?

Well, never again. Now YOU can be the one who's one-up! The savvy traveler everyone envies. The shrewd customer who always heads for the most enjoyable destinations at the lowest possible prices. And the clever consumer who, because each trip costs less, can afford to travel more!

DISCOVER TRAVEL SMART. AND KNOW YOU'RE GETTING TODAY'S BEST TRAVEL DEALS, FOR PLEASURE OR FOR BUSINESS!

TRAVEL SMART is the only publication of its kind. For as little as $29.95, you get a monthly powerhouse of facts, figures and expert recommendations. An "insider's guide" to hotels that have cut their prices drastically ... special discount promotions from airlines, cruise lines, car rental agencies, etc. AND the phone numbers to call!

And that's not just ballyhoo. For example, TRAVEL SMART readers planning to go to England have just been advised to check this bargain steal: British motor tour includes six-nights of accommodations at country inns, breakfast daily, seven-days of an Avis rental car with unlimited mileage, an 80-page Motoring Guide and Directory plus round-trip airfare from the US on a scheduled carrier. All starting at $779 per person! For details, call 1-800-674-8883.

(over, please ...)

Writing inside the reader's experiential background and loading the message with specifics. *(Continued)*

Another, if you're headed to Washington, DC: The Embassy and Windsor Inns are offering a $79/night stay double including continental breakfast, daily newspaper, p.m. sherry and snacks. Just 10 blocks from the White House. 1-800-423-9111.

Check them out (and use them yourself) if you wish.

"O.K. BUT WHAT'S THE CATCH BEHIND THESE GREAT DEALS?"

There isn't any. The simple fact is, like vegetables in a supermarket, travel is perishable. If they aren't sold in time to a customer, they get thrown away. In other words, the unoccupied hotel room ... the empty airplane seat ... the rental car sitting idle on the lot ... the unbooked restaurant table ... they're all wasted. They don't produce a penny in revenue for the companies that own them.

As a result, when unsold -- i.e., unbooked -- travel begins to pile up, the companies give away freebies, slash prices or run specials to bring in paying customers. The only problem is unless you read every newspaper, magazine and travel industry publication, you won't find out about these price-buster deals. Even the best travel agents can't keep track of all of them.

But TRAVEL SMART can. And does. And keeps you informed 365 days a year. What's more ...

WE UNCOVER THE BARGAINS FIRST, SO YOU GET FIRST PICK

Usually, by the time the average traveler hears about a good opportunity, it's gone. Sold out. But not TRAVEL SMART readers. Travel companies come to us first. They respect our 20 years of integrity and reliability. But equally important, they covet our readers -- thousands of active, dedicated, serious travelers whom they would love to have as customers.

In addition, the TRAVEL SMART staff combs through 32 different publications each month (including a daily industry newsletter, which if you could subscribe to, would cost you $752 a year!) to bring you valuable tips and sensational offers. Gems that most people don't know about!

NO ADVERTISING MEANS NO WHITEWASH AND NO BALONEY!

Because TRAVEL SMART doesn't accept any ads, we can give you the straight, unvarnished truth. Having been a member of top management of a prestigious national publication for many years, I can tell you that our real customers were the advertisers who spent hundreds of thousands of dollars with us. If the choice was between candid reporting to our readers -- or protecting an advertiser's interest -- which do you think won?

(Incidentally, when I mention this to students in a publishing course I conduct at a nearby major university, they gasp in disbelief. It serves to remind me how naive even the best-educated people can be!)

So every month we advise you where to go, how to get there, where to stay and where to eat. And also we tell you what's not worth it and what to avoid. For example, we recently sounded the alarm about a highly-touted Jamaican resort that has a rocky bottom, just off the beach, which doesn't show up in its beautiful color brochure. That warning has never been provided by any other travel publication.

(Continued)

We think this honesty does two things: Protects your investment of travel time and money. And helps the industry by alerting negligent companies to get their acts together.

What's more, since we don't have the giant travel companies breathing down our necks, we can also tip you off to some super deals from smaller companies -- growing, well-run operations whose ad budgets aren't big enough yet to make much noise.

For example, in a recent issue TRAVEL SMART readers learned about eight smaller airlines that are just "getting off the ground." One -- Reno Air (1-800-736-6247) -- will fly you L.A. - Seattle for only $204 roundtrip! And if you bring a companion, it's only $106 more!

The "biggies" charge twice or three times as much. Pick up the phone right now and see for yourself! And another nugget:

Try this overseas car-renter -- Kemwel (1-800-678-0678) and gasp at the break you get over many of the big chain renters!

Point being, you're not apt to learn about these low-cost alternatives in magazines and newspapers that are supported by ads from the mega-sized companies. In fact, you may not even learn about them from your travel agent, since many of these "no-frills" companies don't sell through travel agencies.

But TRAVEL SMART readers always get the word, right from the beginning!

WHERE TO STAY ... WHERE TO STAY AWAY ... AND ALL THE REASONS WHY

TRAVEL SMART'S destination articles cover just about every kind of trip or vacation you could have in mind. You'll learn how to get the most from your money in popular spots like London and Paris by avoiding the glitzy, costly, touristy establishments. And you'll get scouting reports from fascinating spots too new to be crowded and over-priced. Along with step-by-step info including addresses and phone numbers.

Naturally, if 5-star luxury is what you're after, we'll guide you to the best big-ticket values around the world. We like opulence, too ... but we're not against saving a buck.

But what's most important to remember, you'll always get the truth. That's an article of faith with Managing Editor Nancy Dunnan, a well-known broadcaster and respected author of over 20 books. She heads a staff of experienced travel writers and gives them a chance -- finally -- to call it as they see it, without worrying about antagonizing any advertisers. Imagine how these veteran reporters unload after years of having to sugar-coat their reviews!

Proof? NEWSWEEK says "TRAVEL SMART pulls no punches damning or praising an airline, hotel or travel agency." U.S. NEWS & WORLD REPORT just referred to us "as crammed with newsy tidbits, like this tour of London ..." THE NY TIMES says we're "the expert in the field of travel complexities." And on and on ... with praise from the likes of CBS, THE WALL STREET JOURNAL, USA TODAY, and BUSINESS WEEK.

Of course, we're far more interested in earning your praise. So we're on the job, day in and day out, to make sure you get the best deal -- the absolute maximum value -- that's out there.

(over, please...)

(Continued)

From special offers just for seniors ... to value-packed tour packages you can trust ... how to avoid single supplements ... perfect places for kids and grandkids ... great "travel freebies" to send for ... and much, much more!

The bottom line is simply this: Whether you take just one trip a year, or several, it will pay you to visit the pages of TRAVEL SMART first. It's the one way to make certain that your dollar goes farthest ... that you go to destinations that have been personally investigated by TRAVEL SMART to assure that they are safe and secure ... and that you will be warmly received as a welcome guest, not just a credit-card number.

ACT NOW AND GET THIS BEST-SELLING $16.95 BOOK FREE AS A BONUS!

Subscribe to TRAVEL SMART today and we'll rush you, while supplies last, the highly-touted book "Fly There for Less, 1995 Edition" -- revealing the ins and outs of airline pricing worldwide. The CHATTANOOGA NEWS - FREE PRESS raved about the 1994 edition: "This guide, whether you travel for business or pleasure, will give you timeless techniques and tips on how to pay the lowest possible airfares every time you fly."

Think of it: you can subscribe to TRAVEL SMART for as little as $29.95 -- and it includes a $16.95 book!

What's more, to make this outstanding offer totally irresistible, you get this iron-clad FULL-REFUND GUARANTEE:

If TRAVEL SMART doesn't make you stand up and shout "Hooray!" ... if it isn't the most fascinating, enjoyable and believable travel publication you've ever seen ... and if it doesn't return its very nominal price many, many times over ... you get your money back.

Not just the "unused portion." But every cent of it. Regardless of how many issues of TRAVEL SMART you've already received. That's how confident we are that this is one travel publication you'll never want to be without again!

To start the ball rolling, just return the enclosed order form. Be sure to respond today -- supplies of "Fly There for Less - 1995 Edition" are limited and you must act promptly to avoid disappointment.

In fact, a better idea is to call us right now TOLL-FREE at 1-800-FARE-OFF (1-800-327-3633).

Sincerely,

Herbert Teison

HJT/sba

Herbert J. Teison
Publisher

P.S. Still Undecided? Here's icing on the cake: you can actually book all of your travel with us - MUCH OF IT AT A DISCOUNT! AND YOU'LL ALWAYS GET KNOWLEDGEABLE, COURTEOUS, AND PROMPT SERVICE! Real peace of mind!

You're always assured of getting a good deal on all your airline and cruise tickets, car rentals, hotels and package tours! And no other publication gives you this advantage!

Chapter 11

Fund Raising

Of all the varieties of direct mail letters, the most challenging is the fund raising letter. This is because all fund raising is competitive with all other fund raising. An individual may respond to a mailed solicitation for garments, sporting goods, insurance, subscriptions, and food—all in the same week—without considering that one gets in the way of another. But most people dedicate a specific amount of money for fund raising of all types. So the local library becomes competitive with the cancer appeal; the college alumni association becomes competitive with the Salvation Army.

This is why we feel that effective fund raising letters are the height of the art. To be a master of fund raising letters, the writer also has to be an instinctive master of human psychology, because asking for money and giving little in return, other than emotional satisfaction (sweepstakes excluded), is a far more difficult task then selling merchandise by mail.

In our opinion, the person who can write an effective, visceral, fund raising appeal could succeed selling almost anything by mail.

That applies to the great majority of the communications we've reprinted in this chapter.

Mailer: Americans Against Human Suffering
Key Words: "Twenty-one months ago"
Writer: Hugh Chewning

The Challenge

Convincing someone to contribute to a cause whose purpose may not be uppermost in that person's mind is a challenge beyond typical fund raising appeals.

Compounding the challenge is the (apparent) dual nature of the plea:

1. Write one's Congressional representative.
2. Contribute.

The Implementation

Using personal tragedy as a rationale is relatively standard in fund raising. In this instance, the drama is considerably heightened by having as the signatory the husband of a woman who died of cancer after a long and painful illness.

The letter develops its premise with a progression from personal episode to universal logic. By including the name of the individual's Congressman, the letter maximizes the benefits of computer-personalization (although, as we point out in our comment, the mechanical aspects of the personalization work well for the Congressman's name, but are not state of the art for the recipient's name and address.

Comment

In evaluating this letter, the editors of this book ignored the primitive personalization, because to do otherwise would be to penalize the writer for the mechanical execution.

Seldom have we seen a more powerful opening:

> Twenty-one months ago, my wife Darlena died of cancer. The picture I've enclosed will give you a better idea what a beautiful woman she was . . .

The concept of this letter is controversial—the right of the terminally ill to withdraw life support.

For many writers this would have been a task so daunting that the text would lapse into an academic argument. That the writer of this letter combined high emotion with dignity is a tribute to his talent.

Figure 11–1. Americans Against Human Suffering

AMERICANS AGAINST HUMAN SUFFERING

2505 Canada Blvd.
P.O. Box 11001
Glendale, CA 91206

MR. FRANCIS J MILLER
1510 EL RITO
GLENDALE, CA 91208

DEAR MR. MILLER,

Twenty-one months ago, my wife Darlena died of cancer.

The picture I've enclosed, will give you a better idea of what a beautiful woman she was. But during her last 10 days, the pain was extraordinary. Then she died in my arms.

But if Darlena had asked, I was mentally prepared to help her escape her agony and suffering. But her request never came.

I know, that if she had asked me, helping her die would have been the right thing to do. But if I had acted to end her pain and suffering, I would have been branded a criminal and could have gone to jail.

And that's why I'm asking you to sign your enclosed letter to your U.S. Congressman. It's addressed to:

CONGRESSMAN CARLOS J. MOORHEAD.

And, it urges him to support our Humane and Dignified Death Act. A law that, when passed, will give the terminally ill the legal right to decide whether life supporting machines and procedures be withheld or withdrawn.

And if necessary, the terminally ill, and only the terminally ill, will have the right to request a physicians' aid in a voluntary, humane and dignified death. Let me explain...

Darlena was a beautiful woman of 39 when she died.

But, what angered me most about her leaving me, was not her death. That was something we had discussed together and learned to accept.

What really angered me was how Darlena was forced to suffer. We both understood that her cancer was terminal. And, although her doctors prescribed drugs, her pain was sometimes unbearable. Even for a woman as strong as Darlena.

My wife loved life and fought to live. Still, she wanted to control her life. But after fighting back with all her strength, it became clear to both of us that only death would end her pain.

As long as the doctors kept her body working, she would suffer. We knew Darlena's remaining days would either be clouded by morphine or spent clenching her fists to fight the pain.

But without taking the chance of being put in jail and

(over please)

A powerful opening gives dignity to a controversial and emotional issue. *(Continued)*

Page 2

branded as criminals, our doctors could do little more than prescribe more drugs.

Because even when a doctor knows that to continue a patient's struggle against a terminal disease only means continued pain with no hope, he must legally keep his patient alive on the machines regardless of what the patient may want.

And when a doctor does decide to help, it's usually done without the patient having control over the decision. Because under the current law, if a physician were to discuss the alternative of death with dignity and without pain with the patient, and then -- on instructions of the patient implement this alternative -- the doctor could be accused of murder. That's the law.

Whatever the doctor decides, the patient too often has absolutely no control over the decision. Either the physician aids death without discussing it with the patient or the patient is forced to endure and suffer.

And that's why I formed Americans Against Human Suffering (A.A.H.S.) to promote the Humane and Dignified Death Act.

Because, I don't want any of your loved ones to suffer the way my wife Darlena was forced to. Darlena was denied the option of a humane and dignified death.

I wish I could have given her that right. But, the law stopped me. And, now I'm asking you to help me change these laws.

First, it's important you understand what the Humane and Dignified Death Act will do.

Our Act applies only to the terminally ill. And, it gives them -- and only them -- the legal right to obtain a physician's aid to a voluntary, humane and dignified end to their suffering.

A terminally ill person will have the legal right to decide whether life sustaining machines and procedures be withheld or withdrawn. And, if needed, the terminally ill will be able to request a physician to administer aid in dying.

The decision to extend the normal life of a terminally ill patient will be the decision of the individual person involved and no one else.

I'm not saying that a terminally ill patient should be denied the use of life extending machines. In fact, they should have them, as long as they want them. But it should be the patient's decision and not the choice of a doctor, hospital administrator, insurance company bureaucrat or anyone else.

The Humane and Dignified Death Act will give you and me this right. It's too late for my wife. But by legalizing what has become known as a "Living Will", you'll be able to instruct your

(next page please)

(Continued)

Page 3

physician to withhold or withdraw life sustaining procedures when they provide nothing medically beneficial to you and only prolong your suffering.

And in cases like my wife's, a terminally ill patient will be able to request a doctor's assistance in a painless and dignified death to end their suffering.

In short, the decision will be the patient's. The terminally ill will be able to determine in advance how long to lie in a coma on a life support machine or how much pain and suffering to endure.

It's not a pleasant subject is it? But I wish my wife, Darlena, had the choice the Humane and Dignified Death Act will give us.

But as you might expect, it's going to be a tough battle getting our Act sponsored and then passed.

Although a recent national Roper survey shows 62% of the American people support the right for a humane and dignified death, Congress and our State Legislatures have refused to debate the issue.

That's where A.A.H.S. comes in. Its job is to mobilize the American public and urge our elected officials to grant the terminally ill the right to make their own decisions.

But, it's not going to be an easy fight. It's an emotional issue that most politicians would rather ignore. A few may even go so far as to accuse A.A.H.S. of trying to kill off helpless terminal patients.

But, I hope by now you know nothing like that could be further from the truth.

I simply want you and your loved ones to have a choice my wife didn't have.

A choice between a painful, hopeless, day-to-day suffering or a life ending humanely and painlessly with dignity.

But to gain this freedom of choice, we must first pass the Humane and Dignified Death Act. And to do that, I need you to do these two things today...

1. Sign the letter I've enclosed addressed to your U.S. Congressman. Your letter urges him to support our Humane and Dignified Death Act and give us the right for a painless and dignified death.

   Once I receive your letter, I'll deliver it to your Congressman along with the letters of other A.A.H.S. supporters. But don't mail your letter separately. We'll have more of an impact with the

(over please)

(Continued)

Page 4

national media if I deliver them all at once.

2. And support Americans Against Human Suffering's national campaign to give you and our loved ones the right to a humane and dignified death. Help me pass the Humane and Dignified Death Act with your contribution of $15, $25, $50 or more today.

Your contribution will help me reach other Americans and gain their support in our fight. But before we can expect our public officials to act, we must prove we have the support of the American public. And to do that, I must contact millions of other Americans urging them to write their own Congressman.

But this will cost money. About $325,500 just to contact the first million Americans in our national campaign.

So please act today. Because every day we wait is another day of pain and suffering for another terminally ill patient. And the longer you wait, the longer our opponents will have to launch an emotional campaign against us.

But frankly, I can do little more without your support. In fact, I had to borrow money just to cover the cost of writing you and other caring Americans. And I'm counting on you to do these two things today:

1. Sign your letter to your U.S. Congressman, and return it to me today.

2. Support our fight against those who deny the terminally ill the right to a painless and dignified death. Return your contribution of $15, $25, $50 or more to me today in the postage-free envelope I've enclosed.

And, please don't delay. We are truly on a shoe-string budget and I fear that without your support, someone near you may be forced to suffer as my wife, Darlena, did.

Please sign your letter to your Congressman and return it to me today with your contribution of $15, $25, $50 or more.

Sincerely,

Robert L. Risley

Bob Risley, President
Americans Against Human Suffering

P.S.: MR. MILLER,

I need you to help me defeat those who deny us the right to a humane and dignified death. Help me pass the Humane and Dignified Death Act to end needless pain and suffering. Please return your signed letter to your U.S. Congressman with your contribution of $15, $25, $50 or more to me today in the postage-free envelope I've enclosed.

Mailer: **The Salvation Army**
Key Words: **"One week a year"**
Writer: **John Yeck**

The Challenge

Does a camp for blind children seem to be a worthy competitor for the fund-raising dollar? The concept itself is foreign to many.

In an appeal-crowded circumstance, the writer's challenge is to make this entreaty one that penetrates typical recipient-apathy.

The Implementation

One of the grand masters of direct mail, the legendary John Yeck, has been the mentor of many of today's successful direct response writers. Painting emotional pictures with words can be the difference between the reader feeling obligated and the reader remaining outside the loop.

When opening the envelope, the viewer sees, on the outside panel of this folded letter, only a double-spaced imperative:

> BEFORE YOU READ THIS LETTER PLEASE SHUT YOUR EYES TIGHT FOR JUST 30 SECONDS.

Unfolding the letter reveals on the next outer panel:

> WHAT IF THAT HAD BEEN 30 YEARS?

In this instance, the outer fold, which might have been left blank, becomes a potent introduction to the letter itself.

Comment

Mr. Yeck, over a long and distinguished career, introduced many of the procedures and techniques today's professional letter-writers accept as a matter of course. This is an example of such techniques and procedures.

The letter generates a haunting feeling which can be relieved only by mailing a donation. And by achieving that extraordinary effect, it becomes one of the great fund raising letters of all time.

Figure 11–2. The Salvation Army

BEFORE YOU READ THIS LETTER

PLEASE SHUT YOUR EYES TIGHT

FOR JUST 30 SECONDS

WHAT IF THAT HAD BEEN 30 YEARS

Overcoming apathy with a dramatic opening statement. *(Continued)*

The Salvation Army

601 Bagley Avenue • Detroit, Michigan 48226

One week a year,
usually in late July,

we "rope" Camp Echo Grove for sightless campers.

It looks funny to us. The rope somehow seems to fence the camp in.

But Edna Sue, one of the sightless, calls the rope "My Life-line" - because it makes life in the out-of-doors, with its smell of grass, sound of birds, and feel of nature,

a taste of heaven for her.

To Edna Sue, and all the other sightless campers, the rope says "Open Sesame" to the world of nature ... a Week of Wonder.

> "Come, friends, with me," the Rope whispers to their hands, "I will lead you, on your own, to the taste and feel and sound of a world you would not reach without me."

Quickly, the Brave; slowly, the Timid; but finally, Each and Every Sightless Camper, makes friends with the rope. And together they explore Echo Grove - the cabins, the dining hall, the nature trails, the pool ... the chapel.

Please, shut your eyes - for just three seconds this time - and see if you can "feel" the joyous, happy, liberating power of that rope.

Thank you.

You know, of course, that this really thrilling experience does not happen every year simply because July once more arrives.

It needs - it must have - help from friends like you, who support Salvation Army work and, with it, that strong and faithful, calm and patient, guiding, caring, taste-of-heaven ... rope.

You've helped us before, I know. I write with thanks, to ask for help again. The rope is ready. The special campers, eager ... and I look forward to your generous support once more,

With many thanks.

Harold E. Shoults

Lt. Col. Harold E. Shoults
Divisional Commander

HES/ybc

P.S. $49 sends a person to camp. $20 buys craft materials for two campers. But send what you can and wish, from $20 or less to $100 or more. It will be well used in service to those who need.

This appeal is for services only partially supported through The United Way.

Need knows no season.

Mailer: **Miami University Fund**

Key Words: **"Just the right instant"**

Writer: **John Yeck**

The Challenge

Drawing a parallel between a war hero and a university fund-raising drive would seem to be an impossible conceit. Why, then, would one of the great letter-writers use such a device?

Tying these pieces together is a challenge not only of generating contributions, but of logic itself.

The Implementation

The writer captures the reader by means of a rhetorical trick. The reader is deep into the text before realizing what the actual purpose of this letter has been.

Empathy generated from the original narrative spills over onto the fund-raising portion of this letter.

The P.S. is a guilt-generator by its suggestion that a "no" response will still be beneficial to the university. Can you imagine any alumnus or alumna sending back a response device marked "No"?

Comment

Before most of today's professional letter-writers had even joined the workforce, John Yeck was writing letters so targeted and so potent that they still would succeed in today's skeptical society.

This letter, originally written in 1974, begins with an episode apparently unrelated to the Miami University Fund; suddenly the reader is forced to acknowledge the relationship, and that acknowledgment, according to our information, produced "waves of checks."

(The asterisk is not really an asterisk because it comes at the end of the letter as a prompting device.)

Figure 11–3. The Miami University Fund

THE MIAMI UNIVERSITY FUND

April, 1974

Just the right instant:

When Eddie Rickenbacker was adrift on that raft in the Pacific, without food or water and all but dead, a ship sailed by in the east. Those on the raft could see the ship, but it was far away. From shipboard they were but a tiny speck on a broad, broad sea.

And the sun was setting on their 22nd - and probably last - day.

Each wave would lift the raft for just an instant, then fall. But there were times during the minute or so while it crossed before the setting sun - when, if someone on the ship had glanced toward it for just one lifted instant, he would have seen, in silhouette, the men on the raft.

Someone glanced!

We know about that instant because someone did look; saw; and acted. So seven lives continued and contributed greatly to the world in the future. Without the look, that moment would have passed unknown.

Now I don't want to seem to overstate the effect of The Miami University Fund on future lives. But honestly, it works just that way.

For one student after another, some Fund action changes lives for the better. Sometimes they know. They tell us. Often no one knows. They can't. A library book opens a mind without the slightest thought of the Fund, but someone's money put it there. A teacher, his technique improved because of a gift from who-knows-who, sparks a student's life-long interest. Miami's Institute of Environmental Sciences, now making real changes in real communities, began with a study paid for with undesignated Fund dollars. Whose check did that?

Somebody's. Waves of checks, really. Through the Fund, small gifts combine to do great things.

Nothing at Miami today is as desperate as Rickenbacker was on the raft. But the opportunities ahead are just as broad, the value to the future just as great, when someone looks; sees; and acts ... with a gift that lifts the student at just the right instant.

Is the chance worth the glance?

Now?*

John E. Dolibois

JED/dgd

John E. Dolibois, Vice President

*A response from you now - with contribution, pledge, or even a "no" - will save Miami the cost of follow-up mailings for this 1974 fund effort. Thank you!

An unusual parallel and an imaginative P.S. make this letter a classic.

Mailer: **Coalition to Stop Gun Violence**
Key Words: **"The situation is frightening"**

The Challenge

Most of those who represent a potential donor-base have been circularized so much by anti-firearm organizations that a numbness to hyper-emotional appeals has dimmed the enthusiasm which might be directed toward any single appeal.

Breaking through the clutter with an approach that overpowers both this numbness on the part of those whose philosophy parallels the organization and apathy on the part of those who may not have a strong original opinion is a massive challenge.

The Implementation

On an oversize (9-1/2" × 14") sheet, this letter sets its typewriter face in larger-than-typical size. This gives a "heroic" impression to the text.

Relentlessly racing in its pace, the letter opens with an appeal to fear, staying in character as it rages through "ordinary citizens are robbed and then gunned down," "How do they get away with it?" "The NRA prevails by pure brute force, deception and money," to its close—"because unless we go after the Congressional buddies of the NRA, they will continue to stall, water down, or defeat important gun control proposals."

Comment

This is one of the strongest and most direct fund-raising letters the editors of this book have seen.

What could be a stronger, more forceful, more direct accusation than this key sentence in boldface: "America is bleeding to death from gun violence and there's only one reason why it's been allowed to continue: the NRA."

One of the rules of activist fund-raising letters: If you can generate anger, and milk it, response will follow . . . provided you mail to the right list of names.

Figure 11–4. Coalition to Stop Gun Violence

COALITION TO STOP GUN VIOLENCE

100 Maryland Avenue, NE, Washington, DC 20002
(202) 544-7190

Coretta Scott King
Honorary Chairperson

Michael K. Beard
Executive Director

Dear Mr. Doshi:

The situation is frightening, even in your neighborhood.

Ordinary citizens are robbed and then gunned down. Perfectly innocent people are slaughtered in fast-food restaurants -- just because they happen to be in the wrong place at the wrong time. And we've all heard far too many tragic stories about toddlers playing at home with loaded weapons.

There are so many accidents and gun crimes that their victims are becoming mere statistics -- or short-lived media sensations.

America is bleeding to death from gun violence and there's only one reason why it's been allowed to continue: the NRA.

The National Rifle Association is the most powerful special interest group in America. And the extremists who control the NRA spend more than $80 million a year to defeat each and every gun control proposal -- no matter how reasonable and important it is.

The NRA's army of lobbyists even fought our efforts to ban mail order machine guns, plastic pistols and cop-killer bullets that are specifically designed to pierce through bullet-proof vests!

And just recently, the NRA defeated our proposal for a 5-day waiting period for gun sales. So law enforcement officers still don't have the time they need to see if a gun buyer has a criminal record or mental disorder -- before they walk away with a gun of their choice.

How do they get away with it? First, the NRA is bankrolled by gun manufacturers and importers. Keep in mind, their 30 full-time lobbyists are also notorious for their arm-twisting tactics.

Additionally, the NRA has produced slick television commercials profiling Charleton Heston which distort the truth about our gun control proposals. And when politicians finally show the courage to stand up to the NRA, they can expect a savage, well-financed campaign against them in the next election.

So the NRA prevails by pure brute force, deception and money.

And the best way a concerned citizen like you can fight back is to take the following three steps:

over, please →

A dramatic appeal to anger that generates powerful response. *(Continued)*

1) Please answer our short survey.

By taking 30 seconds to respond to our national public opinion poll, you will help us prove to the politicians that the NRA does not represent the vast American majority.

2) Take a moment to sign our formal petition to Congress.

Help us send a message to Washington -- that we're fed up with the extremist positions of the NRA and a Congress which has failed to act on gun control issues.

Now that Americans have a new Congress and a sympathetic President in the White House, we finally have the opportunity to defeat the NRA and pass stronger gun control laws. So please sign the petition to Congress.

3) And then include a check for $25, $50 or more when you send back your petition and survey.

The Coalition to Stop Gun Violence was founded nearly 20 years ago -- in response to the public outcry over the murders of Martin Luther King and the Kennedys -- and we are the largest coalition of organizations joined together to stop gun violence.

But the Coalition is solely supported by citizens like you. So please take a moment to respond.

With your help, we will send a powerful message to politicians: the American people want to stop the bloodshed in our streets.

It's gotten so bad that Americans are beginning to feel like hostages in their own homes -- afraid to go to the corner store and too frightened to walk their dog. And this has got to stop!

So please take a moment now to fill out our brief questionnaire, sign the petition and make a special contribution to the Coalition to Stop Gun Violence.

As you will see, the petition is addressed to the Speaker of the House, Tom Foley. He needs to hear our outrage over the unfair influence of the NRA on the political system.

Because unless we go after the Congressional buddies of the NRA, they will continue to stall, water down, or defeat important gun control proposals.

Your help is urgently needed, and greatly appreciated.

Sincerely,

Michael Beard
Executive Director

P.S. Mr. Doshi, we have our best opportunity ever to pass strong gun control laws -- since we now have a friend in the White House and many newly-elected Members of Congress. So please help us to get Saturday Night Specials and assault weapons off of our streets -- by making an extra generous contribution.

Mailer: **Planned Parenthood**
Key Words: **"Urgent"**

The Challenge

Even for those who are philosophically in sync with this organization, fund raising becomes a challenge because some who may agree with the goals may fear public acknowledgement of their agreement.

So an appeal for funds has to take one of two courses—either a quiet, gentle appeal to logic, or an emotional reaction to violence.

The Implementation

In this instance, the writer took full advantage of a violent act and, quite properly, used that act, instead of a less effective standard appeal, to do more than make a point.

The litany of violent acts against Planned Parenthood clinics is presented as a series of carefully orchestrated, brutal attacks. Anyone who is not immediately fanatical in opposition to this organization is a proper target for a letter of this intensity.

Comment

When an organization can tie its appeal to a specific recognizable event—especially a threatening event—response is all but automatic.

This letter, mailed to local members at a time when violence against Planned Parenthood clinics was erupting almost daily, was both timely and convincing. Especially effective is the handwritten "Special thanks" legend to the right of the signature.

The P.S. begins with dynamic terminology—"We can't allow domestic terrorists to impose their will on all of us who disagree with their beliefs." It then closes with a curiously mild call to action.

Figure 11–5. Planned Parenthood

of South Palm Beach & Broward Counties, Inc.

URGENT

January 4, 1995

Dear Friend,

During 1994 we saw a horrifying increase in violent acts by anti-choice fanatics.

*In Vermont, a bomb was found in a **Planned Parenthood** parking lot.*

*In South Dakota, an arson attack occurred at a **Planned Parenthood** clinic.*

In Pensacola, a physician and volunteer escort were murdered by a man who opened fire outside a women's clinic (also wounding the escort's wife) with a 12-gauge shotgun.

Paul Hill, sentenced to death for these murders, publicly supports "whatever force is legitimate to defend the life of an unborn child," and has circulated petitions claiming that killing abortion service providers is justifiable.

The year 1994 concluded with a nightmare . . .

*BROOKLINE, Mass. (AP) - Two women were killed and at least five people wounded in shootings at two abortion clinics Friday morning. Police at the scene said the gunman was still at large. The assailant at both scenes was described by witnesses as a man in his early 30s dressed in black. . . The shootings began at 10:15 a.m. at a **Planned Parenthood** clinic . . . witnesses said a man wielding a shotgun burst in and started firing.*

And 1995 began with a threat . . .

In Fort Lauderdale, a window was smashed at our clinic on the night of December 31st.

We are grateful there were no injuries and only minor damage, but it makes the threat of violence to us real. I spent the early morning hours of this new year boarding up the facility.

On the day of the Massachusetts killings, I requested additional drive-by surveillance and security evaluation from police departments for each of our clinics in Boca Raton, Oakland Park and Pembroke Pines. I have since requested the U.S. Marshal Service to assist in guarding these health care facilities. Although we do not provide abortions in any of our three clinics, statistics show a significant number of clinics like ours have been targets of violence. It is imperative that we take all necessary security precautions and measures to ensure the safety of our patients and staff.

455 N. W. 35th Street • Boca Raton, Florida 33431 • (407) 394-3540 • (305) 480-9744 • FAX (407) 368-2206
Clinic Locations: Fort Lauderdale, Pembroke Pines and Boca Raton

An intense appeal dramatizing a readily recognizable event overcomes reader apathy. *(Continued)*

We cannot ignore this terrifying breakdown of law and order!

The right to choose is meaningless if you cannot safely exercise it.

Planned Parenthood of South Palm Beach & Broward Counties has been doing more to prevent abortion in the past fifteen years than any anti-choice activist ever will. By providing affordable, accessible birth control services and reproductive health care, we are able to reduce the number of unplanned pregnancies. Our education programs address teenagers, young adults and families, providing options and encouraging responsible decision-making.

The fight for safe access to reproductive health care of any nature is getting harder, not easier. One of our primary missions is to empower individuals to make responsible decisions regarding their reproductive health care and to ensure that every child is a loved and wanted child. As one of the leading voices for the right to choose, Planned Parenthood is working to defend your rights. We will not concede an inch to those who want to control the reproductive health choices of women.

Your support is critical. I am asking for your help.

Please send your donation today. We need your financial support to protect a woman's right to control her own body and her life. Your support will help us continue our advocacy work. It will also assist us in implementing the necessary security and safety precautions that are now an absolute necessity because of this escalation of violence. We must ensure that the Freedom of Access to Clinic Entrances Act (F.A.C.E.) is upheld despite pressure from groups to strike it down.

Your support will affirm our mission and provide encouragement for the physicians and staff members who continue to work to make choice a reality for the women and men they serve.

Sincerely,

Marilyn Bonilla Krantz

Marilyn Bonilla Krantz
Executive Director

Special thanks to all who called concerned about our safety.

P.S. We can't allow domestic terrorists to impose their will on all of us who disagree with their beliefs. ***Help us defend the fundamental right of a free society*.** **Give to Planned Parenthood of South Palm Beach & Broward Counties today.**

Mailer: **Los Angeles Mission**
Key Words: **"This is probably your first invitation."**
Writer: **Hugh Chewning**

The Challenge

Most people think missions that feed the homeless are sponsored by organizations who keep that mission well-funded. So the concept of supporting such an organization is not immediately in the mind.

Although the recipient of a letter such as this might have benevolent feelings toward a mission, raising those feelings to the level of actually contributing money requires superimposing education upon attitude—and this is the challenge this letter faced.

The Implementation

This letter hits in short bursts. The typical writer would have opened with the paragraph which begins at the bottom of the first page—"In Los Angeles, 33,000 shuffle through our streets and back alleys." Instead, this writer opened with the provocative, "This is probably your first invitation to an open house in the heart of skid row."

The letter has computer-personalized inserts on pages 1, 2, and 4. The personalized elements are not seamless. Instead, the ink-jet typeface gives us a typical inexpensive "fund-raising" look, as well as ensuring that the personalization stands out from the rest of the letter.

Comment

The first sentence is as ensnaring an opening as we have seen in a fund-raising letter. The second sentence is curiously disarming, causing the reader to feel this will be a "lightweight" appeal.

That makes the personalized demand on the first page even more impactful and dramatic.

Figure 11–6. Los Angeles Mission

DEAR DEVOY J KLASKY,

This is probably your first invitation to an Open House in the heart of Skid Row.

Our new Los Angeles Mission is located at 5th and Wall Streets in downtown Los Angeles -- where the TV show "Hill Street Blues" was once filmed.

I'm hoping you can visit and see firsthand how effectively our program to feed, clothe and shelter Los Angeles' homeless is working.

I've made arrangements for you to park your car inside a secure parking garage. We'll meet you there and drive to the Mission in a chartered bus so you and your car will always be safe.

Your R.S.V.P. card gives all the details.

DEVOY J KLASKY, EVEN IF YOU CAN'T VISIT US, I DESPERATELY NEED YOU TO FURNISH AT LEAST ONE MEAL TO A HUNGRY PERSON.

For only $1.57 you can feed a homeless person a nutritious, home-cooked meal. Twenty people can be fed for $31.40 and every $15.70 you contribute feeds ten hungry people.

There's nothing impractical about what I'm asking you to do. I simply need you to furnish food for at least one hungry person.

In Los Angeles, about 33,000 homeless people shuffle through our streets and back alleys -- more than any place in the country. And before the end of this

(over, please)

A provocative opening followed by short bursts of specific examples gives this letter special impact. *(Continued)* month, over 15,000 tired and hungry people will come to us for food and shelter.

The need is so great that, in the past, we've had to turn people away. And without your support, more people may go hungry again.

This is why I'm asking you to fill out the enclosed "Meal Ticket" and let me know how many hungry people you can help feed.

At the same time, please offer a special word of encouragement to a homeless person by returning the special greeting card I've also enclosed.

DEVOY J KLASKY, I'LL DISPLAY YOUR GREETING CARD IN OUR DINING AREA WHERE THE HOMELESS CAN SEE IT AND FEEL THE WARMTH OF YOUR LOVE.

Many of our homeless are younger men -- their average age is only 28 -- who have family problems or just haven't gotten a hold on life.

> People like David, whose mother was a drug addict. As a child, he was left with friends and even strangers when his mother traveled.

And there are those who have been "discarded" by society -- the unemployed, handicapped, mentally ill, and the retarded.

> Like "Pop," who's in his sixties, has a physical handicap but no family or hope.

Families are huddling together in abandoned buildings and living in cars or cardboard boxes. Mothers with two and three children come to us for clothing, baby formula, and a safe place to stay.

Then there are the Skid Row regulars -- the alcoholics, drug addicts and transients. You can see them sleeping in doorways, on park benches and under freeway overpasses. These are the castaways that no one

(next page)

(Continued)

wants to see.

We feed them, give them a hot shower and clean clothes, and offer free counseling, medical treatment, and our Fresh Start rehabilitation program.

It's our rehab program that helps these men and women get back into society. They spend six months to a year learning a trade, improving their reading and math skills and regaining the self-esteem they need to reenter society.

You'll meet some of these men and women at our Open House. But if for some reason you can't come, here's what our community leaders have witnessed.

Mayor Tom Bradley says:

> "When we see Rev. Mark Holsinger take homeless, hopeless persons off the street, clean them up, find them jobs, and renew their lives, we realize how important the lifesaving work of the mission is."

And Police Chief Daryl Gates says:

> "The Los Angeles Mission has helped save hundreds of homeless citizens from becoming criminal statistics. Rev. Mark Holsinger opens his doors to the castaways and hopeless, those who have given up in life . . . His program rehabilitates desperate citizens and gives them a new chance at life."

We're doing our best, but the Mission gets absolutely no financial assistance from the city, state or federal government.

And in the past two years, the need for food and shelter has been so great, we've had to turn people away. I believe many men and women on Skid Row have the ability to lead productive lives. But to feed them and provide clothing, shelter, and rehabilitation, I need your support.

(over, please)

(Continued)

DEVOY J KLASKY, I NEED YOU TO HELP ME FEED AT LEAST ONE MAN OR WOMAN BY DOING THESE TWO THINGS TODAY:

1. Return your "Meal Ticket" with your tax-deductible contribution of $15.70, $31.40, $62.80 or more to feed the hungry and homeless of Los Angeles.

2. When you return your gift, please sign the greeting card I've enclosed to give a special word of support to the men and women sharing dinner with us.

If you can attend our Open House, please R.S.V.P. to my invitation. You'll meet men from our rehabilitation program and see firsthand how effectively your contribution is working.

But even if you can't visit, we still have people to feed and I need your support to do it.

DEVOY J KLASKY, WE'RE OPERATING FAR BEYOND OUR NORMAL CAPACITY AND WITHOUT YOUR SUPPORT, HUNGRY PEOPLE MAY BE TURNED AWAY.

Please don't let that happen. Rush your "Meal Ticket" and maximum contribution to me today in the brown postage-paid envelope I've enclosed.

Sincerely,

Mark Holsinger

Rev. Mark Holsinger
Director

P.S. You can help feed and shelter the hungry and homeless people of Los Angeles by returning your "Meal Ticket" and tax-deductible contribution of $15.70, $31.40, $62.80 or more. Please respond today so I can be sure there's enough food for everyone.

Mailer: National Taxpayers Union
Key Words: "Private Offer"

The Challenge

Individuals regard their tax problem as . . . well . . . individual.

Everyone hates the Internal Revenue Service and almost everyone considers battling with that organization to be a hopeless exercise.

Beyond that problem is the problem of the IRS specter itself. Horror stories have filtered down through newspapers pinpointing IRS retribution against those who had the temerity to publicize its vicissitudes.

So a letter which asks for money to join the battle not only competes with other fund-raising ventures, but also has to overcome the natural reluctance to make any move that might infuriate the Internal Revenue Service.

The Implementation

This is the longest letter we've included—8 pages.

Written in 1988, it was an early experiment. Crossing the 4-page barrier was regarded as parallel to breaking the "sound" barrier: No one quite knew what would happen. As the twentieth century draws to a close, we have letters of 16 and 32 pages. This is their acknowledged ancestor.

The letter also sets a pace for handwriting within the text. Handwriting is in blue, matching the color of the signature. (Mechanically, the inner pages, which have no handwriting, are printed in black only which may have effected some production savings.)

Comment

With many subheads, indented and short paragraphs, and handwriting, the letter is a "quick read" despite its length.

It opens with a comparative episode, attacking a popular target: the Internal Revenue Service. The letter offers a newsletter. The offer is clarified as early as page 3. Why, then, devote an additional five pages to the message? To intensify, amplify, and justify the offer.

Especially convincing is the signature, a single initial, underscoring the "inside anonymous authority" paralleling the "deep throat" of Watergate notoriety.

Figure 11–7. National Taxpayers' Union

<u>Private offer:</u>
YOURS <u>FREE</u> ---
"How to Save a Fortune"
(retail value $24.00)

Inside information about saving on taxes most IRS agents don't have.

Dear Fellow Taxpayer,

How about this:

Mr. Jones pays his income tax according to the book. He doesn't take a single "questionable" deduction. He doesn't skirt any edges. He hires a conservative accountant who takes no chances on the tax-return.

Jones gets audited and winds up paying a penalty.

Mr. Smith deducts the cost of his children's education. He deducts the cost of maintaining a "mini office" in his home. He deducts car expense far above the normally allowable 21 cents per mile. His income is parallel to Jones, but he pays <u>thousands</u> of dollars less tax.

Smith not only doesn't get audited. If he did, he wouldn't pay another dime.

<u>The Difference Between Jones and Smith</u>

If you were an Internal Revenue special agent you wouldn't turn a hair at this story. You'd have seen it dozens of times.

> The fact is: A handful of taxpayers know how to beat the IRS at its own game. They won't be bullied, <u>and the IRS knows it</u>.
>
> Every decision, every move, is 100% legal, backed by precedent. The IRS knows enough to leave these people alone and bother somebody else.

I'm sure you know from the tax advice <u>you</u> get: One "expert" contradicts another. You don't know what to believe. You don't know what's a safe deduction and what isn't. Even the most astute accountant is bewildered by the multitude of tax laws, regulations, exceptions, exclusions,

1

Many subheads, short paragraphs and a natural target make this a long letter that is sure to get read.

(Continued)

loopholes, and traps.

I propose, in one quick step, to show you how to save hundreds, maybe thousands, of dollars on your income tax this year. I propose to put the power of the National Taxpayers Union behind you, through our plain-talking newsletter, Tax Savings Report. I propose, in short, to line you up with the Smiths instead of the Joneses.

And, oh, yes: I propose to give you your personal copy of "How to Save a Fortune" --- a privately printed book whose $24.00 price-tag can't begin to reflect the money it will save you.

Let me tell you what I have in mind.

Do You Know the Answers?

Do you know the answers to any of these questions? For that matter, does your accountant know the answers to even half of them?

> Question: If one partner in a marriage handles all the finances and signs all the checks --- and the marriage comes unglued --- can the IRS hold the other partner responsible for any deficiencies?
>
> Question: If you get billed for an IRS penalty, what's the best way to get the penalty abated?
>
> Question: Why doesn't it pay to divert some of your income so it's paid in your child's name?
>
> Question: How much Social Security income is taxable?
>
> Question: How can you wind up with more after-tax dollars by reducing your own salary?
>
> Question: How can spending $100 to set up a corporation save you thousands of dollars every year from now on?

Ask an accountant these questions and you'll probably get hems and haws and a whole bunch of "That depends." Oh, and you'll get billed for it.

Here's how you can get the answers. Here's how you can see for

You can bet the IRS won't tell you!

2

(Continued)

yourself how and where you've innocently been paying too much tax.

Tax Savings Report

National Taxpayers Union is a non-profit organization fully recognized by the United States Government.

One key purpose of our organization is: INFORMATION.

We're here in Washington, where survival depends on contacts, inside intelligence one person gets and another doesn't, and knowing who's a dependable source and who isn't.

We're here to tell our members and subscribers what's going on --- which deductions and procedures are safe and which ones aren't --- which areas the Internal Revenue Service probably will attack next --- how to make an airtight case for a deduction you might have thought, when you woke up this morning, couldn't be allowed.

I invite you to join this privileged group.

I invite you to subscribe to our extraordinary newsletter, Tax Savings Report. Read on --- Even better! I invite you to get this astonishingly valuable, useful, money-saving newsletter at a tremendous discount: half the regular price.

The established subscription price of Tax Savings Report is $58 a year. That's a real bargain for eight solid pages of money-saving facts ten times a year. But you don't pay even that. Your special rate is HALF — $29 for a whole year!

That isn't all.

Your Three Big EXTRAS

Three big EXTRAS will prove to you we want you as a subscriber. They'll also prove to you we're confident you'll benefit from taking advantage of this special opportunity.

> (Incidentally, this may be the one and only time you'll have this opportunity.)

EXTRA Number 1:

You don't risk a dime. When you get your first issue of Tax Savings Report, read it through. Make any notes you think will be valuable. Then

3

(Continued)

decide. If you decide Tax Savings Report isn't for you . . . if you don't think it will save you thousands of dollars you'd otherwise pour down the drain in taxes you don't have to pay, just tell us so. We'll cancel your subscription, give you a 100% refund, and that will be the end of the matter.

EXTRA Number 2:

You'll get as our FREE GIFT the confidential book, "How to Save a Fortune." This book sells for $24.00. (This is the actual value.)

EXTRA Number 3:

If ever you decide to discontinue your membership subscription, just tell us so and we'll refund the total unexpired value.

"What's In It for Me?"

You're a sophisticated taxpayer or you wouldn't be on the special list of individuals to whom I'm sending this invitation.

So I'm not surprised if you say, "I know some of it comes from off-the-record 'Deep Throat' conversations with IRS officials. But, specifically, what's in it for me?"

I'll tell you what's in it for you:

If you get even one useful tip . . . if you get even one tax-saving . . . if you get even one pointer alerting you to decisions affecting your taxes . . . you'll pay for your subscription many times over.

The reason I'm so confident: We have inside sources neither you nor any single individual could have. The National Taxpayers Union has spent years developing reliable sources. I've been in Washington a long, long time, and I don't know anyone who has the pipelines we have --- including most IRS officials.

What If You Could Save $5,000 THIS YEAR?

The National Taxpayers Union doesn't deal in theory. We deal in the hard-boiled world of fact.

"What if . . ." questions don't mean much when we're talking about the specifics of tax law. But I'll use the phrase for an example:

4

(Continued)

What if you could save $5,000 to $10,000 this year? I'm not saying you will. But I positively am saying some taxpayers have done just that, armed with the hard-boiled private information in Tax Savings Report.

The difference is: We give you aggressive information, not passive information. Please, please let me explain the difference:

Your accountant or bookkeeper-advisor (if he or she is like 99.4% of the accountants who have business or professional executives as clients) tells you, "We can't do this," or "We're taking a chance if we deduct that." The attitude is one of reaction, not action.

Time after time, our members and subscribers astonish their financial or tax advisors by telling them intricacies of tax law the advisor didn't know. It isn't surprising. This, after all, is why we exist. We're in the "tax marketplace" all day, every day. We live and breathe taxes. We comb the statutes, finding an opening here, a shelter there.

Sure, these openings and shelters have been the quiet private domain of big companies and multimillionaires. They're the ones who may have been instrumental in getting openings and shelters squeezed into the tax laws to start with. But why should they be the only ones to profit from perfectly legal deductions?

How We Edit Tax Savings Report

I can name eleven separate digests, newsletters, and limited-circulation tax publications we scan every month. Just one of these costs FAR more than Tax Savings Report.

Suppose you decide to subscribe to the Journal of Taxation . . . the Executive Tax Report . . . the CPA Digest . . . the Tax Avoidance Digest . . . and some of the others? Would you get the benefits you get from Tax Savings Report?

Consider this, then decide for yourself:

First of all, you'd have to wade through a lot of technical jargon to get at the meat. Second, you'd pay hundreds of dollars each month instead of your special preferred rate of $29 a year (which comes to $2.90 per issue, since we publish 10 times a year).

Third, you wouldn't have the benefit of our contacts which adds recent Tax Court decisions and closely-guarded high-level opinions. And fourth, most of these publications have axes to grind. They're published for

5

(Continued)

profit, and only an expert can sift through their strategies, anticipating which are prudent and which are dangerous.

I wish you could attend some of our meetings. We discuss with our own tax lawyers how our members and subscribers can profit from recent Tax Court decisions. We discuss some of the pertinent points with the highest-level IRS officials, and they give us straight talk, unvarnished by "IRS sales talk."

What filters down to you is the cream --- pure, usable fact.

You Want Plain English, Not Gobbledygook

I know you've seen and been mystified by some of the tax writings, especially articles and advice written since the so-called "Tax Reform" bill.

Many of these articles are written on a professional level. They're written by academicians who just don't care if the person reading their words saves money or not. They're showing off their massive vocabularies in print.

> They analyze. Raw analysis isn't helpful. Telling you what to do, based on the analysis --- that's what's helpful.

Tax Savings Report is written in plain English. The National Taxpayers Union doesn't have to show off for anybody. Our function is to inform, to help, to report. And even though we edit Tax Savings Report for executives, a tremendous number of accountants and tax planners subscribe to it. They know: This is where the information is, distilled and presented for use, not just for filing away.

A Sampler of What You'll Find

I can't predict what nuggets of tax-saving gold you'll see in the pages of Tax Savings Report during the next year. Decisions and changes are flying through the air, not just every month but every day.

That, in fact, is part of the value you get. Your information isn't stale. It's current.

Anyway, here are some of the hard facts on tax saving opportunities you'd have seen if you already were a subscriber:

--- You'd have hard fact on how to get tax-exempt income from

6

(Continued)

stocks and bonds.

--- You'd have hard fact on the advantages and disadvantages of equipment leasing partnerships under the new tax laws.

--- You'd have hard fact on ways to get tax-free money out of a corporation.

--- You'd have hard fact on what you can and can't do with offshore corporations and how to maintain an overseas account the IRS can't touch.

--- You'd have hard fact on how to (safely) deduct foreign travel you may have thought wasn't deductible.

--- You'd have hard fact on how to squeeze the last nickel of car expense by avoiding the "standard" allowance.

--- You'd have hard fact on tax avoidance planning.

Your FREE Book . . . Just for Taking a Look!

Here's solid proof we want you as a subscriber:

When you agree to take a look at a sample issue of Tax Savings Report, we'll send you as our gift your personal copy of "How to Save a Fortune." Please understand:

This is no ordinary book.

You'll wear the pages thin, using the hundreds of tips and moneysavers in this extraordinary book. Some of the ways you can save a bundle: You'll find out how to ---

* Save on the usually enormous cost of college education.
* Save on luxury vacations.
* Save not only on the cost of a car but on car repairs.
* Save on insurance.
* Save on accounting and legal fees.
* Save on designer clothes (you'll buy them at K-Mart prices!)
* Save on real estate and eliminate down payments.

That's what "How to Save a Fortune" is all about --- saving money. Sometimes really big money.

And the best part of all this is you start off by saving money, because

7

(Continued)

instead of paying $24.00 for "How to Save a Fortune" you get it free.

<u>All This Is Yours, At Absolutely NO Risk</u>

When I say "free" I mean <u>free</u>. Suppose you get your first issue of <u>Tax Savings Report</u>. You don't like it. You cancel, and you owe nothing. "How to Save a Fortune" is yours to keep. No strings.

I meant it when I said we want <u>you</u> as a member and subscriber. Chances are, if you ask your next-door neighbor whether he got this same invitation from us, he'll say no. Our computer picked <u>you</u> to get this invitation.

So you have a choice. You can --- as so many millions of taxpayers do --- ignore my invitation and probably pay tens of thousands of dollars in <u>extra</u> taxes over the next few years.

Or you can take me up on my offer. You can see why the National Taxpayers Union has earned the heavy respect of the IRS, as well as lawyers and accountants throughout the United States.

And the best part of all this is: You can get the facts and make your decision without risking a single cent. If you get your first issue of <u>Tax Savings Report</u> and don't like what you see, tell us so and we'll cancel all billing and refund your money.

But if you do see how your special preferred subscription, yours for $29, <u>half</u> the regular subscription rate, can save you hundreds of times its low cost, then you'll be way, way ahead of most Americans. Either way, the fabulous book "How to Save a Fortune" is yours absolutely free, with no strings.

What could be fairer than that?

I hope you'll agree with my logic and take advantage of this opportunity. It may not come your way again.

For the National Taxpayers Union,

M

P.S. I apologize for not naming my contacts at the IRS. Understand: They're high up, and I want to protect them. If you want to take advantage of my offer, mail the Special Preferred Subscription Form in the postage-free envelope I've provided *Before March 31, 1988, please.*

8

National Taxpayers Union 325 Pennsylvania Avenue, S.E. Washington, DC 20003

Mailer: Hong Kong Committee for UNICEF
Key Words: "Can the children count on you?"
Writer: Herschell Gordon Lewis

The Challenge

Any organization faces an eventual "burn-out" point in which its best targets simply take for granted the worth of the organization. This acceptance usually results in lower response or—worse for the fund raiser—absence of response.

To keep the image fresh, a fund raiser whose appeal does not vary from year to year must constantly find new grist for the emotional mill.

The challenge of maintaining a donor base and adding to it is never so pronounced as it is in such circumstances.

The Implementation

The United Nations Children's Fund successfully mounts global appeals by using terminology and episodes familiar to a specific country, unlike some international fund raisers who prepare one appeal and simply translate into the proper language.

This letter, written for the Hong Kong Committee, set a new high in response. We have included the Chinese language version as well, not because we expect the typical reader of this book to know the language, but to exemplify the technique of maximizing response in multi-lingual situations. (Another example: Many fund-raising appeals in the Union of South Africa are mailed with letters printed in both English and Afrikaans.)

Comment

A handwritten overline was a novelty for this committee and, in the Chinese language version the handwriting was so symmetrical it did not really look handwritten. Our information is that this technique was instrumental in bringing the response this letter generated.

Figure 11–8. UNICEF

December, 1993

Can the children count on you?

Dear Friend,

Somewhere in China is a child who can grow tall and strong ... or be cruelly crippled. You are in a position to make that choice.

As we approach "China's Children's Week," I am calling upon the leading citizens of Hong Kong to participate in the future. Please allow me to explain what I mean:

We have dedicated ourselves to a noble goal – eradicating polio in China by the end of 1995. UNICEF and our partners in health have accomplished much. But now, to reach that goal, we need your help.

We <u>can</u> reach the length and breadth of China, immunizing children against this dreaded disease. To do this, we must have millions upon millions of doses of vaccine. We must have refrigerated carriers so the serum will not spoil. We must have depots in various places within the huge country, places where doctors and technicians can get ampoules of the vaccine to carry into the countryside.

> The solution is as simple as having the funds to accomplish our task. So, you see, you <u>are</u> in a position to safeguard some – or many – of these children, depending on the amount of your contribution.

I cannot imagine that someone of your stature will refuse us. I know you understand what a difference every dollar can make ... and I know, too, you can see as I do that every day (in fact, every hour) children are afflicted with polio. If they had been immunized, their lives would not have been ruined.

This is why <u>time</u> is so critical. The supplies are available, if we can pay for them.

To achieve complete coverage by the end of 1995, China needs 125 million doses each year. As you consider the amount of your contribution, please try to

60, Blue Pool Road, 3/F, Happy Valley, Hong Kong. Tel: 833-6139 Fax: 834 0996

Fresh presentation and appeal set a new high in response for this mailer. *(Continued)*

increase it just a little more. Each $250 covers 125 vials of the precious poliomyelitis vaccine.

In the hope that you will become one of our most distinguished supporters, I have enclosed an option to use the "Autopay" System. Your monthly contribution of $100, $200, or more through the Autopay programme will enable UNICEF to move far faster and with greater depth, because we then can count on you for continuing support throughout this so worthwhile campaign of childhood health.

May I tell you why your contribution means so much right now?

Even a generation ago, vaccines against polio didn't exist. Children who were stricken – and their grieving parents – knew that fate had ruled against them. Today, with the availability of effective immunization, allowing even <u>one</u> case of polio to disable a child is inexcusable.

So, to celebrate the special week devoted to China's children, I ask you to join us in this most worthy cause. Please, while you have this message in your hands, don't let the moment pass.

Who knows, in years to come, what races will be won, what towers will be built, because today you cared!

For The Hong Kong Committee for UNICEF,

Dr. Robert H.P. Fung
Chairman

P.S. Please remember – your contribution <u>will</u> make a difference in eliminating the scourge of polio in China, once and for all. On behalf of all the children in China, I thank you.

(Continued)

孩子們能指望您嗎？

親愛的朋友：

一個身處中國某一角落的孩子能健康成長…或不幸地變成跛子，你便是決定他命運的人。

正當我們要進入「中國兒童周」之際，我請求境況優越的香港市民積極參予建設美好的未來。請容許我詳細解釋。

本會致力於一個崇高的目標，就是在一九九五年徹底根絕中國小兒麻痺症。聯合國兒童基金會與其醫療伙伴的合作，已在這方面得到不少成績，但是爲要達到這目標，我們還需要您的協助。

我們可以到達中國的每一個角落，令兒童得到對這種可怕的疾病的免疫能力。然而，我們必須先擁有數以百萬份的疫苗，同時需要冷藏運送設備，以防止血清變壞，我們更需要在幅員龐大的中國領土上的不同地點設立免疫站，以便醫生及技術人員能把疫苗帶進郊區。

> 解決的方法非常簡單，我們只需要足夠的資金，便能完成我們的使命。您有能力保護兒童（人數多少視乎您的捐款數額）免被這可怕的疾病終生摧殘。

以現時香港的經濟發展迅速，實難以想像您會拒絕我們的呼籲。我們明白您一定知道每一塊錢的效用…，同時，我們亦知道您與我一樣，都明白到每一天（事實上，是每小時）都有不少兒童受到小兒麻痺症的侵襲。倘若他們早已接受預防疫苗，就不會被這病魔摧毀一生的幸福。

故此，這個時刻是非常的重要。只要我們有足夠的資金，一切便準備就緒。

爲要在一九九五年年底完成整個計劃，中國需要每年一億二千五百萬份疫苗，當您考慮捐款數額時，請儘量將捐款增加一點。每$250 已足夠購買125 份寶貴的小兒麻痺症疫苗。

60, Blue Pool Road, 3/F, Happy Valley, Hong Kong. Tel: 833-6139 Fax: 834 0996

(Continued)

爲希望您能成爲我們的熱心支持者，我已附上一項「自動轉賬」的選擇辦法。如果您能參與「自動轉賬」計劃，我們便可依賴您對這富有意義的兒童健康運動中作出的每月捐款，而聯合國兒童基金會亦因此而能更迅速和深化地進行這項計劃。

我現在告訴您爲什麼您的參予有著很大的價值？

人類直到上一代，仍未發明對抗小兒麻痺症的疫苗。以前不幸患上這病的兒童和他們的父母，都知道是無法改變的厄運。今天，已發明了有效的預防疫苗，如果我們再縱容這惡疫繼續去蹂躪、殘害我們的兒童，就實在是不可以解釋的。

因此，爲慶祝特別爲中國兒童而設的一周，我邀請您參與這極富意義的運動。當您看到這訊息的時候，不要錯過機會，請即積極參與！

誰會知道未來的日子裡哪個民族會勝出，那些高樓會興建起來，只因您今日的關懷！

馮慶彪

馮慶彪醫生敬啟
主席
一九九三年十二月

附言：請緊記—您的捐款能永久消除小兒麻痺症對中國造成的災害。我謹代表中國國內所有兒童向各位致謝。

Mailer: **NOW**

Key Words: **"Not all the news . . ."**

The Challenge

An organization which dedicates itself to a controversial cause automatically eliminates from its prospective donor base those who either fear controversy or who disagree with its philosophy.

This type of high-profile fund raiser tends to lose members as its cause "wears out" in the popular imagination. Member retention becomes perilous and little short of desperate.

Add to this the lack of urgency and the lack of a life-threatening episode, and it is easy to understand the special challenge facing this type of letter.

The Implementation

This letter was sent to many women (and some men, we understand) who supported NOW in more turbulent times. Many of these individuals may have become complacent from past success. It was important to remind the "faithful" that there "still is work to be done."

Turning a mildly negative election result into a rationale for contributions and combining good news with bad was an effective way to emphasize the need for continued support without appearing fanatical or overly alarmist.

Comment

This letter takes the tone of "reason." Had it struck out in wrath, probably its effectiveness would have been lessened because the reader could not justify a wrathful tone.

By maintaining dignity without sacrificing vigor, this letter became worthy of inclusion in this collection.

Figure 11–9. NOW

National Organization for Women

1000 Sixteenth Street, N.W. • Washington, D.C. 20036

Dear NOW Member,

Not <u>all</u> the news from the 1994 elections was bad.

Only two years ago we were celebrating the victories of the largest group of women legislators ever elected to Congress in our nation's history. Today, conservative politicians elected by a mere 37% of all eligible voters are threatening to turn back the clock on a host of women's issues.

It was especially hard to face this grim political climate at a time when many feminists, full of confidence after our victories in 1992, turned their attentions away from the fight.

And yes, there is good news. Women and men across the country are making the decision to join you and me -- to stand up and be counted as defenders of women's rights. Here at the NOW Action Center our confidence and optimism are growing as we watch our membership increase <u>daily</u>. Right now, over 600 NOW chapters nationwide are taking action in defense of legislation crucial to women.

In the past year, your support has boosted our efforts to protect women's rights. Now more than ever -- the women's movement is in critical need of strong, dedicated members like <u>you</u>!

> **For nearly thirty years, NOW members have stood at the forefront of the struggle for women's rights. Together ... we've fought for equal education, credit and employment opportunities, for reproductive rights, and for an end to violence against women.**
>
> **And your renewed support will help us continue to overcome every obstacle to women's equality.**

Your renewed commitment will help us push forward at a time when the forces in power are determined to push us back. That is why I urge you to <u>renew your NOW membership today</u> by sending your enclosed renewal form right away.

Together, we <u>can make a real difference in women's lives</u>!

The time for action is now. Newt Gingrich and many of his Congressional cronies are specifically targeting some of our key legislative victories -- victories you have helped us win -- for massive funding cuts or even outright repeal. The Republicans' more dangerous plans include:

* repealing the <u>Freedom of Access to Clinic Entrances Law</u>. The radical right wants to take away the only federal protection that clinic staff, doctors and patients have against anti-abortion terrorism.

* bringing back the <u>Gag Rule</u>. Repealed by Clinton, this Bush regulation had prevented federally-funded family planning clinics from even <u>mentioning</u> abortion services. Gingrich's

RECYCLED PAPER

A "reasonable" tone helped this letter overcome donor "wear-out". *(Continued)*

"Contract with America" would bring it back.

* overturning the Family and Medical Leave Act. Some Republicans actually want to remove the guarantee that employees can take unpaid maternity leave or time to care for a sick family member without losing their jobs.

* weakening the Violence Against Women Act. Although funding for this groundbreaking bill has already been approved, refusal to appropriate that money would effectively repeal this crucial anti-violence measure.

NOW is already taking action to protect these important laws.

But we absolutely refuse to limit our goals to the defense of ground we've already won! We plan, with your help, to move forward on many fronts, including:

* **Ending the violence** that controls and limits so many women's lives;

* **Shattering the glass ceiling** of discrimination that keeps women from achieving pay equity with their male co-workers and locks many women and children in poverty;

* **Ensuring civil rights for all people** -- so that no group can be targeted or scapegoated by the purveyors of hate politics;

and, most importantly,

* **Amending the United States Constitution** to ensure the equality of all women -- so that women's fundamental rights will never be at the mercy of the radical right ever again.

But we can't accomplish these goals without you.

Please renew your membership in NOW today. There's never been a better time to stay involved. We can use the challenges before us to generate the same momentum that pushed women's issues forward in the 1960's and '70's. If there is one thing we've learned in our twenty-eight years of action, it's that **when we unite, we're unstoppable!** Let's seize this moment together.

We need you more than ever! Please take a moment to return the enclosed form and renew your support as a "card carrying NOW member." Thanks. PI

Sincerely,

Patricia Ireland

Patricia Ireland
President

Mailer: **WPBT2**
Key Words: **"I'm tempted to say . . ."**
Writers: **Carl Bloom, Dennis Lonergan**

The Challenge

Support for Public Television, whether by its faults or by clever moves on the part of its foes, is no longer an automatic fund-raising reflex for its viewers.

On-air telethons and interminable appeals create as many negatives as they do positives. So the mails become the instrument by which Public TV stations raise funds.

But the challenge goes beyond the medium. Most people know that if Public TV were to disappear altogether, they still would have ample fare on their television screens. So the challenge is to justify continued existence.

The Implementation

This letter takes the posture of utter honesty—statements such as, "We're having a tough time" . . . "that unique public TV format which, regrettably, often interrupts the very programs we're asking you to support" . . . "without members, WPBT just isn't economically possible."

This apparent candor is disarming and, unquestionably, convinced many recipients of the need to continue supporting the station.

Comment

In our opinion, had the letter taken a high-flown, cerebral tone, its effectiveness would have been fragmentary compared with the down-to-earth tone of this approach.

The last sentence—which, readership studies tell us, is read intensively—is as straightforward as any fund raising letter might ever be.

As we have stated before, we generally are opposed to a P.P.S. Here, we have an odd combination of P.S., P.P.S., and handwriting. We wonder whether the station might have set the P.P.S. in a typeface, taking it out of the letter proper, to avoid sharing impact with the P.S.

Figure 11–10. WPBT2

P.O. Box 2
Miami, Florida 33261-0002

George Dooley
President

Dear Friend:

I'm tempted to say we're at our wit's end. But "wit" is one of those precious commodities -- like art, insight and drama -- that we make it our business to keep in abundance at Channel 2.

So I'll just say it as plainly as I can: We're having a tough time understanding why the most precious commodity of all -- your membership support for Channel 2, your public television station -- eludes us.

We've tried all kinds of appeals:

Letter after letter, describing WPBT's exceptional programming and explaining our membership-based economics in every way we can think of.

Membership drive after membership drive, appealing for your membership gift in that unique public TV fundraising format which, regrettably, often interrupts the very programs we're asking you to support.

Yet for all our membership drives, letter writing, special incentives and pleading, we've been unable to inspire you to become a member of Channel 2. And because you aren't alone in your hesitation to join, membership hasn't grown. Program costs, on the other hand, have grown dramatically -- 25% over the past two years!

The dollars we have lost because of a static membership situation are threatening our ability to carry all the programs you enjoy on Channel 2. That's because without your support we can't afford the five- and six-figure price tags that television programs of such high quality cost.

But what I'd much rather do at this point is set the numbers aside and talk frankly and directly to you.

As president of WPBT, I can tell you in all honesty that our programming decisions are made solely to serve our community -- not the mass market, but you and our other discriminating and intelligent viewers.

When our programming staff selects gems from PBS offerings like *Masterpiece Theatre* or *Nature,* and when they rescue popular shows like *I'll Fly Away,* they're searching for the shows you look to Channel 2 for -- the shows you can't find on commercial television services.

But they must also look at our local broadcast budget, a full 63% of which must come from member contributions.

Yes, we care about how many viewers we have -- and how many people

Disarming candor helped this appeal generate high response. *(Continued)*

rave about Channel 2's superior programming. But what matters most is how many members we have because without members, WPBT just isn't economically possible.

That's why we have designed a very special limited time offer: a year's membership for just $30 (that's $10 off the regular membership rate!) And as a thank you for joining, we'll send you a beautiful WPBT2 canvas tote bag.

The individual cost to people like yourself is remarkably small, even though the collective impact of membership support is vital to Channel 2's bottom line.

With that in mind, won't you please join us today? Won't you do your share to keep Channel 2's broadcast excellence alive and well by becoming our newest member, right now?

Some of our staff wanted to send you their own messages inviting you to join Channel 2 (see the enclosed response form). Like me, they're hoping this straightforward appeal succeeds in getting you to take your place among our loyal members.

Please let us know we've made our case and earned your membership. If you do, we'll never be at the end of our wit, art, insight, drama or any of the wonderful programming you've come to count on and enjoy so much.

I can't put it more plainly than that. Join us. We need you. You need us. Together, we'll keep WPBT all we want it to be, and more.

Sincerely,

George Dooley

Some of the most significant words you'll read about Public TV this year!

P.S. Some members of Congress want to "zero out" or drastically cut federal support for public TV. If we are to win what might be the financial fight of our lives, we desperately need your support. Please join us today, and help save quality TV worth watching.

P.P.S. There's never been a better time to join WPBT2. Right now, during our limited time special offer, you can become a member for just $30 ($10 off the regular membership rate!). And we'll send you a handsome WPBT2 canvas tote bag plus all the other benefits of membership: our monthly program guide and the valuable Member Card for discounts at Florida attractions. Please see the enclosed reply form for details.

If you are already a member–or if you have received more than one copy of this letter–please forgive us. We try to avoid duplications but we can't eliminate them totally without spending extra money that could be used for programming. If you wish, you can take this opportunity to renew or send an additional contribution. Thank you for your support.

A Final Word

As you have seen, the word "great" has many facets.

As you have seen, "great" does *not* depend on a gigantic vocabulary. It does *not* depend on deep technical knowledge (in fact, deep technical knowledge can wreak a reverse transformation from greatness to dullness).

No, what these letters have in common is their ability to sweep up the reader in their irresistible approach. Some of the letters in this collection roll with thunder like juggernauts. Some proceed quietly and sedately. All show a mastery of salesmanship, and that such a variety of approaches can exist at all—and succeed—should convince even the most skeptical cynic that the creative process is alive and well.

More to the point: We hope we have convinced you that more than one creative solution to a sales or fund raising problem exists.

If you own this book, you have to be a serious communicator. That means *your* letter may well be in the next edition. We'll look for it.

HGL
CN

Index

C

D

E

I

J

K

L

Q

R

S

T

U

V

W

Y

TITLES OF INTEREST IN MARKETING, DIRECT MARKETING, AND SALES PROMOTION

For further information or a current catalog, write:
NTC Business Books
a division of NTC Publishing Group
4255 West Touhy Avenue
Lincolnwood, Illinois 60646–1975 U.S.A.